Building Microservices with JavaScript

Learn quick and practical methods for developing microservices

Diogo Resende
Paul Osman

BIRMINGHAM - MUMBAI

Building Microservices with JavaScript

First published: May 2019

Production reference: 1170519

Published by Packt Publishing Ltd.
Livery Place
35 Livery Street
Birmingham
B3 2PB, UK.

ISBN 978-1-83882-619-2

www.packtpub.com

`mapt.io`

Mapt is an online digital library that gives you full access to over 5,000 books and videos, as well as industry leading tools to help you plan your personal development and advance your career. For more information, please visit our website.

Why subscribe?

- Spend less time learning and more time coding with practical eBooks and Videos from over 4,000 industry professionals

- Improve your learning with Skill Plans built especially for you

- Get a free eBook or video every month

- Mapt is fully searchable

- Copy and paste, print, and bookmark content

Packt.com

Did you know that Packt offers eBook versions of every book published, with PDF and ePub files available? You can upgrade to the eBook version at `www.packt.com` and as a print book customer, you are entitled to a discount on the eBook copy. Get in touch with us at `customercare@packtpub.com` for more details.

At `www.packt.com`, you can also read a collection of free technical articles, sign up for a range of free newsletters, and receive exclusive discounts and offers on Packt books and eBooks.

Contributors

About the authors

Diogo Resende is a developer with more than 15 years of experience, working with Node.js almost from the beginning. His computer education and experience in many industries and telecommunication projects have given him a wider background knowledge of other architecture components that influence the overall performance.

Paul Osman has been building external and internal platforms for over 10 years. From public APIs targeted at third parties to internal platform teams, he has helped build distributed systems that power large-scale consumer applications. He has managed teams of engineers to rapidly deliver service-based software systems with confidence. Paul has published articles and given multiple conference talks on microservices and DevOps. He is a passionate advocate of open technology platforms and tools.

Packt is searching for authors like you

If you're interested in becoming an author for Packt, please visit `authors.packtpub.com` and apply today. We have worked with thousands of developers and tech professionals, just like you, to help them share their insight with the global tech community. You can make a general application, apply for a specific hot topic that we are recruiting an author for, or submit your own idea.

Table of Contents

Preface

Microservices are a popular way to build distributed systems that power modern web and mobile apps. With the help of this Learning Path, you'll learn how to develop your applications as a suite of independently deployable and scalable services.

Using an example-driven approach, this Learning Path will uncover how you can dismantle your monolithic application and embrace microservice architecture, right from architecting your services and modeling them to integrating them into your application. You'll also explore ways to overcome challenges in testing and deploying these services by setting up deployment pipelines that break down the application development process into several stages. You'll study serverless architecture for microservices and understand its benefits. Furthermore, this Learning Path delves into the patterns used for organizing services, helping you optimize request handling and processing. You'll then move on to learn the fault-tolerance and reliability patterns that help you use microservices to isolate failures in your applications.

By the end of this Learning Path, you'll have the skills necessary to build enterprise-ready applications using microservices.

This Learning Path includes content from the following Packt products:

- Hands-On Microservices with Node.js by Diogo Resende
- Microservices Development Cookbook by Paul Osman

Who this book is for

If you're a JavaScript developer looking to put your skills to work by building microservices and moving away from the monolithic architecture, this book is for you. To understand the concepts explained in this Learning Path, you must have knowledge of Node.js and be familiar with the microservices architecture.

What this book covers

Chapter 1, The Age of Microservices, covers the evolution of computing and how development has changed and shifted from paradigm to paradigm depending on processing capacity and user demand, ultimately resulting in the age of microservices.

Chapter 2, Breaking the Monolith, shows how to make the transition from monolith to microservices, with the recipes focused on architectural design. You'll learn how to manage some of the initial challenges when you begin to develop features using this new architectural style.

Chapter 3, Edge Services, teaches you how to use open source software to expose your services to the public internet, control routing, extend your service's functionality, and handle a number of common challenges when deploying and scaling microservices.

Chapter 4, Modules and Toolkits, introduces you to some modules that help you create a microservice, detailing different approaches: from very raw and simple modules, such as Micro and Express, to full toolkits, such as Hydra and Seneca.

Chapter 5, Building a Microservice, covers the development of a simple microservice using the most common module, Express, with a very simple HTTP interface.

Chapter 6, State and Security, covers the development of our microservice: from using the server filesystem to moving to a more structured database service, such as MySQL.

Chapter 7, Testing, shows how to use Mocha and Chai to add test coverage to our previous microservice.

Chapter 8, Deploying Microservices, introduces you to Docker and helps you create a container image to use to run our microservice.

Chapter 9, Scaling, Sharding, and Replicating, covers the concept of replication when using Docker Swarm and Kubernetes locally to scale our microservice.

Chapter 10, Cloud-Native Microservices, shows how to migrate our microservice from the local Kubernetes to Google Cloud Platform, as an example of a fully cloud-native microservice.

Chapter 11, Design Patterns, enumerates some of the most common architectural design patterns and reviews the continuous integration and deployment loop.

Chapter 12, Inter-Service Communication, discusses recipes that will enable you to confidently handle the various kinds of interactions we're bound to require in a microservice architecture.

Chapter 13, Client Patterns, discusses techniques for modeling dependent service calls and aggregating responses from various services to create client-specific APIs. We'll also discuss managing different microservices environments and making RPC consistent with JSON and HTTP, as well as the gRPC and Thrift binary protocols.

Chapter 14, Reliability Patterns, discusses a number of useful reliability patterns that can be used when designing and building microservices to prepare for and reduce the impact of system failures, both expected and unexpected.

Chapter 15, Security, includes recipes that will help you learn a number of good practices to consider when building, deploying, and operating microservices.

Chapter 16, Monitoring and Observability, introduces several tenants of monitoring and observability. We'll demonstrate how to modify our services to emit structured logs. We'll also take a look at metrics, using a number of different systems for collecting, aggregating, and visualizing metrics.

Chapter 17, Scaling, discusses load testing using different tools. We will also set up autoscaling groups in AWS, making them scalable on demand. This will be followed by strategies for capacity planning.

Chapter 18, Deploying Microservices, discusses containers, orchestration, and scheduling, and various methods for safely shipping changes to users. The recipes in this chapter should serve as a good starting point, especially if you're accustomed to deploying monoliths on virtual machines or bare metal servers.

To get the most out of this book

You should have basic Node.js skills and be somewhat comfortable with the language. We will cover Docker and Kubernetes, and it can be helpful to know the concepts of containers—but it's not mandatory. You need to have Node.js (and npm) installed. We recommend using the current stable version, but you're free to use a previous version if it's an LTS one, with possible adaptions. If you want to deploy Kubernetes locally, you'll need to install it later on.

This books assumes basic knowledge of microservices architectures. Other instructions are mentioned in the respective recipes as needed.

Download the example code files

You can download the example code files for this book from your account at `www.packt.com`. If you purchased this book elsewhere, you can visit `www.packt.com/support` and register to have the files emailed directly to you.

You can download the code files by following these steps:

1. Log in or register at `www.packt.com`.
2. Select the **SUPPORT** tab.
3. Click on **Code Downloads & Errata**.
4. Enter the name of the book in the **Search** box and follow the onscreen instructions.

Once the file is downloaded, please make sure that you unzip or extract the folder using the latest version of:

- WinRAR/7-Zip for Windows
- Zipeg/iZip/UnRarX for Mac
- 7-Zip/PeaZip for Linux

The code bundle for the book is also hosted on GitHub at `https://github.com/TrainingByPackt/BuildingMicroserviceswithJavaScript` .In case there's an update to the code, it will be updated on the existing GitHub repository.

We also have other code bundles from our rich catalogue of books and videos available at `https://github.com/PacktPublishing/`. Check them out!

Downloading the color images of this book

We also provide you with a PDF file that has color images of the screenshots/diagrams used in this book. The color images will help you better understand the changes in the output. You can download this file from `https://www.packtpub.com/sites/default/files/downloads/9781838826192_ColorImages.pdf`

Conventions used

There are a number of text conventions used throughout this book.

`CodeInText`: Indicates code words in text, database table names, folder names, filenames, file extensions, pathnames, dummy URLs, user input, and Twitter handles. Here is an example: "The `input()` method is used to get an input from the user."

A block of code is set as follows:

```
{
"username": "paulosman",
"followings": [
"johnsmith",
"janesmith",
"petersmith"
]
}
```

Any command-line input or output is written as follows:

```
docker build . -t gcr.io/imagini-205120/imagini
```

Bold: Indicates a new term, an important word, or words that you see onscreen. For example, words in menus or dialog boxes appear in the text like this. Here is an example: "If you need something different, click on the **DOWNLOADS** link in the header for all possible downloads: "

Warnings or important notes appear like this.

Tips and tricks appear like this.

Get in touch

Feedback from our readers is always welcome.

General feedback: If you have questions about any aspect of this book, mention the book title in the subject of your message and email us at `customercare@packtpub.com`.

Errata: Although we have taken every care to ensure the accuracy of our content, mistakes do happen. If you have found a mistake in this book, we would be grateful if you would report this to us. Please visit `www.packt.com/submit-errata`, selecting your book, clicking on the Errata Submission Form link, and entering the details.

Piracy: If you come across any illegal copies of our works in any form on the Internet, we would be grateful if you would provide us with the location address or website name. Please contact us at `copyright@packt.com` with a link to the material.

If you are interested in becoming an author: If there is a topic that you have expertise in and you are interested in either writing or contributing to a book, please visit `authors.packtpub.com`.

Reviews

Please leave a review. Once you have read and used this book, why not leave a review on the site that you purchased it from? Potential readers can then see and use your unbiased opinion to make purchase decisions, we at Packt can understand what you think about our products, and our authors can see your feedback on their book. Thank you!

For more information about Packt, please visit `packt.com`.

The Age of Microservices 1

Decades ago, more specifically in 1974, Intel introduced 8080 to the world, which is an 8-bit processor with a 2 MHz clock speed and 64 KB of memory. This processor was used in Altair and began the revolution in personal computers.

It was sold pre-assembled or as a kit for hobbyists. It was the first computer to have enough power to actually be used for calculations. Even though it had some poor design choices and needed an engineering major to be able to use and program it, it started the spread of personal computers to the general public.

The technology evolved rapidly and the processor industry followed Moore's law, almost doubling speed every two years. Processors were still single core, with a low-efficiency ratio (power consumption per clock cycle). Because of this, servers usually did one specific job, called a service, like serving HTTP pages or managing a **Lightweight Directory Access Protocol (LDAP)** directory. Services were the monolith, with very few components, and were compiled altogether to be able to take the most out of the hardware processor and memory.

In the 90s, the internet was still only available for the few. Hypertext, based on HTML and HTTP, was in its infancy. Documents were simple and browsers developed language and protocol as they pleased. Competition for market share was ferocious between Internet Explorer and Netscape. The latter introduced JavaScript, which Microsoft copied as JScript:

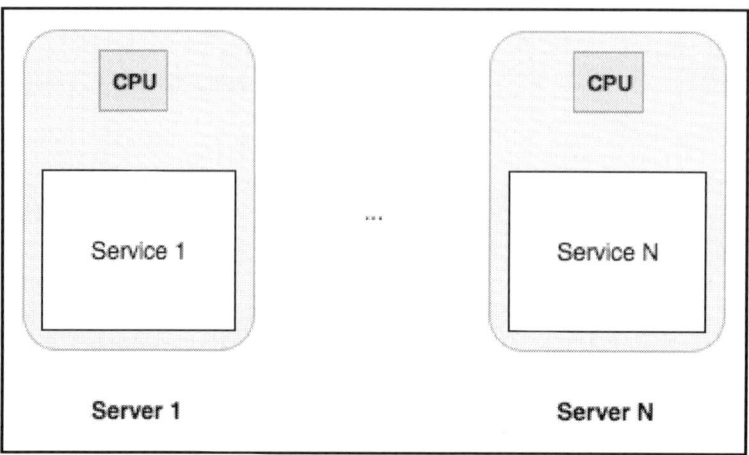

Simple single-core servers

After the turn of the century, processor speed continued to increase, memory grew to generous sizes, and 32-bit became insufficient for allocating memory addresses. The all-new 64-bit architecture appeared and personal computer processors hit the 100 W consumption mark. Servers gained muscle and were able to handle different services. Developers still avoided breaking the service into parts. Interprocess communication was considered slow and services were kept in threads, inside a single process.

The internet was starting to become largely available. Telcos started offering triple play, which included the internet bundled with television and phone services. Cellphones became part of the revolution and the age of the smartphone began.

JSON appeared as a subset of the JavaScript language, although it's considered a language-independent data format. Some web services began to support the format.

The following is an example of servers with a couple of services running, but still having only one processor.

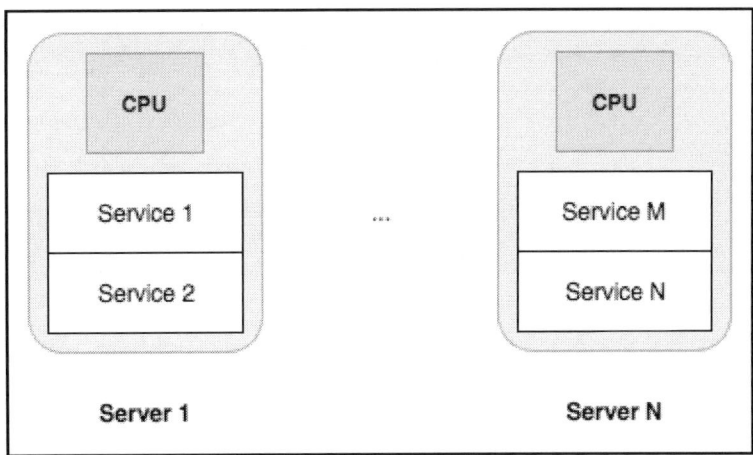

Powerful but single-core servers

Processor evolution then shifted. Instead of the increased speed that we were used to, processors started to appear with two cores, and then four cores. Eight cores followed, and it seemed the evolution of the computer would follow this path for some time.

This also meant a shift in architecture in the development paradigms. Relying on the system to take advantage of all processors is unwise. Services started to take advantage of this new layout and now it's common to see services having at least one processor per core. Just look at any web server or proxy, such as Apache or Nginx.

The internet is now widely available. Mobile access to the internet and its information corresponds to more or less half of all internet access.

In 2012, the **Internet Engineering Task Force (IETF)** began its first drafts for the second version of HTTP or HTTP/2, and **World Wide Web Consortium (W3C)** did the same for HTML/HTML5, as both standards were old and needed a remake. Thankfully, browsers agreed on merging new features and specifications and developers no longer have the burden of developing and testing their ideas on the different browser edge cases.

The following is an example of servers with more services running as we reach a point where each server has more than one processor:

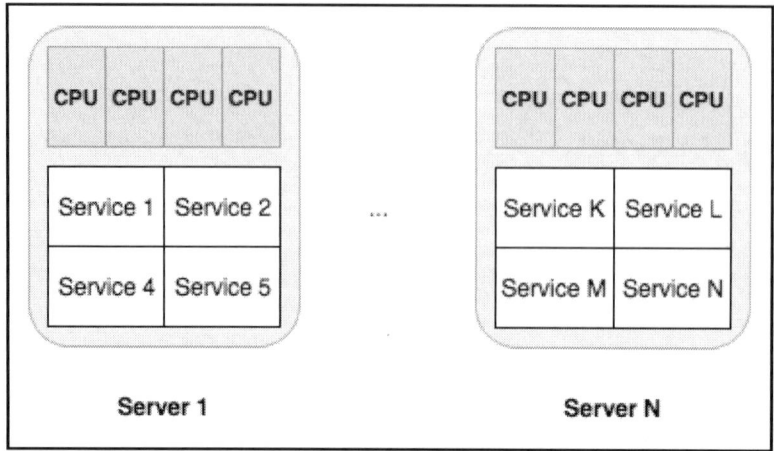

Powerful multi-core servers

Access to information in real time is a growing demand. The **Internet of Things (IoT)** multiplies the number of devices connected to the internet. People now have a couple of devices at home, and the number will just keep rising. Applications need to be able to handle this growth.

On the internet, HTTP is the standard protocol for communication. Routers usually do not block it, as it is considered a low traffic protocol (in contrast with video streams). This is actually not true nowadays, but it's now so widely used that changing this behavior would probably cause trouble.

Nowadays, it's actually so common to have the HTTP serving developer API working with JSON that most programming languages that release any version after 2015 probably support this data format natively.

As a consequence of processor evolution, and because of the data-demanding internet we now have, it's important to not only be able to scale a service or application to the several available cores, but also to scale outside a single hardware machine.

Many developers started using and following the **Service-Oriented Architecture (SOA)** principle. It's a principle where the architecture is focused on services, and each service presents itself to others as an application component and provides information to other application components, passing messages over some standard communication protocol.

Introducing microservices

Microservices, which are a variation of SOA, have become more and more appealing. Many projects have embraced this architecture, and it's not difficult to understand why. With the constant increase in demand for information, applications become more complex, especially with more information being transferred from new data sources to new data visualization devices.

New communication technologies have emerged, social communities spring up like mushrooms, and people expect an application to be able to merge into today's cyber lifestyle.

Microservices come to the rescue by defining a simple strategy: break every complex service into a small, simpler service that is aiming for common functionality. The idea is that services should be small and lightweight - so small that they can be easily maintained, developed, and tested, and so lightweight that they can be responsive and scale more easily:

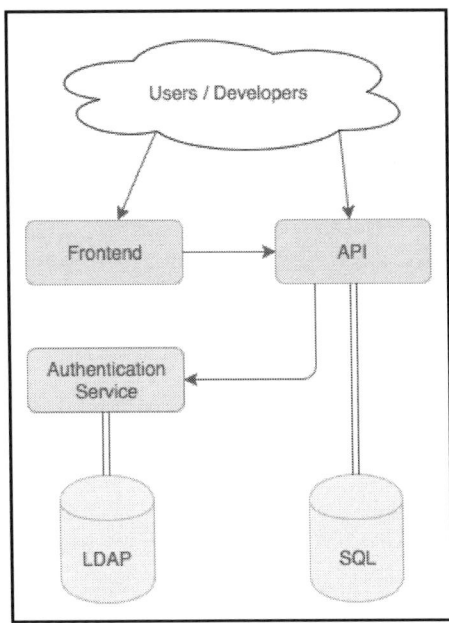

Example of a simple microservices architecture

The preceding diagram is an example of an application that has been split into small microservices (marked as green and blue), with one for the frontend interface, another one for the API, and one just for authentication.

The idea is to decompose the business logic into small and reusable parts, easily understandable in separate chunks, enabling parallel development by different teams or groups. This way, people can develop parts without being worried about breaking an other's code. Each part should be considered a black box to other parts.

It is only important that communication is well-described. It's common for microservices to communicate over HTTP and use JSON as the data format. There are other formats available, such as XML, but they have fallen into desuetude. It's also common to use AMQP as an inter-service communication, but usually not as a public API service.

To summarize, there are several advantages of using this architecture:

- **Maintenance**: Services, when separate, become easier to develop, test, and deploy because they should be simpler and small
- **Design enforcement**: A proper and good design is enforced on the application being developed
- **Knowledge encapsulation**: Services will have specific objectives, such as delivering emails, which will lead to service re-usage and knowledge about specific tasks being grouped together in services
- **Replaceable**: Services become easier to swap because their functionality and communication is well-known
- **Technology agnostic**: Each service can be developed using the best tools and languages to build it correctly
- **Performant**: Services are small and lightweight, and, as mentioned previously, use the best tools available
- **Upgradable**: Services should be interchangeable and upgradable separately
- **Productivity**: When complexity starts to grow, productivity will be better than in a monolith application

There are also costs associated with this architecture, namely:

- **Dependencies**: Because of this architecture being technology agnostic, different dependencies for different services may arise

- **Complexity**: For small applications, the bootstrap complexity is bigger compared to the monolith
- **End-to-end testing**: It becomes more complex to test the application from end to end as the number of services to inter-connect is definitely bigger than in a monolith application

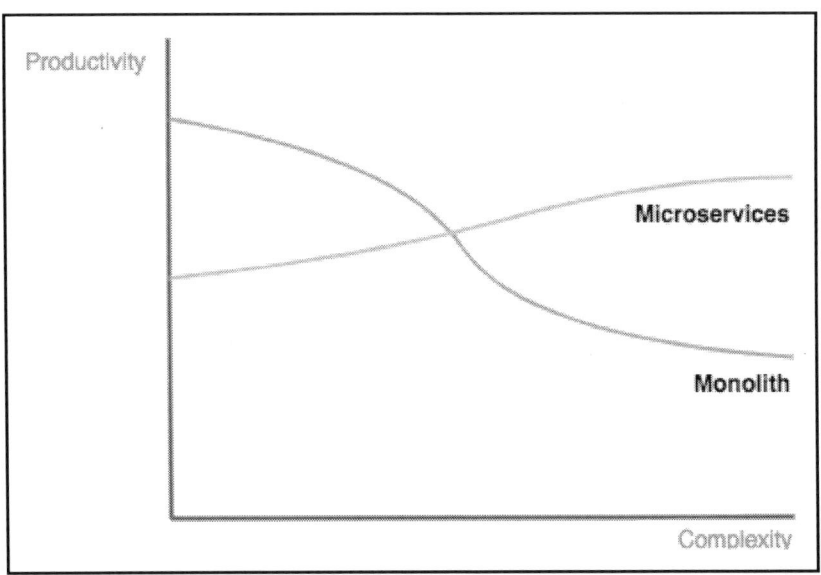

Variation in productivity as complexity grows for both monolith and microservices architecture

The graph is not to be taken very seriously; it's just an approximation of the difference between monolith and microservice architectures. In the beginning, when complexity was just beginning, productivity for microservices was poor as the architecture bootstrap demanded more work and thought.

As complexity started to increase, monolith applications became more difficult to manage and productivity began to decrease. On the other hand, as the microservices architecture started to separate services, productivity increased as the bootstrap already passed and each service was easier to manage.

Some may argue that microservices productivity will not grow as complexity will eventually also hit every service, but that's not true if a team follows the number one rule: if the complexity of a service is too much, split the service into smaller ones.

This architecture design brings long-term advantages if used correctly and across several applications. Services can be reused, which can potentially lead to more intensive usage, which will eventually lead to a more resilient and better-tested service.

Also, future applications can bootstrap faster if a development team has already bootstrapped one before. Previous services can also be integrated, which might lead to gaining an initial application testbed faster.

Using a microservices approach also helps to eliminate any long-term commitment to a technology stack. In the near future, when a team feels the need to change the stack, they can start new services using the new stack, and upgrade the old services one by one if they want to, without compromising the entire application.

Introducing Node.js

Node.js has become a very popular language, so to speak. It's not actually a language, it's a wraparound language, like JavaScript, or ECMAScript. JavaScript was developed for the browser and it is actually small by definition. Then, browsers created a layer of access to the page elements and events, called DOM. That's one of the reasons why people hate the language so much. Node.js takes only the base language and adds an API so that developers have access to I/O, namely, the filesystem and network.

Ryan Dahl started developing Node.js back in 2009. He felt the need for a performant and less blocking program than the ones that were available. Node.js used Google's V8 JavaScript engine from the beginning and was first introduced at the JSConf in Berlin in 2009.

Looking just at the language, it's actually a sound and small, functional, object-oriented, prototype-based language. Everything is an object or inherits from it. Even numbers and functions inherit from an object. The good parts are as follows:

- Functions are first-class objects
- Functions and block-scoped variables
- Closures and anonymous functions
- Loose typing (can be seen as a bad aspect)

Node.js introduced JavaScript to a group of API modules that enable developers to access the filesystem, run and manage processes, and communicate over the network. Since it was first designed to replace a traditional web server, it also has HTTP and HTTPS modules to perform the roles of the client or server. Some other modules exist around these ones, which can be built as separate modules from the core (like DNS or URL), but live and are maintained inside the core.

At first, Node.js was very unstable, and not only the code's stability, but also the API's stability. Methods could change between versions dramatically. Modules got deprecated and replaced by others rapidly (search for the sys module for more information). Only brave developers would use it in production.

By the time it hit version 0.8, it became more reliable and the API had been stabilized. Large companies started supporting it and the community grew. Although there was a fork in 2014 because of internal conflicts, the community survived and the two code trees merged back in 2015:

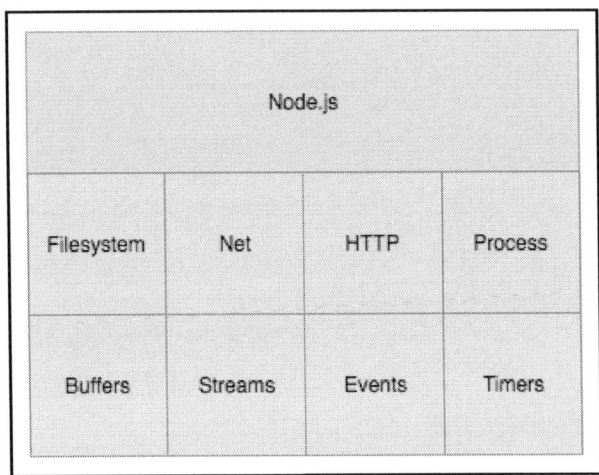

Some of the most frequently used Node.js modules

Because of its use of Google's V8, and because it has a small and stable API, it's very fast and reliable. The reason for having a small API is that one of the guidelines of the community is to only have core functionality in the core API since everything else should go into a module. This has also become a major advantage of Node.js. It has a huge community with hundreds of thousands of modules available.

If you stop and think about it, this is the microservices approach – having separate modules to do one job and one job only, and do it well. You can easily find good, stable, and mature modules for specific needs, which are used by thousands of developers. These mature modules are all easy to deploy and have test suites to ensure they keep stable and functional.

But Node.js is not only about the modules. JavaScript has also evolved in the last couple of years and Google's V8 has always been an early adopter, so Node.js developers get access to the latest new features. Some of them have given developers new ways of simplifying code and removing some of the so-called **callback hell**.

Node.js's **Long Term Support** (LTS) version already has stable support for many new language features. Let's see some of them and how they're useful.

Modules

You develop Node.js code in separate files, called modules. There are three module types:

- Core modules, which you can load anywhere
- Dependency modules, which you can also load anywhere
- Local modules, which you need to load based on the relative path

Modules are loaded synchronously and cached. So, a repeated load will actually not be a load; instead, Node.js will pass you a reference to the already loaded module. This is true for all three types of modules:

```
# loading a JSON file with settings from same path as module
const settings = require("./settings");
```

Local modules are simple files where you need to know the relative or full path. You can also load a path and Node.js will look up the `index.js` file inside it. You can also load JSON files. You don't need to specify the file extension since Node.js will look for `.js` and `.json` files.

A module is nothing more than an object. The module developers decide what to expose and what not to. When you load a module, the code inside can have timers and I/O operations just like your own code. Even without you initializing it, it can run immediately after you load it.

There are hundreds of thousands of modules available. Take some time to search for something you need instead of writing one of your own. Some modules are structured so you can load parts of it (like async and lodash), thereby avoiding the memory footprint of loading everything when you just need a function or two.

Arrow functions

Arrow functions are a shorter expression function syntax without their own function scope, meaning this reference will point to the parent scope. This helps developers avoid saving a reference to the parent scope so they are able to reach it later on.

```
function start() {
    this.uptime = process.uptime();
    setTimeout(() => {
        console.log(this.uptime);
    }, 5000);
}
start();
```

It also helps to write less code for simple operation functions, for example, on array methods. Arrow functions are quite useful when it comes to manipulating arrays of information, whether for filtering, transforming, or reducing them to single values:

```
let double = function (value) {
    return value * 2;
};

[ 1, 2, 3 ].map(double);      // [ 2, 4, 6 ]
[ 1, 2, 3 ].map(v => v * 2);  // [ 2, 4, 6 ]
```

Classes

JavaScript's classes are syntactic sugar over the inheritance model. They introduced a new way of defining object-oriented inheritance that existed in JavaScript but that new developers were not used to. They also introduced a simpler way of extending and defining an object prototype:

```
class Rectangle {
    constructor (w, h) {
        this.w = w;
        this.h = h;
    }
    get area () {
```

```
        return this.w * this.h;
    }
    static clone(r) {
        return new Rectangle(r.w, r.h);
    }
}
```

We just created a Rectangle class, with a constructor to specify dimensions and an area method, too. We also added a static method to clone a Rectangle instance.

Unlike the previous, and still possible, prototype definition, using this syntax will force a stricter development. More specifically:

- There's no hoisting, which means the class must be defined before usage
- There's no prototype redefinition

Promises and async/await

A Promise is an object that represents the completion or failure of an asynchronous operation. The Promise can be chained to perform serial operations, run in parallel until all operations execute, or even race operations and wait only for the first completion or failure:

```
Promise.race([
    new Promise((resolve, reject) => {
        // some possibly long operation
    }),
    new Promise((resolve, reject) => {
        setTimeout(reject, 5000);
    })
]).then(() => {
    console.log("success!");
}, () => {
    console.log("failed");
});
```

More recently, a syntactic sugar was created around Promise to mimic synchronous code syntax. Basically, you can indicate that a function is asynchronously using the async keyword. The function will then return a Promise when called. When the function returns a value, the Promise is resolved with that value. If the function throws an error, the Promise is rejected.

You can then use asynchronous functions inside other asynchronous functions, as follows:

```
function delay(timeout) {
  return new Promise((resolve) => {
    setTimeout(resolve, timeout);
  });
}
async function run() {
  await delay(1000);
  console.log("done");
}
run();
```

Spread and rest syntax

The spread syntax allows an iterable to be expanded in places where arguments (in functions) or elements (in arrays) are expected. It's very useful when, for example, a function accepts an initial set of arguments and then an unlimited one:

```
const concat = (separator, ...parts) => (parts.join(separator));

concat(", ", 1, 2, 3); // "1, 2, 3"
```

This example is especially important in arrow functions since you don't have access to the arguments object. It's also quite useful to merge arrays, as in the following example:

```
const a = [ 1, 2, 3 ];
const b = [ 4, 5, 6 ];

[ ...a, ...b ]; // [ 1, 2, 3, 4, 5, 6 ]
```

Default function parameters

There's no longer the need to use logical operators or check argument types to define default argument values. They can be defined directly in the prototype:

```
function pad(text, len, char = " ") {
    return text.substr(0, len) +
            (text.length < len ? char.repeat(text.length - len) : "");
}
pad("John", 10, "=");
```

If you've developed in languages like Python before, remember default arguments in JavaScript are evaluated at call time, not when defining the function. This means a new object is created every time:

```
function add(value, list = []) {
    list.push(value);
    return list;
}

add(1); // [ 1 ]
add(2); // [ 2 ] , not [ 1, 2 ]
```

Destructuring

Destructuring is the convenient method of constructing (target) or extracting (source) properties from an object. It gives the developer the ability to pick specific object properties from arguments or swap variable values, for example:

```
// head = 1, tail = [ 2, 3, 4]
let [ head, ...tail ] = [ 1, 2, 3, 4 ];

// list = [ "john", "jane" ]
let { users: list } = { users: [ "john", "jane" ] };
```

You can also have more complex destructuring in assignments and function arguments. You can also assign default values:

```
class Rectangle {
    constructor({ width = 100, height = 50 } = {}) {
        this.width = width;
        this.height = height;
    }
}
```

Template literals

Template literals are string literals that allow embedded expressions. Another advantage of these literals is that they can be written in multiple lines:

```
function hello(name) {
    console.log(`Hello ${name}`);
}
```

It's not a simple variable substitution, since it evaluates expressions of any kind:

```
function hello(name, age) {
    console.log(`hi ${name}, you were born in ${(new Date).getFullYear() -
age}`);
}
```

Advantages of using Node.js

Node.js has become a very strong competitor for building all kinds of applications. Large companies use it nowadays to deliver frontend interfaces and information, but also for specific backend services and developer API interfaces. Twitter, LinkedIn, and eBay are examples of these companies.

Let's go through all of the advantages of using Node.js one by one.

Node.js Package Manager

The huge number of modules available today makes it easy to start developing any kind of application or service, and npm ensures you're able to deploy your code in other servers easily. In fact, npm is also one of the advantages of Node.js and is also responsible for its spread.

```
# look how fast it checks dependencies (infinite levels), downloads them
# and installs them locally

$ npm i express
+ express@4.16.2
added 48 packages in 3.129s
```

There has always been some criticism about using Node.js, with people considering it slow and inefficient for some tasks. Some usually point to the fact that the code is single-threaded, but forget that the core API, which is your only way of communicating over the network or with the filesystem, uses a thread pool of workers to handle your actions:

```
const http = require("http");

// request is done in a separate thread, code execution continues
http
.request("http://www.google.com")
.once("response", (res) => {
    console.log(res.headers);
})
```

```
.end();

console.log("getting google.com headers..");
```

Asynchronous I/O

The main purpose and the initial idea behind Node.js was to be able to handle asynchronous I/O effectively. To achieve that goal, Node.js has a very good toolkit. It's built around libuv, which empowers the JavaScript language to do asynchronous I/O.

This means that it's kind of a silver bullet in this field. As long as your application is slim, not very CPU intensive, and is able to handle I/O efficiently, Node.js is the right tool for you.

Although it's true that your code runs in a single thread, as soon as your code needs to open a file or make an HTTP request, it uses other threads to do so. So, to really take advantage of the Node.js architecture, you should use it for writing code that actually needs the core API.

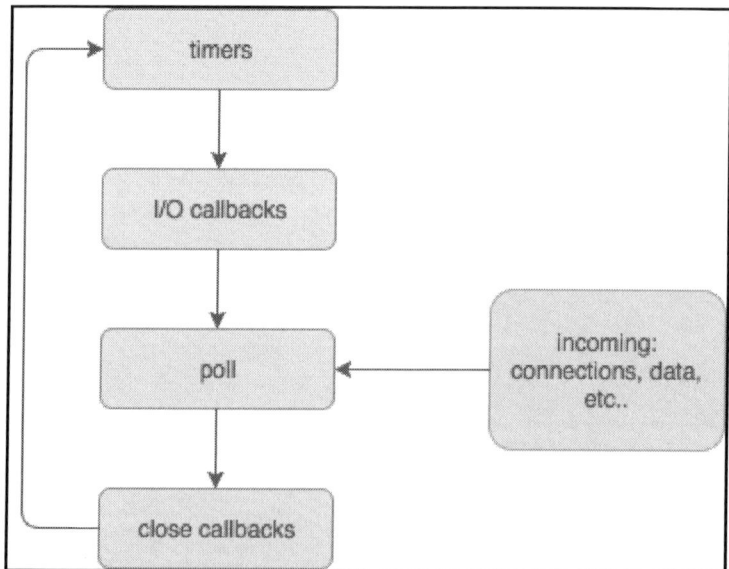

The simplified version of the Node.js Event Loop

The Event Loop is a loop mechanism that is responsible for handling asynchronous I/O code. The code you write synchronously runs immediately. The rest, like connecting to a third-party API, a database, or opening a file, will be queued in the poll. After that, if any timeout occurs (by a `setTimeout` or `setInterval`), they run. After that, run the I/O callbacks, if any. This is data from a file or a socket, for example. Finally, the close callbacks are executed. This is an over-simplified idea of the loop. There are several other tasks in-between (such as `setImmediate` before the close callbacks).

If you're writing code to perform some processor-intensive calculations, with big number manipulation or with fraction precision, Node.js will perform poorly. You may need to find modules to help you address these disadvantages by moving its weak points out of the JavaScript context.

If you still want to use Node.js for performance tasks, try creating a C++ module and use that instead. You can then pass the calculations to this module and still be able to use Node.js for other tasks that you would normally need more code for in C++.

Community

People around the language can also influence it, and in this case positively. There were some strange moments in the past, more specifically, sometime before the `io.js` fork. But the community didn't give up and the commitment to the language has brought it to what it is now.

It's a strong community around a structured language that has gained traction like no other. Developers know what to expect and there's an effort to keep it stable and secure, which, for me, is one of the fundamental principles for a developer to even consider using a language.

Summing up, the advantages of Node.js are as follows:

- A stable and mature language, used and known by web developers for years
- A performant core, based on Google's V8 engine
- A huge community and large module base, with dozens of modules for each task that you can choose from
- An active and maintained core, with a focus on stability and security

From monolith to microservices

As we described previously, a microservices architecture is based on a loosely coupled set of services that work together to achieve a specific target application. At the end of the spectrum, there are monolith applications.

A monolith application is composed of a set of components that are tightly coupled. These components are usually developed using the same language and the application runs as a whole. The first noticeable difference is probably the slow start. Deploying might also be slow since you might need a couple of dependencies before having anything up and running.

Let's imagine an event application, a simple one, an application that lets users define events and be notified when those events are about to start.

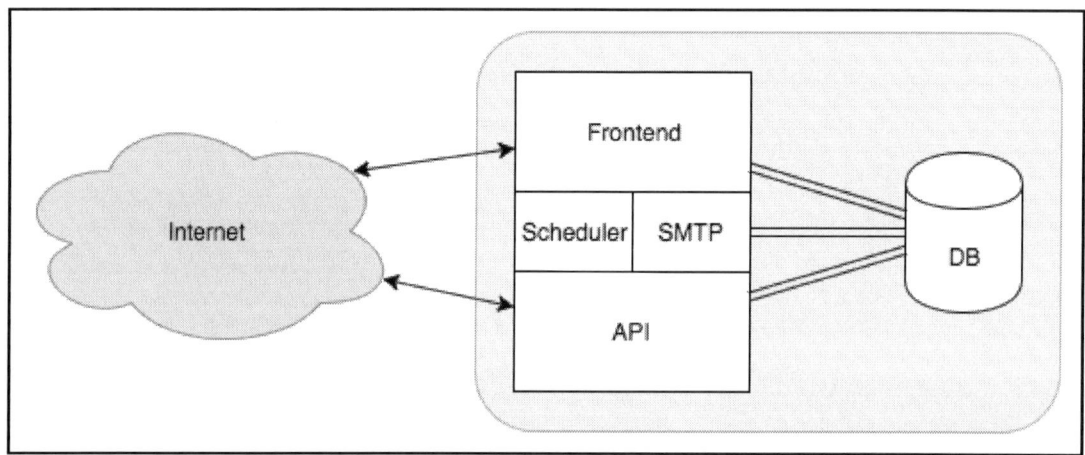

A monolith event application

Let's describe what the event application does:

- It allows users to register themselves and add events to a calendar
- A few minutes before the event starts (that's what the **Scheduler** component is for), the users receive an email with the event information (that's the **SMTP** component)
- Users can use the frontend interface or the **API** interface

Imagine the preceding application as being a monolith (the greyed out area on the right). Imagine that all four parts are part of the same process, even though they could be in separate threads. Imagine that the database is accessed directly across the application. Sound good?

Well, it sounds terrible, perhaps not for a small application, but for a medium one, this would be a representation of chaos. Having a group of developers making new features or improvements would be a nightmare, and for new developers entering the group, it would take some time before having the base knowledge to make some changes.

The first principle that you should follow is the **Don't Repeat Yourself (DRY)** principle. Avoiding multiple components from accessing a data source helps developers in the future. Later on, if there's a need to change the data source or part of its structure, it will be easier if only one component manipulates it. This is not always possible, but if it is possible, you should keep the data source access to a minimum.

In our example, the API should probably have access, and all others should use the API.

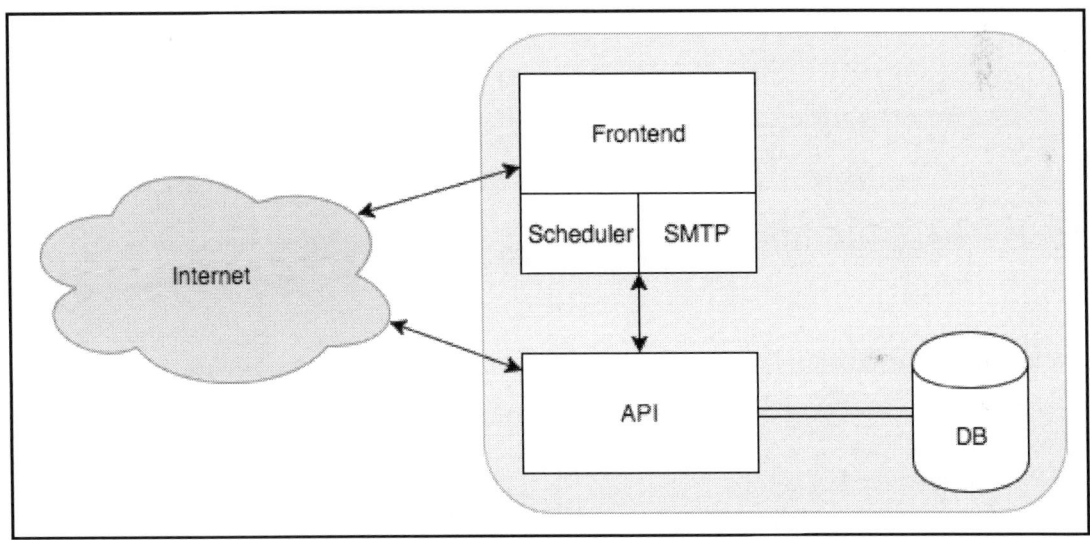

A single service accessing a data source

We now have two services:

- The API, which is the only service accessing the data source
- The frontend, which is the user's interface to change the data source

Although the frontend is used to manage events, it uses the API service to manipulate data sources. Besides having only one service managing data sources, it forces you to think of the API for external developers. It's a win-win.

There is still room for improvement. The **Frontend** could be in a separate service, allowing you to scale the interface according to user traffic, and have the other parts on separate services. **Scheduler** and **SMTP** are both candidates for separate services. **SMTP** should be thought of as a reusable service for other applications you might develop later on.

Let's take a look at how we could build the same application using the microservices approach:

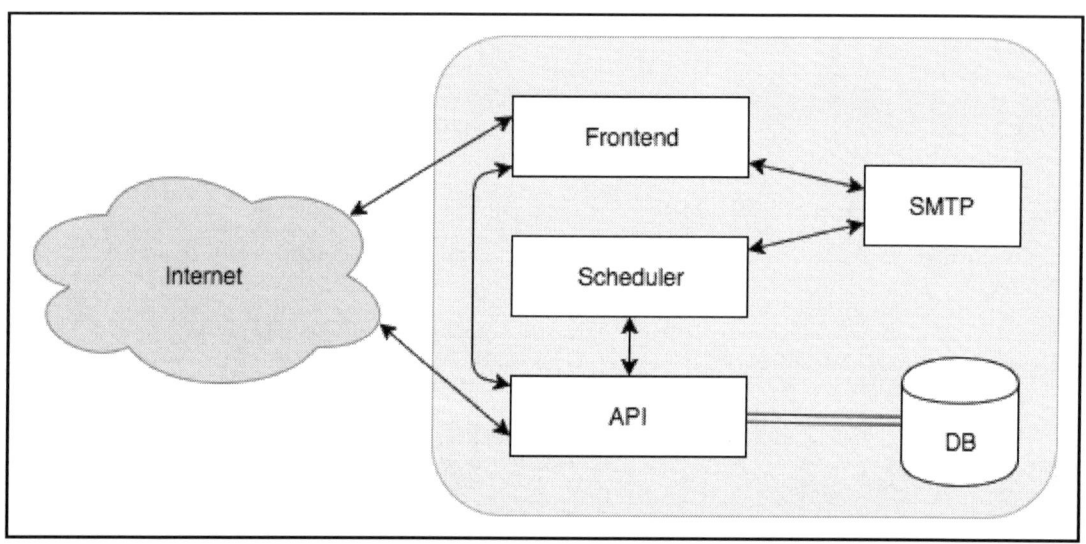

A microservices event application

It looks more complex. Well, the architecture is more complex. The difference is that now, we have loosely coupled components, and each one of them is easily understandable and maintainable. Summing up the changes and advantages:

- The **API** is the only one accessing the database so it can change from SQLite, MongoDB, MySQL, or anything else, and no other component is affected
- **SMTP** can be used from the **Frontend** and **Scheduler**, and if you decide to change it from using a local service to using a third-party email sending **API**, you can make the change easily

- **SMTP** is a candidate for being a reusable service in other applications, meaning you can use it in other applications or event share the same service between multiple applications

You can think of these components as capabilities of your application. They can be swapped, upgraded, maintained, and scaled, all without affecting other components or your application.

A commonly underestimated advantage of using this approach is that your application is much more resilient to failures. In a monolith application, any part can bring your application offline. In this microservices approach, this application might not send emails but can still be running and accessible. Add caching into the mixture and the API can restart in moments.

Patterns of microservices

Microservices architecture, like other archicectures, has a set of patterns that are easily identifiable and form the basis for this application development approach.

Some of these patterns can make the initial bootstrap a burden and can eventually be postponed. Others are essential from the beginning or you will have difficulty, later on, in migrating to a full microservice approach.

The following patterns are not an extensive list but they represent a solid foundation:

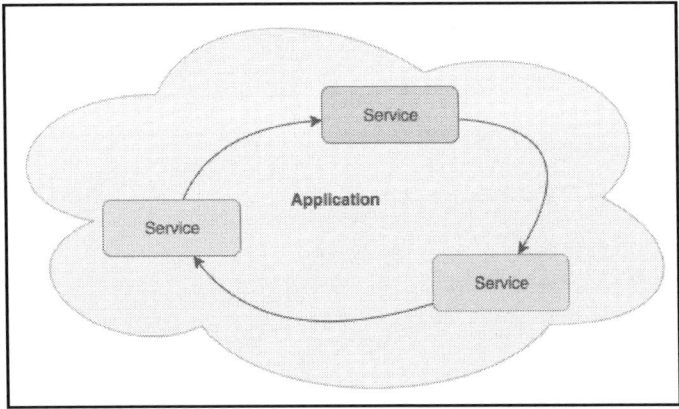

An example of services working together to form an application

Decomposable

The main pattern behind a microservice architecture is the ability to have loosely coupled services. These services are decomposed, separated into smaller parts. This decomposition should create a set of services that implement a set of strongly related functions.

Each service should be small but complete, meaning it should run a set of functions in a given context. Those functions should represent all the functions you need or need to support for that context. What this means is that if you have a service that handles meeting events, all meeting event functions should be done using that service, whether it's creating an event, changing, removing, or getting information about a specific event. This ensures that an implementation change to events will affect that service only.

Decomposing an application can take one of two main approaches:

- By capability, when a service has a specific power or set of powers, such as sending emails, regardless of its content
- By subdomain, when a service has the complete knowledge of a subdomain or module of your application domain

In our previous event application, a service that was decomposed by capability is, for example, the SMTP service. A service decomposed by the domain could be the API service, assuming the application only manages events:

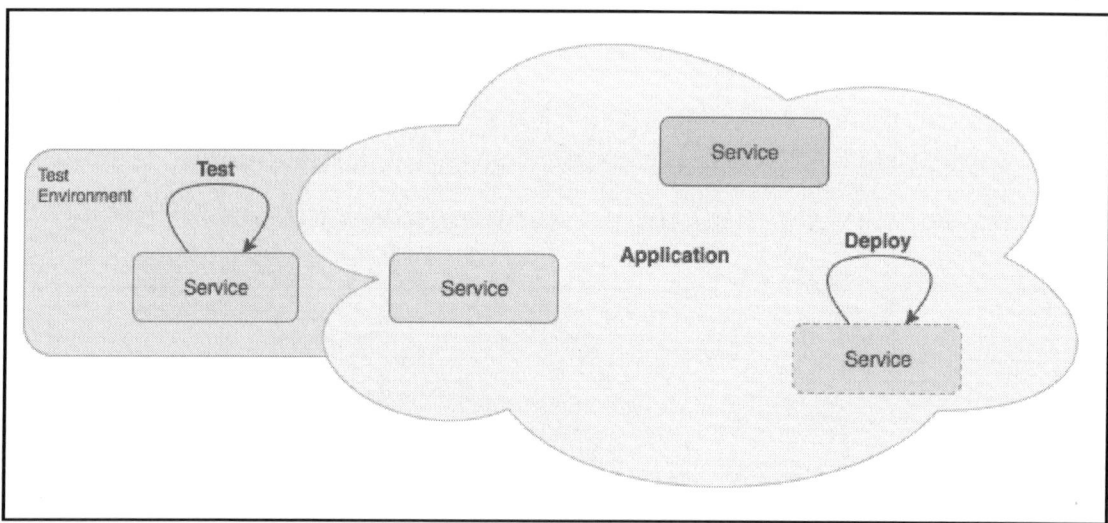

An example of services being tested and deployed autonomously, instead of the whole application

Autonomous

In a microservice architecture, each service should be autonomous. A small team should be able to run it without the other services that make your application. That team should also be able to develop autonomously and make changes to implementation without affecting the application.

The development team should be able to:

- Test, creating business logic and unit tests to ensure the service functions work as expected
- Deploy, upgrading functionality, without restarting other services in the process

Services should be able to evolve regardless of others, keeping backward compatibility, adding new functions, and scaling to several locations, with minimal changes to the architecture:

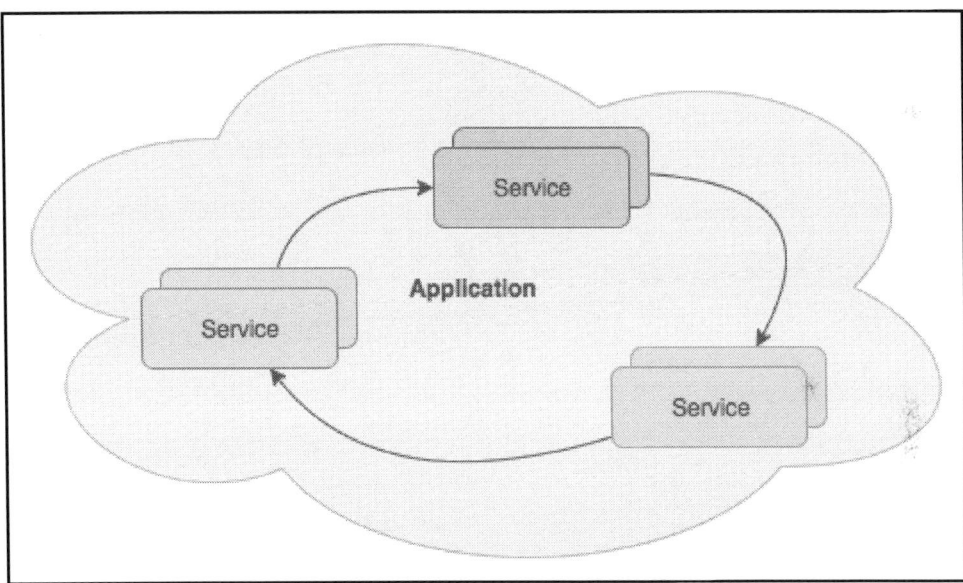

An example of an application with two instances per service, making it fault-tolerant

Scalable

A service should be scalable. At least two instances should be able to run in parallel, enabling failure tolerance and maintenance downtime. A service can also, later on, scale geographically, be near your customers, and improve apparent performance and application response.

For this scaling to be effective, the application platform will need service discovery and routing, a service that could be used by other services to register themselves and expose their capabilities. Other services could, later on, inquire this service directory and know how to reach these capabilities.

To reduce complexity for other services, a service router can redirect requests to service instances. For example, to send emails, you could have three instances and one central router that would redirect requests in a round-robin manner. If any of those instances go offline, the router will stop redirecting to it and the rest of the application doesn't need to care about it.

Another approach could be to use a DNS approach. The name service is capable of handling registrations to a subdomain, and then, when another service makes simple requests, it will receive one or all of the addresses and connect it as if there was only one service operating:

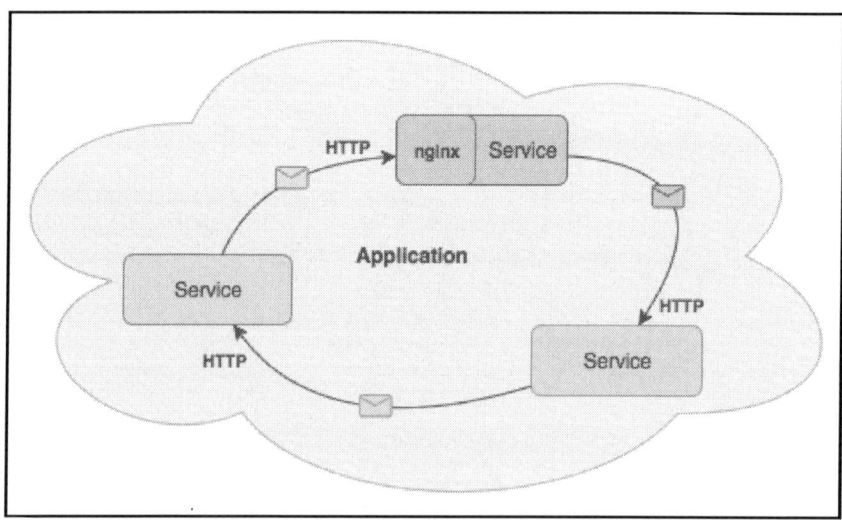

An example of communication between services of an application

Communicable

Usually, services communicate over HTTP using a REST-compliant API. This is not a pattern that you must follow, but it's something that comes naturally based on how common HTTP is nowadays, making it an obvious choice.

There are plenty of HTTP servers out there, making it easy to expose a non-HTTP service with minimum effort.

HTTP is also a mature communication transport layer. It's a stateless protocol, giving developers and operations many features, such as:

- Caching commonly used and often updated resources
- Proxying and routing requests
- Securing communication over TLS

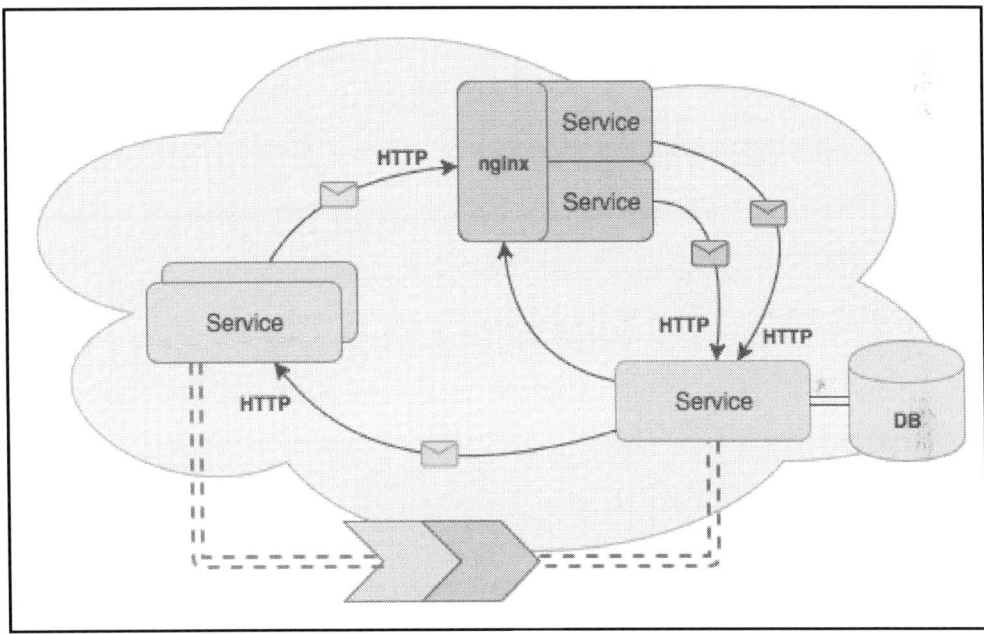

A complex application with several services and streams of communication

Disadvantages of microservices

Microservices have a lot of advantages, and they become more evident in the long term when the application becomes more complex. The microservice patterns primarily introduce complexity and enforce you to be very strict around development in order to avoid losing track of the entire application.

To start with, developers add to the complexity of the distributed system. This distributed system enforces a network communication -- not only do the services need to communicate with each other; they also need to find one another using some kind of service discovery technique.

This adds the need for a stable network to exchange requests. It adds layers of complexity just to exchange a simple request. It will also add an extra layer of security, both for development that needs to support it and for the operations that need to address it. As has been said previously, using bootstrap is harder than using a monolith application.

The operations team can also see some complexity in deployment. It's better to look at several services as separate components for deployment. This is actually as they should look for this architecture. They can, in the long term, even use some of the deployed architecture for new applications. Still, complexity for operations deployment and monitoring is even bigger.

Although not a direct disadvantage, because the architecture is loosely coupled and each service can be built using the best tools for the job, this can increase the heterogeneous environment, which will require operations to have knowledge of a broader technology scope. This can potentially lead to mistakes. Try to look for the second-best tool for the job if that tool is already used in operations.

The operations team will also have to possibly manage more third-party services, such as message queues, as they're commonly used to enable service communication. Other added services that might be added for scalability are service discovery. In a fully scalable application, operations just deploy new services and they register themselves and get used by all of your application's ecosystem.

As you can see, although development might get easier and you'll be able to parallel the application development across teams, there's also an added complexity if you intend to fully scale your application.

As a recommendation, do not plan your application to scale to millions of requests unless you really know it will handle that amount in the near future. Plan your application to have small and lightweight services to start with. It will be easier to do than upgrade the services to scale.

As a possible macro strategy, split your application using these three guidelines:

- Split services by capabilities
- Try to keep subdomains on a single service
- Prepare for scale, but don't scale while there's no need to

Summary

In conclusion, microservices architecture is a good, clear pattern that helps tackle more complex projects. In the long term, it reduces the complexity associated with new projects by appealing to service reuse. It helps to structure an application into loosely coupled services that can be independently developed and tested by small, different teams. It comes at the cost of initial proper planning and a more complex deployment.

We shall now take a look at the recipes mentioned in the next chapter that would explain in much more detail on how to make the transition from monolith to microservices

Breaking the Monolith 2

In this chapter, we will cover the following recipes:

- Organizing your team to embrace microservices
- Decomposing by business capability
- Identifying bounded contexts
- Migrating data in production
- Refactoring your monolith
- Evolving your monolith into services
- Evolving your test suite
- Using Docker for local development
- Routing requests to services

Introduction

One of the hardest things about microservices is getting started. Many teams have found themselves building features into an ever-growing, hard-to-manage monolithic code base and don't know how to start breaking it apart into more manageable, separately deployable services. The recipes in this chapter will explain how to make the transition from monolith to microservices. Many of the recipes will involve no code whatsoever; instead, they will be focused on architectural design and how best to structure teams to work on microservices.

You'll learn how to begin moving from a single monolithic code base to suites of microservices. You'll also learn how to manage some of the initial challenges when you begin to develop features using this new architectural style.

Organizing your team

Conway's law tells us that organizations will produce designs whose structure is a copy of their communication structure. This often means that the organizational chart of an engineering team will have a profound impact on the structure of the designs of the software it produces. When a new startup begins building software, the team is small—sometimes it is comprised of just one or two engineers. In this setup, engineers work on everything, including frontend and backend systems, as well as operations. Monoliths suit this organizational structure very well, allowing engineers to work on any part of the system at any given time without moving between code bases.

As a team grows, and you start to consider the benefits of microservices, you can consider employing a technique commonly referred to as an the **Inverse Conway Maneuver**. This technique recommends evolving your team and organizational structure to encourage the kind of architectural style you want to see emerge. With regard to microservices, this will usually involve organizing engineers into small teams that you will eventually want to be responsible for a handful of related services. Setting your team up for this structure ahead of time can motivate engineers to build services by limiting communication and decision-making overhead within the team. Simply put, monoliths continue to exist when the cost of adding features as services is greater than the cost of adding a feature to the monolith. Organizing your teams in this way reduces the cost of developing services.

This recipe is aimed at managers and other leaders in companies who have the influence to implement changes to the structure of the organization.

How to do it...

Re-organizing a team is never a simple task, and there are many non-obvious factors to consider. Factors such as personality, individual strengths and weaknesses, and past histories are outside the scope of this recipe, but they should be considered carefully when making any changes. The steps in this recipe provide one possible way to move a team from being organized around a monolithic code base to being optimized for microservices, but there is no one-size-fits-all recipe for every organization.

Use the following steps as a guide if you think they apply, but otherwise use them for inspiration and to encourage thought and discussion:

1. Working with other stakeholders in your organization, build out a product roadmap. You may have limited information about the challenges your organization will face in the short term, but do the best you can. It's perfectly natural to be very detailed for short-term items on a roadmap and very general for the longer term.

2. Using the product roadmap, try to identify technical capabilities that will be required to help you deliver value to your users. For example, you may be planning to work on a feature that relies heavily on search. You may also have a number of features that rely on content uploading and management. This means that search and uploading are two technical capabilities you know you will need to invest in.

3. As you see patterns emerge, try to identify the main functional areas of your application, paying attention to how much work you anticipate will go into each area. Assign higher priorities to the functional areas you anticipate will need a lot of investment in the short to medium term.

4. Create new teams, ideally consisting of four to six engineers, who are responsible for one of the functional areas within your application. Start with the functional areas that you anticipate will require the most work over the next quarter or so. These teams can be focused on the backend services or they can be cross-functional teams that include the mobile and web engineers. The benefit of having cross-functional teams is that the team can then deliver the entire vertical component of the application autonomously. The combination of service engineers with engineers consuming their services will also enable more information sharing, and hopefully, empathy.

Discussion

Using this approach, you should end up with small, cohesive, and focused teams responsible for core areas of your application. The nature of teams is that individuals within the team should start to see the benefit of creating separately managed and deployed code bases that they can work in autonomously without the costly overhead of coordinating changes and deployments with other teams.

To help illustrate these steps, imagine your organization builds an image-messaging application. The application allows users to take a photo with their smart phone and send it, along with a message, to a friend in their contacts list. Their friends can also send them photos with messages. A fictional roadmap for this fictional product could involve the need to add support for short videos, photo filters, and support for emojis. You now know that the ability to record, upload, and play videos, the ability to apply photo filters, and the ability to send rich text will be important to your organization. Additionally, you know from experience that users need to register, log in, and maintain a friends list.

Using the preceding example, you may decide to organize engineers into a media team, responsible for uploading, processing and playing, filters, and storage and delivery, a messaging team, responsible for the sending of photo or video messages with associated text, and a users team, responsible for providing reliable authentication, registration, on-boarding, and social features.

Decomposing by business capability

In the early stages of product development, monoliths are the best suited to delivering features to users as quickly and simply as possible. This is appropriate, as at this point in a products development you do not have luxury problems of having to scale your teams, code bases or ability to serve customer traffic. Following good design practices, you separate your applications concerns into easy-to-read, modular code patterns. Doing so allows engineers to work on different sections of the code autonomously and limits the possibility of having to untangle complicated merge conflicts when it comes time to merge your branch into the master and deploy your code.

Microservices require you to go a step further than the good design practices you've already been following in your monolith. To organize your small, autonomous teams around microservices, you should consider first identifying the core business capabilities that your application provides. Business capability is a business school term that describes the various ways your organization produces value. For example, your internal order management is responsible for processing customer orders. If you have a social application that allows users to submit user-generated content such as photos, your photo upload system provides a business capability.

When thinking about system design, business capabilities are closely related to the **Single Responsibility Principle (SRP)** from **object-oriented design (OOD)**. Microservices are essentially SRP extended to code bases. Thinking about this will help you design appropriately sized microservices. Services should have one primary job and they should do it well. This could be storing and serving images, delivering messages, or creating and authenticating user accounts.

How to do it...

Decomposing your monolith by business capability is a process. These steps can be carried out in parallel for each new service you identify a need for, but you may want to start with one service and apply the lessons you learn to subsequent efforts:

1. Identify a business capability that is currently provided by your monolith. This will be the target for our first service. Ideally this business capability is something that has some focus on the roadmap you worked on in the previous recipe and ownership can be given to one of your newly created teams. Let's use our fictional photo messaging service as an example and assume we'll start with the ability to upload and display media as our first identified business capability. This functionality is currently implemented as a single model and controller in your **Ruby on Rails** monolith:

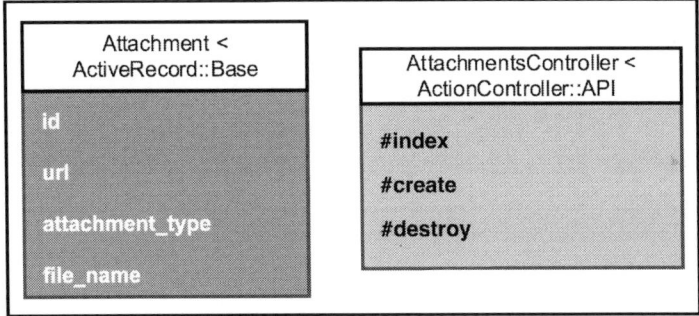

2. In the preceding screenshot, **AttachmentsController** has four methods (called **actions** in Ruby on Rails lingo), which roughly correspond to the **create, retrieve, update, delete (CRUD)** operations you want to perform on an **Attachment** resource. We don't strictly need it, and so will omit the update action. This maps very nicely to a RESTful service, so you can design, implement, and deploy a microservice with the following API:

```
POST /attachments
GET /attachments/:id
DELETE /attachments/:id
```

3. With the new microservice deployed (migrating data is discussed in a later recipe), you can now begin modifying client code paths to use the new service. You can begin by replacing the code in the **AttachmentsController** action's methods to make an HTTP request to our new microservice. Techniques for doing this are covered in the *Evolving your monolith into services* recipe later in this chapter.

Identifying bounded contexts

When designing microservices, a common point of confusion is how big or small a service should be. This confusion can lead engineers to focus on things such as the number of lines of code in a particular service. Lines of code are an awful metric for measuring software; it's much more useful to focus on the role that a service plays, both in terms of the business capability it provides and the domain objects it helps manage. We want to design services that have low coupling with other services, because this limits what we have to change when introducing a new feature in our product or making changes to an existing one. We also want to give services a single responsibility.

When decomposing a monolith, it's often useful to look at the data model when deciding what services to extract. In our fictional image-messaging application, we can imagine the following data model:

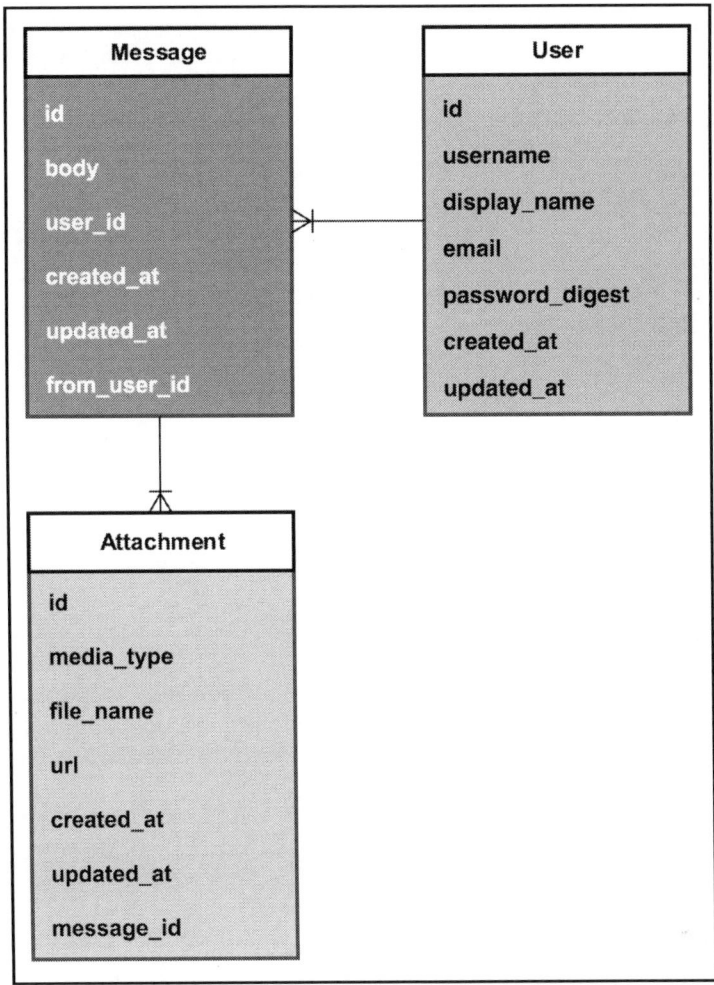

We have a table for messages, a table for users, and a table for attachments. The **Message** entity has a one-to-many relationship with the **User** entity; every user can have many messages that originate from or are targeted at them, and every message can have multiple attachments. What happens as the application evolves and we add more features? The preceding data model does not include anything about social graphs. Let's imagine that we want a user to be able to follow other users. We'll define the following as a asymmetric relationship, just because user 1 follows user 2, that does not mean that user 2 follows user 1.

There are a number of ways to model this kind of relationship; we'll focus on one of the simplest, which is an adjacency list. Take a look at the following diagram:

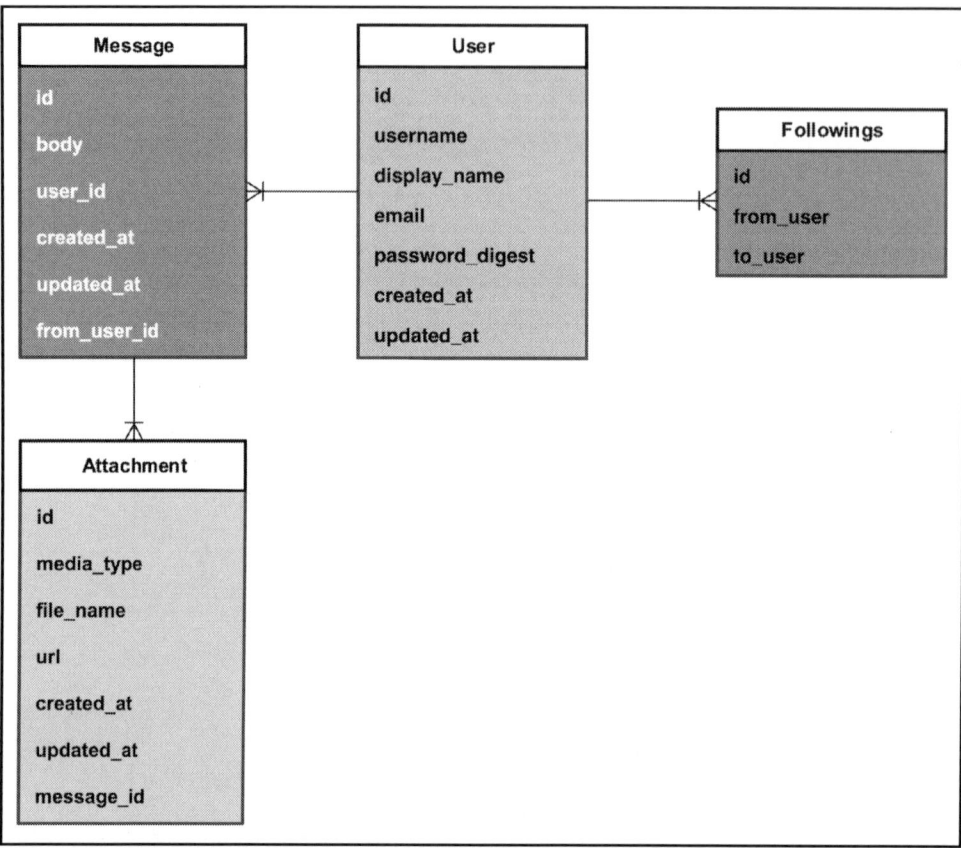

We now have an entity, **Followings**, to represent a follow relationship between two users. This works perfectly in our monolith, but introduces a challenge with microservices. If we were to build two new services, one to handle attachments, and another to handle the social graph (two distinct responsibilities), we now have two definitions of the user. This duplication of models is often necessary. The alternative is to have multiple services access and make updates to the same model, which is extremely brittle and can quickly lead to unreliable code.

This is where bounded contexts can help. A bounded context is a term from **Domain-Driven Design (DDD)** and it defines the area of a system within which a particular model makes sense. In the preceding example, the social-graph service would have a **User** model whose bounded context would be the users social graph (easy enough). The media service would have a **User** model whose bounded context would be photos and videos. Identifying these bounded contexts is important, especially when deconstructing a monolith—you'll often find that as a monolithic code base grows, the previously discussed business capabilities (uploading and viewing photos and videos, and user relationships) would probably end up sharing the same, bloated **User** model, which will then have to be untangled. This can be a tricky but enlightening and important process.

How to do it...

Deciding on how to define bounded contexts within a system can be a rewarding endeavor. The process itself encourages teams to have many interesting discussions about the models in a system and the various interactions that must happen between various systems:

1. Before a team can start to define the bounded contexts it works with, it should first start listing the models that are owned by the parts of the system it works on. For example, the media team will obviously own the **Attachment** model, but it will also need to have information about users, and messages. The **Attachment** model may be entirely maintained within the context of the media teams services, but the others will have to have a well-defined bounded context that can be communicated to other teams if necessary.
2. Once a team has identified potentially shared models, it's a good idea to have a discussion with other teams that use similar models or the same model.
3. In those discussions, hammer out the boundaries of the model and decide whether it makes sense to share a model implementation (which in a microservice world would necessitate a service-to-service call) or go their separate ways and develop and maintain separate model implementations. If the choice is made to develop separate model implementations, it'll become important to clearly define the bounded context within which the model applies.
4. The team should document clear boundaries in terms of teams, specific parts of the application, or specific code bases that should make use of the model.

Migrating data in production

Monolith code bases usually use a primary relational database for persistence. Modern web frameworks are often packaged with **object-relational mapping (ORM)**, which allows you to define your domain objects using classes that correspond to tables in the database. Instances of these model classes correspond to rows in the table. As monolith code bases grow, it's not uncommon to see additional data stores, such as document or key value stores, be added.

Microservices should not share access with the same database your monolith connects to. Doing so will inevitably cause problems when trying to coordinate data migrations, such as schema changes. Even schema-less stores will cause problems when you change the way data is written in one code base but not how data is read in another code base. For this and other reasons, it's best to have microservices fully manage the data stores they use for persistence.

When transitioning from a monolith to microservices, it's important to have a strategy for how to migrate data. All too often, a team will extract the code for a microservice and leave the data, setting themselves up for future pain. In addition to difficulty managing migrations, a failure in the monolith relational database will now have cascading impacts on services, leading to difficult-to-debug production incidents.

One popular technique for managing large-scale data migrations is to set up dual writing. When your new service is deployed, you'll have two write paths–one from the original monolith code base to its database and one from your new service to its own data store. Make sure that writes go to both of these code paths. You'll now be replicating data from the moment your new service goes into production, allowing you to backfill older data using a script or a similar offline task. Once data is being written to both data stores, you can now modify all of your various read paths. Wherever the code is used to query the monolith database directly, replace the query with a call to your new service. Once all read paths have been modified, remove any write paths that are still writing to the old location. Now you can delete the old data (you have backups, right?).

How to do it...

Migrating data from a monolith database to a new store fronted by a new service, without any impact on availability or consistency, is a difficult but common task when making the transition to microservices. Using our fictional photo-messaging application, we can imagine a scenario where we want to create a new microservice responsible for handling media uploads. In this scenario, we'd follow a common dual-writing pattern:

1. Before writing a new service to handle media uploads, we'll assume that the monolith architecture looks something like the following diagram, where HTTP requests are being handled by the monolith, which presumably reads the multipart/form-encoded content body as a binary object and stores the file in a distributed file store (Amazon's S3 service, for example). Metadata about the file is then written to a database table, called **attachments**, as shown in the following diagram:

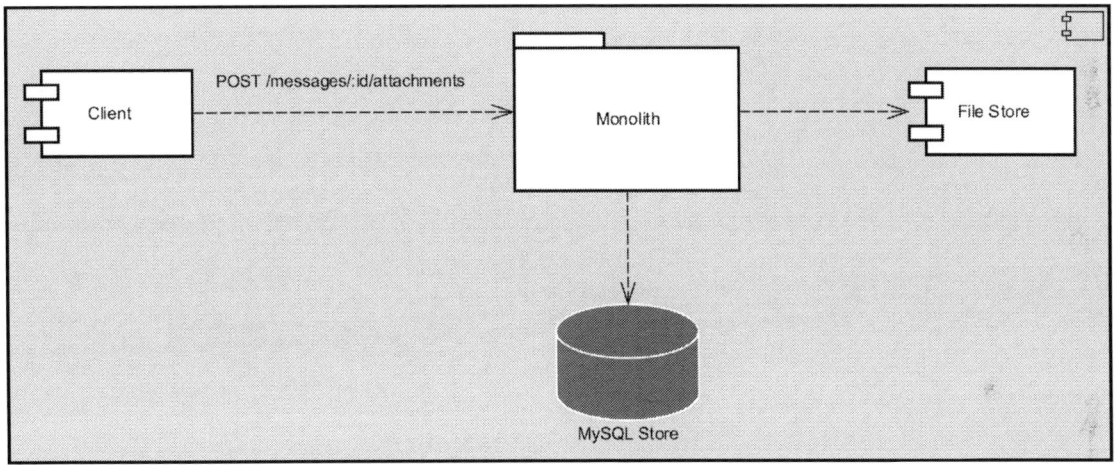

2. After writing a new service, you now have two write paths. In the write path in the monolith, make a call to your service so that you're replicating the data in the monolith database as well as the database fronted by your new service. You're now duplicating new data and can write a script to backfill older data. Your architecture now looks something like this:

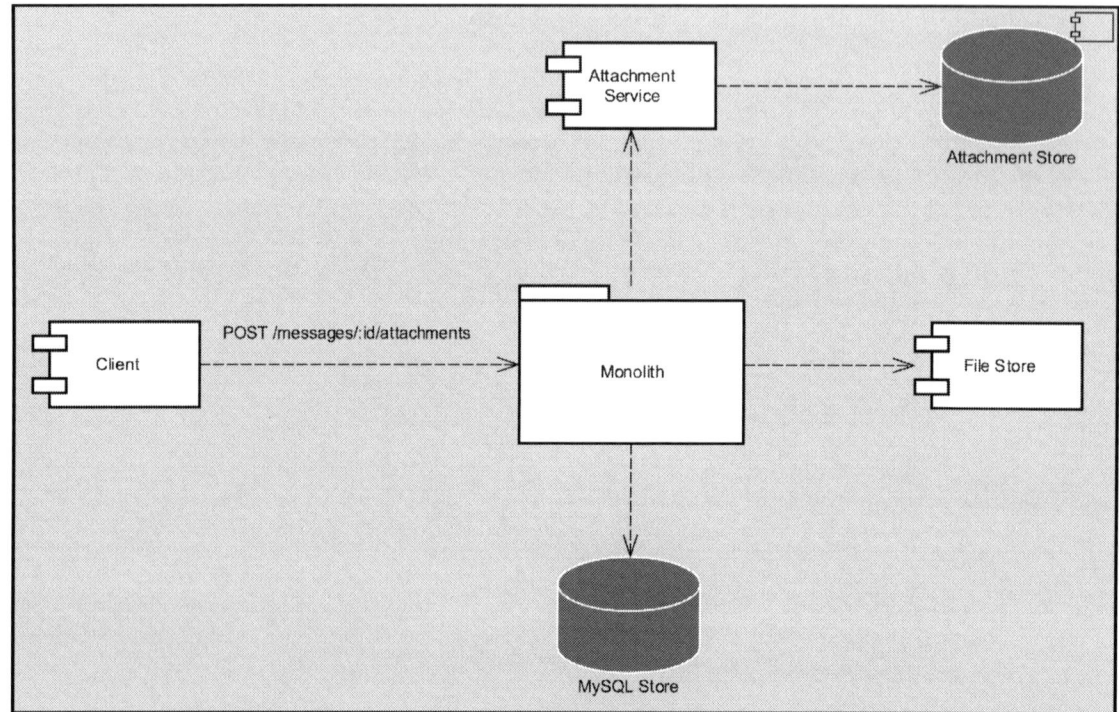

3. Find all read paths in your **Client** and **Monolith** code, and update them to use your new service. All reads will now be going to your service, which will be able to give consistent results.

4. Find all write paths in your **Client** and **Monolith** code, and update them to use your new service. All reads and writes are now going to your service, and you can safely delete old data and code paths. Your final architecture should look something like the following (we'll discuss edge proxies in later chapters):

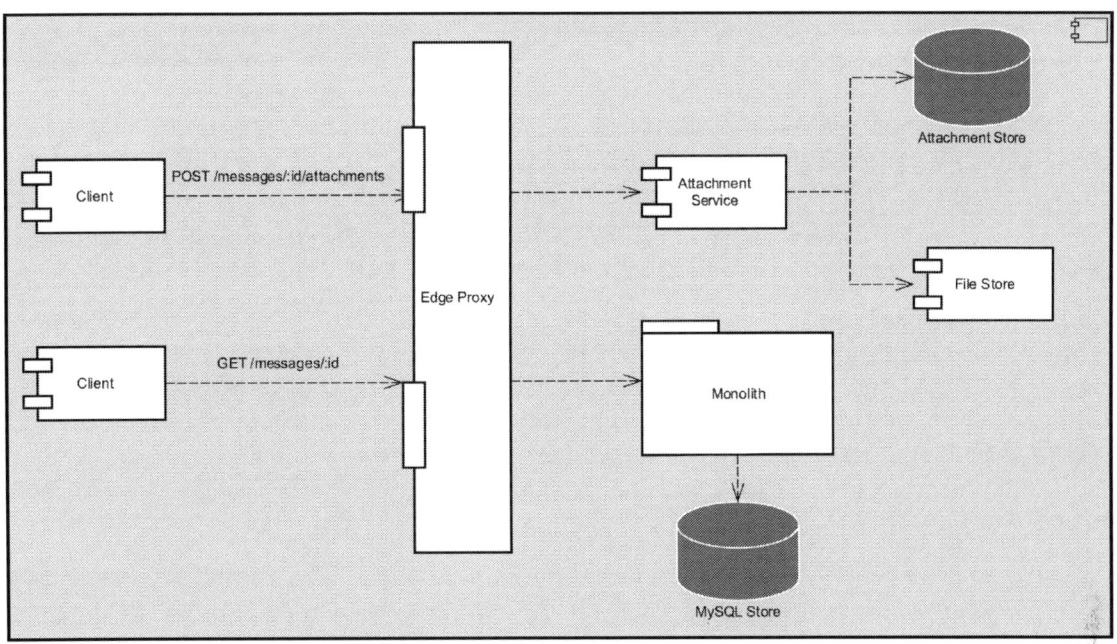

Using this approach, you'll be able to safely migrate data from a monolith database to a new store created for a new microservice without the need for downtime. It's important not to skip this step; otherwise, you won't truly realize the benefits of microservice architectures (although, arguably, you'll experience all the downsides!).

Refactoring your monolith

A common mistake when making the transition to microservices is to ignore the monolith and just build new features as services. This usually happens when a team feels that the monolith has gotten so out of control, and the code so unwieldy, that it would be better to declare bankruptcy and leave it to rot. This can be especially tempting because the idea of building green field code with no legacy baggage sounds a lot nicer than refactoring brittle, legacy code.

Resist the temptation to abandon your monolith. To successfully decompose your monolith by business capability and start evolving it into a set of nicely factored, single-responsibility microservices, you'll need to make sure that your monolith code base is in good shape and is well factored, and well tested. Otherwise, you'll end up with a proliferation of new services that don't model your domain cleanly (because they overlap with functionality in the monolith), and you'll continue to have trouble working with any code that exists in your monolith. Your users won't be happy and your teams' energy will most likely start to decline as the weight of technical debt becomes unbearable.

Instead, take constant, proactive steps to refactor your monolith using good, solid design principles. Excellent books have been written on the subject of refactoring (I recommend *Refactoring* by Martin Fowler and *Working Effectively with Legacy Code* by Michael Feathers), but the most important thing to know is that refactoring is never an all-or-nothing effort. Few product teams or companies will have the patience or luxury to wait while an engineering team stops the world and spends time making their code easier to change, and an engineering team that tries this will rarely be successful. Refactoring has to be a constant, steady process.

However your team schedules its work, make sure you're reserving an appropriate time for refactoring. A guiding principle is, whenever you go to make a change, first make the change easy to make, then make the change. Your goal is to make your monolith code easier to work with, easier to understand, and less brittle. You should also be able to develop a robust test suite that will come in handy.

Once your monolith is in better shape, you can start to continuously shrink the monolith as you factor out services. Another aspect of most monolith code bases is serving dynamically generated views and static assets served through browsers. If your monolith is responsible for this, consider moving your web application component into a separately served JavaScript application. This will allow you to shrink your monolith from multiple directions.

How to do it...

Refactoring any code base is a process. For monoliths, there are a few techniques that can work quite well. In this example, we'll document the steps that can be taken to make refactoring a Ruby on Rails code base easy:

1. Using the techniques described in previous recipes, identify business capabilities and bounded contexts within your application. Let's focus on the ability to upload pictures and videos.

2. Create a directory called `app/services` alongside `controllers`, `models`, and `views`. This directory will hold all of your service objects. Service objects are a pattern used in many Rails applications to factor out a conceptual service into a ruby object that does not inherit any Ruby on Rails functionality. This will make it easier to move the functionality encapsulated within a service object into a separate microservice. There is no one way to structure your service objects. I prefer to have each object represent a service, and move operations I want that service to be responsible for to that service object as methods.

3. Create a new file called `attachments_service.rb` under `app/services` and give it the following definition:

```
class AttachmentsService

  def upload
    # ...
  end

  def delete!
    # ...
  end

end
```

4. Looking at the source code for the `AttachmentsController#create` method in the `app/controllers/attachments_controller.rb` file, it currently handles the responsibility for creating the `Attachment` instance and uploading the file data to the attachment store, which in this case is an Amazon S3 bucket. This is the functionality that we need to move to the newly created service object:

```
# POST /messages/:message_id/attachments
def create
  message = Message.find_by!(params[:message_id], user_id:
  current_user.id)
  file = StorageBucket.files.create(
    key:  params[:file][:name],
    body: StringIO.new(Base64.decode64(params[:file][:data]),
    'rb'),
    public: true
  )
  attachment = Attachment.new(attachment_params.merge!(message:
  message))
  attachment.url = file.public_url
  attachment.file_name = params[:file][:name]
```

```
    attachment.save
    json_response({ url: attachment.url }, :created)
  end
```

5. Open the newly created service object in
   the app/services/attachments_service.rb file and move the responsibility
   for uploading the file to the AttachmentsService#upload method:

```
class AttachmentsService

  def upload(message_id, user_id, file_name, data, media_type)
    message = Message.find_by!(message_id, user_id: user_id)
    file = StorageBucket.files.create(
      key:   file_name,
      body: StringIO.new(Base64.decode64(data), 'rb'),
      public: true
    )
    Attachment.create(
      media_type: media_type,
      file_name:  file_name,
      url:        file.public_url,
      message:    message
    )
  end

  def delete!
  end
end
```

6. Now upload the AttachmentsController#create method in
   app/controllers/attachments_controller.rb to use the newly created
   AttachmentsService#upload method:

```
# POST /messages/:message_id/attachments
def create
  service = AttachmentService.new
  attachment = service.upload(params[:message_id], current_user.id,
    params[:file][:name], params[:file][:data],
    params[:media_type])
  json_response({ url: attachment.url }, :created)
end
```

7. Repeat this process for code in the `AttachmentsController#destroy` method, moving the responsibility to the new service object. When you're finished, no code in `AttachmentsController` should be interacting with the `Attachments` model directly; instead, it should be going through the `AttachmentsService` service object.

You've now isolated responsibility for the management of attachments to a single service class. This class should encapsulate all of the business logic that will eventually be moved to a new attachment service.

Evolving your monolith into services

One of the most complicated aspects of transitioning from a monolith to services can be request routing. In later recipes and chapters, we'll explore the topic of exposing your services to the internet so that the mobile and web client applications can communicate directly with them. For now, however, having your monolith act as a router can serve as a useful intermediary step.

As you break your monolith into small, maintainable microservices, you can replace code paths in your monolith with calls to your services. Depending on the programming language or framework you used to build your monolith, these sections of code can be called controller actions, views, or something else. We'll continue to assume that your monolith was built in the popular Ruby on Rails framework; in which case, we'll be looking at controller actions. We'll also assume that you've begun refactoring your monolith and have created one or more service objects as described in the previous recipe.

It's important when doing this to follow best practices. In later chapters, we'll introduce concepts, such as circuit breakers, that become important when doing service-to-service communication. For now, be mindful that HTTP calls from your monolith to a service could fail, and you should consider how best to handle that kind of situation.

How to do it...

1. Open the service object we created in the previous recipe. We'll modify the service object to be able to call an external microservice responsible for managing attachments. For the sake of simplicity, we'll use an HTTP client that is provided in the Ruby standard library. The service object should be in the app/services/attachments_service.rb file:

```
class AttachmentsService

  BASE_URI = "http://attachment-service.yourorg.example.com/"

  def upload(message_id, user_id, file_name, data, media_type)
    body = {
      user_id: user_id,
      file_name: file_name,
      data: StringIO.new(Base64.decode64(params[:file]
      [:data]), 'rb'),
      message: message_id,
      media_type: media_type
    }.to_json
    uri = URI("#{BASE_URI}attachment")
    headers = { "Content-Type" => "application/json" }
    Net::HTTP.post(uri, body, headers)
  end

end
```

2. Open the attachments_controller.rb file, located in pichat/app/controllers/, and look at the following create action. Because of the refactoring work done, we require only a small change to make the controller work with our new service object:

```
class AttachmentsController < ApplicationController
  # POST /messages/:message_id/attachments
  def create
    service = AttachmentService.new
    response = service.upload(params[:message_id], current_user.id,
    params[:file][:name], params[:file][:data],
    params[:media_type])
    json_response(response.body, response.code)
  end
  # ...
end
```

Evolving your test suite

Having a good test suite in the first place will help tremendously as you move from a monolith to microservices. Each time you remove functionality from your monolith code base, your tests will need to be updated. It's tempting to replace unit and functional tests in your Rails app with tests that make external network calls to your services, but this approach has a number of downsides. Tests that make external calls will be prone to failures caused by intermittent network connectivity issues and will take an enormous amount of time to run after a while.

Instead of making external network calls, you should modify your monolith tests to stub microservices. Tests that use stubs to represent calls to microservices will be less brittle and will run faster. As long as your microservices satisfy the API contracts you develop, the tests will be reliable indicators of your monolith code base's health. Making backwards-incompatible changes to your microservices is another topic that will be covered in a later recipe.

Getting ready

We'll use the webmock gem for stubbing out external HTTP requests in our tests, so update your monolith gemfile to include the webmock gem in the test group:

```
group :test do
  # ...
  gem 'webmock'
end
```

You should also update spec/spec_helper.rb to disable external network requests. That will keep you honest when writing the rest of your test code:

```
require 'webmock/rspec'
WebMock.disable_net_connect!(allow_localhost: false)
```

How to do it...

Now that you have `webmock` included in your project, you can start stubbing HTTP requests in your specs. Once again, open `specs/spec_helper.rb` and add the following content:

```
stub_request(:post, "attachment-service.yourorg.example.com").
  with(body: {media_type: 1}, headers: {"Content-Type" => /image\/.+/}).
  to_return(body: { foo: bar })
```

Using Docker for local development

As we've discussed, microservices solve a particular set of problems but introduce some new challenges of their own. One challenge that engineers on your team will probably run into is doing local development. With a monolith, there are fewer moving parts that have to be managed—usually, you can get away with just running a database and an application server on your workstation to get work done. As you start to create new microservices, however, the situation gets more complicated.

Containers are a great way to manage this complexity. Docker is a popular, open source software containerization platform. Docker allows you to specify how to run your application as a container—a lightweight standardized unit for deployment. There are plenty of books and online documentation about Docker, so we won't go into too much detail here, just know that a container encapsulates all of the information needed to run your application. As mentioned, a monolith application will often require an application server and a database server at a minimum—these will each run in their own container.

Docker Compose is a tool for running multicontainer applications. Compose allows you to define your applications containers in a YAML configuration file. Using the information in this file, you can then build and run your application. Compose will manage all of the various services defined in the configuration file in separate containers, allowing you to run a complex system on your workstation for local development.

Getting ready

Before you can follow the steps in this recipe, you'll need to install the required software:

1. Install Docker. Download the installation package from the Docker website (`https://www.docker.com/docker-mac`) and follow the instructions.
2. Install `docker-compose` by executing the following command line on macOS X:

```
brew install docker-compose
```

On Ubuntu Linux, you can execute the following command line:

```
apt-get install docker-compose
```

With those two packages installed, you'll be ready to follow the steps in this recipe.

How to do it...

1. In the root directory of your Rails application, create a single file called `Dockerfile` with the following contents:

```
FROM ruby:2.3.3
RUN apt-get update -qq && apt-get install -y build-essential
libpq-dev nodejs
RUN mkdir /pichat
WORKDIR /pichat
ADD Gemfile /pichat/Gemfile
ADD Gemfile.lock /pichat/Gemfile.lock
RUN bundle install
ADD . /pichat
```

2. Create a file called `docker-compose.yml` with the following contents:

```
version: '3'
services:
  db:
    image: mysql:5.6.34
    ports:
      - "3306:3306"
    environment:
      MYSQL_ROOT_PASSWORD: root

  app:
    build: .
    environment:
```

```
      RAILS_ENV: development
  command: bundle exec rails s -p 3000 -b '0.0.0.0'
  volumes:
    - .:/pichat
  ports:
    - "3000:3000"
  depends_on:
    - db
```

3. Start your application by running the `docker-compose up app` command. You should be able to access your monolith by entering `http://localhost:3000/` in your browser. You can use this approach for new services that you write.

Routing requests to services

In previous recipes, we focused on having your monolith route requests to services. This technique is a good start since it requires no client changes to work. Your clients still make requests to your monolith and your monolith marshals the request to your microservices through its controller actions. At some point, however, to truly benefit from a microservices architecture, you'll want to remove the monolith from the critical path and allow your clients to make requests to your microservices. It's not uncommon for an engineer to expose their organization's first microservice to the internet directly, usually using a different hostname. However, this starts to become unmanageable as you develop more services and need a certain amount of consistency when it comes to monitoring, security, and reliability concerns.

Internet-facing systems face a number of challenges. They need to be able to handle a number of security concerns, rate limiting, periodic spikes in traffic, and so on. Doing this for each service you expose to the public internet will become very expensive, very quickly. Instead, you should consider having a single edge service that supports routing requests from the public internet to internal services. A good edge service should support common features, such as dynamic path rewriting, load shedding, and authentication. Luckily, there are a number of good open source edge service solutions. In this recipe, we'll use a Netflix project called **Zuul**.

How to do it...

1. Create a new Spring Boot service called `Edge Proxy` with a main class called `EdgeProxyApplication`.

2. Spring Cloud includes an embedded Zuul proxy. Enable it by adding the `@EnableZuulProxy` annotation to your `EdgeProxyApplication` class:

```
package com.packtpub.microservices;

import org.springframework.boot.SpringApplication;
import
org.springframework.boot.autoconfigure.SpringBootApplication;
import org.springframework.cloud.netflix.zuul.EnableZuulProxy;

@EnableZuulProxy
@SpringBootApplication
public class EdgeProxyApplication {

    public static void main(String[] args) {
        SpringApplication.run(EdgeProxyApplication.class, args);
    }

}
```

3. Create a file called `application.properties` under `src/main/resources/` with the following contents:

```
zuul.routes.media.url=http://localhost:8090
ribbon.eureka.enabled=false
server.port=8080
```

In the preceding code, it tells `zuul` to route requests to `/media` to a service running on port `8090`. We'll touch on that `eureka` option in later chapters when we discuss service discovery, for now just make sure it's set to `false`.

At this point, your service should be able to proxy requests to the appropriate service. You've just taken one of the biggest steps toward building a microservices architecture. Congratulations!

3
Edge Services

In this chapter, we will cover the following recipes:

- Controlling access to your service with an edge proxy server
- Extending your services with sidecars
- Using API Gateway to route requests to services
- Rate limiting with an edge proxy server
- Stopping cascading failure with Hystrix
- Using a service mesh to factor out shared concerns

Introduction

Now that you've had some experience breaking a monolith into microservices, you've seen that many of the challenges exist outside the monolith or service code bases themselves. Exposing your service to the internet, controlling routing, and building in resiliency are all concerns that can be addressed by what are commonly called **edge services**. These are services that exist at the edge of our architecture, generally handling requests from the public internet. Luckily, because many of these challenges are so common, open source projects exist to handle most of them for us. We'll use a lot of great open source software in this chapter.

With the recipes in this chapter, you'll learn how to use open source software to expose your services to the public internet, control routing, extend your service's functionality, and handle a number of common challenges when deploying and scaling microservices. You'll also learn about techniques for making client development against services easier and how to standardize the monitoring and observability of your microservice architecture.

Controlling access to your service with an edge proxy server

In `Chapter 2`, *Breaking the Monolith*, we modified a monolith code base to provide easy routing to our microservices. This approach works and requires little effort, making it an ideal intermediary step. Eventually, your monolith will become a bottleneck in the development and resiliency of your architecture. As you try to scale your service and build more microservices, your monolith will need to be updated and deployed every time you make an API change to your service. Additionally, your monolith will have to handle connections to your services and is probably not well-configured to handle edge concerns such as load shedding or circuit breaking. In the *Routing requests to services* recipe of `Chapter 2`, *Breaking the Monolith*, we introduced the concept of edge proxies. Using an edge proxy server to expose your service to the public internet allows you to factor out most of the shared concerns a publicly exposed service must address. Requirements such as request routing, load shedding, back pressure, and authentication can all be handled in a single edge proxy layer instead of being duplicated by every service you need to have exposed to the internet.

An edge proxy is a proxy server that sits on the edge of your infrastructure, providing access to internal services. You can think of an edge proxy as the "front door" to your internal service architecture—it allows clients on the internet to make requests to internal services you deploy. There are multiple open source edge proxies that have a robust feature set and community, so we don't have to write and maintain our own edge proxy server. One of the most popular open source edge proxy servers is called **Zuul** and is built by Netflix. Zuul is an edge service that provides dynamic routing, monitoring, resiliency, security, and more. Zuul is packaged as a Java library. Services written in the Java framework Spring Boot can use an embedded Zuul service to provide edge-proxy functionality. In this recipe, we'll walk through building a small Zuul edge proxy and configuring it to route requests to our services.

Operational notes

Continuing with our example application from the previous chapter, imagine that our photo-messaging application (we'll call it `pichat` from now on) was originally implemented as a Ruby on Rails monolithic code base. When the product first launched, we deployed the application to Amazon Web Services behind a single **Elastic Load Balancer** (**ELB**). We created a single **Auto Scale Group** (**ASG**) for the monolith, called `pichat-asg`.

Each EC2 instance in our ASG is running NGINX, which handles requests for static files (images, JavaScript, CSS) and proxies requests to unicorns running on the same host that is serving our Rails application. SSL is terminated at the ELB, and HTTP requests are forwarded to NGINX. The ELB is accessed through the DNS `monolith.pichat-int.me` name from within the **Virtual Private Cloud** (**VPC**).

We've now created a single `attachment-service`, which handles videos and images attached to messages being sent through the platform. The `attachment-service` is written in Java, using the Spring Boot platform and is deployed in its own ASG, called `attachment-service-asg`, that has its own ELB. We've created a private DNS record, called `attachment-service.pichat-int.me`, that points to this ELB.

With this architecture and topology in mind, we now want to route requests from the public internet to our Rails application or our newly created attachment service, depending on the path.

How to do it...

1. To demonstrate using Zuul to route requests to services, we'll first create a basic Java application that will serve as our edge proxy service. The Java project Spring Cloud provides an embedded Zuul service, making it pretty simple to create a service that uses the `zuul` library. We'll start by creating a basic Java application. Create the `build.gradle` file with the following content:

```
group 'com.packtpub.microservices'
version '1.0-SNAPSHOT'

buildscript {
    repositories {
        mavenCentral()
    }
    dependencies {
        classpath "org.springframework.boot:spring-boot-gradle-
plugin:1.4.4.RELEASE"
        classpath "io.spring.gradle:dependency-management-
plugin:0.5.6.RELEASE"
    }
}

apply plugin: 'java'
apply plugin: 'org.springframework.boot'
apply plugin: 'io.spring.dependency-management'
```

```
sourceCompatibility = 1.8

repositories {
    mavenCentral()
}

dependencyManagement {
    imports {
        mavenBom 'org.springframework.cloud:spring-cloud-
netflix:1.4.4.RELEASE'
    }
}

dependencies {
    compile group: 'org.springframework.boot', name: 'spring-boot-
starter-web', version: '1.4.4.RELEASE'
    compile group: 'org.springframework.cloud', name: 'spring-
cloud-starter-zuul'
    testCompile group: 'junit', name: 'junit', version: '4.12'
}
```

2. Create a single class called EdgeProxyApplication. This will serve as the entry
   point to our application:

```
package com.packtpub.microservices.ch02.edgeproxy;

import org.springframework.boot.SpringApplication;
import
org.springframework.boot.autoconfigure.SpringBootApplication;
import org.springframework.cloud.netflix.zuul.EnableZuulProxy;

@EnableZuulProxy
@SpringBootApplication
public class EdgeProxyApplication {
    public static void main(String[] args) {
        SpringApplication.run(EdgeProxyApplication.class, args);
    }
}
```

3. Create a file called `application.yml` in the `src/main/resources` directory of your application. This file will specify your route configurations. In this example, we'll imagine that our monolith application can be accessed on the `monolith.pichat-int.me` internal host and we want to expose the `/signup` and `/auth/login` paths to the public internet:

```
zuul:
  routes:
    signup:
      path: /signup
      url: http://monolith.pichat-int.me
    auth:
      path: /auth/login
      url: http://monolith.pichat-int.me
```

4. Start the project with `./gradlew bootRun` and you should be able to access the `/signup` and `/auth/login` URLs, which will be proxied to our monolith application.

5. We want to expose the `attachment-service` URLs to the internet. The attachment service exposes the following endpoints:

```
POST / # Creates an attachment
GET / # Fetch attachments, can filter by message_id
DELETE /:attachment_id # Deletes the specified attachment
GET /:id # Get the specific attachment
```

6. We'll need to decide which paths we want to use in our public API. Modify `application.properties` to add the following entries:

```
zuul:
  routes:
    signup:
      path: /signup
      url: http://monolith.pichat-int.me
    auth:
      path: /auth/login
      url: http://monolith.pichat-int.me
    attachments:
      path: /attachments/**
      url: http://attachment-service.pichat-int.me
```

7. Now all requests to `/attachments/*` will be forwarded to the attachment service and signup, and `auth/login` will continue to be served by our monolith application.

8. We can test this by running our service locally and sending requests to `localhost:8080/signup`, `localhost:8080/auth/login`, and `localhost:8080/attachments/foo`. You should be able to see that requests are routed to the respected services. Of course, the service will respond with an error because `attachment-service.pichat-int.me` cannot be resolved, but this shows that the routing is working as expected:

```
$ curl -D - http://localhost:8080/attachments/foo
HTTP/1.1 500
X-Application-Context: application
Content-Type: application/json;charset=UTF-8
Transfer-Encoding: chunked
Date: Tue, 27 Mar 2018 12:52:21 GMT
Connection: close

{"timestamp":1522155141889,"status":500,"error":"Internal Server
Error","exception":"com.netflix.zuul.exception.ZuulException","mess
age":"attachment-service.pichat-int.me"}%
```

Extending your services with sidecars

When you start developing microservices, it's common to embed a certain amount of boilerplate into each service. Logging, metrics, and configuration are all functionalities that are commonly copied from service to service, resulting in a large amount of boilerplate and copied and pasted code. As your architecture grows and you develop more services, this kind of setup becomes harder and harder to maintain. The usual result is that you end up with a bunch of different ways of doing logging, metrics, service discovery, and so on, which results in systems that are hard to debug and maintain. Changing something as simple as a metrics namespace or adding a feature to your service discovery clients can require the coordination of multiple teams and code bases. More realistically, your microservices architecture will continue to grow with inconsistent logging, metrics, and service discovery conventions, making it harder for developers to operate, contributing to overall operational pain.

The sidecar pattern describes a pattern whereby you extend the functionality of a service with a separate process or container running on the same machine. Common functionalities, such as metrics, logging, service discovery, configuration, or even network RPC, can be factored out of your application and handled by a sidecar service running alongside it. This pattern makes it easy to standardize shared concerns within your architecture by implementing them in a separate process that can be used by all of your services.

A common method for implementing a sidecar is to build a small, separate process that exposes some functionality over a commonly used protocol, such as HTTP. Imagine, for instance, that you want all of your services to use a centralized service-discovery service instead of relying on DNS hosts and ports to be set in each application's configuration. To accomplish this, you'd need to have up-to-date client libraries for your service-discovery service available in all of the languages that your services and monolith are written in. A better way would be to run a sidecar parallel to each service that runs a service-discovery client. Your services could then proxy requests to the sidecar and have it determine where to send them. As an added benefit, you could configure the sidecar to emit consistent metrics around network RPC requests made between services.

This is such a common pattern that there are multiple open source solutions available for it. In this recipe, we'll use `spring-cloud-netflix-sidecar`, a project that includes a simple HTTP API that allows non-JVM applications to use JVM client libraries. The Netflix sidecar assumes you are using Eureka, a service registry designed to support the service-discovery needs of clients. We'll discuss service discovery in more detail in later chapters. The sidecar also assumes your non-JVM application is serving a health-check endpoint and will use this to advertise its health to Eureka. Our Rails application exposes such an endpoint, /health, which, when running normally, will return a small JSON payload with a key status and the UP value.

How to do it...

1. Start by creating a basic Spring Boot service. Include the Spring Boot Gradle plugin and add dependencies for Spring Boot and the Spring Cloud Netflix sidecar project:

```
group 'com.packtpub.microservices'
version '1.0-SNAPSHOT'

buildscript {
    repositories {
        mavenCentral()
    }
    dependencies {
        classpath "org.springframework.boot:spring-boot-gradle-
plugin:1.4.4.RELEASE"
        classpath "io.spring.gradle:dependency-management-
plugin:0.5.6.RELEASE"
    }
}

apply plugin: 'java'
```

```
apply plugin: 'org.springframework.boot'
apply plugin: 'io.spring.dependency-management'

sourceCompatibility = 1.8

repositories {
    mavenCentral()
}

dependencyManagement {
    imports {
        mavenBom 'org.springframework.cloud:spring-cloud-
netflix:1.4.4.RELEASE'
    }
}

dependencies {
    compile group: 'org.springframework.boot', name: 'spring-boot-
starter-web', version: '1.4.4.RELEASE'
    compile group: 'org.springframework.cloud', name: 'spring-
cloud-netflix-sidecar', version: '1.4.4.RELEASE'
    testCompile group: 'junit', name: 'junit', version: '4.12'
}
```

2. We're ready to create a simple Spring Boot application. We'll use the @EnableSidecar annotation, which also includes the @EnableZuulProxy, @EnableCircuitBreaker, and @EnableDiscoveryClient annotations:

```
package com.packtpub.microservices;

import org.springframework.boot.SpringApplication;
import
org.springframework.boot.autoconfigure.EnableAutoConfiguration;
import org.springframework.cloud.netflix.sidecar.EnableSidecar;
import org.springframework.stereotype.Controller;

@EnableSidecar
@Controller
@EnableAutoConfiguration
public class SidecarController {
    public static void main(String[] args) {
        SpringApplication.run(SidecarController.class, args);
    }
}
```

3. The Netflix sidecar application requires a few configuration settings to be present. Create a new file called `application.yml` with the following content:

```
server:
  port: 5678

sidecar:
  port: 3000
  health-uri: http://localhost:3000/health
```

4. The sidecar will now expose an API that allows non-JVM applications to locate services registered with Eureka. If our `attachment-service` is registered with Eureka, the sidecar will proxy requests to `http://localhost:5678/attachment/1234` to `http://attachment-service.pichat-int.me/1234`.

Using API Gateways for routing requests to services

As we've seen in other recipes, microservices should provide a specific business capability and should be designed around one or more domain concepts, surrounded by a bounded context. This approach to designing service boundaries works well to guide you toward simple, independently-scalable services that can be managed and deployed by a single team dedicated to a certain area of your application or business.

When designing user interfaces, clients often aggregate related but distinct entities from various backend microservices. In our fictional messaging application, for instance, the screen that shows an actual message might have information from a message service, a media service, a likes service, a comments service, and so on. All of this information can be cumbersome to collect and can result in a large number of round-trip requests to the backend.

Porting a web application from a monolith with server-side-rendered HTML to a single-page JavaScript application, for example, can easily result in hundreds of `XMLHttpRequests` for a single page load:

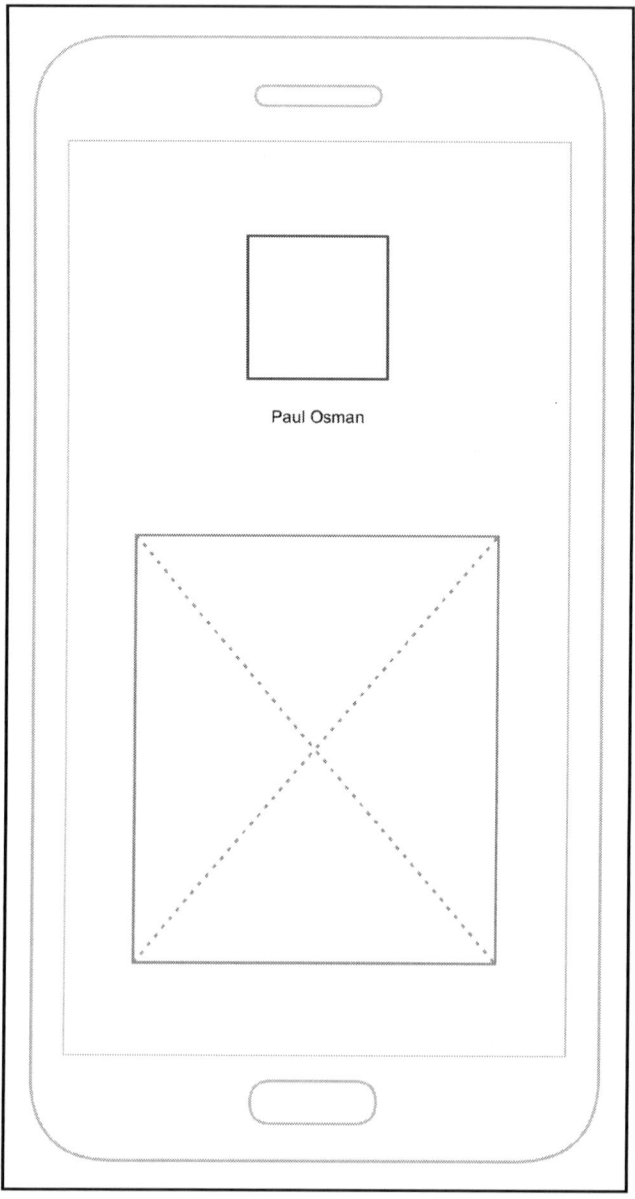

To reduce the amount of round-trip requests to the backend services, consider creating one or more API Gateways that provide an API that is catered to the client's needs. API Gateways can be used to present a single view of backend entities in a way that makes it easier for clients who use the API. In the preceding example, a request to a single message endpoint could return information about the message itself, media included in the message, likes and comments, and other information.

These entities can be concurrently collected from various backend services using a fan-out request pattern:

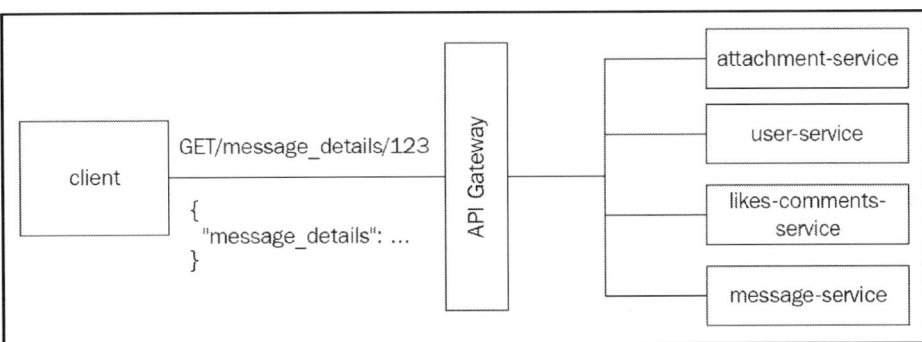

Design considerations

One of the benefits of using an API Gateway to provide access to microservices is that you can create a single, cohesive API for a specific client. In most cases, you'll want to create a specific API for mobile clients, perhaps even one API for iOS and one for Android. This implementation of API Gateways is commonly referred to as the **Backend for Frontend (BFF)** because it provides a single logical backend for each frontend application. A web application has very different needs than a mobile device.

In our situation, we'll focus on creating one endpoint that provides all the data needed by the message-view screen. This includes the message itself as well as the attachment(s), the user details of the sender, and any additional recipients of the message. If the message is public, it can also have likes and comments, which we'll imagine are served by a separate service. Our endpoint could look something like this:

```
GET /message_details/:message_id
```

The endpoint will return a response similar to the following:

```json
{
  "message_details": {
    "message": {
      "id": 1234,
      "body": "Hi There!",
      "from_user_id": "user:4321"
    },
    "attachments": [{
      "id": 4543,
      "media_type": 1,
      "url": "http://..."
    }],
    "from_user": {
      "username": "paulosman",
      "profile_pic": "http://...",
      "display_name": "Paul Osman"
    },
    "recipients": [
      ...
    ],
    "likes": 200,
    "comments": [{
      "id": 943,
      "body": "cool pic",
      "user": {
        "username": "somebody",
        "profile_pic": "http://..."
      }
    }]
  }
}
```

This response should have everything a client needs to show our message-view screen. The data itself comes from a variety of services, but, as we'll see, our API Gateway does the hard work of making those requests and aggregating the responses.

How to do it...

An API Gateway is responsible for exposing an API, making multiple service calls, aggregating the results, and returning them to the client. The **Finagle Scala** framework makes this natural by representing service calls as futures, which can be composed to represent dependencies. To stay consistent with other examples in this book, we'll build a small example gateway service in Java using the Spring Boot framework:

1. Create the project skeleton. Create a new Java project and add the following dependencies and plugins to the Gradle build file. We'll be using Spring Boot and Hystrix in this recipe:

```
plugins {
    id 'org.springframework.boot' version '1.5.9.RELEASE'
}

group 'com.packtpub.microservices'
version '1.0-SNAPSHOT'

apply plugin: 'java'

sourceCompatibility = 1.8

repositories {
    mavenCentral()
}

dependencies {
    compile group: 'org.springframework.boot', name: 'spring-boot-
starter-web', version: '1.5.9.RELEASE'
    compile group: 'com.netflix.hystrix', name: 'hystrix-core',
version: '1.0.2'
    testCompile group: 'junit', name: 'junit', version: '4.12'
}
```

    Looking at the JSON example in the previous section, it's clear that we are collecting and aggregating some distinct domain concepts. For the purposes of this example, we'll imagine that we have a message service that retrieves information about messages, including likes, comments, and attachments, and a user service. Our gateway service will be making a call to the message service to retrieve the message itself, then calls to the other services to get the associated data, which we'll stitch together in a single response. For the purposes of this recipe, imagine the message service is running on port 4567 and the user service on port 4568. We'll create some stub services to mock out the data for these hypothetical microservices.

2. Create a model to represent our Message data:

```
package com.packtpub.microservices.gateway.models;

import com.fasterxml.jackson.annotation.JsonIgnoreProperties;
import com.fasterxml.jackson.annotation.JsonProperty;

@JsonIgnoreProperties(ignoreUnknown = false)
```

```
public class Message {

    private String id;
    private String body;

    @JsonProperty("from_user_id")
    private String fromUserId;

    public String getId() {
        return id;
    }

    public void setId(String id) {
        this.id = id;
    }

    public String getBody() {
        return body;
    }

    public void setBody(String body) {
        this.body = body;
    }

    public String getFromUserId() {
        return fromUserId;
    }

    public void setFromUserId(String fromUserId) {
        this.fromUserId = fromUserId;
    }
}
```

It's important that non-dependent service calls be done in a non-blocking, asynchronous manner. Luckily, Hystrix has an option to execute commands asynchronously, returning Future<T>.

3. Create a new package, say, com.packtpub.microservices.gateway.commands with the following classes:

   - Create the AttachmentCommand class with the following content:

   ```
   package com.packtpub.microservices.gateway.commands;

   import com.netflix.hystrix.HystrixCommand;
   import com.netflix.hystrix.HystrixCommandGroupKey;
   ```

```java
import org.springframework.http.ResponseEntity;
import org.springframework.web.client.RestTemplate;

public class AttachmentCommand extends HystrixCommand<String> {
    private String messageId;

    public AttachmentCommand(String messageId) {
super(HystrixCommandGroupKey.Factory.asKey("AttachmentCommand"));
        this.messageId = messageId;
    }

    @Override
    public String run() {
        RestTemplate template = new RestTemplate();
        String attachmentsUrl = "http://localhost:4567/message/" +
messageId + "/attachments";
        ResponseEntity<String> response =
template.getForEntity(attachmentsUrl, String.class);
        return response.getBody();
    }
}
```

- **Create the** `CommentCommand` **class with the following content:**

```java
package com.packtpub.microservices.commands;

import com.netflix.hystrix.HystrixCommand;
import com.netflix.hystrix.HystrixCommandGroupKey;
import org.springframework.http.ResponseEntity;
import org.springframework.web.client.RestTemplate;

public class CommentCommand extends HystrixCommand<String> {

    private String messageId;

    public CommentCommand(String messageId) {
super(HystrixCommandGroupKey.Factory.asKey("CommentGroup"));
        this.messageId = messageId;
    }

    @Override
    public String run() {
        RestTemplate template = new RestTemplate();
        String commentsUrl = "http://localhost:4567/message/" +
messageId + "/comments";
        ResponseEntity<String> response =
template.getForEntity(commentsUrl, String.class);
        return response.getBody();
```

```
    }
}
```

- Create the `LikeCommand` class with the following content:

```
package com.packtpub.microservices.commands;

import com.netflix.hystrix.HystrixCommand;
import com.netflix.hystrix.HystrixCommandGroupKey;
import org.springframework.http.ResponseEntity;
import org.springframework.web.client.RestTemplate;

public class LikeCommand extends HystrixCommand<String> {

    private String messageId;

    public LikeCommand(String messageId) {
        super(HystrixCommandGroupKey.Factory.asKey("Likegroup"));
        this.messageId = messageId;
    }

    @Override
    public String run() {
        RestTemplate template = new RestTemplate();
        String likesUrl = "http://localhost:4567/message/" +
messageId + "/likes";
        ResponseEntity<String> response =
template.getForEntity(likesUrl, String.class);
        return response.getBody();
    }
}
```

- Our `MessageClient` class is a bit different than the previous examples—instead of returning the JSON string from the service response, it'll return an object representation, in this case, an instance of our `Message` class:

```
package com.packtpub.microservices.commands;

import com.netflix.hystrix.HystrixCommand;
import com.netflix.hystrix.HystrixCommandGroupKey;
import com.packtpub.microservices.models.Message;
import org.springframework.web.client.RestTemplate;

public class MessageClient extends HystrixCommand<Message> {

    private final String id;
```

```
    public MessageClient(String id) {
super(HystrixCommandGroupKey.Factory.asKey("MessageGroup"));
        this.id = id;
    }

    @Override
    public Message run() {
        RestTemplate template = new RestTemplate();
        String messageServiceUrl = "http://localhost:4567/message/"
+ id;
        Message message = template.getForObject(messageServiceUrl,
Message.class);
        return message;
    }
}
```

- Create the `UserCommand` class with the following content:

```
package com.packtpub.microservices.commands;

import com.netflix.hystrix.HystrixCommand;
import com.netflix.hystrix.HystrixCommandGroupKey;
import org.springframework.http.ResponseEntity;
import org.springframework.web.client.RestTemplate;

public class UserCommand extends HystrixCommand<String> {

    private String id;

    public UserCommand(String id) {
        super(HystrixCommandGroupKey.Factory.asKey("UserGroup"));
        this.id = id;
    }

    @Override
    public String run() {
        RestTemplate template = new RestTemplate();
        String userServiceUrl = "http://localhost:4568/user/" + id;
        ResponseEntity<String> response =
template.getForEntity(userServiceUrl, String.class);
        return response.getBody();
    }
}
```

4. Stitch together the execution of these Hystrix commands in a single controller that exposes our API as the `/message_details/:message_id` endpoint:

```
package com.packtpub.microservices;

import com.fasterxml.jackson.databind.ObjectMapper;
import com.packtpub.microservices.commands.*;
import com.packtpub.microservices.models.Message;
import org.springframework.boot.SpringApplication;
import org.springframework.http.MediaType;
import
org.springframework.boot.autoconfigure.SpringBootApplication;
import org.springframework.web.bind.annotation.PathVariable;
import org.springframework.web.bind.annotation.RequestMapping;
import org.springframework.web.bind.annotation.RestController;

import java.io.IOException;
import java.io.StringWriter;
import java.util.HashMap;
import java.util.Map;
import java.util.concurrent.ExecutionException;
import java.util.concurrent.Future;

@SpringBootApplication
@RestController
public class MainController {

    @RequestMapping(value = "/message_details/{id}", produces =
MediaType.APPLICATION_JSON_UTF8_VALUE)
    public Map<String, HashMap<String, String>>
messageDetails(@PathVariable String id)
            throws ExecutionException, InterruptedException,
IOException {

        Map<String, HashMap<String, String>> result = new
HashMap<>();
        HashMap<String, String> innerResult = new HashMap<>();

        Message message = new MessageClient(id).run();
        String messageId = message.getId();

        Future<String> user = new
UserClient(message.getFromUserId()).queue();
        Future<String> attachments = new
AttachmentClient(messageId).queue();
        Future<String> likes = new LikeClient(messageId).queue();
        Future<String> comments = new
CommentClient(messageId).queue();
```

```java
        ObjectMapper mapper = new ObjectMapper();
        StringWriter writer = new StringWriter();
        mapper.writeValue(writer, message);

        innerResult.put("message", writer.toString());
        innerResult.put("from_user", user.get());
        innerResult.put("attachments", attachments.get());
        innerResult.put("comments", comments.get());
        innerResult.put("likes", likes.get());

        result.put("message_details", innerResult);

        return result;
    }

    public static void main(String[] args) {
        SpringApplication.run(MainController.class, args);
    }
}
```

5. There you have it. Run the service with `./gradlew bootRun` and test it by making a request to:

    ```
    $ curl -H "Content-Type: application/json"
    http://localhost:8080/message_details/1234
    ```

Stopping cascading failures with Hystrix

Failures in a complex system can be hard to diagnose. Often, the symptom can appear far away from the cause. Users might start experiencing higher-than-normal error rates during login because of some downstream service that manages profile pictures or something else tangentially related to user profiles. An error in one service can often propagate needlessly to a user request and adversely impact user experience and therefore trust in your application. Additionally, a failing service can have cascading effects, turning a small system outage into a high-severity, customer-impacting incident. It's important when designing microservices to consider failure isolation and decide how you want to handle different failure scenarios.

A number of patterns can be used to improve the resiliency of distributed systems. Circuit breakers are a common pattern used to back off from making requests to a temporarily overwhelmed service. Circuit breakers were first described in Michael Nygard's book *Release It!*. A calling service defaults to a closed state, meaning requests are sent to the downstream service.

If the calling service receives too many failures too quickly, it can change the state of its circuit breaker to open, and start failing fast. Instead of waiting for the downstream service to fail again and adding to the load of the failing service, it just sends an error to upstream services, giving the overwhelmed service time to recover. After a certain amount of time has passed, the circuit is closed again and requests start flowing to the downstream service.

There are many available frameworks and libraries that implement circuit breakers. Some frameworks, such as Twitter's Finagle, automatically wrap every RPC call in a circuit breaker. In our example, we'll use the popular Netflix library, hystrix. Hystrix is a general-purpose, fault-tolerance library that structures isolated code as commands. When a command is executed, it checks the state of a circuit breaker to decide whether to issue or short circuit the request.

How to do it...

Hystrix is made available as a Java library, so we'll demonstrate its use by building a small Java Spring Boot application:

1. Create a new Java application and add the dependencies to your build.gradle file:

```
plugins {
    id 'org.springframework.boot' version '1.5.9.RELEASE'
}

group 'com.packetpub.microservices'
version '1.0-SNAPSHOT'

apply plugin: 'java'

sourceCompatibility = 1.8

repositories {
    mavenCentral()
}

dependencies {
    compile group: 'org.springframework.boot', name: 'spring-boot-
starter-web', version: '1.5.9.RELEASE'
    compile group: 'com.netflix.hystrix', name: 'hystrix-core',
version: '1.0.2'
    testCompile group: 'junit', name: 'junit', version: '4.12'
}
```

2. We'll create a simple `MainController` that returns a simple message. This is a contrived example, but it demonstrates an upstream service making downstream calls. At first, our application will just return a hardcoded `Hello, World!` message. Next, we'll move the string out to a Hystrix command. Finally, we'll move the message to a service call wrapped in a Hystrix command:

```
package com.packtpub.microservices;

import org.springframework.boot.SpringApplication;
import
org.springframework.boot.autoconfigure.EnableAutoConfiguration;
import
org.springframework.boot.autoconfigure.SpringBootApplication;
import org.springframework.web.bind.annotation.RequestMapping;
import org.springframework.web.bind.annotation.RestController;

@SpringBootApplication
@EnableAutoConfiguration
@RestController
public class MainController {
    @RequestMapping("/message")
    public String message() {
        return "Hello, World!";
    }

    public static void main(String[] args) {
        SpringApplication.run(MainController.class, args);
    }
}
```

3. Move the message out to `HystrixCommand`:

```
package com.packtpub.microservices;

import com.netflix.hystrix.HystrixCommand;
import com.netflix.hystrix.HystrixCommandGroupKey;

public class CommandHelloWorld extends HystrixCommand<String> {

    private String name;

    CommandHelloWorld(String name) {
super(HystrixCommandGroupKey.Factory.asKey("ExampleGroup"));
        this.name = name;
    }

    @Override
```

```
        public String run() {
            return "Hello, " + name + "!";
        }
    }
```

4. Replace the method in `MainController` to use `HystrixCommand`:

```
@RequestMapping("/message")
public String message() {
    return new CommandHelloWorld("Paul").execute();
}
```

5. Move the message generation to another service. We're hardcoding the hypothetical message service URL here, which is not a good practice but will do for demonstration purposes:

```
package com.packtpub.microservices;

import com.netflix.hystrix.HystrixCommand;
import com.netflix.hystrix.HystrixCommandGroupKey;
import org.springframework.http.ResponseEntity;
import org.springframework.web.client.RestTemplate;

public class CommandHelloWorld extends HystrixCommand<String> {

    CommandHelloWorld() {
    super(HystrixCommandGroupKey.Factory.asKey("ExampleGroup"));
    }

    @Override
    public String run() {
        RestTemplate restTemplate = new RestTemplate();
        String messageResourceUrl = "http://localhost:4567/";
        ResponseEntity<String> response =
    restTemplate.getForEntity(messageResourceUrl, String.class);
        return response.getBody();
    }

    @Override
    public String getFallback() {
        return "Hello, Fallback Message";
    }
}
```

6. Update the `MainController` class to contain the following:

```
package com.packetpub.microservices;

import org.springframework.boot.SpringApplication;
import
org.springframework.boot.autoconfigure.EnableAutoConfiguration;
import
org.springframework.boot.autoconfigure.SpringBootApplication;
import org.springframework.web.bind.annotation.RequestMapping;
import org.springframework.web.bind.annotation.RestController;

@SpringBootApplication
@EnableAutoConfiguration
@RestController
public class MainController {

    @RequestMapping("/message")
    public String message() {
        return new CommandHelloWorld().execute();
    }

    public static void main(String[] args) {
        SpringApplication.run(MainController.class, args);
    }

}
```

7. Our `MainController` class now makes a service call, wrapped in a Hystrix command, to generate a message to send back to the client. You can test this by creating a very simple service that generates a message string. `sinatra` is a simple-to-use Ruby library ideal for creating test services. Create a new file called `message-service.rb`:

```
require 'sinatra'

get '/' do
  "Hello from Sinatra"
end
```

8. Run the service by running `ruby message-service.rb` and then make a few sample requests to your Hystrix-enabled service. You can simulate a failure by modifying the service to return a `503`, indicating that it is temporarily overwhelmed:

```ruby
require 'sinatra'

get '/' do
  halt 503, 'Busy'
end
```

Your Spring service should now attempt to reach the service but use the value in the fallback when it encounters a `503`. Furthermore, after a number of attempts, the command's circuit breaker will be tripped and the service will start defaulting to the fallback for a period of time.

Rate limiting

In addition to techniques such as circuit breaking, rate limiting can be an effective way to prevent cascading failures in a distributed system. Rate limiting can be effective at preventing spam, protecting against **Denial of Service (DoS)** attacks, and protecting parts of a system from becoming overloaded by too many simultaneous requests. Typically implemented as either a global or per-client limit, rate limiting is usually part of a proxy or load balancer. In this recipe, we'll use NGINX, a popular open source load balancer, web server, and reverse proxy.

Most rate-limiting implementations use the *leaky-bucket algorithm*—an algorithm that originated in computer network switches and telecommunications networks. As the name suggests, the leaky-bucket algorithm is based on the metaphor of a bucket with a small leak in it that controls a constant rate. Water is poured into the bucket in bursts, but the leak guarantees that water exists in the bucket at a steady, fixed rate. If the water is poured in faster than the water exits the bucket, eventually the bucket will overflow. In this case, the overflow represents requests that are dropped.

It's certainly possible to implement your own rate-limiting solution; there are even implementations of the algorithms out there that are open source and available to use. It's a lot easier, however, to use a product such as NGINX to do rate limiting for you. In this recipe, we'll configure NGINX to proxy requests to our microservice.

How to do it...

1. Install NGINX by running the following command:

   ```
   apt-get install nginx
   ```

2. nginx has a config file, nginx.conf. On an Ubuntu-based Linux system, this will probably be in the /etc/nginx/nginx.conf directory. Open the file and look for the http block and add the following content:

   ```
   limit_req_zone $binary_remote_addr zone=mylimit:10m rate=10r/s;
   server {
       location /auth/signin {
           limit_req zone=mylimit;
           proxy_pass http://my_upstream;
       }
   }
   ```

   As you can see from the preceding code, rate limiting is implemented with two configuration directives. The limit_req_zone directive defines the parameters for rate limiting. In this example, we're implementing a rate limit, based on the client's IP address, of 10 requests per second. The limit_req directive applies our rate limiting to a specific path or location. In this case, we're applying it to all requests to /auth/signin, presumably because we don't want bots scripting the creation of accounts!

Using service mesh for shared concerns

As web services' frameworks and standards evolve, the amount of boilerplate or shared application concerns is reduced. This is because, collectively, we figure out what parts of our applications are universal and therefore shouldn't need to be re-implemented by every programmer or team. When people first started networking computers, programmers writing network-aware applications had to worry about a lot of low-level details that are now abstracted out by the operating system's networking stack. Similarly, there are certain universal concerns that all microservices share. Frameworks such as Twitter's Finagle wrap all network calls in a circuit breaker, increasing fault tolerance and isolating failures in systems. Finagle and Spring Boot, the Java framework we've been using for most of these recipes, both support exposing a standard metrics endpoint that standardizes basic network, JVM, and application metrics collected for microservices.

Every microservice should consider a number of shared application concerns. From an observability perspective, services should strive to emit consistent metrics and structured logs. To improve the reliability of our systems, services should wrap network calls in circuit breakers and implement consistent retry and back-off logic. To support changes in network and service topology, services should consider implementing client-side load balancing and use centralized service discovery.

Instead of implementing all of these features in each of our services, it would be ideal to abstract them out to something outside our application code that could be maintained and operated separately. Like the features of our operating systems network stack, if each of these features is implemented by something our application could rely on being present, we would not have to worry about them being available. This is the idea behind a service mesh.

Running a service mesh configuration involves running each microservice in your system behind a network proxy. Instead of services speaking directly to one another, they communicate via their respective proxies, which are installed as sidecars. Practically speaking, your service would communicate with its own proxy running on localhost. As network requests are sent through a services proxy, the proxy can control what metrics are emitted and what log messages are output. The proxy can also integrate directly with your service registry and distribute requests evenly among active nodes, keeping track of failures and opting to fail fast when a certain threshold has been reached. Running your system in this kind of configuration can ease the operational complexity of your system while improving the reliability and observability of your architecture.

Like most of the recipes discussed in this chapter, there are numerous open source solutions for running a service mesh. We'll focus on **Linkerd**, an open source proxy server built and maintained by buoyant. The original authors of Linkerd worked at Twitter before forming buoyant and as such, Linkerd incorporates many of the lessons learned by teams at Twitter. It shares many features with the Finagle Scala framework, but can be used with services written in any language. In this recipe, we'll walk through installing and configuring Linkerd and discuss how we can use it to control communication between our Ruby on Rails monolith API and our newly developed media service.

How to do it...

To demonstrate running a service behind a proxy, we'll install and run an instance of Linkerd and configure it to handle requests to and from your service. There are instructions on the Linkerd website for running it in Docker, Kubernetes, and other options. To keep things simple, we'll focus on running Linkerd and our service locally:

1. Download the latest Linkerd release at `https://github.com/linkerd/linkerd/releases`.

2. Extract the tarball by executing the following command:

   ```
   $ tar xvfz linkerd-1.3.4.tgz
   $ cd linkerd-1.3.4
   ```

3. By default, `linkerd` ships with a configuration that uses file-based service discovery. We'll discuss alternatives to this approach next, but, for now, create a new file called `disco/media-service` with the following contents:

   ```
   localhost 8080
   ```

4. This maps the hostname and port to a service called `media-service`. Linkerd uses this file to look up services by name and determines the hostname and port mappings.

5. Run Linkerd as follows:

   ```
   $ ./linkerd-1.3.4-exec config/linkerd.yaml
   ```

6. Start the service on port `8080`. Change into the `media-service` directory and run the service:

   ```
   $ ./gradlew bootRun
   ```

7. Linkerd is running on port `4140`. Test that proxying is working with the following request:

   ```
   $ curl -H "Host: attachment-service" http://localhost:4140/
   ```

4
Modules and Toolkits

Now we'll review a couple of options and build a more or less simple microservice so that we can point out advantages and disadvantages for each approach.

We'll look at four different modules:

- **Express**: One of the most commonly used modules in the Node.js ecosystem
- **Micro**: A very minimalistic microservices approach
- **Seneca**: A microservice toolkit based on property matching
- **Hydra**: A package that bundles a couple of modules to help you resolve many microservices concerns, such as distribution and monitoring

Express

If you're familiar with Node.js, you probably know of one module that is the core for most Node.js platforms and applications that are around. You have probably heard of Express, and it's not by accident. It's eight years old and it's been there since the beginning of Node.js.

Express is a rock-solid layer that helps you create applications faster. As it states on its website, it's a *fast, unopinionated,* and *minimalist web framework*.

Node.js has an HTTP module that you can use to create a simple HTTP server. The problem is that it's too raw and you'll have to do a ton of work so that you can make it usable and modular. Instead of you creating that layer, you can use Express.

To install Express, create a folder and run the following command:

```
npm init -y
npm install express —save
```

Then, create a file called `app.js` and place the following code inside it:

```
let express = require("express");
let app     = express();

app.get("/", (req, res) => {
    res.send("Hello World");
});

app.listen(80);
```

Then, run your code using the following command:

```
node app
```

Go to your browser and type the address `http://localhost:3000/`. You should see something like the following:

With Express, you can associate functions to routes. A route is a URL with a specific HTTP verb, but it doesn't necessarily have to. You can have automatic parameters parsing inside routes. You can even associate more functions to the same route and have them be called sequentially. You can also stop the sequence at any time. It's up to you; remember, Express is not opinionated.

Change your `app.js` to the following code and run it again:

```js
let express = require("express");
let app     = express();
let stack   = [];

app.post("/stack", (req, res, next) => {
    let buffer = "";

    req.on("data", (data) => {
        buffer += data;
    });
    req.on("end", () => {
        stack.push(buffer);
        return next();
    });
});

app.delete("/stack", (req, res, next) => {
    stack.pop();
    return next();
});

app.get("/stack/:index", (req, res) => {
    if (req.params.index >= 0 && req.params.index < stack.length) {
        return res.end("" + stack[req.params.index]);
    }
    res.status(404).end();
});

app.use("/stack", (req, res) => {
    res.send(stack);
});

app.listen(3000);
```

You'll have trouble testing it in the browser because we're using POST and DELETE verbs. Instead, let's use curl and make requests in the command line. Follow this sequence and see if you understood the preceding code:

```
● ● ●                    2. nazgul.home: /Users/dresende (bash)
~ > curl http://localhost:3000/stack
[]~ >
~ > curl --data zero http://localhost:3000/stack
["zero"]~ >
~ > curl --data one http://localhost:3000/stack
["zero","one"]~ >
~ > curl http://localhost:3000/stack/1
one~ >
~ > curl http://localhost:3000/stack/2 -v
*   Trying ::1...
* TCP_NODELAY set
* Connected to localhost (::1) port 3000 (#0)
> GET /stack/2 HTTP/1.1
> Host: localhost:3000
> User-Agent: curl/7.54.0
> Accept: */*
>
< HTTP/1.1 404 Not Found
< X-Powered-By: Express
< Date: Mon, 15 Jan 2018 21:31:26 GMT
< Connection: keep-alive
< Content-Length: 0
<
* Connection #0 to host localhost left intact
~ > _
```

We first make a request to /stack just to see if it will return an empty array. Then, we use --data to pass zero as the HTTP request body and curl assumes it's a POST. We do it again, this time, with body one. For both requests, we get the final stack result. We then request stack index 1 and it returns one. We then request index 2 and, as you can see by the -v parameter, our code returns a proper 404 Not Found error.

You might have wondered how the stack is returned on both GET and POST requests and that's the reason for calling next (), which tells Express to pass to the next route (if there are any) available. In our case, it's the route that's been defined that's using the use method. This is a catch all for all HTTP verbs. Remember: route definition order is important and that's why the catch all is done at the end.

As you can see, we can scale pretty fast to complex logic. It's important to note that although Express really helps you create an HTTP service easier, it's still just an improved layer over the http and https modules that are available.

To help you even more, it has an integrated modular system, called middleware, and hundreds of compatible published modules that help you create services even faster, such as session handling, templating, caching, and security modules.

Let's make our example a little bit more complex so that you can see what I mean. First, install some middleware:

```
npm i body-parser --save
```

Now, change your code to this:

```
let express = require("express");
let body    = require("body-parser");
let route   = express.Router();
let app     = express();
let stack   = [];

app.use(body.text({ type: "*/*" }));

route.post("/", (req, res, next) => {
    stack.push(req.body);

    return next();
});

route.delete("/", (req, res, next) => {
    stack.pop();

    return next();
});

route.get("/:index", (req, res) => {
    if (req.params.index >= 0 && req.params.index < stack.length) {
        return res.end("" + stack[req.params.index]);
    }
    res.status(404).end();
```

```
});

route.use((req, res) => {
    res.send(stack);
});

app.use("/stack", route);
app.listen(3000);
```

It has the same number of lines, but we improved our code by making two important changes:

- Instead of reading the request body, we now use a middleware, `body-parser`, which handles it for us and supports several body types and compression.
- We created an `express.Route` and attached it to our service at the last but one line. We can use this to move our route definition to a separate file and make it URL agnostic (see how we only mention /`stack` once, when attaching).

Micro

Let's look at another interesting tool. This module is called micro and was created by ZEIT, a team of some of the most influential Node.js developers. It is meant to be a minimalistic framework to create slim and fast microservices.

Let's repeat our first example. Create a folder and run the following command:

```
npm init -y
npm install --save micro
```

Now, create a file called `app.js` and write the following code inside it:

```
module.exports = (req, res) => {
    res.end("Hello World");
};
```

Change your `scripts` property in `package.json` to this:

```
"scripts": {
    "start": "micro"
},
```

Now, just run this:

```
npm start
```

You'll see something like this, which indicates that a micro is running on its default port, 3000:

```
micro: Accepting connections on port 3000
```

You can now refresh your browser and you will get the same page you saw earlier. But now, you have it with only three lines of code (and some configuration).

That's it. Micro is very minimalistic. You'll have to declare and install all your dependencies as it won't do anything other than enable you to write very slim microservices. This is handy if you don't want to carry the 2.3 MB of dependencies from our first Express example.

Seneca

Now it's time for a completely different approach. Let's look at another framework called Seneca. This framework was designed to help you develop message-based microservices. It has two distinct characteristics:

- **Transport agnostic**: Communication and message transport is separated from your service logic and it's easy to swap transports
- **Pattern matching**: Messages are JSON objects and each function exposes what sort of messages they can handle based on object properties

Being able to change transports is not a big deal; many tools allow you to do so. What is really interesting about this framework is its ability to expose functions based on object patterns. Let's start by installing Seneca:

```
npm install seneca
```

For now, let's forget the transport and create a producer and consumer in the same file. Let's look at an example:

```
const seneca  = require("seneca");
const service = seneca();

service.add({ math: "sum" }, (msg, next) => {
    next(null, {
        sum : msg.values.reduce((total, value) => (total + value), 0)
    });
});

service.act({ math: "sum", values: [ 1, 2, 3 ] }, (err, msg) => {
    if (err) return console.error(err);
```

```
        console.log("sum = %s", msg.sum);
    });
```

There's a lot to absorb. The easy part comes first as we include the `seneca` module and create a new service.

We then expose a producer function that matches an object that has `math` equal to `sum`. This means that any request object to the service that has the property `math` and that is equal to `sum` will be passed to this function. This function accepts two arguments. The first, which we called `msg`, is the request object (the one with the `math` property and anything else the object might have). The second argument, `next`, is the callback that the function should invoke when finished or in case of an error. In this particular case, we're expecting an object that also has a `values` list and we're returning the sum of all values by using the `reduce` method that's available in arrays.

Finally, we invoke `act`, expecting it to consume our producer. We pass an object with the `math` equal to `sum` and a list of `values`. Our producer should be invoked and should return the sum.

Assuming you have this code in `app.js`, if you run this in the command line, you should see something like this:

```
$ node app

sum = 6
```

Let's try and replicate our previous stack example. This time, instead of having the consumer and producer in the code, we'll use `curl` as the consumer, just like we did previously.

First, we need to create our `service`. We do that, as we've seen before, by loading Seneca and creating an instance:

```
const seneca  = require("seneca");
const service = seneca({ log: "silent" });
```

We explicitly tell it that we don't care about logging for now. Now, let's create a variable to hold our stack:

```
const stack = [];
```

We then create our producers. We'll create three of them: one for adding an element to the stack, called push; one to remove the last element from the stack, called pop; and one to see the stack, called get. Both push and pop will return the final stack result. The third producer is just a helper function so that we can see the stack without performing any operations.

To add elements to the stack, we define:

```
service.add("stack:push,value:*", (msg, next) => {
    stack.push(msg.value);

    next(null, stack);
});
```

There are a few new things to see here:

- We defined our pattern as a string instead of an object. This action string is a shortcut to the extended object definition.
- We explicitly indicate that we need a value.
- We also indicate that we don't care what the value is (remember, this is pattern matching).

We now define a simpler function to remove the last element of the stack:

```
service.add("stack:pop", (msg, next) => {
    stack.pop();

    next(null, stack);
});
```

This one is simpler as we don't need a value, we're just removing the last one. We're not addressing the case where the stack is empty already. An empty array won't throw an exception, but perhaps, in a real scenario, you would want another response.

Our third function is even simpler as we just return the `stack`:

```
service.add("stack:get", (msg, next) => {
    next(null, stack);
});
```

Finally, we need to tell our `service` to listen for messages. The default transport is HTTP and we just indicate port `3000` as we did in our previous examples:

```
service.listen(3000);
```

Wrap all this code in a file and try it out. You can use curl or just try it in your browser. Seneca won't differentiate between HTTP verbs in this case. Let's begin by checking our `stack`. The URL describes an action (`/act`) we want to perform and the query parameter gets converted to our pattern:

We can then try adding the value one to our stack and see the final stack:

We can continue and add the value two and see how the stack grows:

If we then try to remove the last element, we'll see the `stack` shrinking:

As in Express, Seneca also has middleware that you can install and use. In this case, the middleware is called plugins. By default, Seneca includes a number of core plugins for transport, and both HTTP and TCP transports are supported. There are more transports available, such as **Advanced Message Queuing Protocol** (**AMQP**) and Redis.

There are also storage plugins for persistent data and there's support for several database servers, both relational and non-relational. Seneca exposes an **object-relational mapping** (**ORM**)-like interface to manage data entities. You can manipulate entities and use a simple storage in development and then move to production storage later on. Let's see a more complex example of this:

```
const async   = require("async");
const seneca  = require("seneca");
const service = seneca();

service.use("basic");
service.use("entity");
service.use("jsonfile-store", { folder : "data" });

const stack = service.make$("stack");

stack.load$((err) => {
    if (err) throw err;

    service.add("stack:push,value:*", (msg, next) => {
        stack.make$().save$({ value: msg.value }, (err) => {
            return next(err, { value: msg.value });
```

```
        });
    });

    service.add("stack:pop,value:*", (msg, next) => {
        stack.list$({ value: msg.value }, (err, items) => {
            async.each(items, (item, next) => {
                item.remove$(next);
            }, (err) => {
                if (err) return next(err);

                return next(err, { remove: items.length });
            });
        });
    });

    service.add("stack:get", (msg, next) => {
        stack.list$((err, items) => {
            if (err) return next(err);

            return next(null, items.map((item) => (item.value)));
        });
    });

    service.listen(3000);
});
```

Just run this new code and we'll see how this code behaves by making some requests to test it. First, let's see how our `stack` is by requesting it:

Nothing different. Now, let's add the value one to the stack:

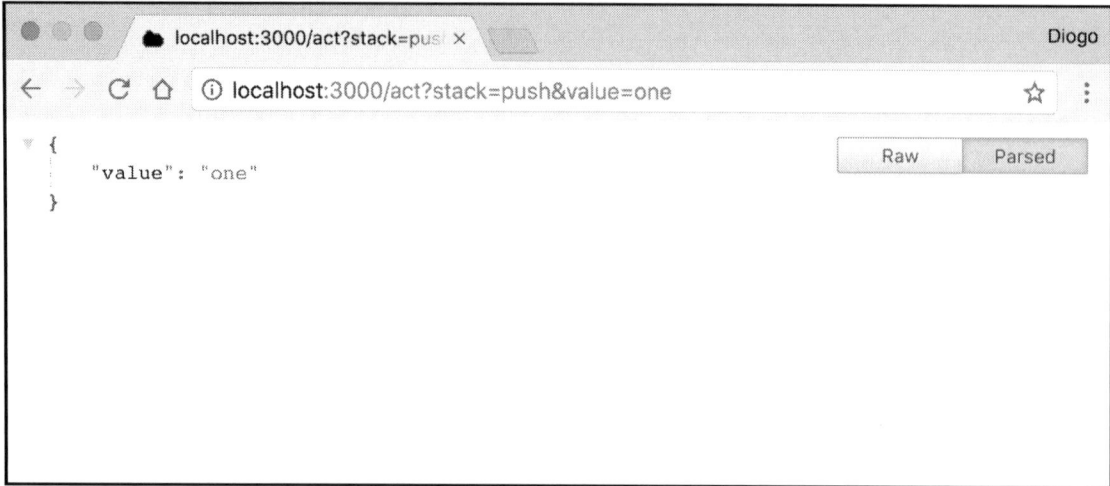

Well, we haven't received the final stack. We could, but instead we changed the service to return the exact item that was added. It's actually a good way to confirm what we just did. Let's add another one:

Again, it returns the value we just added. Now, let's see how our stack is:

Our `stack` now has our two values. Now comes one big difference compared with the previous code. We're using *entities*, an API exposed by Seneca, which helps you store and manipulate data objects using a simple abstraction layer similar to an ORM, or to people who are familiar with Ruby, an `ActiveRecord`.

Our new code, instead of just popping out the last value, removes a value we indicate. So, let's remove the value `one` instead of `two`:

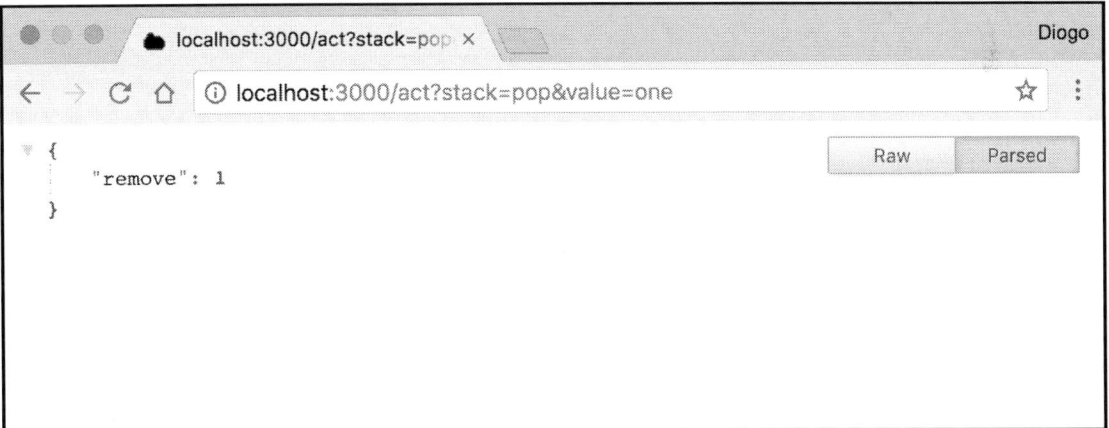

Success! We removed exactly one item. Our code will remove all items from the `stack` that match the value (it has no duplication check so you can have repeated items). Let's try to remove the same item again:

No more items match `one`, so it didn't remove anything. We can now check our `stack` and confirm that we still have the value `two`:

Correct! And, as a bonus, you can stop and restart the code and your stack will still have the value `two`. That's because we're using the JSON file store plugin.

 When testing using Chrome or any other browser, be aware that sometimes, browsers make requests in advance while you're typing. Because we already tested our first code, which had the same URL addresses, the browser might duplicate requests and you might get a stack with duplicated values without knowing why. This is why.

Hydra

Let's get back to Express. As you've seen before, it's a rock-solid layer on top of the `http` module. Although it adds an important base layer in the somewhat raw module, it still lacks many features you need to make a good microservice.

As there are lots of plugins out there to extend Express, it can be hard to pick a useful list for us to use.

After picking the right list, you'll still need to make other decisions:

- How can I distribute my service with multiple instances?
- How can the service be discovered?
- How can I monitor whether my service is running properly?

Enter Hydra, a framework that facilitates building distributed microservices. Hydra leverages the power of Express and helps you create microservices or communicate with microservices.

It will, out of the box, enable you to:

- Do service registration and service discovery, allowing your microservices to discover and be discoverable
- Communicate with microservices and load balance communication between multiple instances, taking care of failed instances and automatically rerouting requests to other running instances
- Monitor instances, checking whether the microservice is available and operating normally

Unlike the other modules we've reviewed so far, Hydra has a dependency that is not installable directly using the NPM. Hydra uses Redis to accomplish its goal. Look for information on the Redis website at `https://redis.io/` to install it on your operating system before continuing. If you have macOS and use Homebrew, type the following to install `redis`:

```
1. nazgul.home: /Users/dresende (bash)
~ > brew install redis
==> Downloading https://homebrew.bintray.com/bottles/redis-4.0.6.high_sierra.bottle.tar.gz
Already downloaded: /Users/dresende/Library/Caches/Homebrew/redis-4.0.6.high_sierra.bottle.tar.gz
==> Pouring redis-4.0.6.high_sierra.bottle.tar.gz
==> Caveats
To have launchd start redis now and restart at login:
  brew services start redis
Or, if you don't want/need a background service you can just run:
  redis-server /usr/local/etc/redis.conf
==> Summary
🍺 /usr/local/Cellar/redis/4.0.6: 13 files, 2.8MB
~ > _
```

Now, let's make sure `redis` has successfully started:

```
1. nazgul.home: /Users/dresende (bash)
~ > brew services start redis
==> Successfully started `redis` (label: homebrew.mxcl.redis)
~ > _
```

After that, we need to install Hydra command-line tools:

```
sudo npm install -g yo generator-fwsp-hydra hydra-cli
```

We now need to configure the connection to Redis. We do this by creating a configuration. Type in the command and follow the instructions. If you installed it locally (or used the preceding instructions), you should answer something similar to the following screenshot:

```
●  ●  ●          1. nazgul.home: /Users/dresende (bash)
~ › hydra-cli config local
redisUrl: 127.0.0.1
redisPort: 6379
redisDb: 15
~ › _
```

Now, let's create a very simple microservice, just to see what the workflow is like. Hydra has a scaffolding tool using yeoman. To create a service, type the following command and follow the instructions:

```
●  ●  ●          1. nazgul.home: /Users/dresende (bash)
~ › yo fwsp-hydra
fwsp-hydra generator v0.3.1   yeoman-generator v2.0.2   yo v2.0.0
? Name of the service (`-service` will be appended automatically) hello
? Your full name?
? Your email address?
? Your organization or username? (used to tag docker images)
? Host the service runs on?
? Port the service runs on? 0
? What does this service do?
? Does this service need auth? No
? Is this a hydra-express service? Yes
? Set up a view engine? No
? Set up logging? No
? Enable CORS on serverResponses? No
? Run npm install? No
   create hello-service/specs/test.js
   create hello-service/specs/helpers/chai.js
   create hello-service/.editorconfig
   create hello-service/.eslintrc
   create hello-service/.gitattributes
   create hello-service/.nvmrc
   create hello-service/.gitignore
   create hello-service/package.json
   create hello-service/README.md
   create hello-service/hello-service.js
   create hello-service/config/sample-config.json
   create hello-service/config/config.json
   create hello-service/scripts/docker.js
   create hello-service/routes/hello-v1-routes.js

Done!
'cd hello-service' then 'npm install' and 'npm start'

~ › _
```

On the name of the service, just type **hello**. Just hit *Enter* to the rest of the questions to use the defaults. In the end, enter the folder that was created and install the dependencies:

```
● ● ●                  1. nazgul.home: /Users/dresende/hello-service (bash)
~ > cd hello-service/
~/hello-service > npm i
added 338 packages in 6.56s
~/hello-service > _
```

The service is now ready to start. You might have already seen the instructions when scaffolding the service. Let's start the service:

```
● ● ●                  1. nazgul.home: /Users/dresende/hello-service (node)
~/hello-service > npm start

> hello-service@0.0.1 start /Users/dresende/hello-service
> node hello-service.js

INFO
{ event: 'start',
  message: 'hello-service (v.0.0.1) server listening on port 45394' }
INFO
{ event: 'info', message: 'Using environment: development' }
serviceInfo { serviceName: 'hello-service',
  serviceIP: '192.168.1.108',
  servicePort: 45394 }

_
```

As we can see from the preceding screenshot, the service has started and has been attached to a local IP (**192.168.1.108**) and port (**45394**). Open up the folder in your code editor:

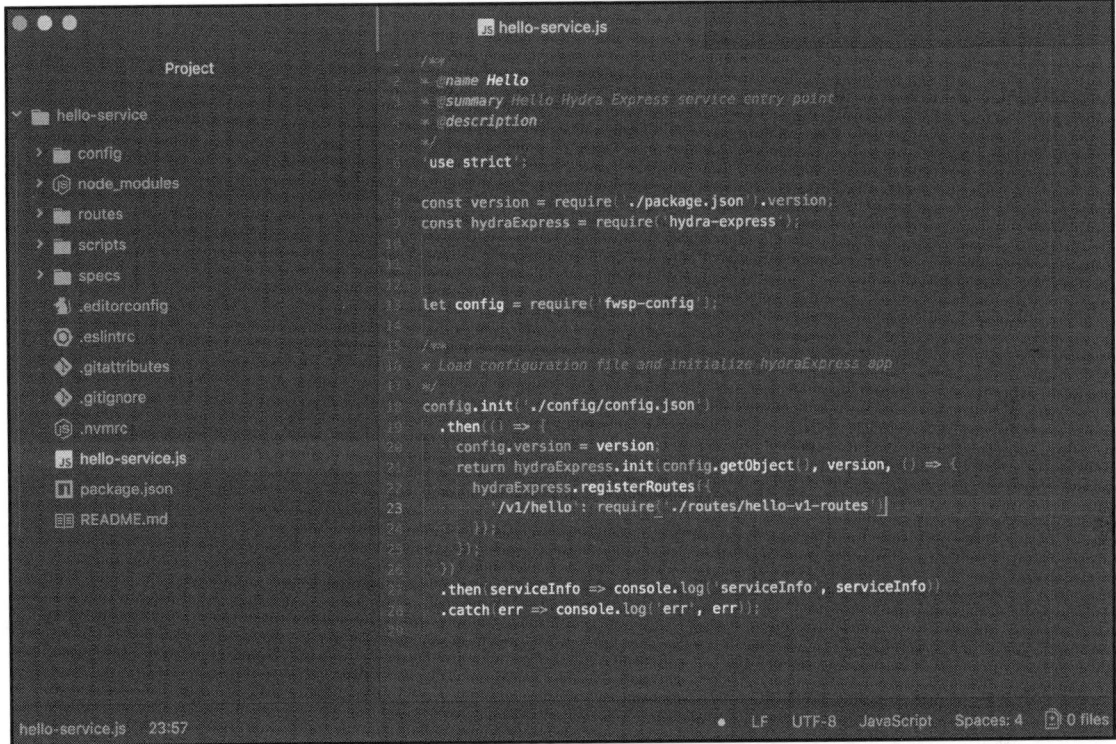

You'll see a file in the base folder called `hello-service.js`, which has the service routes inside it. You'll find the `/v1/hello` route, which points to another file in `routes/hello-v1-routes.js`:

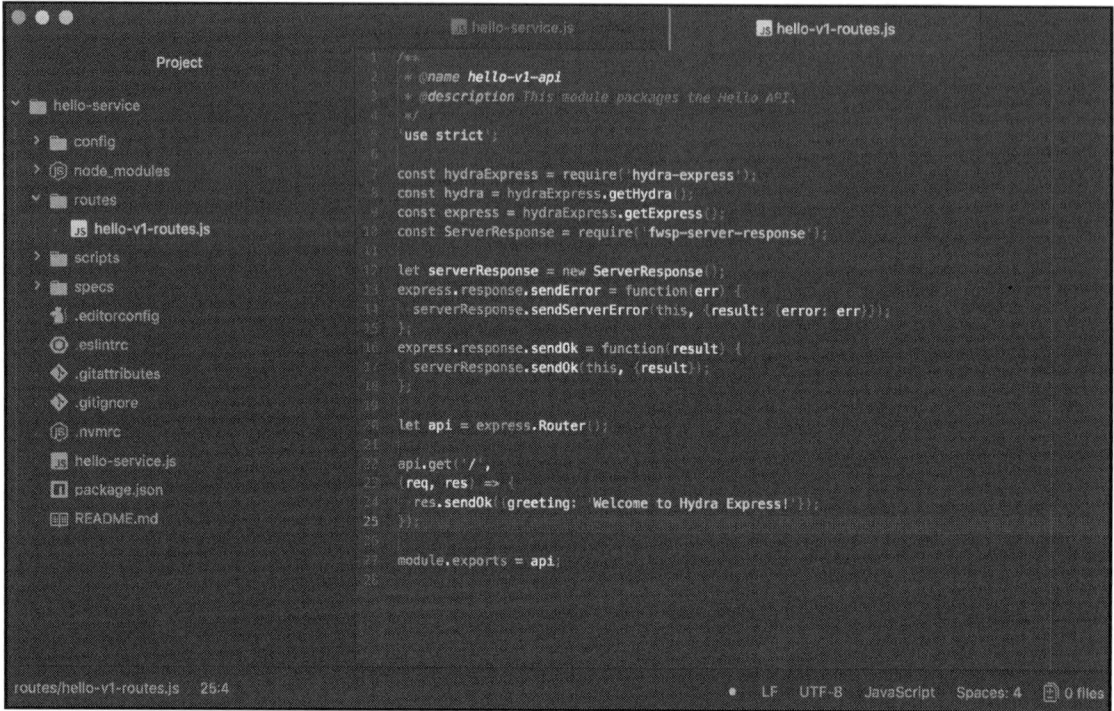

Inside that file, you'll see the response to that route. Now, let's jump to a web browser and see if it's up and running:

What we saw in the file is inside the result property of the JSON response. We just deployed our first Hydra microservice without writing a single line of code!

Summary

We've just covered a range of different modules and toolkits to help develop microservices. From the tiny Micro, through patterns in Seneca, to the Hydra bundle, many approaches are available.

They all target different audiences and fill different needs. I would advise you to experiment with some of them to help you make a better choice instead of just picking one.

Let's dig into some of these tools and start creating a more complete microservice. In the next chapter, we'll be making a useful microservice, covering different use cases, while we develop a fully functional and distributed microservice.

5
Building a Microservice

Now that we've seen some examples of building microservices using some tools, let's dig deeper and create a microservice from scratch using these tools. To accomplish our goal, we'll first use Express, then see how we could refactor it using Hydra, and finally, we'll create our microservice using the Seneca approach.

There are many microservices we could create, but some are more interesting than others. More specifically, a microservice that you can use in several applications is obviously more useful.

Let's create an image processing microservice. We'll start with a simple thumbnail service, and then we'll evolve to make some simple image transformations. We'll be covering how to:

- Build a microservice using Express
- Use external modules to manipulate images
- Build our previous microservice in Hydra and Seneca

The microservice name is very important, as it gives identity. Let's name it *imagini*, the Latin name for image.

Using Express

As we've seen before, Express gives us a very simple but very useful layer on top of the default Node.js HTTP module. Let's create an empty folder, initialize our `package.json` file, and install Express:

```
● ● ●                    1. nazgul.home: /Users/dresende/imagini (bash)
~/imagini > npm init -y
Wrote to /Users/dresende/imagini/package.json:

{
  "name": "imagini",
  "version": "1.0.0",
  "description": "",
  "main": "index.js",
  "scripts": {
    "test": "echo \"Error: no test specified\" && exit 1"
  },
  "keywords": [],
  "author": "",
  "license": "ISC"
}


~/imagini > npm install express --save
npm WARN imagini@1.0.0 No description
npm WARN imagini@1.0.0 No repository field.

+ express@4.16.2
added 49 packages in 2.297s
~/imagini > _
```

To help us get around images, we'll use the sharp module, a very fast image manipulation tool for the modern web. It will allow us to easily transform and resize images in a simple serial interface. Let's just install it now:

Let's start by exposing an address to return thumbnails. We'll need to first define our default parameters. Later on, we'll allow the user to change the default values. Our service will run on port 3000 and will accept thumbnail requests on both PNG and JPEG formats. Here's our not-so-simple service:

```
const express = require("express");
const sharp   = require("sharp");
const app     = express();

app.get(/\/thumbnail\.(jpg|png)/, (req, res, next) => {
    let format    = (req.params[0] == "png" ? "png" : "jpeg");
    let width     = 300;
    let height    = 200;
    let border    = 5;
    let bgcolor   = "#fcfcfc";
    let fgcolor   = "#ddd";
    let textcolor = "#aaa";
    let textsize  = 24;
    let image     = sharp({
        create : {
            width      : width,
            height     : height,
            channels   : 4,
            background : { r: 0, g: 0, b: 0 },
        }
    });
```

```
    const thumbnail = new Buffer(
`<svg width="${width}" height="${height}">
    <rect
        x="0" y="0"
        width="${width}" height="${height}"
        fill="${fgcolor}" />
    <rect
        x="${border}" y="${border}"
        width="${width - border * 2}" height="${height - border * 2}"
        fill="${bgcolor}" />
    <line
        x1="${border * 2}" y1="${border * 2}"
        x2="${width - border * 2}" y2="${height - border * 2}"
        stroke-width="${border}" stroke="${fgcolor}" />
    <line
        x1="${width - border * 2}" y1="${border * 2}"
        x2="${border * 2}" y2="${height - border * 2}"
        stroke-width="${border}" stroke="${fgcolor}" />
    <rect
        x="${border}" y="${(height - textsize) / 2}"
        width="${width - border * 2}" height="${textsize}"
        fill="${bgcolor}" />
    <text
        x="${width / 2}" y="${height / 2}" dy="8"
        font-family="Helvetica" font-size="${textsize}"
        fill="${textcolor}" text-anchor="middle">${width} x
${height}</text>
</svg>`
    );

    image.overlayWith(thumbnail)[format]().pipe(res);
});

app.listen(3000, () => {
    console.log("ready");
});
```

We start by getting access to both express and sharp modules. We then initialize our Express application:

```
const express = require("express");
const sharp   = require("sharp");
const app     = express();
```

We then create a route to get an image, with a regular expression that will catch the address `/thumbnail.png` and `/thumbnail.jpg`. We'll use the extension to ascertain what image type the user wants. We define some default parameters, such as sizes and colors:

```
let format    = (req.params[0] == "png" ? "png" : "jpeg");
let width     = 300;
let height    = 200;
let border    = 5;
let bgcolor   = "#fcfcfc";
let fgcolor   = "#ddd";
let textcolor = "#aaa";
let textsize  = 24;
```

We then create an empty image using `sharp`:

```
let image = sharp({
    create : {
        width       : width,
        height      : height,
        channels    : 4,
        background  : { r: 0, g: 0, b: 0 },
    }
});
```

We then create an SVG file with an outer border, two crossing lines, and a text in the middle with the size of the image. Next, we overlay the SVG on our empty image, and output the result to the user:

```
image.overlayWith(thumbnail)[format]().pipe(res);
```

Finally, we initialize our service on port 3000:

```
app.listen(3000, () => {
    console.log("ready");
});
```

Save the full code shown previously as `imagini.js`, and run it on the console:

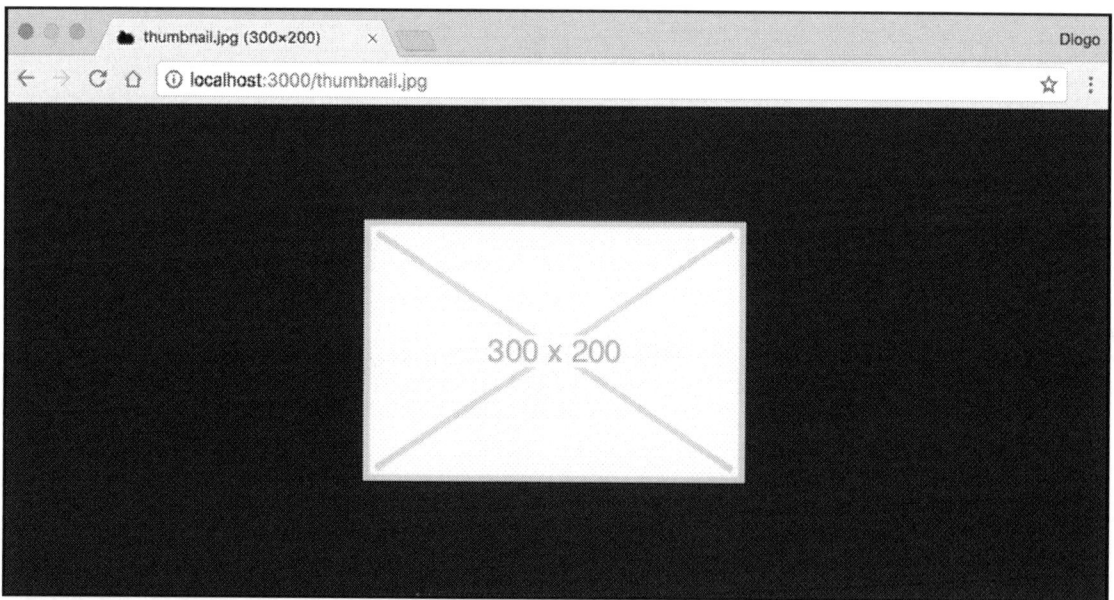

You can now head to your web browser and just type the address of our service, and you'll see something like the following image:

We can now start accepting some changes. Let's change our default variables to something like this:

```
let width    = +req.query.width  || 300;
let height   = +req.query.height || 200;
let border   = +req.query.border || 5;
```

```
let bgcolor    = req.query.bgcolor || "#fcfcfc";
let fgcolor    = req.query.fgcolor || "#ddd";
let textcolor  = req.query.textcolor || "#aaa";
let textsize   = +req.query.textsize || 24;
```

> The preceding code is not safe for production. Use it only for demonstration purposes. We'll take a look at security in the next chapter.

Restart our service and play with query parameters to see the result. Here's an example of changing the width to 500 px, the border to 2 px, and the foreground color to cyan:

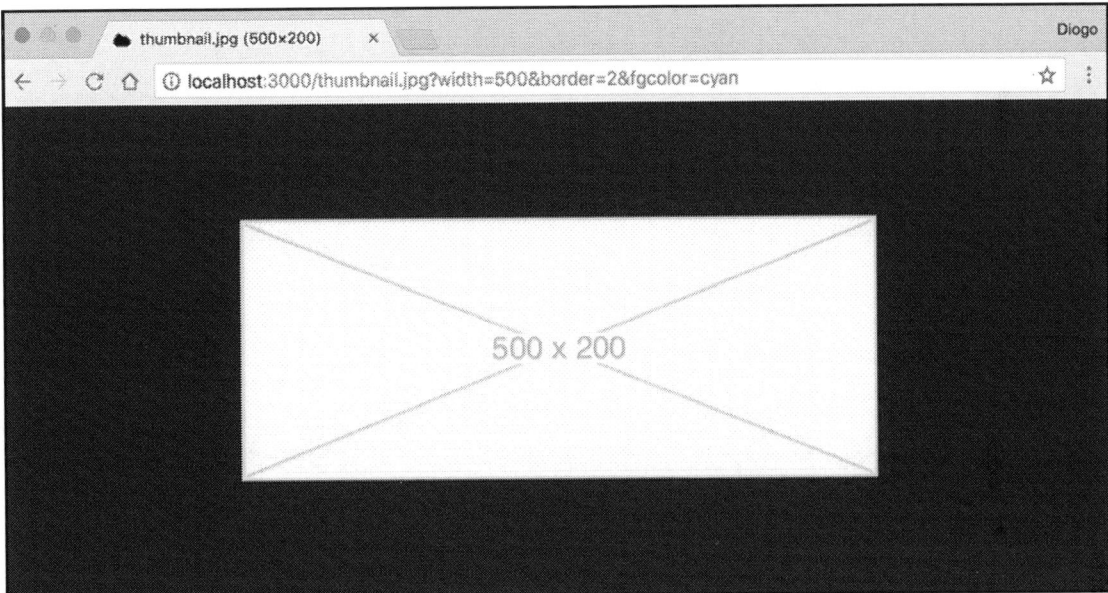

Well, it looks awesome, but it's not very useful as it is, as it just shows the same empty image. Though perhaps more applicable for prototyping, in the real world, it would be more useful if it could create thumbnails from images we upload. Let's do that.

To do so, we need to be able to:

- Upload images, which should be stored somewhere
- Check whether an image exists
- Download an image thumbnail

To simplify, we'll create dynamic routes in a specific path, and we'll use HTTP verbs (GET, POST, DELETE, and so on) to distinguish the actions. When uploading images, we'll use POST and the body should have the image data. To check if an image exists, we'll use HEAD. To download an image thumbnail, we'll use GET.

Uploading images

Let's first add our route to handle uploading images. We'll use a body parser module that will handle compressed requests automatically for us.

```
npm install body-parser --save
```

We'll include it along with other core modules that we'll need. Add these lines on the top of our `service` file:

```
const bodyparser = require("body-parser");
const path       = require("path");
const fs         = require("fs");
```

We can now create the function that will handle our upload:

```
app.post("/uploads/:image", bodyparser.raw({
    limit : "10mb",
    type  : "image/*"
}), (req, res) => {
    let image = req.params.image.toLowerCase();

    if (!image.match(/\.(png|jpg)$/)) {
        return res.status(403).end();
    }

    let len = req.body.length;
    let fd  = fs.createWriteStream(path.join(__dirname, "uploads",
    image), {
        flags    : "w+",
        encoding : "binary"
    });

    fd.write(req.body);
    fd.end();

    fd.on("close", () => {
        res.send({ status : "ok", size: len });
    });
});
```

We're expecting an HTTP POST on the /uploads path. It must be an image with a maximum size of 10 MB. Let's analyze the code in detail.

```
let image = req.params.image.toLowerCase();

if (!image.match(/\.(png|jpg)$/)) {
    return res.status(403).end();
}
```

We start by checking whether the image name passed ends with .png or .jpg. If not, we reply with an HTTP 403 response code, which means **forbidden**, as we're just accepting those types of images:

```
let len = req.body.length;
let fd  = fs.createWriteStream(path.join(__dirname, "uploads", image), {
    flags    : "w+",
    encoding : "binary"
});
```

We then create a stream to the local file where we'll save our image. The name of the file will be the name of the image. We also store the image size so we can return that to the user when we finish saving. This enables the microservice user to check if we received all the data.

```
fd.write(req.body);
fd.end();

fd.on("close", () => {
    res.send({ status : "ok", size: len });
});
```

Lastly, we write the image to file and, after properly closing the stream, we reply to the user with a JSON response with a status and a size property.

Don't forget to create the uploads folder inside the microservice folder. Then, restart the service. We'll continue to use curl to test our services. We'll need an image to try it out. I searched for a Google image and saved it locally. I then uploaded it to our service using this command:

```
curl -X POST -H 'Content-Type: image/png' \
    --data-binary @example.png \
    http://localhost:3000/uploads/example.png
```

We're telling `curl` that we want to:

- Send a `POST` request
- Define the `Content-Type` header saying it's a PNG image
- Add the content of the `example.png` file (I downloaded) inside the request body
- Send the request to the `/upload/example.png` path of our microservice

After executing the command, I received a JSON response. The size matches my file:

```
{ "status" : "ok", "size" : 55543 }
```

We can't see the image using our microservice just yet, but we can check it locally. You should have a copy of the file in the `uploads` folder. For reference, here's the image I'm using:

Checking an image exists in the folder

We can now create a route to check whether an image exists in our `uploads` folder. We'll use the HEAD verb. If you're not familiar with it, it's just like a `GET` request, but without a body (no content). It's used to request only information (headers) from a path.

```
app.head("/uploads/:image", (req, res) => {
    fs.access(
        path.join(__dirname, "uploads", req.params.image),
        fs.constants.R_OK ,
        (err) => {
            res.status(err ? 404 : 200);
            res.end();
        }
    );
});
```

We'll look for a similar route, but this time we're only handling HEAD requests. This is a simple check. We just question if the current process has read access to the local file.

```
fs.access(path, mode, callback);
```

If so, we'll reply with HTTP response code 200, which means *Found*. If not, we'll reply with HTTP response code 404, which means *Not Found*:

```
res.status(err ? 404 : 200);
```

Add the preceding code and restart the service.

If you use `curl` to check for our previously uploaded file, you'll receive something like this:

```
curl --head 'http://localhost:3000/uploads/example.png'

HTTP/1.1 200 OK
X-Powered-By: Express
Content-Length: 0
Connection: keep-alive
```

If you change the path to something else, you should receive something like this:

```
curl --head 'http://localhost:3000/uploads/other.png'

HTTP/1.1 404 Not Found
X-Powered-By: Express
Connection: keep-alive
```

Downloading images

Now that we have uploaded our file and checked whether it's stored on the server, we want to be able to download it anytime. Let's create a route to download it. It will be just like the HEAD route we created, but now using the GET verb. Here's an example of how we can implement the route:

```
app.get("/uploads/:image", (req, res) => {
    let ext = path.extname(req.params.image);

    if (!ext.match(/^\.(png|jpg)$/)) {
        return res.status(404).end()
    }

    let fd = fs.createReadStream(path.join(__dirname, "uploads",
    req.params.image));
```

```
    fd.on("error", (e) => {
        if (e.code == "ENOENT") {
            return res.status(404).end()
        }

        res.status(500).end();
    });

    res.setHeader("Content-Type", "image/" + ext.substr(1));

    fd.pipe(res);
});
```

We first start by checking the image extension:

```
let ext = path.extname(req.params.image);
```

If the extension is not .png or .jpg, we immediately return an HTTP response code 404, which means *Not Found*:

```
if (!ext.match(/^\.(png|jpg)$/)) {
    return res.status(404).end();
}
```

If the extension is acceptable, we create a readable stream to the image file path:

```
let fd = fs.createReadStream(path.join(__dirname, "uploads",
req.params.image));
```

We then attach an error handler that will catch errors when reading the local file. If the error code is ENOENT, it means the file does not exist, so we again return an HTTP response code 404. For any other error codes, we return an HTTP response code 500, which means *Internal Server Error*:

```
fd.on("error", (e) => {
    if (e.code == "ENOENT") {
        return res.status(404).end()
    }

    res.status(500).end();
});
```

Returning code 500 is up to you. Perhaps you prefer to always return a 404 and hide the error differences from the user. That's a design decision; it depends on how you want your users to see your microservice and what target users will use it.

Then, we use the previously stored extension to set the content type returned to the user, in order to identify the image type we're sending. The content type should be in the format image/extension (without a dot):

```
res.setHeader("Content-Type", "image/" + ext.substr(1));
```

Finally, we pipe the file content to the response. This is a helper method that will trigger reads from the file stream and write them to the response. When the whole file has been read, the response is ended automatically:

```
fd.pipe(res);
```

Let's try it out. Restart our service and open your web browser. If you point to the previously uploaded image, you should get a copy of it:

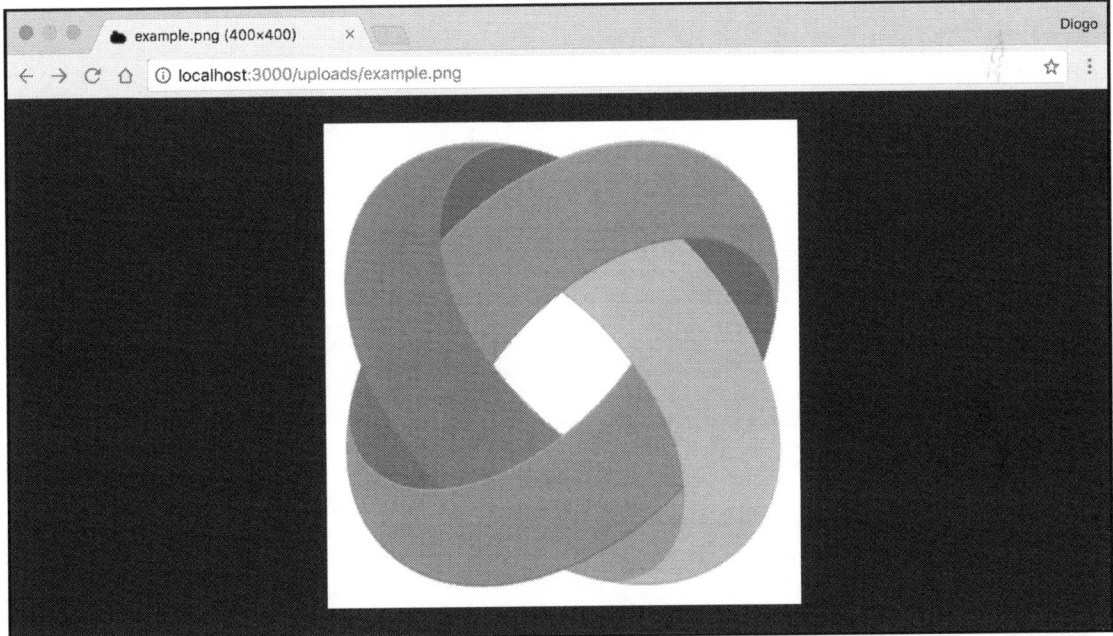

If you change the path to something that you haven't uploaded, you should get an **HTTP ERROR 404**:

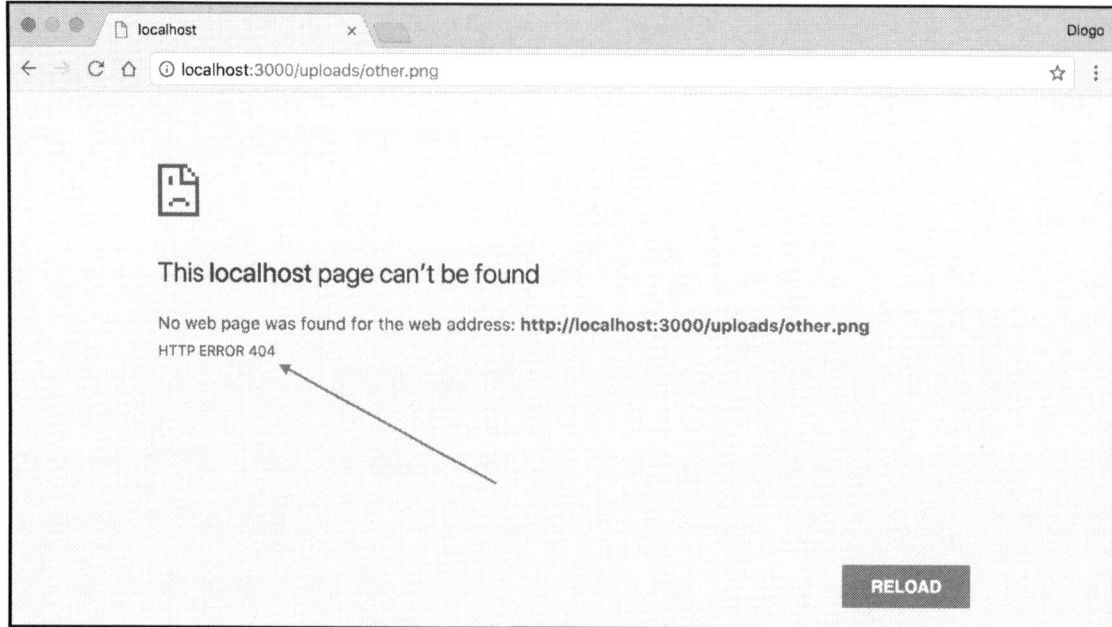

This is not very appealing. We can change our error handler to check whether the request might accept HTML content and return a custom message:

```
fd.on("error", (e) => {
    if (e.code == "ENOENT") {
        res.status(404);

        if (req.accepts('html')) {
            res.setHeader("Content-Type", "text/html");

            res.write("<strong>Error:</strong> image not found");
        }

        return res.end();
    }

    res.status(500).end();
});
```

You should now receive a nicer response:

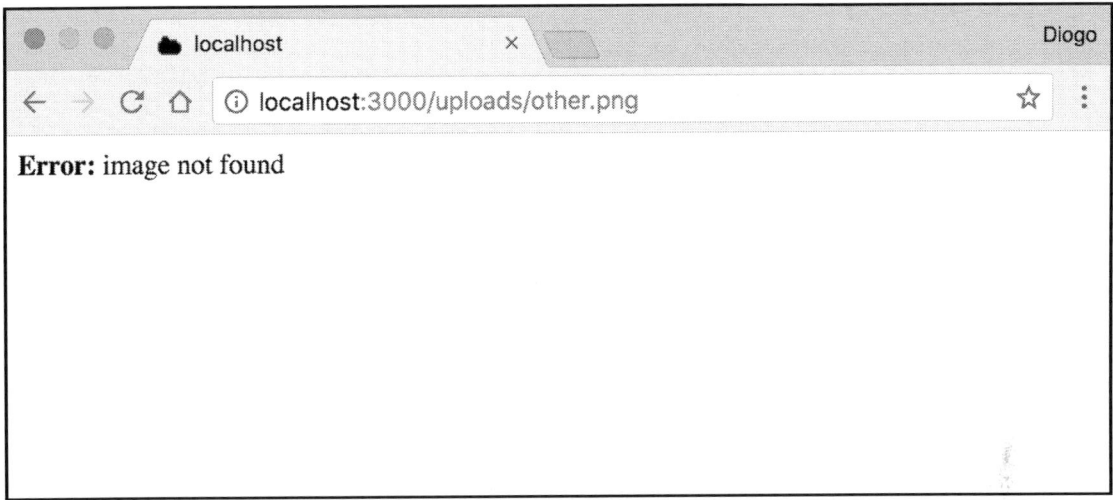

If you're familiar with Express, you could instead use a render engine and define a custom error template, or look for error handler modules that generate beautiful error pages.

Using route parameters

Now that we've written more than 100 lines of code, let's take a step back and look at it. There's certainly space for optimizations. Let's use another awesome feature of Express – route parameters. They allow you to preprocess any route that uses a parameter and check whether it's valid, and do all kinds of stuff such as fetching additional information from a database or another server.

We'll use it to validate our image name for now:

```
app.param("image", (req, res, next, image) => {
    if (!image.match(/\.(png|jpg)$/i)) {
        return res.status(req.method == "POST" ? 403 : 404).end();
    }

    req.image    = image;
    req.localpath = path.join(__dirname, "uploads", req.image);

    return next();
});
```

We start by checking whether the name matches a PNG or JPG image and, if not, we immediately reply with a 403 (for POST requests) or 404 error code (for anything else). If the name is acceptable, we store the image and the expected local path in the request object, for consulting it later.

We can now rewrite our routes, so let's start with our upload route:

```
app.post("/uploads/:image", bodyparser.raw({
    limit : "10mb",
    type  : "image/*"
}), (req, res) => {
    let fd  = fs.createWriteStream(req.localpath, {
        flags    : "w+",
        encoding : "binary"
    });

    fd.end(req.body);

    fd.on("close", () => {
        res.send({ status : "ok", size: req.body.length });
    });
});
```

Our initial check was completely removed since the parameter was pre-validated. Also, we can now use req.localpath. I also optimized code by removing an unnecessary variable allocation (len) and just using .end() by avoiding .write().

```
app.head("/uploads/:image", (req, res) => {
    fs.access(req.localpath, fs.constants.R_OK , (err) => {
        res.status(err ? 404 : 200).end();
    });
});
```

Our image check route looks almost exactly the same. This route had no security, so at least we introduced the pre-validation automatically. It's still far from acceptable for production, but it's a good start:

```
app.get("/uploads/:image", (req, res) => {
    let fd = fs.createReadStream(req.localpath);

    fd.on("error", (e) => {
        res.status(e.code == "ENOENT" ? 404 : 500).end();
    });

    res.setHeader("Content-Type", "image/" +
path.extname(req.image).substr(1));
```

```
        fd.pipe(res);
    });
```

Our image download route got a bit smaller. I removed the fancy error to keep the service clean as it will most probably be used by other services and programs, not users directly.

The change we introduced centralizes the image parameter check. We can go a little further and see if the name has special characters that would allow a malicious user to fetch a file from a location other than our local uploads folder. Let's save that for the next chapter.

Generating thumbnails

We created upload and download routes, but they do nothing to the image other than storing it locally. Picking on our first thumbnail route, let's change our download route to be able to tell us the size we want for the image:

```
app.param("width", (req, res, next, width) => {
    req.width = +width;

    return next();
});

app.param("height", (req, res, next, height) => {
    req.height = +height;

    return next();
});
```

We start by defining two parameters, width, and height. These are numbers, so we'll assume they can be casted to a number type and stored in the request object.

Since we want to be able to specify sizes, let's create different routes using the route parameters we just introduced. To keep our code DRY, let's create a function to download the image and enable us to avoid repeating a very similar code. Our function will be able to handle optional resize:

```
function download_image(req, res) {
    fs.access(req.localpath, fs.constants.R_OK , (err) => {
        if (err) return res.status(404).end();

        let image = sharp(req.localpath);

        if (req.width && req.height) {
            image.ignoreAspectRatio();
        }
```

```
        if (req.width || req.height) {
            image.resize(req.width, req.height);
        }

        res.setHeader("Content-Type", "image/" +
        path.extname(req.image).substr(1));

        image.pipe(res);
    });
}
```

Our function first starts by checking whether the image exists. This will avoid the `sharp` module from throwing for non-existent images. We then initialize the image processing by passing its local path. We then do something interesting:

```
if (req.width && req.height) {
    image.ignoreAspectRatio();
}
```

First, if we receive both width and height, we tell `sharp` to ignore aspect ratio and resize as we tell it. Otherwise, it would maintain aspect ratio and center the image in the final size. You can check the difference by commenting out those first three lines:

```
if (req.width || req.height) {
    image.resize(req.width, req.height);
}
```

Second, if we receive one of the `width` or `height` parameters, we resize the image. We can resize with only one of the parameters. The `sharp` module is also able to resize using only one of the parameters if the other is undefined, so the line just works and will maintain aspect ratio.

We then just do what we did before: set the content type response header and send the image to the user. Now, we can create multiple routes for this function.

We'll allow three different download scenarios:

- A particular fixed-size image
- An aspect ratio resize by passing only width or height
- A full-size image

For the first scenario, we'll use our previous `width` and `height` parameters:

```
app.get("/uploads/:width(\\d+)x:height(\\d+)-:image", download_image);
```

This will allow a route address similar to the following:

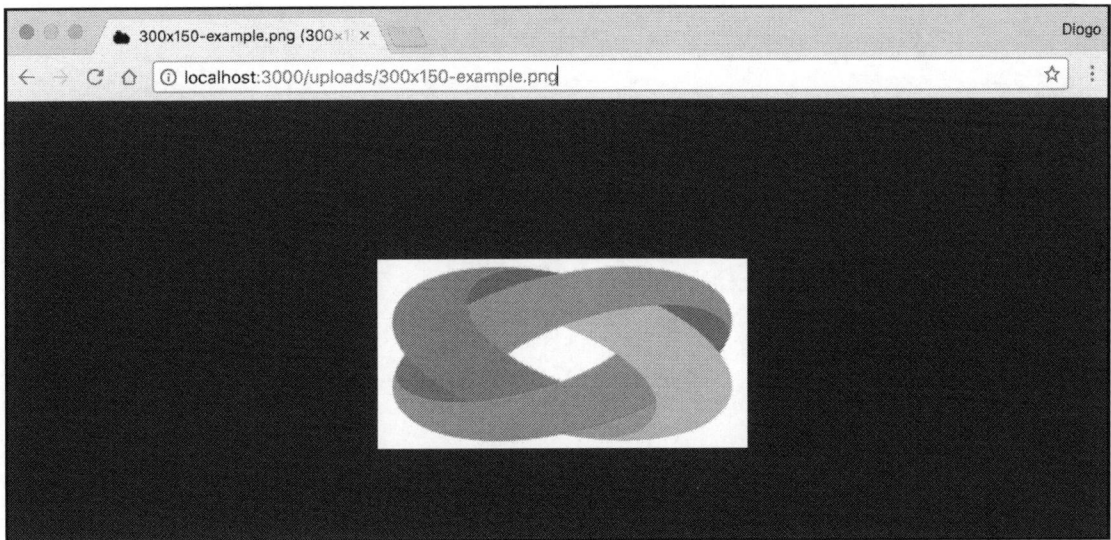

For the second scenario, we'll use similar routes, where the missing parameter is replaced by an underscore:

```
app.get("/uploads/_x:height(\\d+)-:image", download_image);
app.get("/uploads/:width(\\d+)x_-:image", download_image);
```

These will allow routes similar to the one as follows:

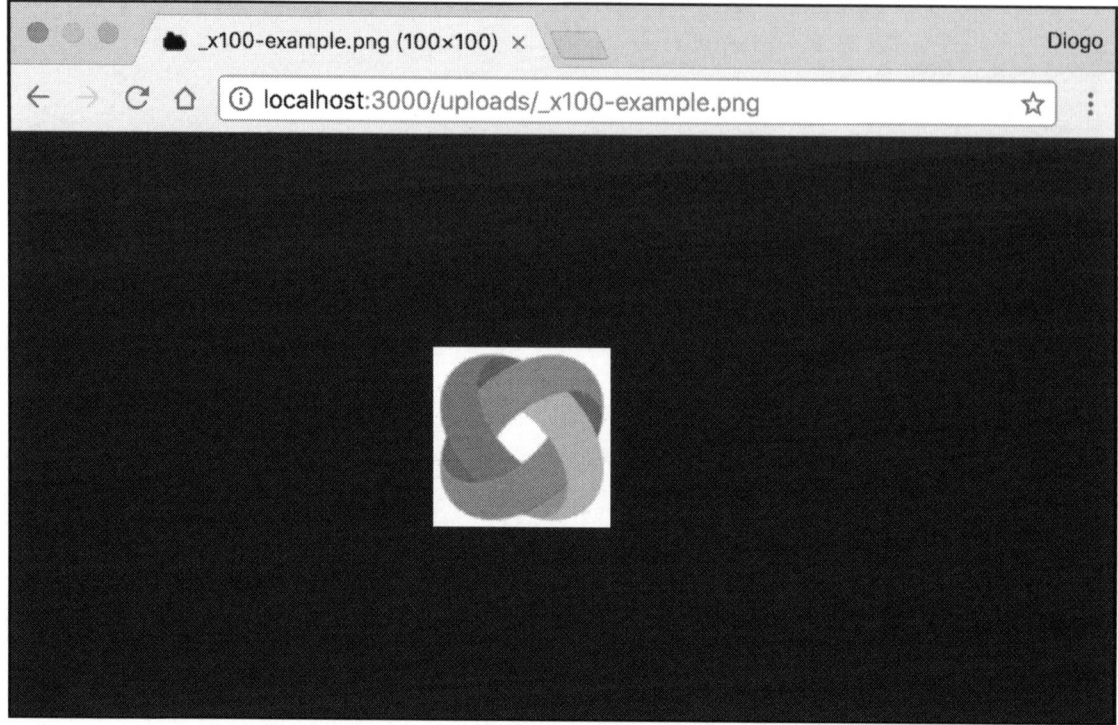

For the third and final scenario, we'll keep the same route:

```
app.get("/uploads/:image", download_image);
```

These four routes must be defined in this order. This is important because route parameters are based on regular expressions and they're greedy, so we need to define our more complicated routes first, and then the simpler ones.

Playing around with colors

Let's have some more fun and add a simple effect: greyscale. Let's add a parameter that will indicate to our service that the user wants the image in shades of grey:

```
app.param("greyscale", (req, res, next, greyscale) => {
    if (greyscale != "bw") return next("route");

    req.greyscale = true;
```

```
        return next();
    });
```

Our parameter will only match the bw string. If it matches, it will mark a flag in the request object.

We can now change our image download function to handle this parameter, if defined:

```
function download_image(req, res) {
    fs.access(req.localpath, fs.constants.R_OK , (err) => {
        if (err) return res.status(404).end();

        let image = sharp(req.localpath);

        if (req.width && req.height) {
            image.ignoreAspectRatio();
        }

        if (req.width || req.height) {
            image.resize(req.width, req.height);
        }

        if (req.greyscale) {
            image.greyscale();
        }

        res.setHeader("Content-Type", "image/" +
        path.extname(req.image).substr(1));

        image.pipe(res);
    });
}
```

Finally, for every one of our four download routes, we need to add another one to enable grey scaling. This means our user can take advantage of our resizing options and can greyscale the image if he prefers:

```
app.get("/uploads/:width(\\d+)x:height(\\d+)-:greyscale-:image",
download_image);
app.get("/uploads/:width(\\d+)x:height(\\d+)-:image", download_image);
app.get("/uploads/_x:height(\\d+)-:greyscale-:image", download_image);
app.get("/uploads/_x:height(\\d+)-:image", download_image);
app.get("/uploads/:width(\\d+)x_-:greyscale-:image", download_image);
app.get("/uploads/:width(\\d+)x_-:image", download_image);
app.get("/uploads/:greyscale-:image", download_image);
app.get("/uploads/:image", download_image);
```

For every one of our initial four routes, we added a similar route before that, with the greyscale parameter. The user just has to prefix the image name with `bw-` to automatically enable `greyscale`.

In the end, excluding our first generated thumbnail, you should have something similar to the following code. I removed the code blocks inside the routes and our download function, so you're able to see the base structure:

```
const bodyparser = require("body-parser");
const path      = require("path");
const fs        = require("fs");
const express   = require("express");
const sharp     = require("sharp");
const app       = express();

app.param("image", (req, res, next, image) => { ... });
app.param("width", (req, res, next, width) => { ... });
app.param("height", (req, res, next, height) => { ... });
app.param("greyscale", (req, res, next, greyscale) => { ... });

app.post("/uploads/:image", bodyparser.raw({ limit: "10mb", type: "image/*"
}), (req, res) => { ... });

app.head("/uploads/:image", (req, res) => { ... });

app.get("/uploads/:width(\\d+)x:height(\\d+)-:greyscale-:image",
download_image);
app.get("/uploads/:width(\\d+)x:height(\\d+)-:image", download_image);
app.get("/uploads/_x:height(\\d+)-:greyscale-:image", download_image);
app.get("/uploads/_x:height(\\d+)-:image", download_image);
app.get("/uploads/:width(\\d+)x_-:greyscale-:image", download_image);
app.get("/uploads/:width(\\d+)x_-:image", download_image);
app.get("/uploads/:greyscale-:image", download_image);
app.get("/uploads/:image", download_image);

app.listen(3000, () => {
    console.log("ready");
});

function download_image(req, res) {
    ...
}
```

You can now restart our service and make some tests. Taking our first image as an example, we can request a `greyscale` version:

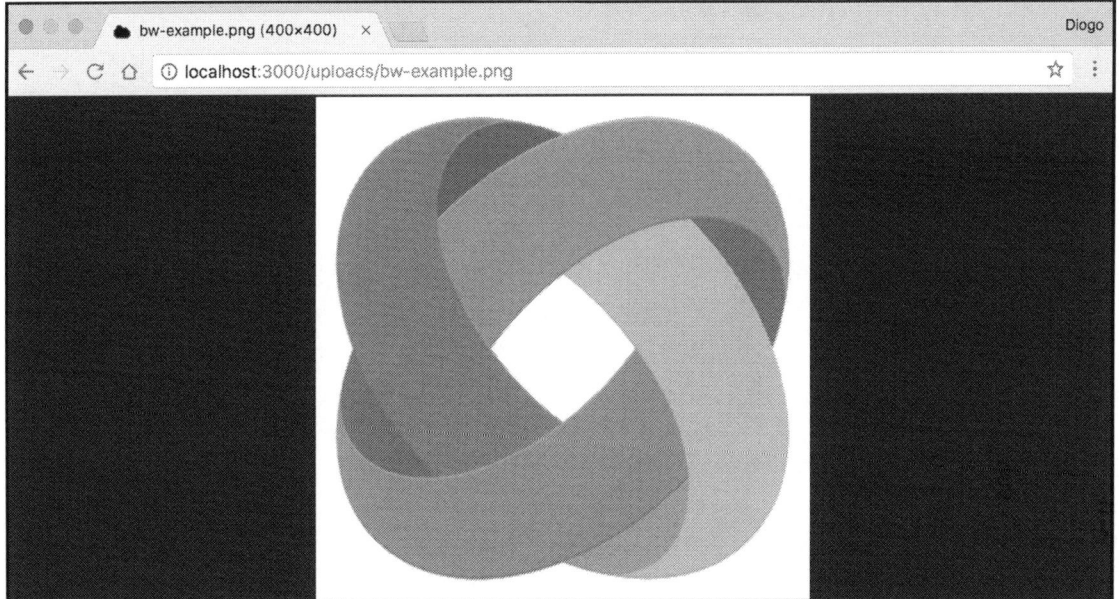

You can still resize the image as we did before, with the optional `greyscale` filter:

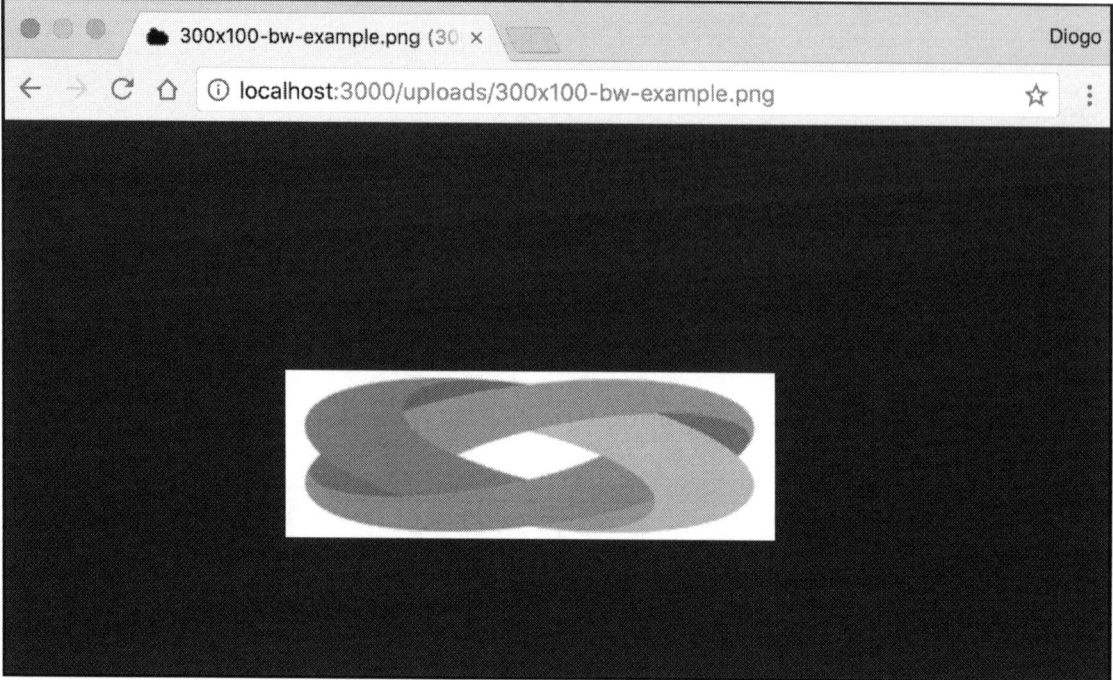

We can take advantage of the `sharp` module and add some more interesting image manipulations for our service. This way, we can use it in more projects as it evolves to a full-featured image manipulation service.

We can start by adding a blurring option, something that will make the image seem unfocused. We can also do the opposite, and make the image sharper. We can also flip the image horizontally and vertically.

Refactor routes

These options look neat but, following the route we're doing, it will probably be a mess to create all the path possibilities. We're also narrowing on the image names as we're creating virtual prefixes for these image manipulations options.

Let's make a change while we're at the beginning. Instead of using route parameters, let's use query parameters. They can be added in the order we want, and don't affect the path. We could also use request headers, but these would be harder to test both on the browser and using fetching modules such as request.

So, before we add our neat image manipulations, let's refactor our code to use query parameters. Express handles and decodes query parameters automatically, so we just need to change our download `image` function:

```
function download_image(req, res) {
    fs.access(req.localpath, fs.constants.R_OK , (err) => {
        if (err) return res.status(404).end();

        let image    = sharp(req.localpath);
        let width    = +req.query.width;
        let height   = +req.query.height;
        let greyscale = (req.query.greyscale == "y");

        if (width > 0 && height > 0) {
            image.ignoreAspectRatio();
        }

        if (width > 0 || height > 0) {
            image.resize(width || null, height || null);
        }

        if (greyscale) {
            image.greyscale();
        }

        res.setHeader("Content-Type", "image/" +
        path.extname(req.image).substr(1));

        image.pipe(res);
    });
}
```

We're not validating as we probably should, but we're ensuring the width and height are positive numbers. For greyscaling, we're checking whether the query parameter equals `y`. If you prefer to support more options on greyscaling such as `yes` or `true`, change the line to something like the following:

```
let greyscale = [ "y", "yes", "1", "on"].includes(req.query.greyscale);
```

Now, we can drop the `width`, `height`, and `greyscale` route parameters we added before, and just keep the `image` parameter. Also, all our download routes can be removed, and we just keep the simpler one. In the end, we'll have something like this:

```
const bodyparser = require("body-parser");
const path       = require("path");
const fs         = require("fs");
const express    = require("express");
const sharp      = require("sharp");
const app        = express();

app.param("image", (req, res, next, image) => {
    if (!image.match(/\.(png|jpg)$/i)) {
        return res.status(req.method == "POST" ? 403 : 404).end();
    }

    req.image     = image;
    req.localpath = path.join(__dirname, "uploads", req.image);

    return next();
});

app.post("/uploads/:image", bodyparser.raw({
    limit : "10mb",
    type  : "image/*"
}), (req, res) => {
    let fd = fs.createWriteStream(req.localpath, {
        flags    : "w+",
        encoding : "binary"
    });

    fd.end(req.body);

    fd.on("close", () => {
        res.send({ status : "ok", size: req.body.length });
    });
});

app.head("/uploads/:image", (req, res) => {
    fs.access(req.localpath, fs.constants.R_OK , (err) => {
```

```
        res.status(err ? 404 : 200).end();
    });
});

app.get("/uploads/:image", download_image);

app.listen(3000, () => {
    console.log("ready");
});
```

Let's try it out now. You should be able to do a resize like we did before, but with a different address:

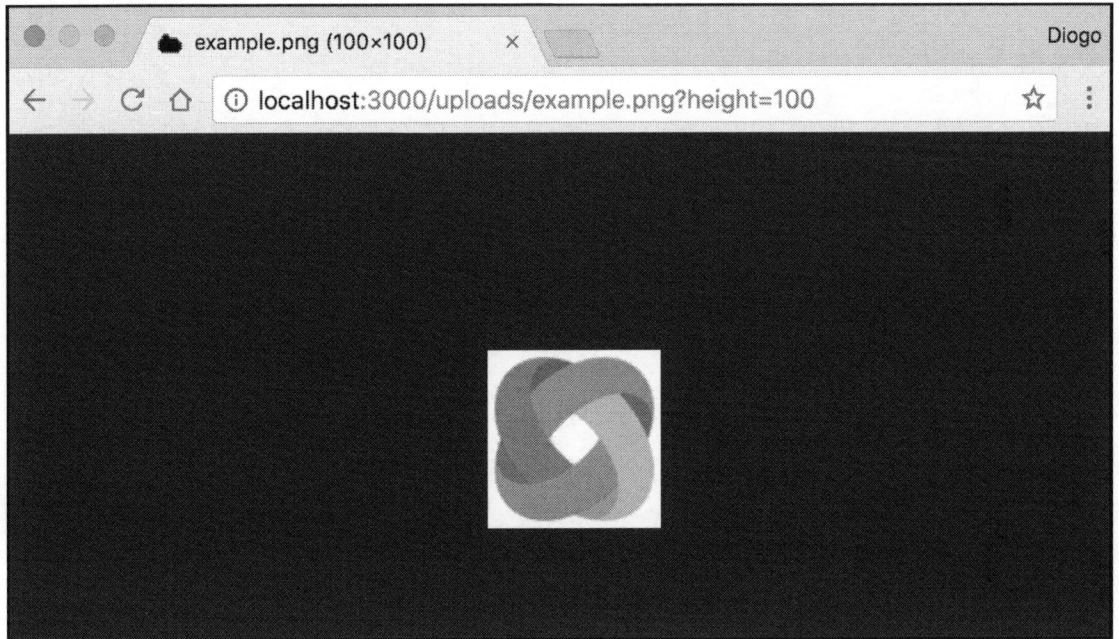

We can also add the `greyscale` function to it:

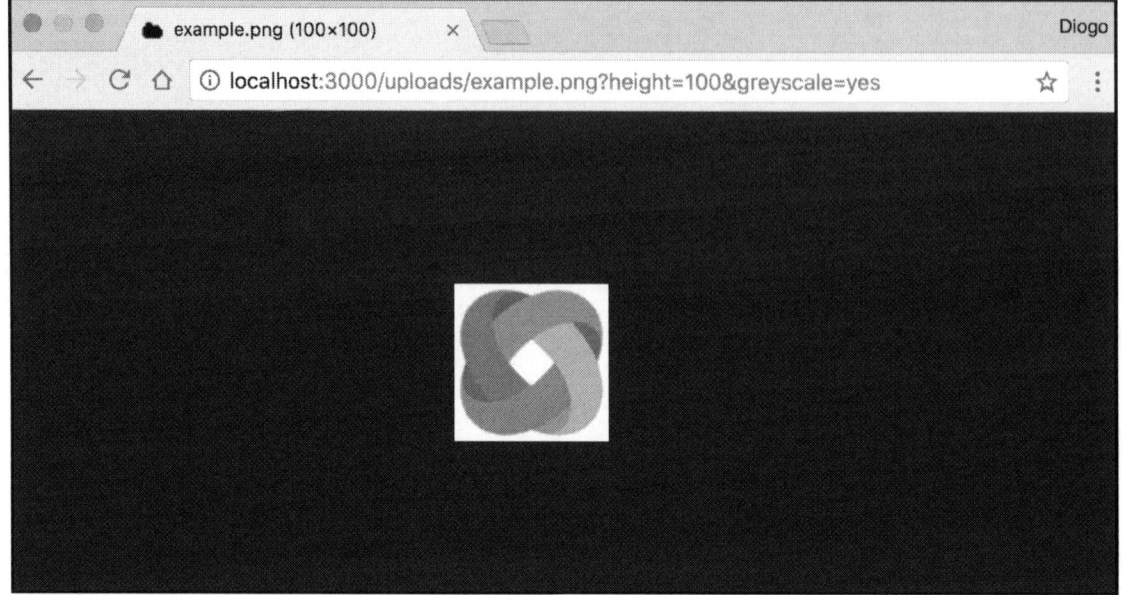

Manipulating images

Let's add the other image manipulation options we mentioned before. Let's use the Sharp naming for flipping. We'll use the query parameter `flip` to flip the image vertically, and the query parameter `flop` to flip it horizontally. We'll also add the optional query parameters `blur` and `sharpen`, which should be positive numbers.

Our image download function can be reintegrated directly in our download route, since we only have one route now. In the end, we would end up with something like this:

```
app.get("/uploads/:image", (req, res) => {
    fs.access(req.localpath, fs.constants.R_OK , (err) => {
        if (err) return res.status(404).end();

        let image     = sharp(req.localpath);
        let width     = +req.query.width;
        let height    = +req.query.height;
        let blur      = +req.query.blur;
        let sharpen   = +req.query.sharpen;
        let greyscale = [ "y", "yes", "1",

      "on"].includes(req.query.greyscale);
        let flip      = [ "y", "yes", "1",
      "on"].includes(req.query.flip);
        let flop      = [ "y", "yes", "1",
      "on"].includes(req.query.flop);

        if (width > 0 && height > 0) {
            image.ignoreAspectRatio();
        }

        if (width > 0 || height > 0) {
            image.resize(width || null, height || null);
        }

        if (flip)         image.flip();
        if (flop)         image.flop();
        if (blur > 0)     image.blur(blur);
        if (sharpen > 0)  image.sharpen(sharpen);
        if (greyscale)    image.greyscale();

        res.setHeader("Content-Type", "image/" +
        path.extname(req.image).substr(1));

        image.pipe(res);
    });
});
```

We should be able to play with it now; flipping and sharpening the image leads to something like this:

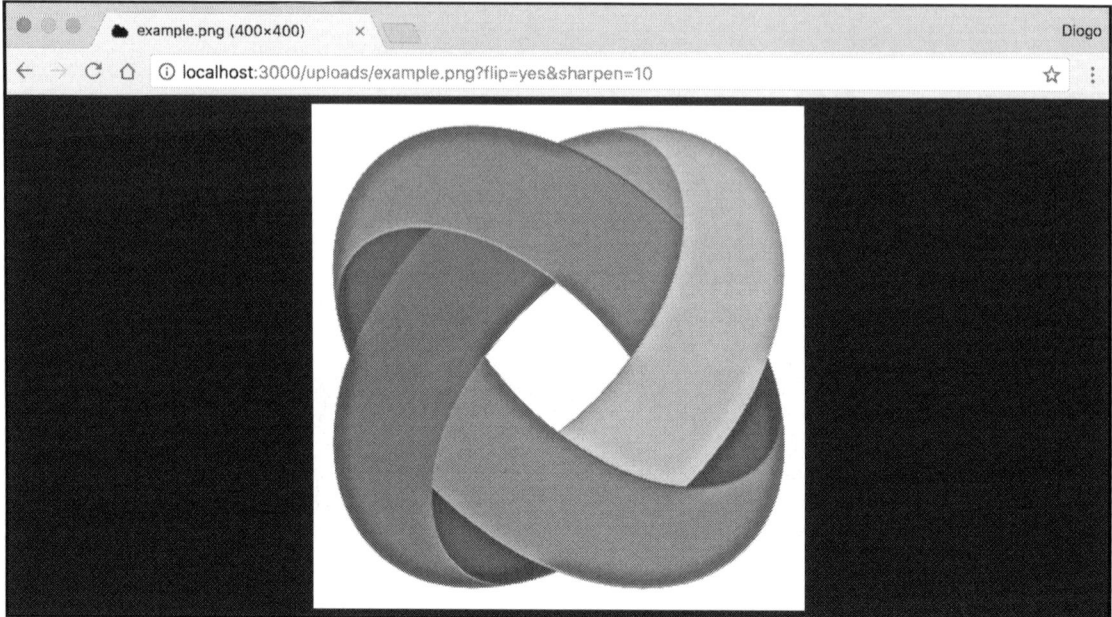

Blurring the image leads to something similar to this:

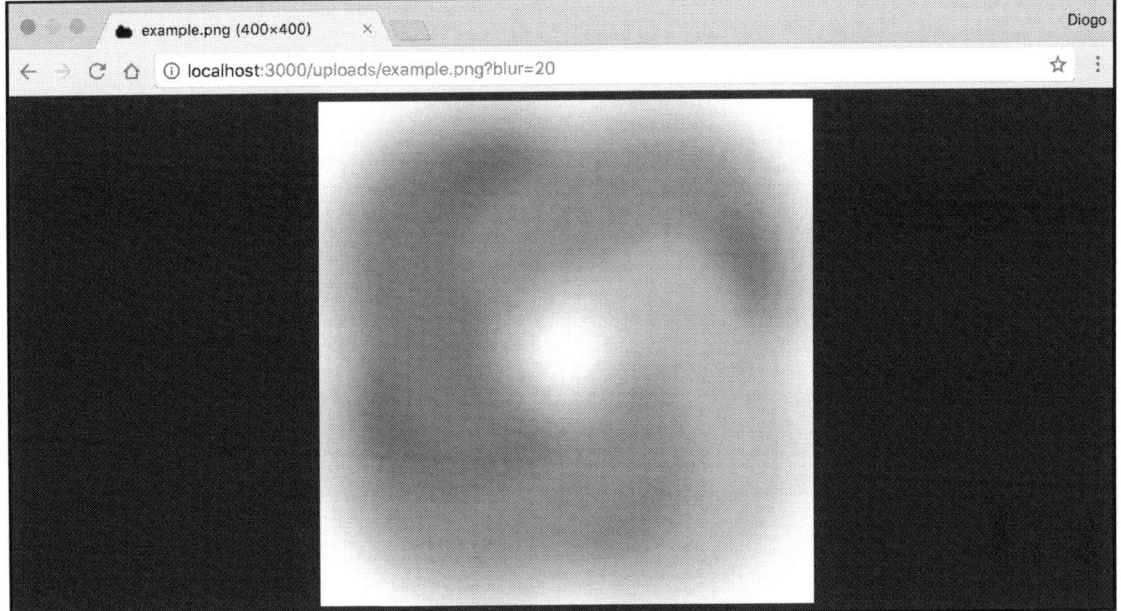

Well, that looks awesome for a first iteration. Let's see what it would look like if we use Hydra instead.

Using Hydra

As you may remember, Hydra has a scaffolding command that helps to bootstrap our service quickly. Let's use it, and prepare our base layout. Run yo fwsp-hydra and answer the questions. You can leave most of them as default. Depending on the versions you'll use, you should get something similar to the lines shown here:

```
fwsp-hydra generator v0.3.1    yeoman-generator v2.0.2    yo v2.0.1
? Name of the service (`-service` will be appended automatically) imagini
? Your full name? Diogo Resende
? Your email address? dresende@thinkdigital.pt
? Your organization or username? (used to tag docker images) dresende
? Host the service runs on?
? Port the service runs on? 3000
? What does this service do? Image thumbnail and manipulation
? Does this service need auth? No
? Is this a hydra-express service? Yes
? Set up a view engine? No
? Set up logging? No
? Enable CORS on serverResponses? No
? Run npm install? No
   create imagini-service/specs/test.js
   create imagini-service/specs/helpers/chai.js
   create imagini-service/.editorconfig
   create imagini-service/.eslintrc
   create imagini-service/.gitattributes
   create imagini-service/.nvmrc
   create imagini-service/.gitignore
   create imagini-service/package.json
   create imagini-service/README.md
   create imagini-service/imagini-service.js
   create imagini-service/config/sample-config.json
   create imagini-service/config/config.json
   create imagini-service/scripts/docker.js
   create imagini-service/routes/imagini-v1-routes.js

Done!

'cd imagini-service' then 'npm install' and 'npm start'
```

Well, let's do just that. Let's enter our service folder and install dependencies. If you then start it using `npm start`, and open the browser and point it to our service, you should get something like this:

Not surprising, because Hydra created a different base route. To enable versioning and having different services running on the same HTTP backend, Hydra scaffolding created a route under the `/v1/imagini` prefix. Remember, we scaffolded Hydra with Express integration, so many of the terms we discussed earlier will be the same here:

Before we pick our previous code and integrate into Hydra, we need to add our Sharp dependency to `package.json`. Look up the `dependencies` property and add `sharp`. You should end up with something along these lines:

```
(…)
"dependencies": {
    "sharp"                : "^0.19.0",
    "body-parser"          : "^1.18.2",
    "fwsp-config"          : "1.1.5",
    "hydra-express"        : "1.5.5",
    "fwsp-server-response" : "2.2.6"
},
(…)
```

Now, run `npm install` to install Sharp. Then, open the `imagini-v1-routes.js` file, which is under the `routes` folder. Basically, what it does is get a handler for Hydra and Express, prepare a generic JSON server response (that's what the `fwsp-server-response` module is), create an Express router, attach the / route, and then export it.

We'll keep this structure for now. I refactored the file as I'm a bit picky about indentation and quotes. I added our image route parameter and added the image upload route. I changed our previous route code to drop the /uploads route prefix, and use the new `sendOk` and `sendError` functions you see in the preceding code:

```
/**
 * @name         imagini-v1-api
 * @description  This module packages the Imagini API.
 */
"use strict";

const fs             = require("fs");
const path           = require("path");
const sharp          = require("sharp");
const bodyparser     = require("body-parser");
const hydraExpress   = require("hydra-express");
const ServerResponse = require("fwsp-server-response");
const hydra          = hydraExpress.getHydra();
const express        = hydraExpress.getExpress();

let serverResponse = new ServerResponse();

express.response.sendError = function (err) {
    serverResponse.sendServerError(this, { result : { error : err }});
};

express.response.sendOk = function (result) {
```

```
        serverResponse.sendOk(this, { result });
};

let api = express.Router();

api.param("image", (req, res, next, image) => {
    if (!image.match(/\.(png|jpg)$/i)) {
        return res.sendError("invalid image type/extension");
    }

    req.image     = image;
    req.localpath = path.join(__dirname, "../uploads", req.image);

    return next();
});

api.post("/:image", bodyparser.raw({
    limit : "10mb",
    type  : "image/*"
}), (req, res) => {
    let fd = fs.createWriteStream(req.localpath, {
        flags    : "w+",
        encoding : "binary"
    });

    fd.end(req.body);

    fd.on("close", () => {
        res.sendOk({ size: req.body.length });
    });
});

module.exports = api;
```

Then, we restart our microservice, create the `uploads` folder under the `imagini-service` folder, and try to upload an image. Like before, I used `curl` to test it:

```
curl -X POST -H 'Content-Type: image/png' \
    --data-binary @example.png \
    http://localhost:3000/v1/imagini/example.png
```

As expected, I received a JSON response with our `size` property:

```
{
    "statusCode"        : 200,
    "statusMessage"     : "OK",
    "statusDescription" : "Request succeeded without error",
    "result" : {
```

```
                "size" : 55543
        }
    }
```

We can have our uploaded file in our `uploads` folder. We're getting there; just two more routes:

```
api.head("/:image", (req, res) => {
    fs.access(req.localpath, fs.constants.R_OK , (err) => {
        if (err) {
            return res.sendError("image not found");
        }

        return res.sendOk();
    });
});
```

Our check route is very similar. We just changed the return methods to use the methods defined previously:

```
api.get("/:image", (req, res) => {
    fs.access(req.localpath, fs.constants.R_OK , (err) => {
        if (err) {
            return res.sendError("image not found");
        }

        let image     = sharp(req.localpath);
        let width     = +req.query.width;
        let height    = +req.query.height;
        let blur      = +req.query.blur;
        let sharpen   = +req.query.sharpen;
        let greyscale = [ "y", "yes", "true", "1",
        "on"].includes(req.query.greyscale);
        let flip      = [ "y", "yes", "true", "1",
        "on"].includes(req.query.flip);
        let flop      = [ "y", "yes", "true", "1",
        "on"].includes(req.query.flop);

        if (width > 0 && height > 0) {
            image.ignoreAspectRatio();
        }

        if (width > 0 || height > 0) {
            image.resize(width || null, height || null);
        }

        if (flip)        image.flip();
        if (flop)        image.flop();
```

```
    if (blur > 0)    image.blur(blur);
    if (sharpen > 0) image.sharpen(sharpen);
    if (greyscale)   image.greyscale();

    res.setHeader("Content-Type", "image/" +
    path.extname(req.image).substr(1));

    image.pipe(res);
  });
});
```

Our image download method is equally similar. For this route, we're not using the JSON responses, and instead just return our image directly. This allows us to try it out on our browser:

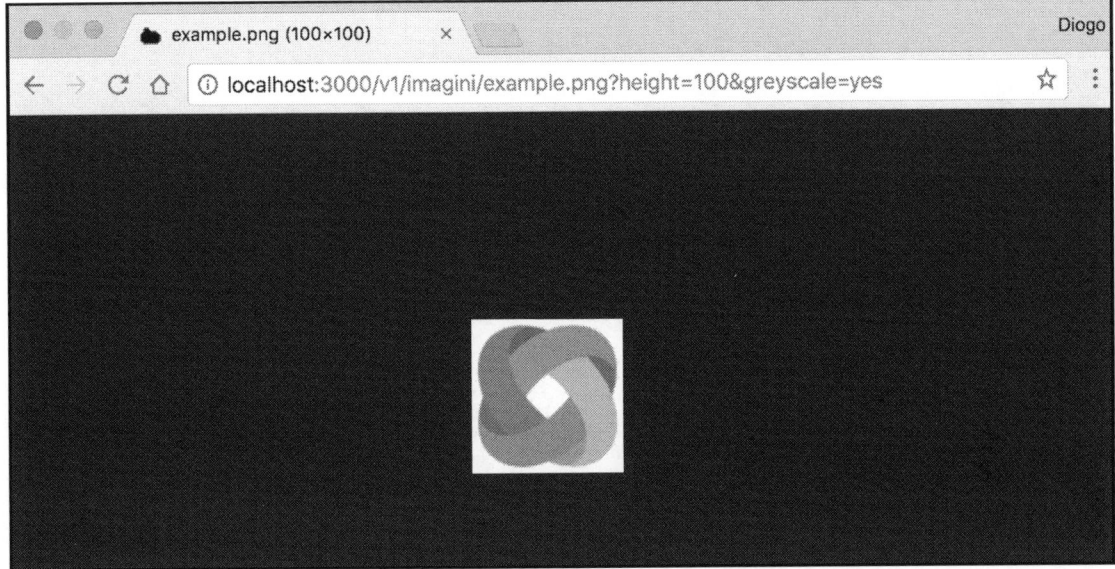

We just migrated our service from Express to Hydra. Not much of a difference, but Hydra gives you a more robust layout, about which we'll find out more later on. Let's take a look at our third framework: Seneca.

Using Seneca

Remember that routing on this framework is all about patterns. Let's keep it simple for now and use a role property to indicate what we want to do (upload, check, or download).

By default, every message should be JSON-encoded, so we'll encode the image in base64 to pass it as a string inside the JSON messages to upload and download.

Create a folder for our Seneca service, and then create a child folder called uploads. Then, install seneca and sharp on that folder by running the following command:

```
npm install seneca sharp --save
```

Then, create a file called imagini.js with the following content:

```
const seneca  = require("seneca");
const sharp   = require("sharp");
const path    = require("path");
const fs      = require("fs");
const service = seneca();

service.add("role:upload,image:*,data:*", function (msg, next) {
    let filename = path.join(__dirname, "uploads", msg.image);
    let data = Buffer.from(msg.data, "base64");

    fs.writeFile(filename, data, (err) => {
        if (err) return next(err);

        return next(null, { size : data.length });
    });
});

service.listen(3000);
```

What this does is initiate a simple service with a route for uploading. Since we're receiving all the image content directly on an object property, I used fs.writeFile. It's a simpler method and gives me an error whether something incorrect happens, which we can pass on to the route response.

I also used Buffer.from to convert our image data, which we'll be uploading in base64.

So, let's just start it as we did with the others. I included the same example.png image and used curl to test this out.

```
curl -H "Content-Type: application/json" \
--data '{"role":"upload","image":"example.png","data":"'"$( base64
```

```
example.png)"'"}' \
http://localhost:3000/act
```

Seneca promptly replied with the following:

```
{"size":55543}
```

This is the image size. Notice I'm taking advantage of bash interpolation (variable substitution) to directly convert the image file to `base64` and pass it to `curl`, which then sends that JSON piece of data to our service:

```
service.add("role:check,image:*", function (msg, next) {
    let filename = path.join(__dirname, "uploads", msg.image);

    fs.access(filename, fs.constants.R_OK , (err) => {
        return next(null, { exists : !err });
    });
});
```

Our check route is very similar. Instead of just replying with an HTTP 404 response code, we reply with a stringified JSON object with a boolean property exists, which will indicate if the image was found.

Here, we are checking for our image using `curl`:

```
curl -H "Content-Type: application/json" \
    --data '{"role":"check","image":"example.png"}' \
    http://localhost:3000/act
```

We will respond with the following:

```
{"exists":true}
```

If you change the image name, it will respond with `false`:

```
service.add("role:download,image:*", function (msg, next) {
    let filename = path.join(__dirname, "uploads", msg.image);

    fs.access(filename, fs.constants.R_OK , (err) => {
        if (err) return next(err);

        let image      = sharp(filename);
        let width      = +msg.width;
        let height     = +msg.height;
        let blur       = +msg.blur;
        let sharpen    = +msg.sharpen;
        let greyscale  = !!msg.greyscale;
        let flip       = !!msg.flip;
```

```
let flop        = !!msg.flop;

if (width > 0 && height > 0) {
    image.ignoreAspectRatio();
}

if (width > 0 || height > 0) {
    image.resize(width || null, height || null);
}

if (flip)         image.flip();
if (flop)         image.flop();
if (blur > 0)     image.blur(blur);
if (sharpen > 0)  image.sharpen(sharpen);
if (greyscale)    image.greyscale();

image.toBuffer().then((data) => {
    return next(null, { data: data.toString("base64") });
});
    });
});
```

Our downloaded route has some changes:

- Instead of query parameters, we check directly on msg. One noticeable advantage is that we have types and not just strings, so we can use Boolean and numbers directly.
- Instead of returning the image in binary, so that we could just open in the browser, we convert it to base64 and pass it on the JSON response.

We need some tools to test this on the command line. Since I use JSON a lot, I have jq installed. I strongly recommend you install it too and take a look at the tutorials. It will make your life easier. Using the base64 command we previously used to encode, we can decode the content and pipe the data to a local file:

```
● ● ●                2. nazgul.home: /Users/dresende/imagini (bash) 🔔
Last login: Tue Feb 13 21:44:17 on ttys002
~ > cd imagini/
~/imagini >
~/imagini > curl -H "Content-Type: application/json" \
> --data '{"role":"download","image":"example.png","greyscale":true,"height":100}' \
> http://localhost:3000/act \
> | jq -r '.data' | base64 --decode > example.png
  % Total    % Received % Xferd  Average Speed   Time    Time     Time  Current
                                 Dload  Upload   Total   Spent    Left  Speed
100  7430  100  7359  100    71   262k   2597 --:--:-- --:--:-- --:--:--  266k
~/imagini > _
```

We can then open the folder and see the image is there. Notice I added `greyscale` and resized the image just by passing two more JSON parameters:

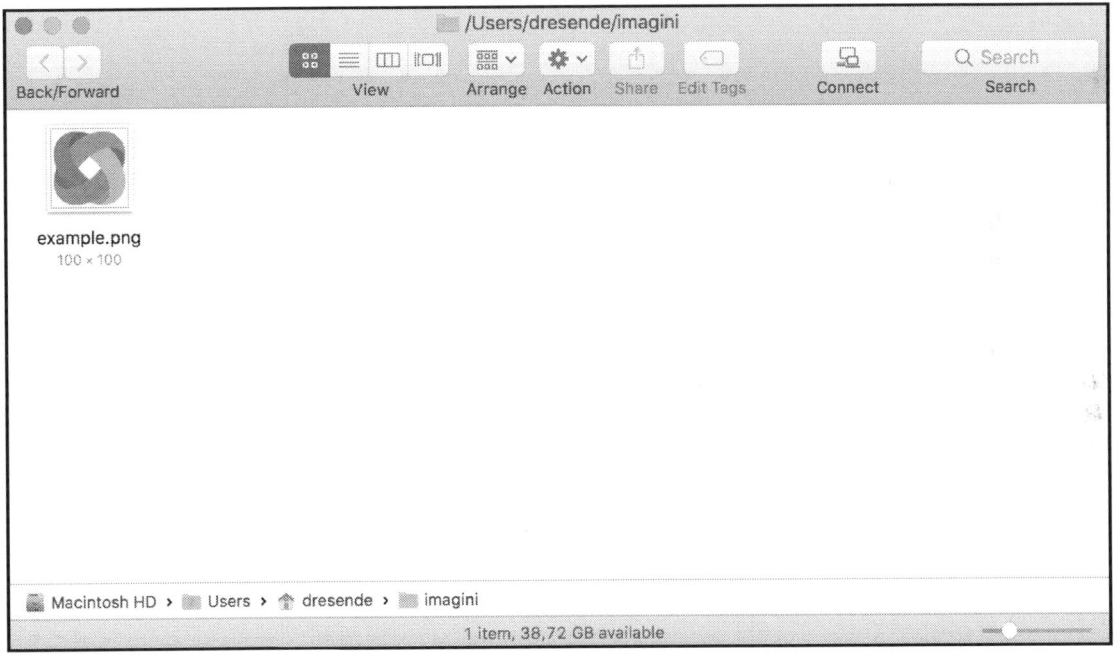

Plugins

In the spirit of Seneca, we should make a plugin for our `imagini` service. Let's split our code into two parts:

- The `imagini` plugin, a service that manipulates images
- A Seneca microservice, which exposes the `imagini` plugin, and possibly others later on

There's lot of room for improvement on our code, starting with code we repeated constantly. It's important to detect repetitions while our service is still very small.

The most repeated part is the local filename. This is actually something you might want to configure when starting the service, so let's change that to a function. Start by changing our `imagini.js` file to be a plugin. Clear all content and write this code:

```
const sharp    = require("sharp");
const path     = require("path");
const fs       = require("fs");

module.exports = function (settings = { path: "uploads" }) {
    // plugin code goes here
};
```

This is the basis of our plugin. We're loading the modules we need, but not Seneca, because our plugin will have access to the service directly. Seneca itself will load the plugin by calling our exported function. Following the idea of being able to configure the local image folder, we define an optional `settings` parameter, which will default to an object with the property `path` equal to `uploads`, which is the folder we've been using so far.

Now, let's add the content of our plugin, inside the preceding function:

```
const localpath = (image) => {
    return path.join(settings.path, image);
}
```

We start by defining a function that will convert our image parameter to the local path. We can actually reduce the function to be written in one single line:

```
const localpath = (image) => (path.join(settings.path, image));
```

Then, let's create another function that will check whether we have access to a local file, and return a Boolean (if it exists or not) and the filename we provided:

```
const access = (filename, next) => {
    fs.access(filename, fs.constants.R_OK , (err) => {
        return next(!err, filename);
    });
};
```

We can use this for our image check, and for our image download. This way, we can improve or even cache the results for greater performance, avoiding excessive filesystem hits. Our image check route can now be written in a very concise way:

```
this.add("role:check,image:*", (msg, next) => {
    access(localpath(msg.image), (exists) => {
        return next(null, { exists : exists });
    });
});
```

Notice that we're referring to the `this` object. Our Seneca service will call our plugin function and reference itself to `this`. Again, we can write it in a more concise way:

```
this.add("role:check,image:*", (msg, next) => {
    access(localpath(msg.image), (exists) => (next(null, { exists }))));
});
```

Our upload route is fairly simple and has no changes:

```
this.add("role:upload,image:*,data:*", (msg, next) => {
    let data = Buffer.from(msg.data, "base64");

    fs.writeFile(localpath(msg.image), data, (err) => {
        return next(err, { size : data.length });
    });
});
```

The download route uses our previously created helper functions to avoid storing our local filename. We also made some tweaks to how `width` and `height` were treated:

```
this.add("role:download,image:*", (msg, next) => {
    access(localpath(msg.image), (exists, filename) => {
        if (!exists) return next(new Error("image not found"));

        let image    = sharp(filename);
        let width    = +msg.width || null;
        let height   = +msg.height || null;
        let blur     = +msg.blur;
        let sharpen  = +msg.sharpen;
```

```
        let greyscale = !!msg.greyscale;
        let flip      = !!msg.flip;
        let flop      = !!msg.flop;

        if (width && height) image.ignoreAspectRatio();
        if (width || height) image.resize(width, height);
        if (flip)            image.flip();
        if (flop)            image.flop();
        if (blur > 0)        image.blur(blur);
        if (sharpen > 0)     image.sharpen(sharpen);
        if (greyscale)       image.greyscale();

        image.toBuffer().then((data) => {
            return next(null, { data: data.toString("base64") });
        });
    });
});
```

There are actually a lot of variables we're using where we could just check the message parameter instead. We can rewrite our download function and get one-third reduction:

```
this.add("role:download,image:*", (msg, next) => {
    access(localpath(msg.image), (exists, filename) => {
        if (!exists) return next(new Error("image not found"));

        let image    = sharp(filename);
        let width    = +msg.width || null;
        let height   = +msg.height || null;

        if (width && height) image.ignoreAspectRatio();
        if (width || height) image.resize(width, height);
        if (msg.flip)        image.flip();
        if (msg.flop)        image.flop();
        if (msg.blur > 0)    image.blur(blur);
        if (msg.sharpen > 0) image.sharpen(sharpen);
        if (msg.greyscale)   image.greyscale();

        image.toBuffer().then((data) => {
            return next(null, { data: data.toString("base64") });
        });
    });
});
```

In the end, you should have an `imagini.js` file with the following content:

```
const sharp   = require("sharp");
const path    = require("path");
const fs      = require("fs");
```

```javascript
module.exports = function (settings = { path: "uploads" }) {
    const localpath = (image) => (path.join(settings.path, image));
    const access    = (filename, next) => {
        fs.access(filename, fs.constants.R_OK , (err) => {
            return next(!err, filename);
        });
    };

    this.add("role:check,image:*", (msg, next) => {
        access(localpath(msg.image), (exists) => (next(null, { exists })));
    });

    this.add("role:upload,image:*,data:*", (msg, next) => {
        let data = Buffer.from(msg.data, "base64");

        fs.writeFile(localpath(msg.image), data, (err) => {
            return next(err, { size : data.length });
        });
    });

    this.add("role:download,image:*", (msg, next) => {
        access(localpath(msg.image), (exists, filename) => {
            if (!exists) return next(new Error("image not found"));

            let image      = sharp(filename);
            let width      = +msg.width || null;
            let height     = +msg.height || null;

            if (width && height) image.ignoreAspectRatio();
            if (width || height) image.resize(width, height);
            if (msg.flip)        image.flip();
            if (msg.flop)        image.flop();     .
            if (msg.blur > 0)    image.blur(blur);
            if (msg.sharpen > 0) image.sharpen(sharpen);
            if (msg.greyscale)   image.greyscale();

            image.toBuffer().then((data) => {
                return next(null, { data: data.toString("base64") });
            });
        });
    });
};
```

We just need to create our Seneca service and use our plugin. This is actually very straightforward. Create a file called `seneca.js`, and add the following:

```
const seneca  = require("seneca");
const service = seneca();

service.use("./imagini.js", { path: __dirname + "/uploads" });

service.listen(3000);
```

What the code does, line by line, is as follows:

1. Loads the `seneca` module
2. Creates a Seneca `service`
3. Loads the `imagini.js` plugin and passes our desired path
4. Starts `service` on port `3000`

That's it, our service is now a plugin and could be used by any Seneca service! You should now start our `service` by running the new file and not `imagini.js` directly:

```
node seneca
```

Summary

As you can see, writing a service does not change much between frameworks. Our code is very similar, with minor changes. Seneca is stricter about message format and content, so we used `base64` to encode our image inside the JSON message. Other than that, everything is the same.

For tools such as Express, which is a broader tool in terms of doing everything you might need, and not just microservices, you'll need to find the right plugins, and perhaps write several more plugins, in order to help you reach a production-ready microservice. You get the advantage of being able to choose everything about the service, but you need to write a lot of code. To facilitate the task, Hydra might be a good start for an initial set of plugins.

For other tools such as Seneca, some aspects of the microservice (for instance, the communication using JSON messages and service composition) are already packed. This comes at the price of a stricter service definition.

In the next chapter, we will discuss the security of our three service versions, and how we can store state.

6
State and Security

Now that we have created our microservice base layout on different frameworks, it's time to read our code more carefully and see if everything looks good. It's easy to just keep writing code and stop thinking about what we're doing, but later on, when we do stop for a while, we'll be wasting time deleting repeated code and reorganizing our service.

It's always better to think before we code. This is something you'll learn with time, to value the time you dedicate to plan your service or think about a new feature. It's never a good idea to just start coding. In theory, your **Service** should be inside a **Security** layer, with a good and stable connection to **State**:

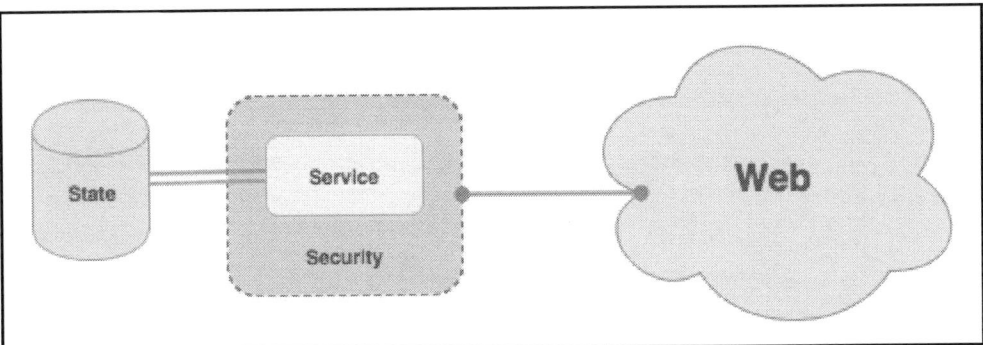

State

Think of state as a person's memory. Usually, a service has state, which means it has memory of actions and information it's serving. The idea is that our service will run indefinitely, but sometimes we're forced to restart it or even stop it for some time because of maintenance or an upgrade.

Ideally, a service should resume without losing state, giving its users the perception that it never stopped. This is achieved by doing one of two things:

- Having state stored in a persistent storage
- Saving state in a persistent storage before stopping and loading that state after restarting

The first option will make your service a bit slower (nothing is faster than state in system memory) but should give you a more consistent state across restarts.

The second option is trickier, because sometimes our service might stop abruptly and be unable to save that state, but for those use cases, you may not care about the state. It's up to you.

There are a lot of options to store state; it will depend on what you want to store. For a microservice, you should avoid the filesystem so as to make your service more compatible with multiple operating systems.

Storing state

Depending on your service, you can store state using:

- A **relational database management system (RDBMS)**, such as MySQL or PostgreSQL
- A **non-relational database management system**, or NoSQL, such as MongoDB or RethinkDB
- An **in-memory database (IMDB)**, such as Redis or Memcached

The first option is still the most commonly used one. You'll rely on stable and more than proven database systems that run in multiple systems and that you can find on any cloud service where you might want to deploy your microservice. Apart from the maturity of most solutions, a relational database, if properly set up, should give you consistency.

The second option is more recent compared to the first one. Usually, there are no fixed tables as in RDBMS, and you normally work with collections of documents that are just common JSON structures. It's more agile as there are usually no restrictions, and each document might have a different structure. The more agile, the less consistent.

All three options, depending on the specific system you choose, support replication, which should enable fault tolerance and improve speed in geographically spaced instances.

Let's try each of the three options using one of the suggested systems. Let's begin with the relational database, and use MySQL.

MySQL

Installing MySQL is very simple. Just head to the official website and follow the instructions. You'll usually be asked for a password for the root user, which you can use later on to manage the server settings and user accounts.

There are some options to connect to a MySQL server using Node.js, but the best tools are the mysql and mysql2 modules. They both serve the required purpose, and neither is the next version of the other, they're just a bit different in design and supported features.

First, let's add the dependency to our service. On the terminal, go to our service folder and type:

```
npm install mysql --save
```

We can now include our dependency and configure a connection to the database. To avoid having the credentials in our code, we can create a separate file and put settings there that we may change in the future, and that shouldn't belong in the code. We can take advantage of Node.js being able to include JSON files, and just write our settings in JSON.

Create a file called settings.json, and add the following content:

```
{
    "db": "mysql://root:test@localhost/imagini"
}
```

We defined a setting called db that has a database URI, which is a handy way of defining our database access and credentials using an address similar to any website address. Our database uses mysql; it's at localhost (using the default port), which can be accessed using the username root and the password test, and our database name is called imagini. We can now include the module and settings, and create the connection:

```
const settings = require("./settings");
const mysql    = require("mysql");
const db       = mysql.createConnection(settings.db);
```

This module only connects to the database when you make a query. This means the service would start and you wouldn't know whether your connection settings are correct until you make the first query. We don't want to figure out we can't connect to the database only when the service is used later on, so let's force a connection and check if the server is running and accepts our connection:

```
db.connect((err) => {
    if (err) throw err;

    console.log("db: ready");

    // ...
    // the rest of our service code
    // ...

    app.listen(3000, () => {
        console.log("app: ready");
    });
});
```

This way, if anything is wrong with the database, the service won't start and will throw an exception, which will notify you to check what's wrong. Here's an example of a possible error:

```
Error: ER_ACCESS_DENIED_ERROR: Access denied for user 'root'@'localhost'
(using password: YES)
```

This indicates you probably typed the password incorrectly, or the user doesn't match, or even the hostname or database may be wrong. Ensuring you connect to the database before setting up the service means your service won't be exposed to the public without a proper state.

Our microservice has a very simple state, so to speak. Our state is the images previously uploaded. Instead of using the filesystem, we can now use the database and create a table to store them all:

```
db.query(
    `CREATE TABLE IF NOT EXISTS images
    (
        id INT(11) UNSIGNED NOT NULL AUTO_INCREMENT,
        date_created TIMESTAMP NOT NULL DEFAULT CURRENT_TIMESTAMP,
        date_used TIMESTAMP NULL DEFAULT NULL,
        name VARCHAR(300) NOT NULL,
        size INT(11) UNSIGNED NOT NULL,
        data LONGBLOB NOT NULL,

        PRIMARY KEY (id),
```

```
        UNIQUE KEY name (name)
    )
    ENGINE=InnoDB DEFAULT CHARSET=utf8`
);
```

We can issue this query every time the service starts because it will create the images table only if it doesn't exist already. If we don't change its structure, it's fine to always do this.

You can see we're creating a table with a unique identification number (`id`), a creation date (`date_created`), a date to know when our image has been used(`date_used`), the `name` of the image, the `size` of it in bytes, and the image `data`. The size is a little redundant here as we could just check the data length, but bear with me, this is just an example.

We also defined our name as a unique key, meaning it has an index for quickly finding images by name, and also ensures our name does not repeat and that no one can overwrite an image (without removing it first).

Having the images stored this way on a database table gives you several advantages, such as regarding:

- How many images you have
- The size of every image and the total size
- When the images were created and last used

It also enables you to improve your service; for example, you can delete images that are not used for longer than a specific time period. You can also make this dependent on the image sizes. Later, you can add authentication (mandatory or not) and have user-specific rules.

It's also easy to back up and replicate the state to another site. There are plenty of tools for backing up databases, and you can have another MySQL server acting as a slave to this one and have your images replicated in real time to another geographical location.

Let's change our service from the previous chapter to use our table instead of the previously used folder on our filesystem. We can remove our `fs` module dependency (don't remove the path dependency for now):

```
app.param("image", (req, res, next, image) => {
    if (!image.match(/\.(png|jpg)$/i)) {
        return res.status(403).end();
    }

    db.query("SELECT * FROM images WHERE name = ?", [ image ], (err,
    images) => {
        if (err || !images.length) {
            return res.status(404).end();
```

```
        }

        req.image = images[0];

        return next();
    });
});
```

Our `app.param` is completely different. We now validate the `image` against our `image` table. If it doesn't find it, it returns code `404`. If it does find it, it stores the `image` information in `req.image`. We can now change our `image` upload to store the `image` on our table:

```
app.post("/uploads/:name", bodyparser.raw({
    limit : "10mb",
    type : "image/*"
}), (req, res) => {
    db.query("INSERT INTO images SET ?", {
        name : req.params.name,
        size : req.body.length,
        data : req.body,
    }, (err) => {
        if (err) {
            return res.send({ status : "error", code: err.code });
        }

        res.send({ status : "ok", size: req.body.length });
    });
});
```

Uploading images no longer use the filesystem and instead creates a new row on our table. We don't need to specify the `id` as it's automatic. Our creation date is also automatic as it defaults to the current timestamp. Our use date defaults to NULL, which means we haven't used the `image` yet:

```
app.head("/uploads/:image", (req, res) => {
    return res.status(200).end();
});
```

Our `image` check method now gets extremely simple as it relies on the previous `app.param` to check whether the `image` exists, so, if we get to this point, we already know the image exists (it's on `req.image`), so we just need to return the code `200`.

Before updating our image `fetch` method, let's try our service. If you start it on the console, you can immediately open any MySQL administration tool and check our database. I'm using Sequel Pro for macOS. Although there's a Pro in the name, it's free software and it's damn good:

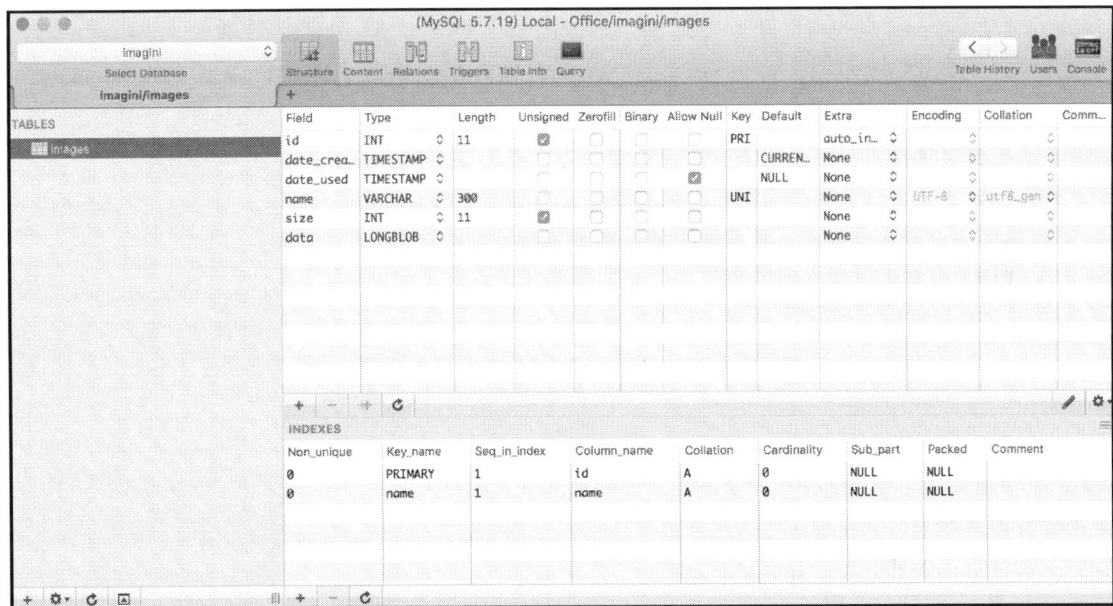

Our table was created, and you can check it has all the properties and indexes we defined. Let's now upload an `image` once again:

As before, it returns a JSON response with a success status and the size of the image. If you look at Sequel again, on the content separator, you'll see our **images** data:

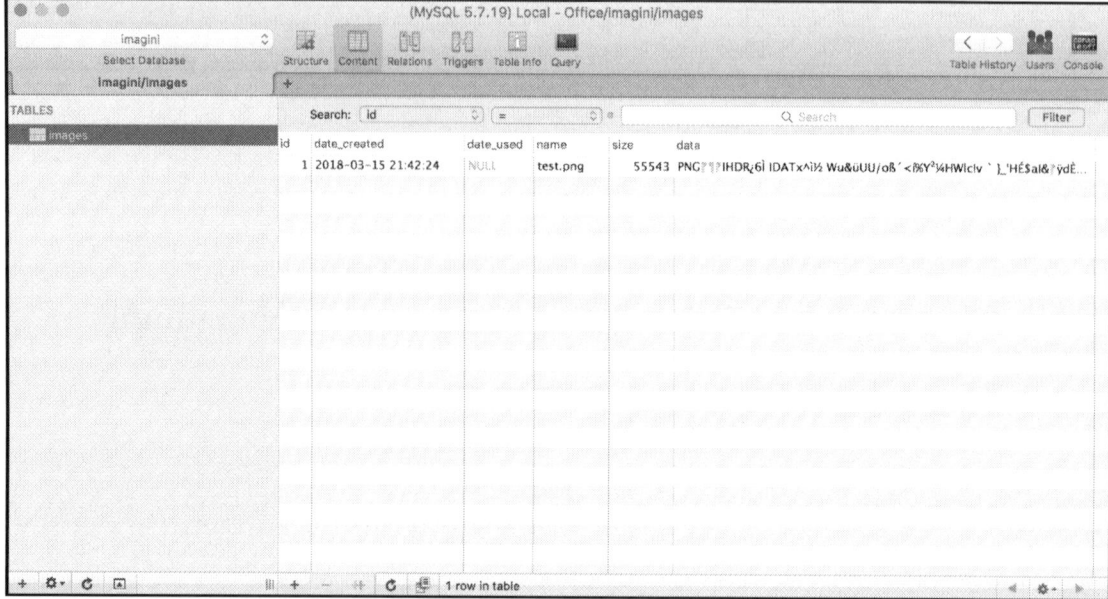

Let's try and upload the image again. Previously, our service would just overwrite it. Now, because of our unique index, it should deny an INSERT with the same name:

Great! The ER_DUP_ENTRY is the MySQL code for duplicate insertion. We can rely on that and deny overwriting images.

We can also check whether our `image` exists using the `check` method:

```
● ● ●                                    2. nazgul.home: /Users/dresende (bash)
~ > curl --head http://localhost:3000/uploads/test.png
HTTP/1.1 200 OK
X-Powered-By: Express
Date: Thu, 15 Mar 2018 21:56:32 GMT
Connection: keep-alive

~ > _
```

If we use another name, we'll get a code `404`:

```
● ● ●                                    2. nazgul.home: /Users/dresende (bash)
~ > curl --head http://localhost:3000/uploads/test.png
HTTP/1.1 200 OK
X-Powered-By: Express
Date: Thu, 15 Mar 2018 21:56:40 GMT
Connection: keep-alive

~ > curl --head http://localhost:3000/uploads/other.png
HTTP/1.1 404 Not Found
X-Powered-By: Express
Date: Thu, 15 Mar 2018 21:56:44 GMT
Connection: keep-alive

~ > _
```

It looks like everything is working great. Let's now change our final method, the `image` manipulation one. This method is almost the same; we just don't have to read the `image` file, as it's already available:

```
app.get("/uploads/:image", (req, res) => {
    let image     = sharp(req.image.data);
    let width     = +req.query.width;
    let height    = +req.query.height;
    let blur      = +req.query.blur;
    let sharpen   = +req.query.sharpen;
    let greyscale = [ "y", "yes", "true", "1",
    "on"].includes(req.query.greyscale);
    let flip      = [ "y", "yes", "true", "1",
    "on"].includes(req.query.flip);
    let flop      = [ "y", "yes", "true", "1",
    "on"].includes(req.query.flop);

    if (width > 0 && height > 0) {
        image.ignoreAspectRatio();
    }
```

```
    if (width > 0 || height > 0) {
        image.resize(width || null, height || null);
    }

    if (flip)         image.flip();
    if (flop)         image.flop();
    if (blur > 0)     image.blur(blur);
    if (sharpen > 0)  image.sharpen(sharpen);
    if (greyscale)    image.greyscale();

    db.query("UPDATE images " +
            "SET date_used = UTC_TIMESTAMP " +
            "WHERE id = ?", [ req.image.id ]);

    res.setHeader("Content-Type", "image/" +
path.extname(req.image.name).substr(1));

    image.pipe(res);
});
```

You can see how we used the path dependency to get the extension of the image name. The rest is the same. We just add an update to our image every time we request this method.

We can use a web browser to test our method and see our previously uploaded image:

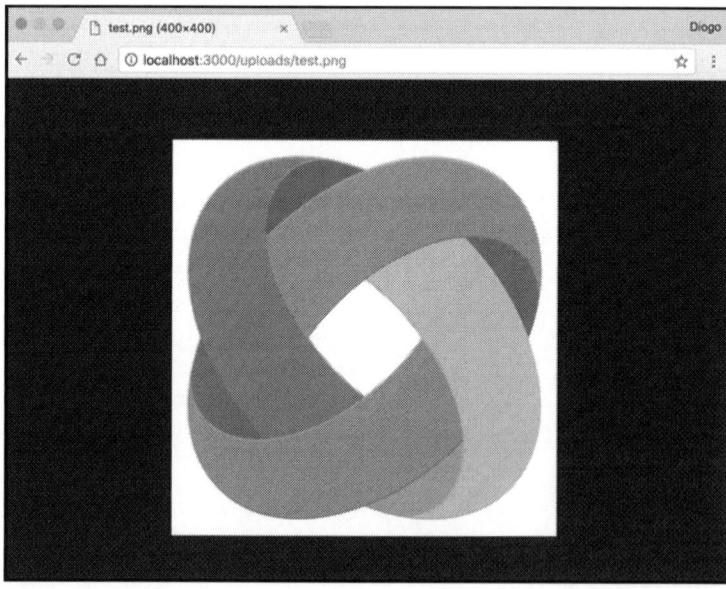

Everything should just work as before because we haven't changed our image manipulation dependency, so blurring and the other actions should work as expected:

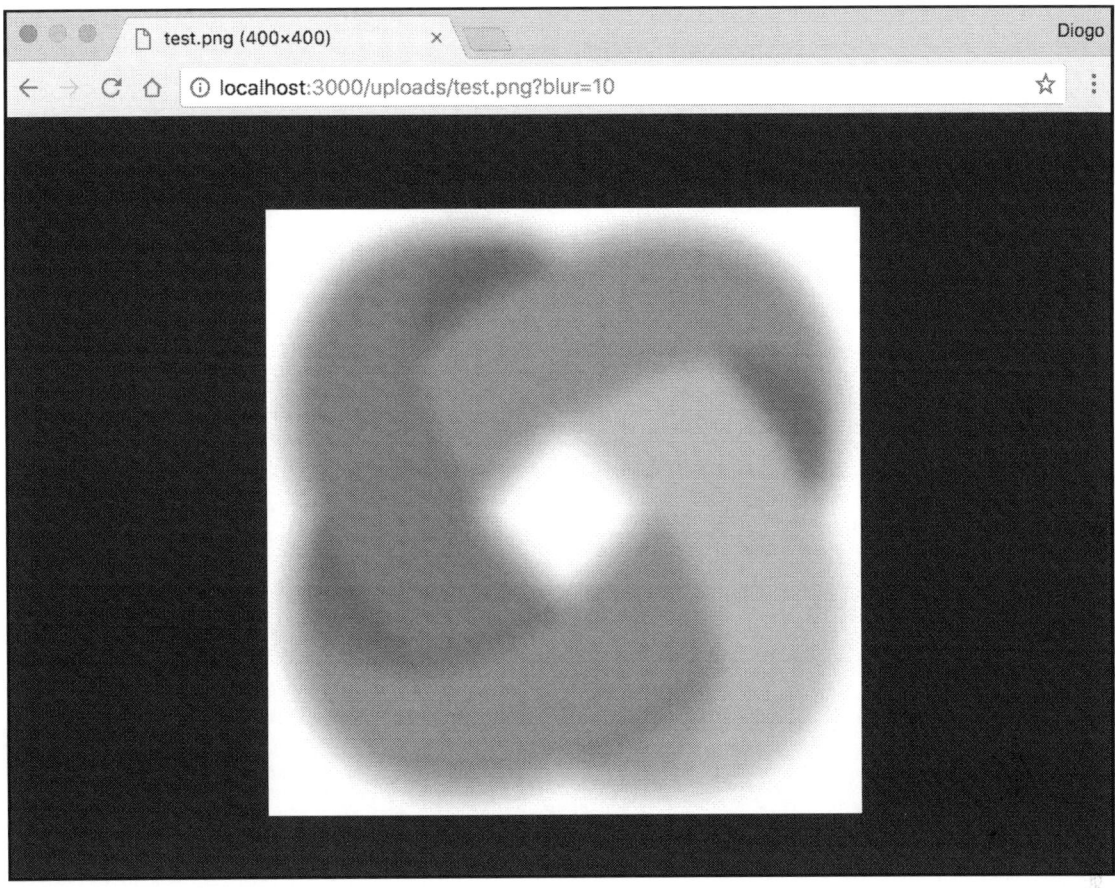

We can now improve our service and add a method we didn't expose before: deleting an `image`. To do that, we can use the DELETE verb from HTTP and just remove the `image` from our table:

```
app.delete("/uploads/:image", (req, res) => {
    db.query("DELETE FROM images WHERE id = ?", [ req.image.id ], (err)
    => {
        return res.status(err ? 500 : 200).end();
    });
});
```

We just have to check whether the query resulted in an error. If so, we respond with a code 500 (internal server error). If not, we respond with the usual code 200.

Let's restart our microservice and try to delete our `image`:

```
                                    2. nazgul.home: /Users/dresende (bash)
~ > curl -v -X DELETE http://localhost:3000/uploads/test.png
*   Trying ::1...
* TCP_NODELAY set
* Connected to localhost (::1) port 3000 (#0)
> DELETE /uploads/test.png HTTP/1.1
> Host: localhost:3000
> User-Agent: curl/7.54.0
> Accept: */*
>
< HTTP/1.1 200 OK
< X-Powered-By: Express
< Date: Fri, 16 Mar 2018 22:44:08 GMT
< Connection: keep-alive
< Content-Length: 0
<
* Connection #0 to host localhost left intact
~ > _
```

It looks like it worked; it responded with a code 200. If we try to open our image in the web browser, we should see something like this:

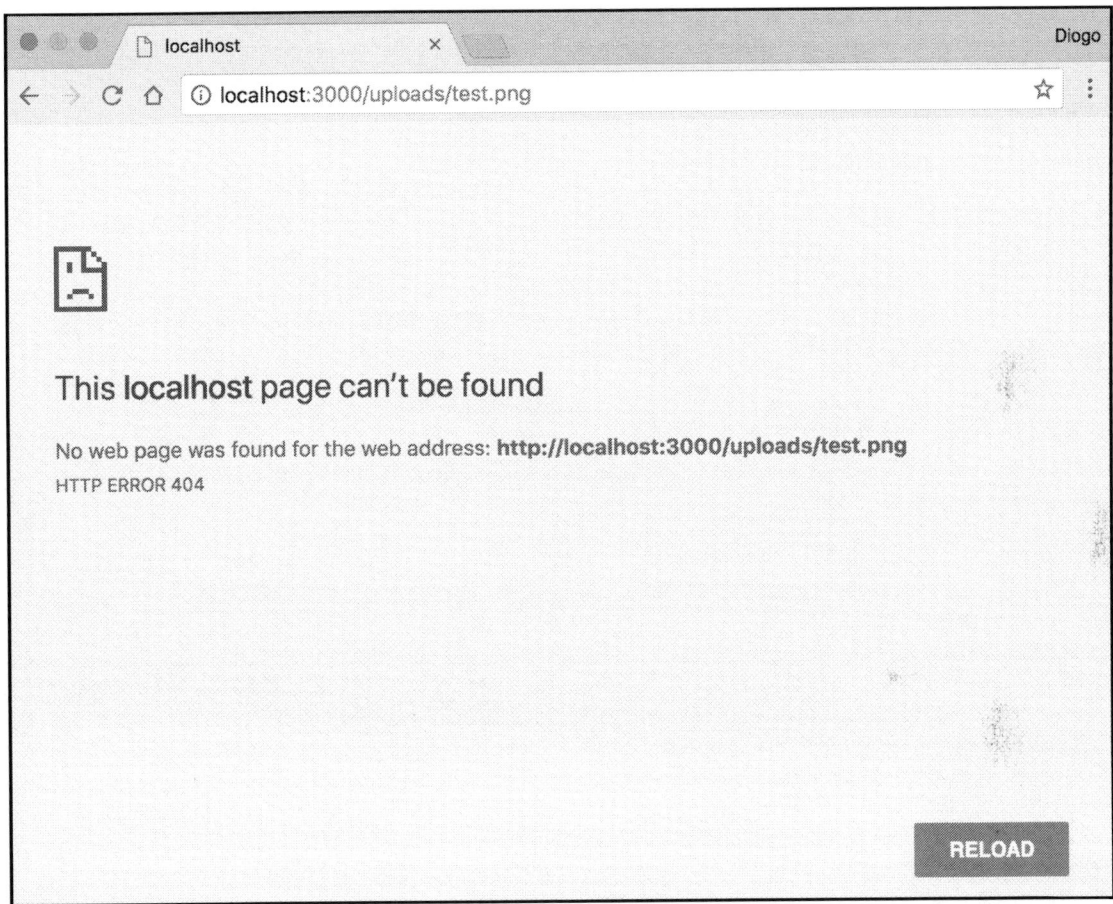

On Sequel, the table should now be empty too:

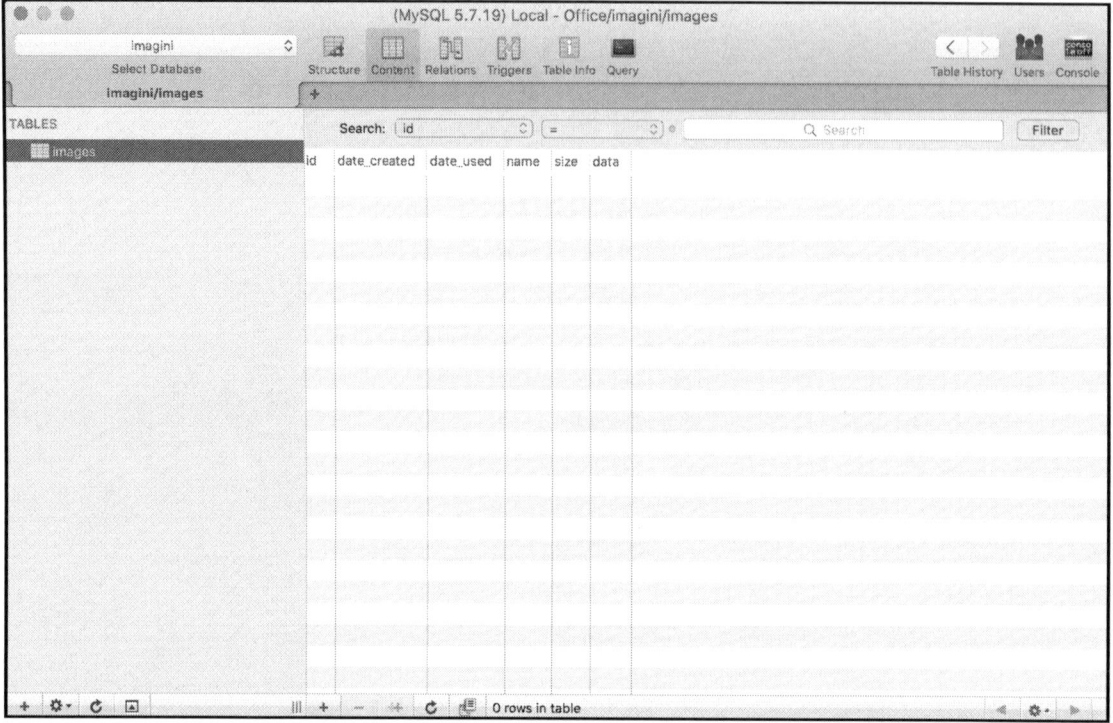

We now have a functional microservice with a state that persists across restarts, as we intended. You can now deploy to any cloud service with no dependency on the filesystem, just a database.

You could easily change MySQL to another database or use an **object relational mapping (ORM)** module to enable you to change database server without changing your code. An ORM is a library that allows you to use a common interface to access different types of databases. Usually, this kind of abstraction involves not using SQL at all and reducing your interaction with the databases to simpler queries (to allow for interoperability between database servers).

Let's take this opportunity to go a little further and add a few methods that got simplified by this migration to the database. Let's create a method that exposes statistics about our database, and let's remove old images.

Our first statistics method should just return a JSON structure with some useful information. Let's expose the following:

- The total number of images
- The total size of the images
- How long our service is running
- When the last time was that we uploaded an image

Here's an example of how our statistics method could look:

```
app.get("/stats", (req, res) => {
    db.query("SELECT COUNT(*) total" +
             ", SUM(size) size " +
             ", MAX(date_created) last_created " +
             "FROM images",
    (err, rows) => {
        if (err) {
            return res.status(500).end();
        }

        rows[0].uptime = process.uptime();

        return res.send(rows[0]);
    });
});
```

Restart the service, and let's try it:

```
● ● ●                    2. nazgul.lan: /Users/dresende (bash)
~ > curl http://localhost:3000/stats
{"total":0,"size":null,"last_used":null,"uptime":4.957}~ > _
```

As we can see, we have no images as we just removed our image previously. There's no size because we have no images. There's also no used date, and the service uptime is 5 seconds.

If we upload our previous image, we will get different results, something like the following screenshot:

```
2. nazgul.lan: /Users/dresende (bash)
~ > curl http://localhost:3000/stats
{"total":1,"size":55543,"last_used":null,"uptime":961.091}~ >
~ > _
```

Now, for our second task, deleting old images, we need to check our database periodically. We'll use an interval timer and just run a DELETE query. The intervals mentioned in the following query are just an example; you can write the conditions you want.

```
setInterval(() => {
    db.query("DELETE FROM images " +
            "WHERE (date_created < UTC_TIMETSTAMP - INTERVAL 1 WEEK
            AND date_used IS NULL) " +
            " OR (date_used < UTC_TIMETSTAMP - INTERVAL 1 MONTH)");
}, 3600 * 1000);
```

This query deletes images that were not used in the past month (but were used before) or images that were not used in the past week (and never used before). This means that images uploaded need to be used at least once or they will get removed quickly.

You can think of a different strategy, or use no strategy and delete manually if you want. Now that we've seen MySQL, let's move on and look at another kind of database server.

RethinkDB

Let's see the differences for a non-relational database using RethinkDB. If you don't have it, just install it by following the official documentation (https://www.rethinkdb.com/docs/). Let's just start the server:

```
rethinkdb
```

This will start the server, which comes with a very nice administration console on port `8080`. You can open it in the web browser:

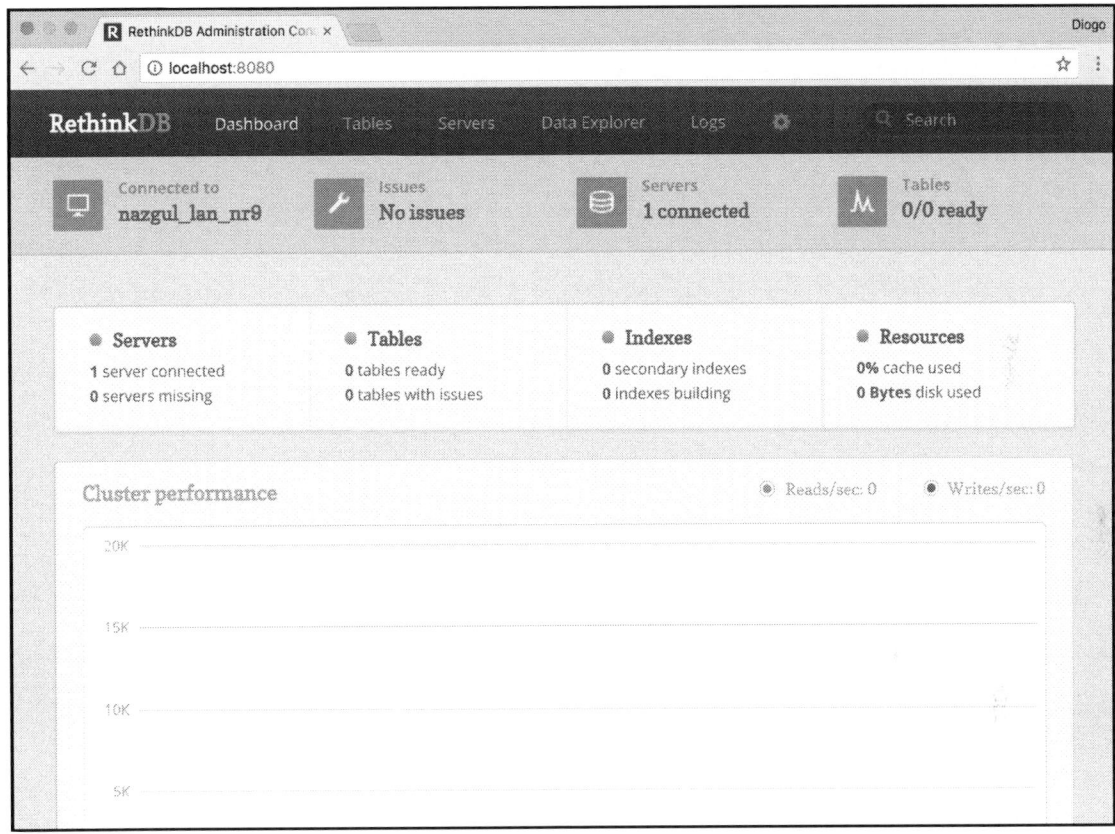

Go to the **Tables** section on top to see the databases:

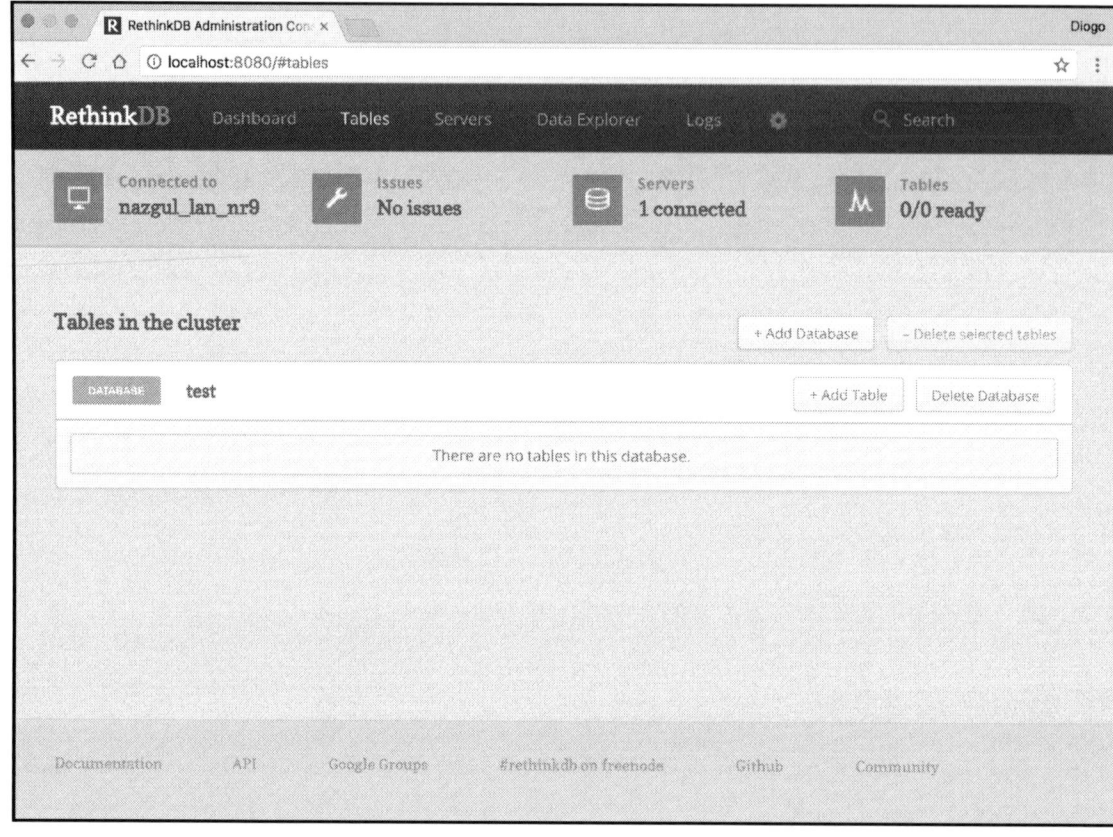

Create a database called `imagini` using the **Add Database** button. You should now have our database ready. You need nothing else here:

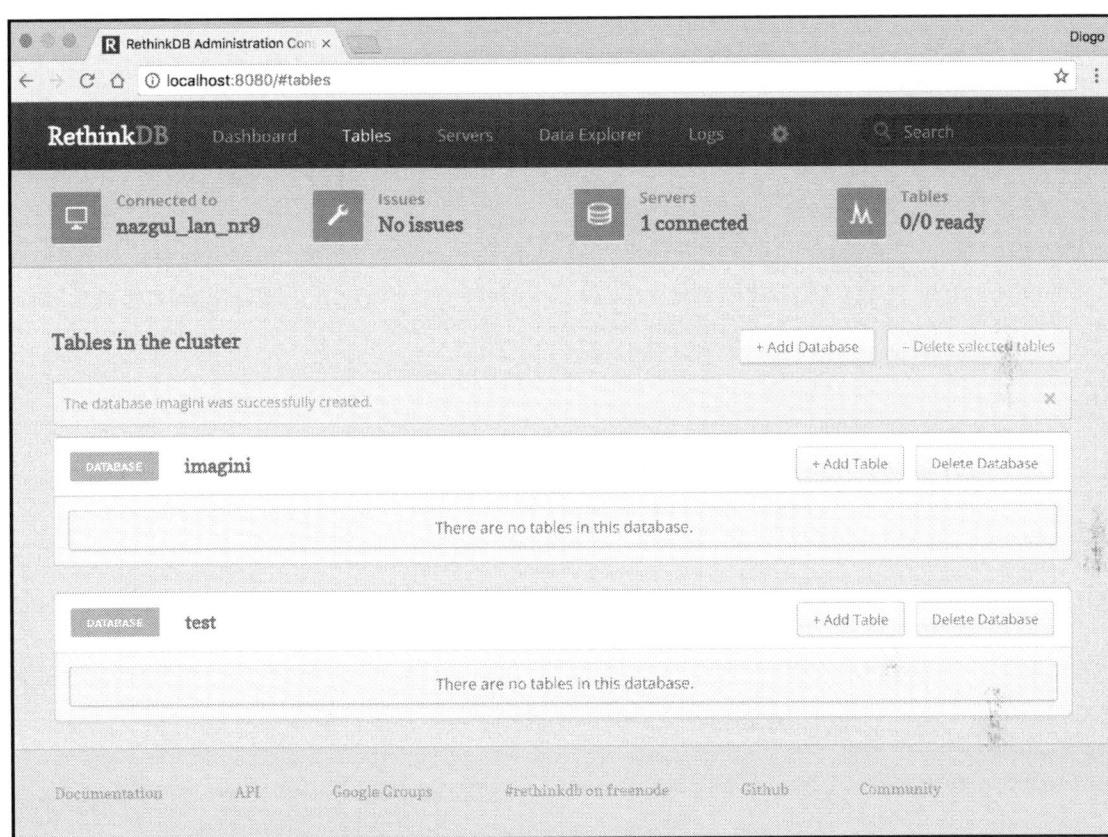

To use our new database, we need to install the `rethinkdb` dependency. You can remove the MySQL dependency:

```
npm uninstall mysql --save
npm install rethinkdb --save
```

Now, let's change our `settings` file. This module doesn't accept a connection string, so we'll use a JSON structure:

```
{
    "db": {
        "host" : "localhost",
        "db" : "imagini"
    }
}
```

To include our dependency, we just need to include the module:

```
const rethinkdb = require("rethinkdb");
```

Then, use this to connect to our server:

```
rethinkdb.connect(settings.db, (err, db) => {
    if (err) throw err;

    console.log("db: ready");

    // ...
    // the rest of our service code
    // ...

    app.listen(3000, () => {
        console.log("app: ready");
    });
});
```

After connecting, we can create our table as we did before. This time, we don't need to specify any structure:

```
rethinkdb.tableCreate("images").run(db);
```

The `rethinkdb` object is the one we'll use to manipulate our table, and the `db` object is a connection object used to reference the connection and to indicate where to run our manipulations.

If you restart our service just like this, you'll see a new table on our previously created database:

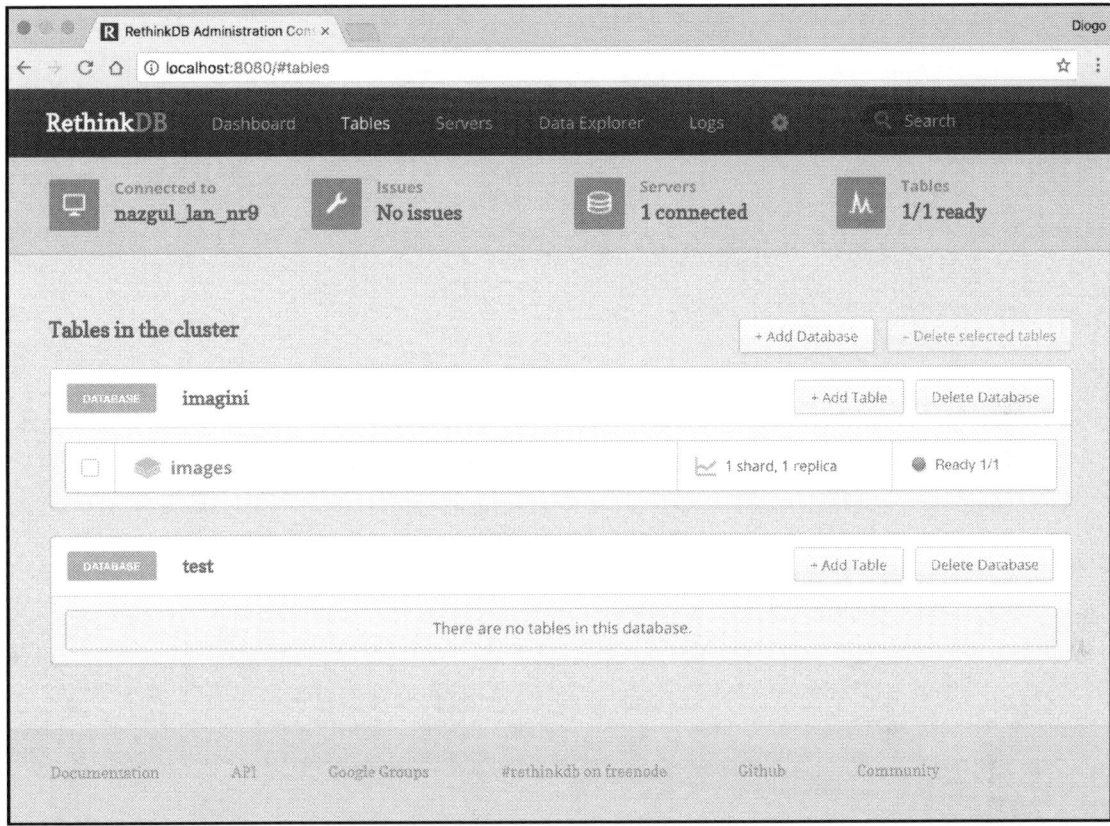

If you restart our service again, you'll get an error trying to create the table that already exists. We need to check whether it already exists, and only issue the command if not:

```
rethinkdb.tableList().run(db, (err, tables) => {
    if (err) throw err;

    if (!tables.includes("images")) {
        rethinkdb.tableCreate("images").run(db);
    }
});
```

Moving on, our upload method should be changed slightly to something like the following:

```
app.post("/uploads/:name", bodyparser.raw({
    limit : "10mb",
    type : "image/*"
}), (req, res) => {
    rethinkdb.table("images").insert({
        name : req.params.name,
        size : req.body.length,
        data : req.body,
    }).run(db, (err) => {
        if (err) {
            return res.send({ status : "error", code: err.code });
        }

        res.send({ status : "ok", size: req.body.length });
    });
});
```

If you restart the server just like this, you should be able to upload an image:

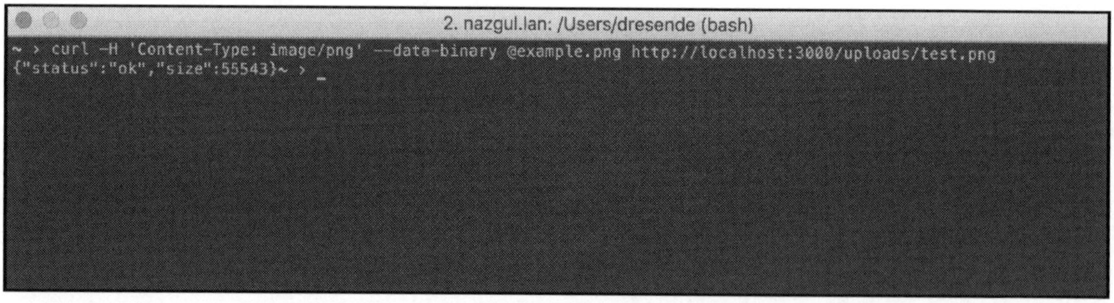

We receive the same response, just like with MySQL. We can go to the **Data Explorer** section in the administration console and get our record to see whether it's there:

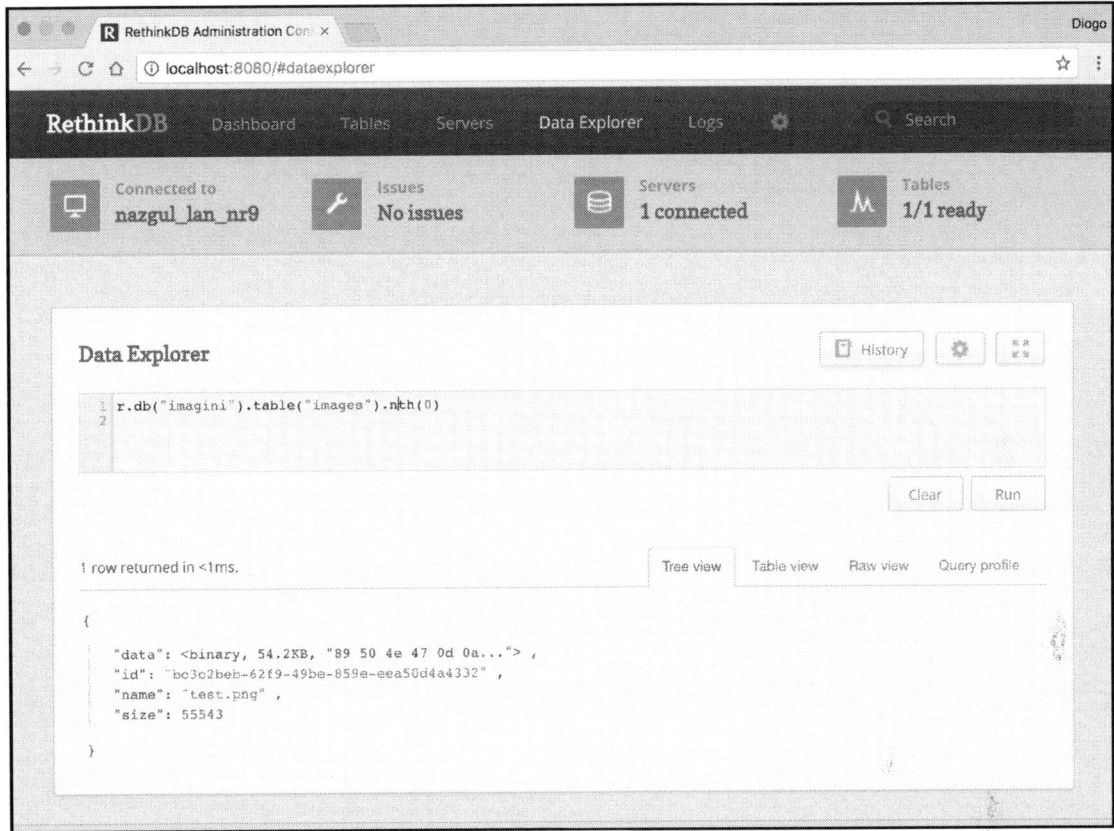

Looks good. Notice our record ID is not a number, it's a **Universally Unique Identifier (UUID)**. This is because RethinkDB has support for sharding (our table is sharded by default if there was more than one server) and it's easier to shard unique identifiers than an incremental number.

Moving on to our Express parameter:

```
app.param("image", (req, res, next, image) => {
    if (!image.match(/\.(png|jpg)$/i)) {
        return res.status(403).end();
    }

    rethinkdb.table("images").filter({
        name : image
    }).limit(1).run(db, (err, images) => {
        if (err) return res.status(404).end();

        images.toArray((err, images) => {
```

```
            if (err) return res.status(500).end();
            if (!images.length) return res.status(404).end();

            req.image = images[0];

            return next();
        });
    });
});
```

With this change, we can now restart our service and see whether our `image` exists:

```
● ● ●                 2. nazgul.lan: /Users/dresende (bash)
~ > curl --head http://localhost:3000/uploads/test.png
HTTP/1.1 200 OK
X-Powered-By: Express
Date: Sat, 17 Mar 2018 22:04:07 GMT
Connection: keep-alive

~ > _
```

We need to change the download just a little bit. We need to remove the previous query to update our usage date and replace it with a new one:

```
app.get("/uploads/:image", (req, res) => {
    let image     = sharp(req.image.data);
    let width     = +req.query.width;
    let height    = +req.query.height;
    let blur      = +req.query.blur;
    let sharpen   = +req.query.sharpen;
    let greyscale = [ "y", "yes", "true", "1",
    "on"].includes(req.query.greyscale);
    let flip      = [ "y", "yes", "true", "1",
    "on"].includes(req.query.flip);
    let flop      = [ "y", "yes", "true", "1",
    "on"].includes(req.query.flop);

    if (width > 0 && height > 0) {
        image.ignoreAspectRatio();
    }

    if (width > 0 || height > 0) {
        image.resize(width || null, height || null);
```

```
    }

    if (flip)         image.flip();
    if (flop)         image.flop();
    if (blur > 0)     image.blur(blur);
    if (sharpen > 0)  image.sharpen(sharpen);
    if (greyscale)    image.greyscale();

    rethinkdb.table("images").get(req.image.id).update({ date_used :
    Date.now() }).run(db);

    res.setHeader("Content-Type", "image/" +
    path.extname(req.image.name).substr(1));

    image.pipe(res);
});
```

We can now download our image using the web browser:

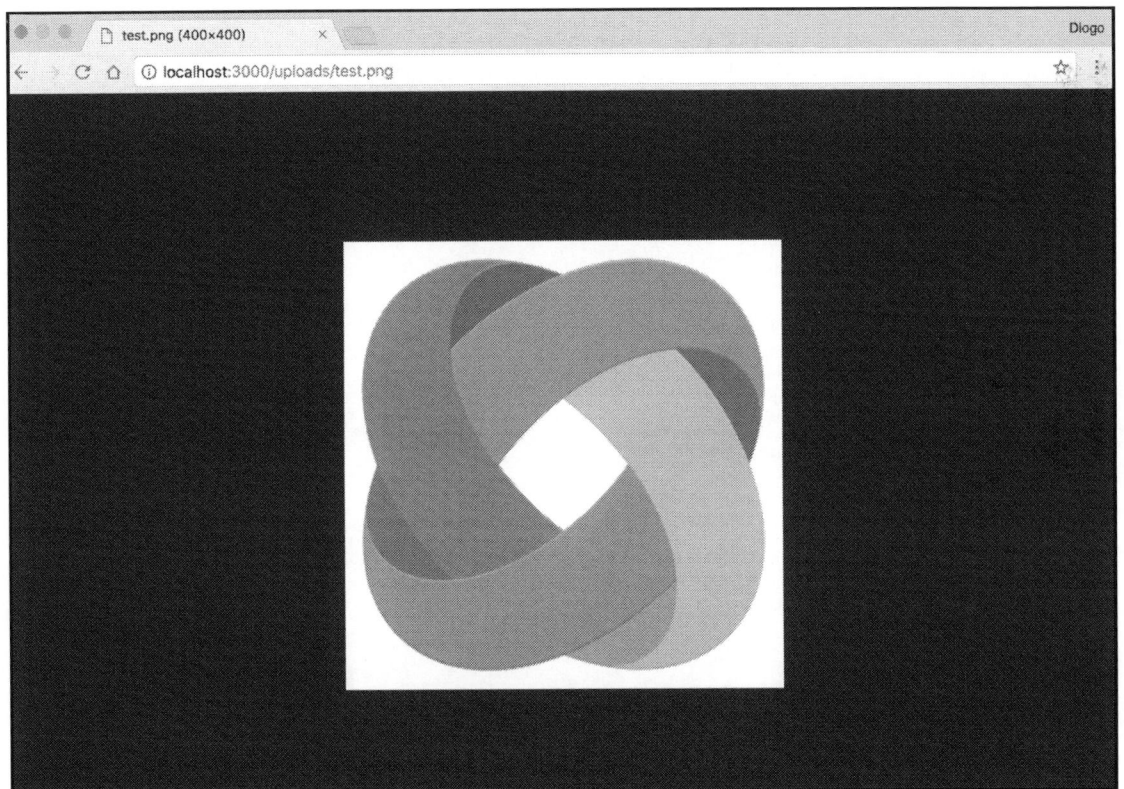

Next, we need to update our image removal method. It's as easy as our upload:

```
app.delete("/uploads/:image", (req, res) => {
    rethinkdb.table("images").get(req.image.id).delete().run(db, (err)
    => {
        return res.status(err ? 500 : 200).end();
    });
});
```

This time, we used the image unique ID to remove it. If we try again using the `curl` command, we'll receive a code `200`:

If we try to get the first record of our table, we'll see there's nothing there:

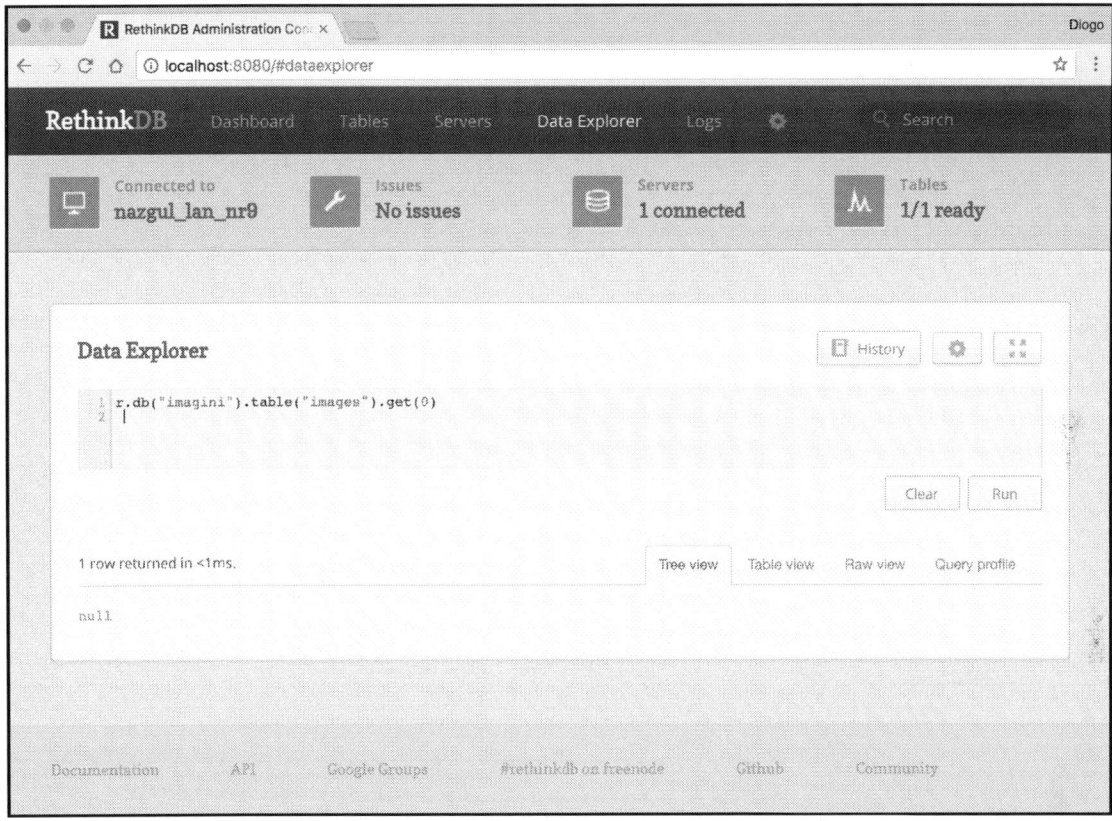

Finally, there are our two extra features that we added after introducing MySQL: the statistics and removing old unused images.

Our statistics method is not so simple as running an SQL query with aggregations. We must calculate each of our statistics:

```
app.get("/stats", (req, res) => {
    let uptime = process.uptime();

    rethinkdb.table("images").count().run(db, (err, total) => {
        if (err) return res.status(500).end();

        rethinkdb.table("images").sum("size").run(db, (err, size) => {
            if (err) return res.status(500).end();

            rethinkdb.table("images").max("date_created").run(db, (err,
            last_created) => {
                if (err) return res.status(500).end();
```

```
                    last_created = (last_created ? new
                    Date(last_created.date_created) : null);

                    return res.send({ total, size, last_created, uptime });
                });
            });
        });
    });
```

We should have a similar result to before:

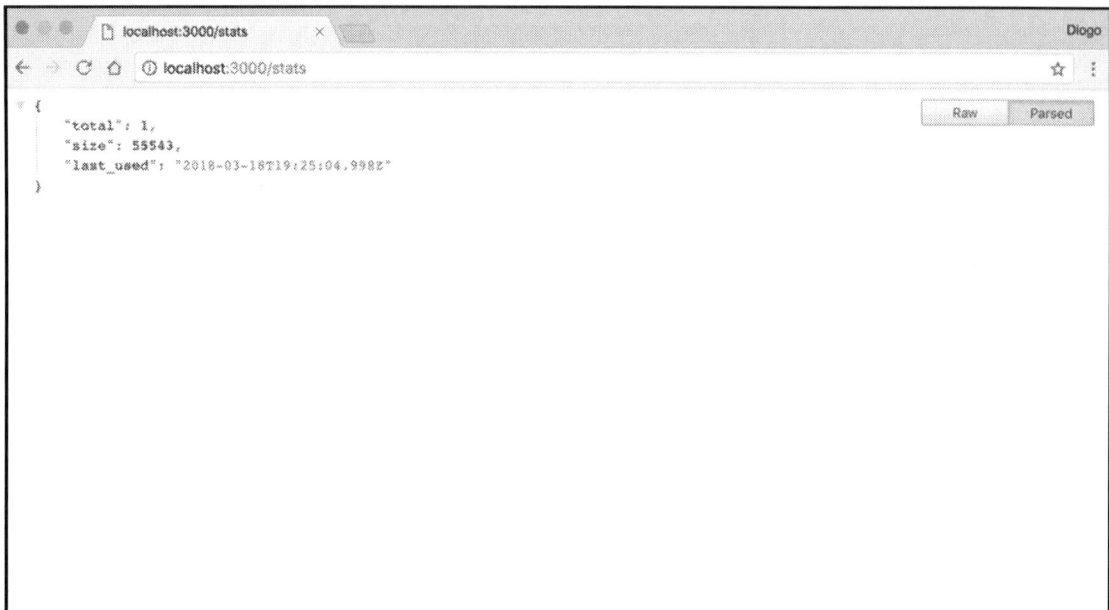

Removing old images is more or less easy; we just need to filter the images we want to remove, and then remove them:

```
setInterval(() => {
    let expiration = Date.now() - (30 * 86400 * 1000);

    rethinkdb.table("images").filter((image) => {
        return image("date_used").lt(expiration);
    }).delete().run(db);
}, 3600 * 1000);
```

I simplified the previous strategy and am just removing `images` older than 1 month (30 days, times 86,400 seconds a day, times 1,000 milliseconds).

Redis

In-memory databases are different from the previous two types, as they're usually not structured, which means you have no tables. What you have is normally lists of some kind that you can look up and manipulate, or simple hash tables.

Taking advantage of the Redis instance we installed previously for Hydra, let's see another drawback, or actually feature, of this kind of database. Let's connect to our Redis instance and make the following sequence of instructions:

```
● ● ●                    1. nazgul.home: /Users/dresende (redis-cli)
~ > redis-cli
127.0.0.1:6379> get counter
(nil)
127.0.0.1:6379> incr counter
(integer) 1
127.0.0.1:6379> incr counter
(integer) 2
127.0.0.1:6379> get counter
"2"
127.0.0.1:6379> shutdown
not connected>
~ > redis-server --daemonize yes
20676:C 19 Mar 21:14:28.654 # oO0oOO0oO0Oo Redis is starting oO0oOO0oO0Oo
20676:C 19 Mar 21:14:28.655 # Redis version=4.0.6, bits=64, commit=00000000, modified=0, pid=20676, just started
20676:C 19 Mar 21:14:28.655 # Configuration loaded
~ > redis-cli
127.0.0.1:6379> get counter
(nil)
127.0.0.1:6379> _
```

What we did here was to:

1. Connect to the Redis service using `redis-cli`.
2. Get the content of the counter, which is nil (nothing), because we haven't defined it yet.
3. Increment the counter, which is now automatically defined and set to 1.
4. Increment the counter again, which is now 2.
5. Get the content of the counter, which is of course 2.
6. Shut down the Redis service.
7. Start the Redis service.
8. Connect to the Redis service again.
9. Get the content of the counter, which is nil (nothing).

Where's our counter? Well, this is an in-memory database, so everything is gone when we shut down the Redis service. This is the design of almost all kinds of in-memory databases.

They're designed to be fast and in-memory. Their purpose is normally to cache data that is expensive to get, such as some complex calculations, or extensive to download, and we want that to be available faster (in-memory).

I wasn't completely fair with Redis as it actually allows your data to be saved between service restarts. So, let's see how far we can go in using it to save our microservice state.

As before, let's uninstall `rethinkdb` and install the `redis` module:

```
npm uninstall rethinkdb --save
npm install redis --save
```

Let's ignore our `settings.json` file (you can remove it if you prefer) and assume Redis will be on our local machine.

First, we need to include the `redis` module and create a `Client` instance:

```
const redis = require("redis");
const db    = redis.createClient();
```

We then need to wait until it connects:

```
db.on("connect", () => {
    console.log("db: ready");

    // ...
    // the rest of our service code
    // ...

    app.listen(3000, () => {
        console.log("app: ready");
    });
});
```

There are a couple of ways we can use Redis to store our data. To make it simple, as we don't have tables, let's use hashes to store our images. Each image will have a different hash, and the name of the hash will be the name of the image.

As there are no tables in this kind of database, our initialization code can just be removed.

Next, let's change our upload method to store data on Redis. As I mentioned, let's store it in a hash with the name of the `image`:

```
app.post("/uploads/:name", bodyparser.raw({
```

```
    limit : "10mb",
    type : "image/*"
}), (req, res) => {
    db.hmset(req.params.name, {
        size : req.body.length,
        data : req.body.toString("base64"),
    }, (err) => {
        if (err) {
            return res.send({ status : "error", code: err.code });
        }

        res.send({ status : "ok", size: req.body.length });
    });
});
```

The `hmset` command lets us set multiple fields of a hash, in our case, `size` and `data`. Notice we're storing our image content in `base64` encoding, otherwise we'll lose data. If we restart our service and try to upload our test `image`, it should work fine:

```
● ● ●                          2. nazgul.home: /Users/dresende (bash)
~ > curl -H 'Content-Type: image/png' --data-binary @example.png http://localhost:3000/uploads/test.png
{"status":"ok","size":55543}~ > _
```

We can then use `redis-cli` and see whether our image is there. Well, we're checking to see whether our hash has the field size and matches our image size:

```
● ● ●                          2. nazgul.home: /Users/dresende (redis-cli)
~ > redis-cli
127.0.0.1:6379> hget test.png size
"55543"
127.0.0.1:6379> _
```

Great! We can now change our Express parameter to look for the `image` hash:

```
app.param("image", (req, res, next, name) => {
    if (!name.match(/\.(png|jpg)$/i)) {
        return res.status(403).end();
    }
```

```
    db.hgetall(name, (err, image) => {
        if (err || !image) return res.status(404).end();

        req.image      = image;
        req.image.name = name;

        return next();
    });
});
```

Our `image` check method should work now. And, for our download method to work, we just need to change the image loading to decode our previous `base64` encoding:

```
app.get("/uploads/:image", (req, res) => {
    let image     = sharp(Buffer.from(req.image.data, "base64"));
    let width     = +req.query.width;
    let height    = +req.query.height;
    let blur      = +req.query.blur;
    let sharpen   = +req.query.sharpen;
    let greyscale = [ "y", "yes", "true", "1",
"on"].includes(req.query.greyscale);
    let flip      = [ "y", "yes", "true", "1",
"on"].includes(req.query.flip);
    let flop      = [ "y", "yes", "true", "1",
"on"].includes(req.query.flop);

    if (width > 0 && height > 0) {
        image.ignoreAspectRatio();
    }

    if (width > 0 || height > 0) {
        image.resize(width || null, height || null);
    }

    if (flip)         image.flip();
    if (flop)         image.flop();
    if (blur > 0)     image.blur(blur);
    if (sharpen > 0)  image.sharpen(sharpen);
    if (greyscale)    image.greyscale();

    db.hset(req.image.name, "date_used", Date.now());

    res.setHeader("Content-Type", "image/" +
path.extname(req.image.name).substr(1));

    image.pipe(res);
});
```

Our images are now being served from Redis. As a bonus, we're adding/updating a
date_used field in our image hash to indicate when it was last used:

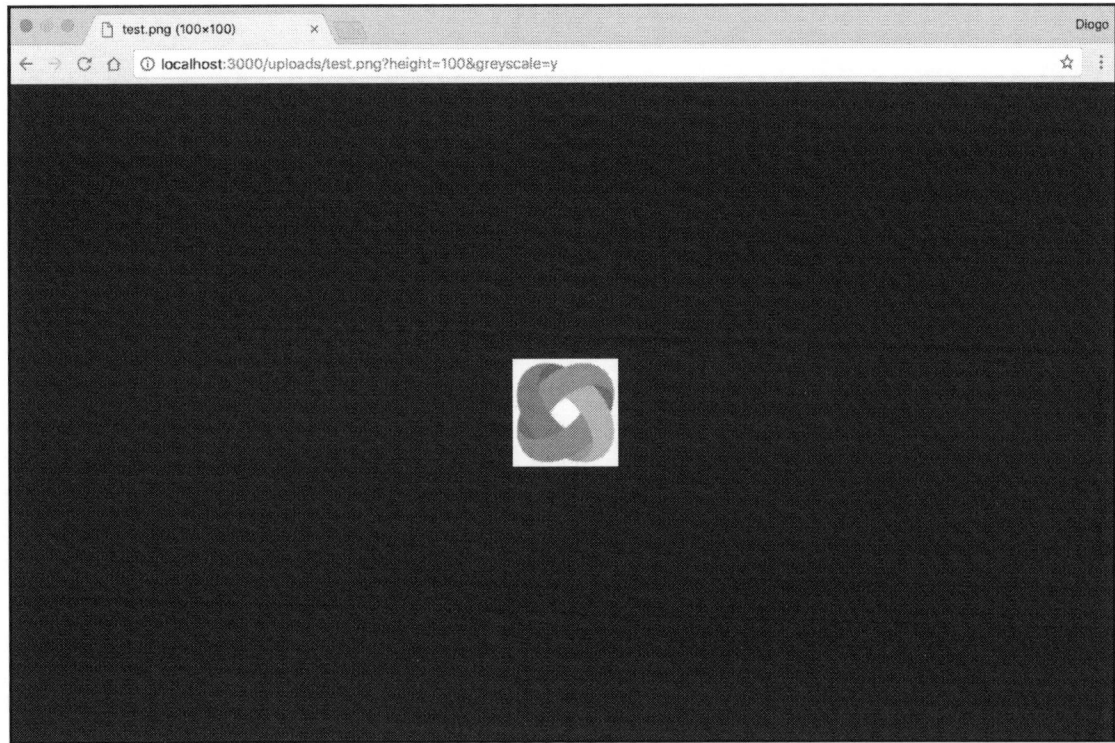

Removing our image is as simple as removing our hash:

```
app.delete("/uploads/:image", (req, res) => {
    db.del(req.image.name, (err) => {
        return res.status(err ? 500 : 200).end();
    });
});
```

We can then try to remove our `test` image:

```
3. nazgul.home: /Users/dresende (bash)
~ > curl -v -X DELETE http://localhost:3000/uploads/test.png
* Trying ::1...
* TCP_NODELAY set
* Connected to localhost (::1) port 3000 (#0)
> DELETE /uploads/test.png HTTP/1.1
> Host: localhost:3000
> User-Agent: curl/7.54.0
> Accept: */*
>
< HTTP/1.1 200 OK
< X-Powered-By: Express
< Date: Mon, 19 Mar 2018 22:07:52 GMT
< Connection: keep-alive
< Content-Length: 0
<
* Connection #0 to host localhost left intact
~ > _
```

Using `redis-cli` to check whether the hash exists, we see that it's gone:

```
3. nazgul.home: /Users/dresende (redis-cli)
~ > redis-cli
127.0.0.1:6379> get test.png
(nil)
127.0.0.1:6379> _
```

The only two features missing are the statistics and removing old images.

For the statistics, that could be hard as we're using generic hash tables and we can't be sure how many hash tables are defined, and if all or any have image data. We would have to scan all hash tables, which is complex for large sets.

To remove old images, the problem is the same as there's no way of looking for hash tables with a specific condition, such as a field value.

There are still other paths available to tackle this problem. For example, we could have another hash table with just our image names and use dates. But, the complexity would increase, and the integrity could be at risk as we're splitting information through different hash tables with no certainty of making **Atomicity**, **Consistency**, **Isolation**, and **Durability** (**ACID**) operations.

Conclusion

As we've seen, there are plenty of options to store our microservice state. Depending on the type of information we're manipulating, there are databases better-prepared to handle our data.

It all depends on a few different questions we should ask ourselves:

- Is our data integrity important?
- Is our data structure complex?
- How and what type of information do we need to acquire?

If our data integrity is important or the data structure is complex, do not use in-memory databases. Depending on the complexity, see if you need a non-relational database, or whether you can go with a relational database that can handle more complex manipulation and data aggregation operations, which will help you to achieve the last point.

Security

One good practice is to write code iteratively, testing every time we make a new small feature or improvement, and always write code thinking of all the features we envision for our service.

Thinking about the service roadmap allows you to prepare the service for future improvements, reducing the amount of code wasted or replaced later on.

For instance, in terms of security:

- Is our service secure? Is it prepared for some types of malicious attacks?
- Is our service private? Should it have some kind of authentication or authorization mechanism?

Luckily, our frameworks allow our code to be composed and allow us to add layers of security later. For example, using Express or Hydra, we can add a precedent routing function that will run before any of our service methods, allowing us to enforce, for example, authentication.

Looking at our service, since it exposes its methods using HTTP, there are a couple of improvements we can add to it, for example:

- **Authentication**: Forcing anyone that uses it to identify themselves. Or, just the upload and removal methods. It's up to you. There could also be user accounts, and each user would see their respective list of images.
- **Authorization**: Restricting, for example, what networks could access the service, independently of having a valid authentication or not.
- **Confidentiality**: Giving your users protection against prying eyes over the network traffic.
- **Availability**: Restricting the maximum usage frequency of the service, per client, to ensure a single client cannot block your entire service.

To introduce these improvements, you may add an authentication module such as the Passport module, and use a certificate to give your users a more secure HTTPS experience.

Other types of insecurity come directly from your code and don't improve by adding a certificate or forcing authentication. I'm referring to:

- Bugs, programming logic flaws, and use cases not properly tested, which can lead to minor or serious problems
- Dependency bugs, which you might not be aware of but can still ruin your service and may force you to look for alternative dependencies, which is never a pleasant task

To minimize these events, you should always keep evolving your test suite, adding use cases as they show up, ensuring a new bug that is solved does not reappear later. Regarding dependency bugs, you can subscribe to the Node Security Project and even integrate it with your code to always know when one of your dependencies is a risk.

If there were source code commandments, the next four would surely be on the list:

- Keep the code simple. If the code is getting complex, stop, look back, and split the code into simpler parts.
- Validate external input, whether it's the user or another service. Never trust data from the outside.
- Deny by default and not the opposite, checking whether someone has access to a resource and denying anyone that is not.
- Add test cases from the beginning of the project.

Summary

The state is part of any service, and state is built upon data. For a more cloud-native experience, a service cannot depend on a traditional filesystem and needs to use other kinds of storage structures to store data. Databases are a natural progress, and there are some types of databases to choose from, depending on how important and complex our data is.

Assuming our state is securely stored in a database service of some kind, it's also important to ensure our data cannot be corrupted using our service. There can be security flaws and bugs in our service that may put our data at risk, so it's important to write simple code, validate input, and think about security in general when planning the service roadmap.

To progress our service, let's introduce something we haven't done yet, and should, which is a proper test suite. In the next chapter, we'll see some good options and create a test suite, establishing whether anything needs to change in order to make our service as secure as possible.

7
Testing

When you're developing an application, it will eventually form a structure and evolve into a stable product that you can use in production and sell to your customers. In the beginning, everything may seem simple and many tend to postpone the construction of a proper test suite.

"Debugging is twice as hard as writing the code in the first place."

—*Brian W. Kernighan and P. J. Plauger in The Elements of Programming Style*

Later on, the application may become just sufficiently complex for you to hesitate to begin testing. You may eventually give up and never test your application. It may be frustrating, especially if you have never seen or used any test suite before.

Proper testing gives you more than a little bit of quality assurance. Proper testing gives you:

- **Predictability**: This means that your code execution, no matter if it's an application or just a module, will have an expected result. As you evolve the tests and introduce different test cases, you begin to fulfill all the uses for your code, and you ensure its results were as intended.
- **Feature coverage**: This means that you can measure what parts of your code are tested or not. There are plenty of tools to inspect your code and tell you what parts of it haven't been used in your test suite, which helps you create specific tests for specific parts of the code that are not yet covered.
- **Safe evolution**: This is a side effect. When your code gets complex, if your test suite has good code coverage, you can make changes and add features without compromising stability, as you can continuously run the test suite and see if it breaks anything.

There's a developing methodology that involves first creating a test for a new feature and then making sure the test passes. This way, you can focus on how you think your code should be used (in the new test) and then evolve it (actually develop it) so the test stops failing and gives proper results.

So, let's begin by looking at some testing methodologies, and then write our first test. Then, let's see how code coverage can help in the testing process. Finally, we'll look at how you can mock parts of your code.

Types of testing methodologies

There are several types of testing methodologies. You can have tests to measure performance by stressing your application with specific actions and checking whether it achieves the expected minimum results. Those are important, but not at this stage. We should focus on other kinds of tests.

Our goal is to have a test suite that ensures our code behaves as we designed it. To ensure that, we must have:

- Unit tests, to check individual code units, such as some functions
- Integration tests, to check whether external actions produce the expected results

Using these two types of test, and having a full code coverage, we'll be able to develop new features and run regression tests, which is just a fancy way of saying that our test suite still passes, and our new code does not break (there's no regression).

You may see these regression tests as and when you run the test suite on your laptop and the results are OK, and then you commit your code to GitHub, for example, and Travis runs the same test suite on different environments to see if nothing breaks. If you're pushing to a pull request on GitHub, you'll be unable to merge your changes unless every test result passes.

To achieve full test coverage, you'll necessarily have test cases in the same language as the one used to develop the application, which in our case is Node.js. It's not mandatory, but it simplifies a lot of the tools used to run the test cases use the same language, as this creates a friendlier environment for other developers.

When using open source modules, it's not uncommon for others to find issues and try to fix them. Having test frameworks that involve installing third-party software will lower the interest in helping to fix them. On the other hand, if the user just needs to clone the repository, fix and run the tests, that will be a much more enjoyable experience.

Using frameworks

There are a couple of test frameworks available for Node.js. What they do is give you an environment where you can focus on the test cases. Some frameworks will even do code coverage more or less automatically.

One of the most commonly used frameworks is mocha, which is a simple yet powerful framework. It can be used for general unit testing, but also for performance, as it is able to highlight slow tests.

Let's try it out and prepare our microservice for the tests. You can use any of the previous versions; it should not matter for the storage model we're using, only the microservice interface. First of all, let's install mocha as a development dependency. We're also using an assertion library called chai, which has a plugin specifically for HTTP testing:

```
npm install –save-dev mocha chai chai-http
```

Then, change your package.json file to update the scripts part to something similar to this:

```
"scripts": {
    "test": "node test/run"
},
```

This tells NPM that, to test our microservice, it should run the node test/run command. We now need to create this file (test/run.js) so it will actually work. Create the test folder, add the run.js file, and add only this line to it:

```
console.log("ok");
```

Now, go to a console on our microservice folder and run the test command:

```
npm test
> imagini@1.0.0 test /Users/dresende/imagini
> node test/run

Ok
```

The first step is complete. This is not actually a test, but we now have the initial structure.

Integrating tests

We will now create our first integration tests. Each of our tests will run separately, meaning they should not depend on any other test and should follow a predictable workflow. First, we need to change our run.js file to run all test files. For that, we'll use mocha and add all files found in the integration folder:

```
const fs    = require("fs");
const path  = require("path");
const mocha = require("mocha");
const suite = new mocha();

fs.readdir(path.join(__dirname, "integration"), (err, files) => {
    if (err) throw err;

    files.filter((filename) =>
    (filename.match(/\.js$/))).map((filename) => {
        suite.addFile(path.join(__dirname, "integration", filename));
    });

    suite.run((failures) => {
        process.exit(failures);
    });
});
```

Then, let's create the integration folder inside our test folder, and let's create our first test file, called image-upload.js. Add this content to the file:

```
describe("Uploading image", () => {
    it("should accept only images");
});
```

If we now run the tests again, we should see the default mocha response with no tests passing and no tests failing:

```
npm test
> imagini@1.0.0 test /Users/dresende/imagini
> node test/run

0 passing (2ms)
```

To avoid repeating code, let's create a tools.js file inside the test folder, so we can export common tasks that every test file can use. Out of the box, I'm thinking about our microservice location and a sample image:

```
const fs    = require("fs");
const path  = require("path");
```

```
exports.service = require("../imagini.js");
exports.sample  = fs.readFileSync(path.join(__dirname, "sample.png"));
```

Create a `sample.png` image in the `test` folder. When a test needs to upload an image, it will use that sample. In the future, we could have different kinds of samples, such as huge images, to test performance and limitations.

Using chai

We also need to make a little change to our microservice. We need to export its app so that the HTTP plugin from `chai` can load it and were able to test it without the need to run in a separate console. Add this to the end of our microservice file:

```
module.exports = app;
```

You should have a folder hierarchy similar to the following screenshot:

We should now change our `image-upload.js` test file to create our first real test:

```
const chai  = require("chai");
const http  = require("chai-http");
const tools = require("../tools");

chai.use(http);

describe("Uploading image", () => {
    beforeEach((done) => {
        chai
        .request(tools.service)
        .delete("/uploads/test_image_upload.png")
        .end(() => {
            return done();
        });
    });

    it ("should accept a PNG image", function (done) {
        chai
        .request(tools.service)
        .post("/uploads/test_image_upload.png")
        .set("Content-Type", "image/png")
        .send(tools.sample)
        .end((err, res) => {
            chai.expect(res).to.have.status(200);
            chai.expect(res.body).to.have.status("ok");

            return done();
        });
    });
});
```

We start by first including the `chai` modules and our `tools` file:

```
const chai  = require("chai");
const http  = require("chai-http");
const tools = require("../tools");

chai.use(http);
```

Then, we describe our test file as `Uploading image`:

```
describe("Uploading image", () => {
```

We'll add the different use cases we can think of, related to the uploading of images.

Inside, we use `beforeEach`, which is a `mocha` method that will be called before every test in this file. Remember, we want our tests to be consistent, so we add this method to remove our image before running every test. We don't care whether the image exists:

```
beforeEach((done) => {
    chai
    .request(tools.service)
    .delete("/uploads/test_image_upload.png")
    .end(() => {
        return done();
    });
});
```

Look how we use the `tools.service`, which points to our microservice. If, later on, we change the name or somehow make it more complex, we just need to change the `tools` file, and everything should work.

Then, we add our first `integration` file's test – a simple image upload:

```
it("should accept a PNG image", (done) => {
    chai
    .request(tools.service)
    .post("/uploads/test_image_upload.png")
    .set("Content-Type", "image/png")
    .send(tools.sample)
    .end((err, res) => {
        chai.expect(res).to.have.status(200);
        chai.expect(res.body).to.have.status("ok");

        return done();
    });
});
```

It checks whether the HTTP response code is `200` and if the response body, which is a JSON structure, has the status property set to `ok`. And we're done!

Let's run our test suite again and see how it goes.

Adding code coverage

Now that our test suite is working and has one test, let's introduce code coverage. Adding this from the beginning of development is very easy and will help us focus on parts of the code that need to be tested, especially some use cases that involve specific conditions (such as `if-then-else` statements in our code). Having it all set up from the start of development is easy. On the other hand, if you have a fully working code and want to add tests and coverage, it will be harder and will take quite some time.

To add code coverage, we'll introduce another module. We'll install it globally to be able to run the tests with it directly:

```
npm install -g nyc
```

We can now run our tests with the following instrumentation:

```
nyc npm test
```

This should run our tests with the instrumentation installed. In the end, you'll get a nice console report.

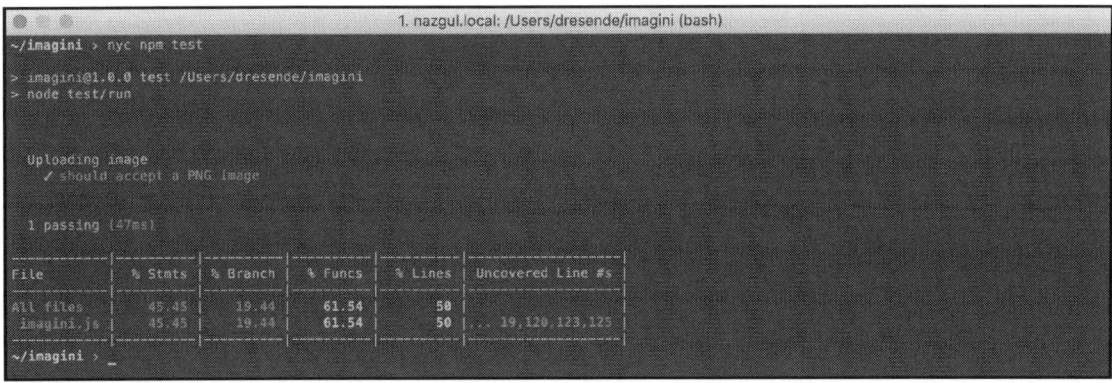

The coverage results are stored inside in a `.nyc_output` folder. This enables you to look at the last test results without running tests again. This is useful if your test suite is big and takes some time to finish.

To see the results, you just run `nyc report`:

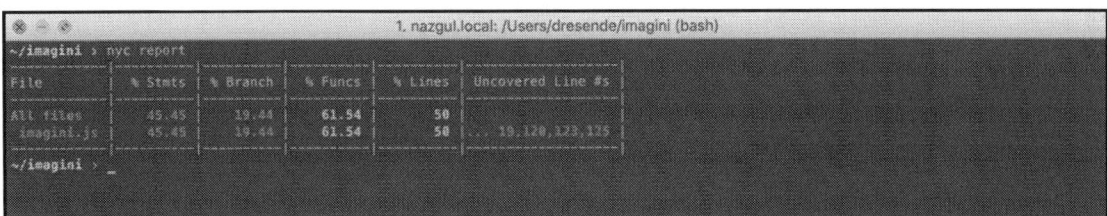

The result is a console report. There are several other styles of reports. One particularly useful one is the `html` report. Let's generate it:

```
nyc report --reporter=html
```

You should now have a `coverage` folder with an `index.html` file. Open that in your browser, and you should see something like the following screenshot:

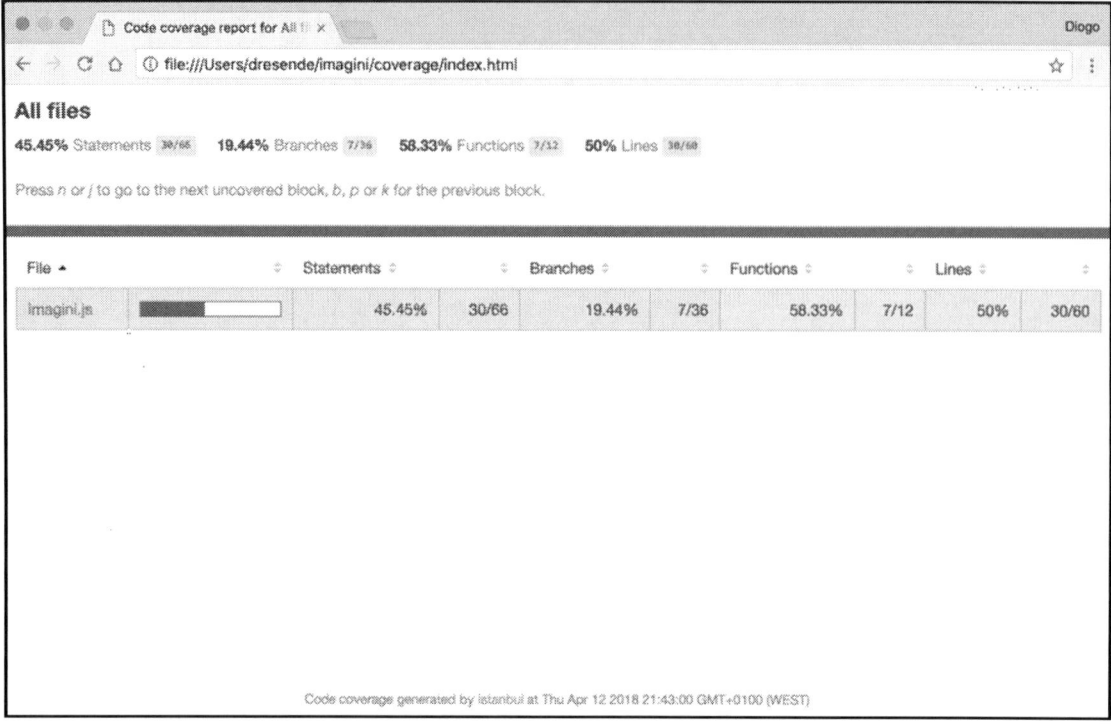

We only have one file that represents our microservice. If we had more, they would be listed hierarchically. There are global average statistics for every file.

There are three important groups of columns:

- **Statements**: Which represent code statements (conditions, assignments, assertions, calls, and so on)
- **Branches**: Which represent possible code control workflows, such as if-then-else or switch-case statement possibilities
- **Functions**: Which represent our actual code functions and callbacks

You can click in our file, look at the specific details of it and, more specifically, see the code and information line by line:

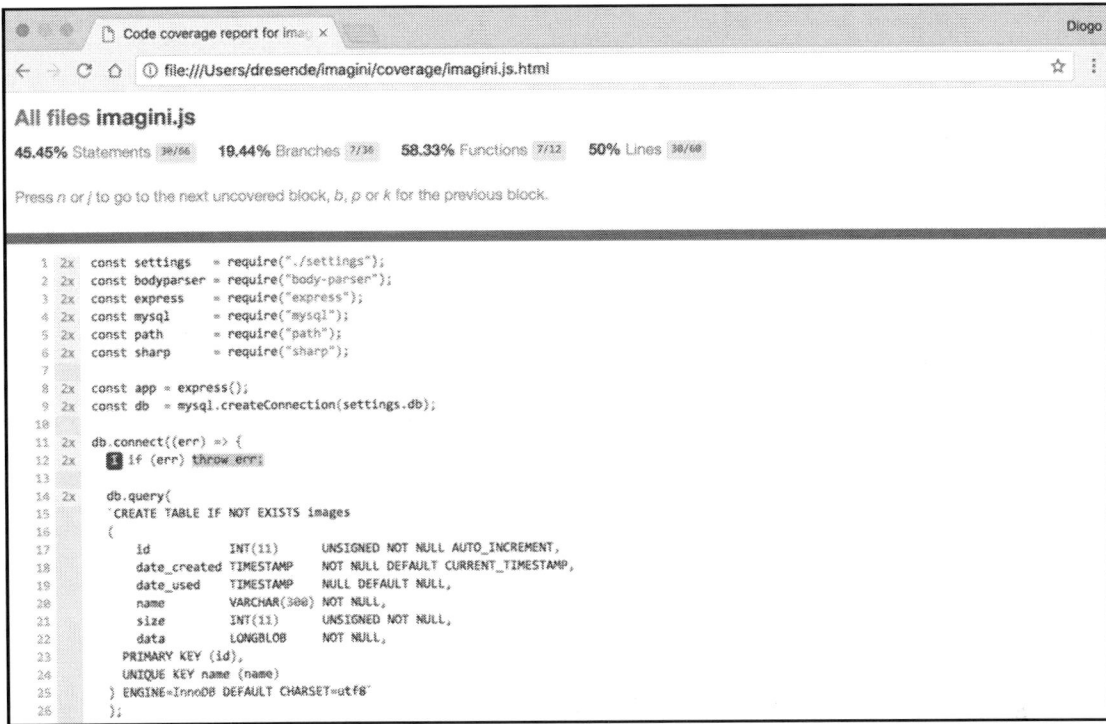

To the right of every line number, you see a gray area and, in this case, you see 2x in some of the lines. This is the execution count for that line. The execution has passed by that line twice. This is actually not that important, unless you're looking for bits of code that get largely executed and you want to do some kind of optimization.

You can also see that *line 12* has two changes. First, there's a pinkish background in the back of `throw err`. That means that statement never got executed, which is normal for now as we always successfully connected to the database. The mark before the `if` statement means that the condition never got executed:

If you scroll a few lines down, we'll see more lines with marks. For example, we can see our image upload method got almost completely covered. The only statement missing is the error handling.

As we delete our test image before running the tests, our image deletion method is also covered. Again, the only missing branch is if the database returns an error to our `DELETE` query.

Before going any further with the image upload, let's add another `integration` test file called `image-parameter.js`, and add some tests to increase our coverage:

```
const chai = require("chai");
const http = require("chai-http");
const tools = require("../tools");

chai.use(http);

describe("The image parameter", () => {
    beforeEach((done) => {
        chai
        .request(tools.service)
        .delete("/uploads/test_image_parameter.png")
        .end(() => {
            return done();
        });
    });

    it("should reply 403 for non image extension", (done) => {
        chai
        .request(tools.service)
        .get("/uploads/test_image_parameter.txt")
        .end((err, res) => {
            chai.expect(res).to.have.status(403);

            return done();
        });
    });

    it("should reply 404 for non image existence", (done) => {
        chai
        .request(tools.service)
        .get("/uploads/test_image_parameter.png")
        .end((err, res) => {
            chai.expect(res).to.have.status(404);

            return done();
        });
    });
});
```

Let's run our test suite and see how it goes:

Refresh the HTML report page and look at our parameter method:

As you can see, we now cover the following condition:

```
if (!image.match(/\.(png|jpg)$/i)) {
```

The following condition:

```
if (err || !images.length) {
```

We now have full coverage on this method.

There are other coverage lines that are harder to test, such as timers (you can see one on *line 28*), `catch` statements, or external errors coming from databases or other storage sources. There are ways of mocking those events, and we'll cover them later on.

Covering all code

For now, let's focus on adding coverage to our code. It's important to have it covered as much as possible when it's still just a small service. If we start adding tests and coverage when it's already big, you'll be frustrated, and it will be hard to find the motivation to cover it all.

This way, you'll find it rewarding to cover it in the beginning and keep the coverage percentage as high as possible along with code evolution.

Let's get back to our image upload test, and add another test:

```
it("should deny duplicated images", (done) => {
    chai
    .request(tools.service)
    .post("/uploads/test_image_upload.png")
    .set("Content-Type", "image/png")
    .send(tools.sample)
    .end((err, res) => {
        chai.expect(res).to.have.status(200);
        chai.expect(res.body).to.have.status("ok");

        chai
        .request(tools.service)
        .post("/uploads/test_image_upload.png")
        .set("Content-Type", "image/png")
        .send(tools.sample)
        .end((err, res) => {
            chai.expect(res).to.have.status(200);
            chai.expect(res.body).to.have.status("error");
            chai.expect(res.body).to.have.property("code",
            "ER_DUP_ENTRY");
```

```
                    return done();
                });
            });
        });
```

This will upload the same image twice in a row and we should receive an error from the database saying there's a duplicate. Let's run the tests again:

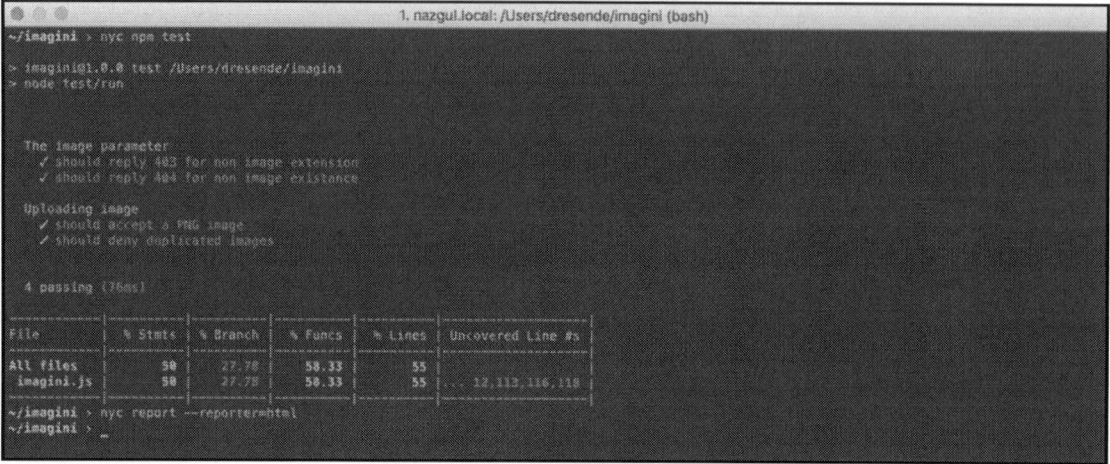

Now, let's open the initial page of the coverage report:

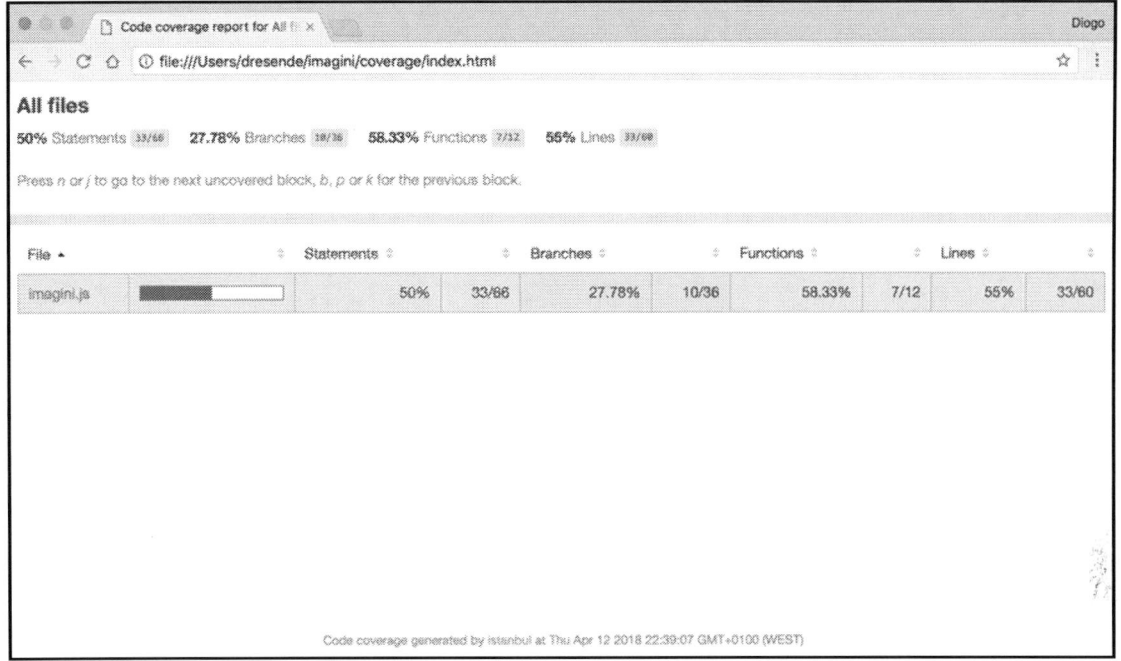

Notice that our file is no longer in a red background. This means the statement coverage has reached *50%*. Let's click on our file and see how our image upload method is covered:

It's complete! We can now move on. Just a reminder before we move to another method: having full coverage does not mean there are no bugs. That's something you need to understand. You might have a use case that you're not expecting, and so, you have no code for it, so there's no obvious coverage.

For example, the `bodyparser` module will not limit the type of content. If we upload a text file with an image name on it, our code will accept it and store it in the database without noticing. Think of this use case as your homework, and try to create a test to cover that use case and then fix the code.

Let's move to the next method we see after our upload method: the image check on *line 67*. Let's create a new integration test file called `image-check.js`, and add a simple test:

```
const chai = require("chai");
const http = require("chai-http");
const tools = require("../tools");

chai.use(http);
```

```
describe("Checking image", () => {
    beforeEach((done) => {
        chai
        .request(tools.service)
        .delete("/uploads/test_image_check.png")
        .end(() => {
            return done();
        });
    });

    it("should return 404 if it doesn't exist", (done) => {
        chai
        .request(tools.service)
        .head("/uploads/test_image_check.png")
        .end((err, res) => {
            chai.expect(res).to.have.status(404);

            return done();
        });
    });

    it("should return 200 if it exists", (done) => {
        chai
        .request(tools.service)
        .post("/uploads/test_image_check.png")
        .set("Content-Type", "image/png")
        .send(tools.sample)
        .end((err, res) => {
            chai.expect(res).to.have.status(200);
            chai.expect(res.body).to.have.status("ok");

            chai
            .request(tools.service)
            .head("/uploads/test_image_check.png")
            .end((err, res) => {
                chai.expect(res).to.have.status(200);

                return done();
            });
        });
    });
});
```

Let's run the test suite:

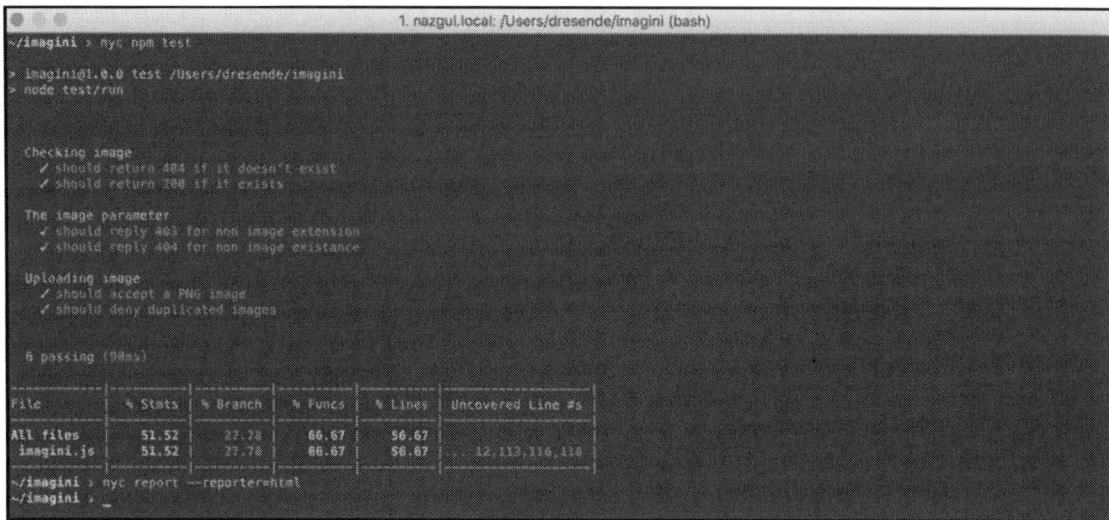

We can see our console report is getting bigger. As we're creating new integration test files and having a description for each one, `mocha` writes a nice tree view showing how the tests run. On the bottom, we can see the coverage report:

```
64        });
65      });
66
67  2x  app.head("/uploads/:image", (req, res) => {
68  2x    return res.status(200).end();
69      });
70
71  2x  app.delete("/uploads/:image", (req, res) => {
72  6x    db.query("DELETE FROM images WHERE id = ?", [ req.image.id ], (err) => {
73  6x      return res.status(err ? 500 : 200).end();
74        });
75      });
76
77  2x  app.get("/uploads/:image", (req, res) => {
78        let image     = sharp(req.image.data);
79        let width     = +req.query.width;
80        let height    = +req.query.height;
81        let blur      = +req.query.blur;
82        let sharpen   = +req.query.sharpen;
83        let greyscale = [ "y", "yes", "true", "1", "on"].includes(req.query.greyscale);
84        let flip      = [ "y", "yes", "true", "1", "on"].includes(req.query.flip);
85        let flop      = [ "y", "yes", "true", "1", "on"].includes(req.query.flop);
86
87        if (width > 0 && height > 0) {
88          image.ignoreAspectRatio();
89        }
90        if (width > 0 || height > 0) {
91          image.resize(width || null, height || null);
92        }
93        if (flip)        image.flip();
94        if (flop)        image.flop();
95        if (blur > 0)    image.blur(blur);
96        if (sharpen > 0) image.sharpen(sharpen);
97        if (greyscale)   image.greyscale();
```

Looking at the check method, we see it's now fully covered. This one was very simple.

We're still in the middle of statement coverage as our top method; the image manipulation one is almost half of our code. This means that when we start covering it, the coverage will significantly rise.

Let's create an `integration` test for it:

```
const chai = require("chai");
const http = require("chai-http");
const tools = require("../tools");

chai.use(http);

describe("Downloading image", () => {
    beforeEach((done) => {
        chai
        .request(tools.service)
        .delete("/uploads/test_image_download.png")
        .end(() => {
            chai
            .request(tools.service)
            .post("/uploads/test_image_download.png")
            .set("Content-Type", "image/png")
            .send(tools.sample)
            .end((err, res) => {
                chai.expect(res).to.have.status(200);
                chai.expect(res.body).to.have.status("ok");

                return done();
            });
        });
    });

    it("should return the original image size if no parameters given",
    (done) => {
        chai
        .request(tools.service)
        .get("/uploads/test_image_download.png")
        .end((err, res) => {
            chai.expect(res).to.have.status(200);
            chai.expect(res.body).to.have.length(tools.sample.length);

            return done();
        });
    });
});
```

Before each test, we're deleting the image (if it exists) and then uploading a fresh sample one. Then, for each test, we'll download it and test the output according to what we asked for.

Let's try and run it:

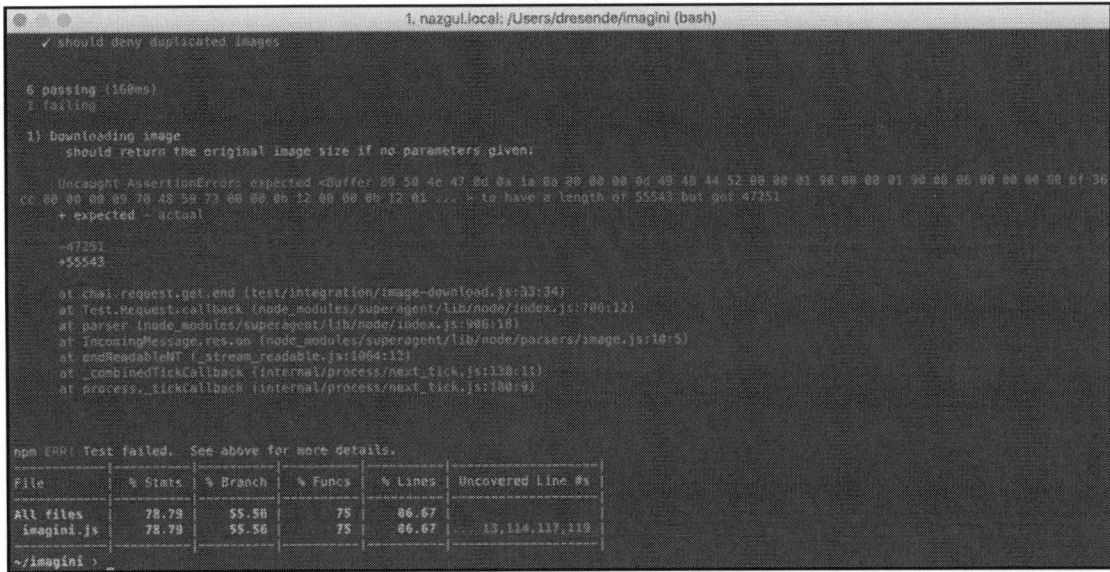

Well, that was unexpected. The test fails because our length check does not match. This is actually a good example of something we just notice when we start to execute testing.

What happens is that, when we request an image, we use the `sharp` module to make any manipulation on the image, according to query parameters. In this case, we're not asking for any manipulation, but when we output the image (through `sharp`), it actually returns the same image in size, but perhaps with a little bit less quality, or maybe it just knows how to better encode our image and remove data from the file that is not needed.

We don't know exactly, but let's assume we want the original image, untouched. We need to change our download method. Let's assume that if no query parameters are defined at all, we just return the original image. Let's add a condition to the top of our method:

```
if (Object.keys(req.query).length === 0) {
    db.query("UPDATE images " +
            "SET date_used = UTC_TIMESTAMP " +
            "WHERE id = ?",
            [ req.image.id ]);

    res.setHeader("Content-Type", "image/" +
    path.extname(req.image.name).substr(1));

    return res.end(req.image.data);
}
```

If we run it now, we should have no failures:

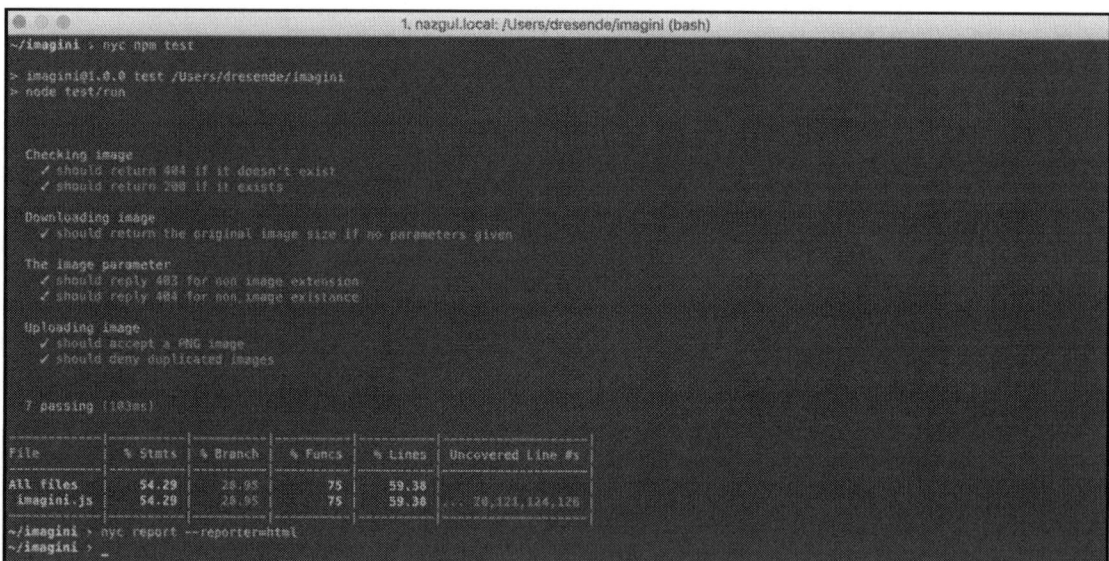

Our statement coverage did not rise much because we actually created a condition on top of the method and returned immediately, so our previous method is still untested:

Looking at *line 78*, you should see a new mark, an E that means that the condition in that line never executed the `else` statement, which is the rest of our code. Let's add a test to this integration and resize our image.

We will need `sharp` to help us check whether the results are correct. Let's include it on the top of our file:

```
const sharp = require("sharp");
```

Then, add a resize test:

```
it("should be able to resize the image as we request", (done) => {
    chai
    .request(tools.service)
    .get("/uploads/test_image_download.png?width=200&height=100")
    .end((err, res) => {
        chai.expect(res).to.have.status(200);

        let image = sharp(res.body);

        image
        .metadata()
        .then((metadata) => {
            chai.expect(metadata).to.have.property("width", 200);
            chai.expect(metadata).to.have.property("height", 100);

            return done();
        });
    });
});
```

Let's run our test suite:

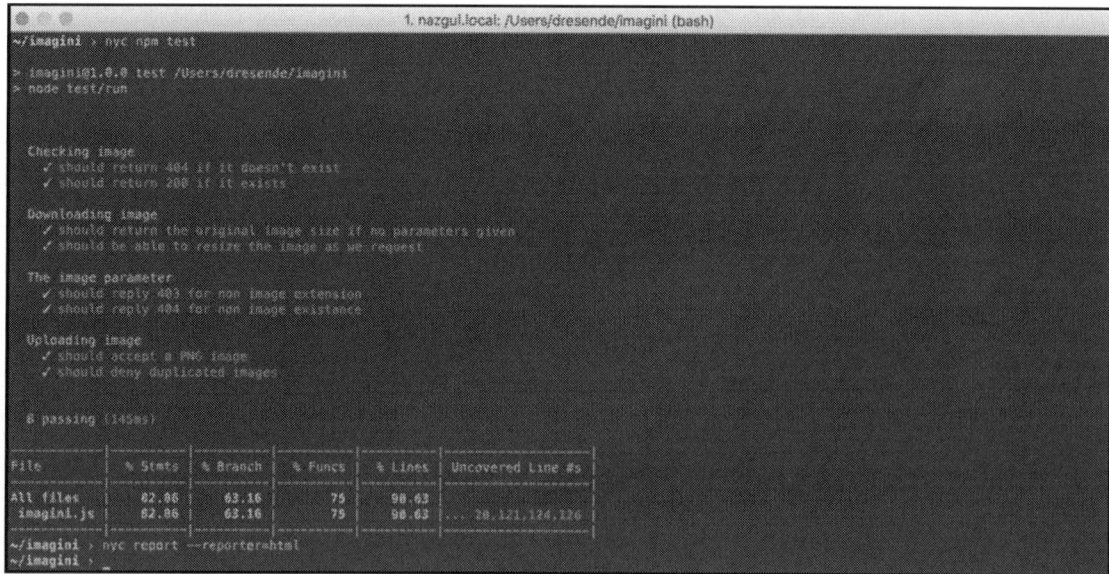

It now looks very good. From the console report, we can see some green. Let's look at the front page of the coverage report:

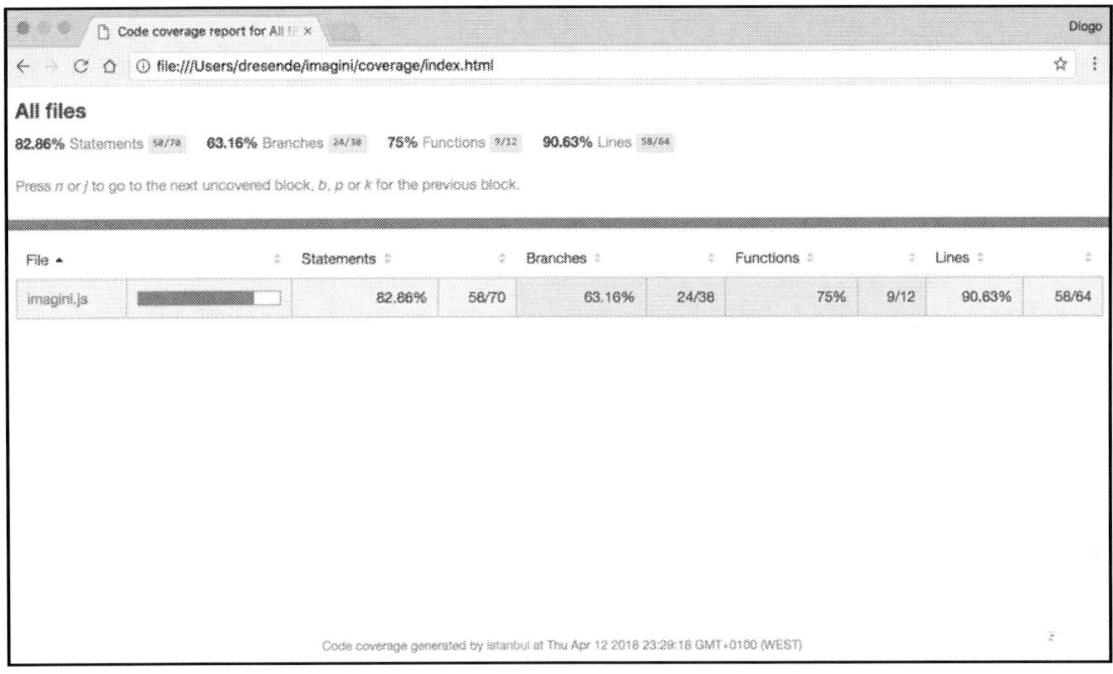

We see green here as well. Having more than *80%* coverage is good, but we can still go further. Let's see the file:

It's more or less covered. We still need to cover all the effects. We can actually run them all at once. The first two conditions also have an E marker, but that should disappear after adding a test without resizing. Let's add it:

```
it("should be able to add image effects as we request", (done) => {
    chai
    .request(tools.service)
    .get("/uploads/test_image_download.png?
    flip=y&flop=y&greyscale=y&blur=10&sharpen=10")
    .end((err, res) => {
        chai.expect(res).to.have.status(200);

        return done();
    });
});
```

Looking at our report now, we see the coverage is almost complete:

To cover those yellow nulls there, we need to resize the image with only `width` or `height`. We can add two tests for those:

```
it("should be able to resize the image width as we request", (done) => {
    chai
    .request(tools.service)
    .get("/uploads/test_image_download.png?width=200")
    .end((err, res) => {
        chai.expect(res).to.have.status(200);

        let image = sharp(res.body);

        image
        .metadata()
        .then((metadata) => {
            chai.expect(metadata).to.have.property("width", 200);

            return done();
        });
    });
});
```

Add a similar one for the `height`, and run the test suite. You should not see the statement coverage go up, only the branch coverage:

The only method missing is the statistics method. This one is simple. We could eventually run a more specific test, by asking statistics, making a change such as an upload, and asking for statistics again to compare. I'll leave that to you. Let's just add a simple request test:

```
const chai = require("chai");
const http = require("chai-http");
const tools = require("../tools");

chai.use(http);

describe("Statistics", () => {
    it("should return an object with total, size, last_used and
    uptime", (done) => {
        chai
        .request(tools.service)
        .get("/stats")
        .end((err, res) => {
            chai.expect(res).to.have.status(200);
            chai.expect(res.body).to.have.property("total");
            chai.expect(res.body).to.have.property("size");
```

```
            chai.expect(res.body).to.have.property("last_used");
            chai.expect(res.body).to.have.property("uptime");

            return done();
        });
    });
});
```

Now, running our test suite should give all green:

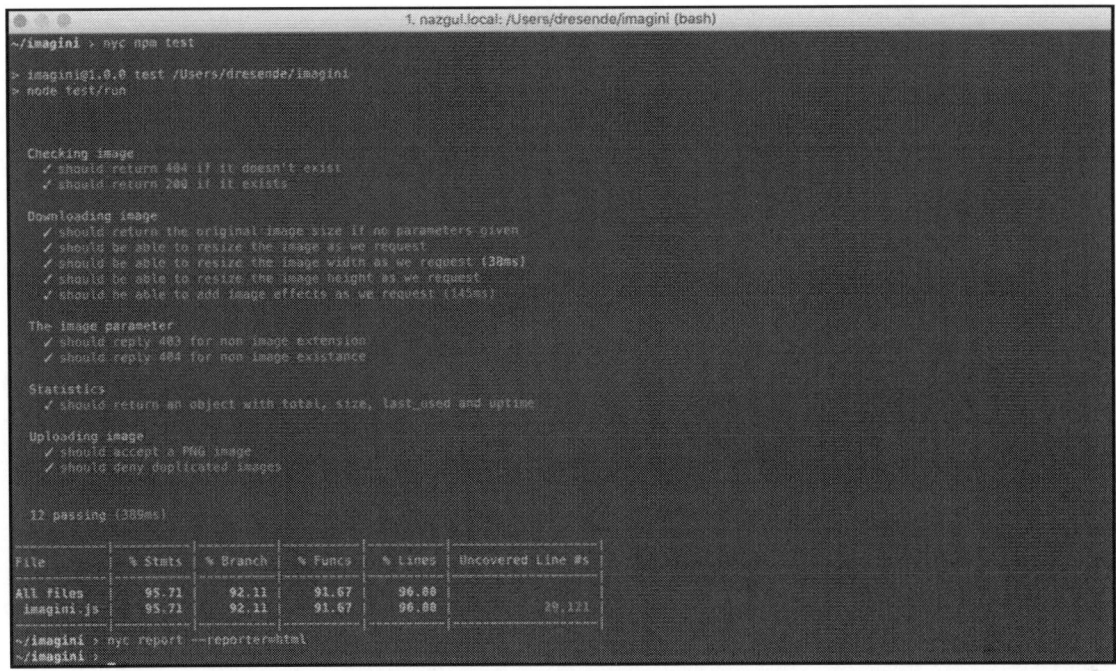

We see there are only two lines uncovered: `29.121`. The first one is our timer and the second one is on the statistics method. Let's refresh our HTML report:

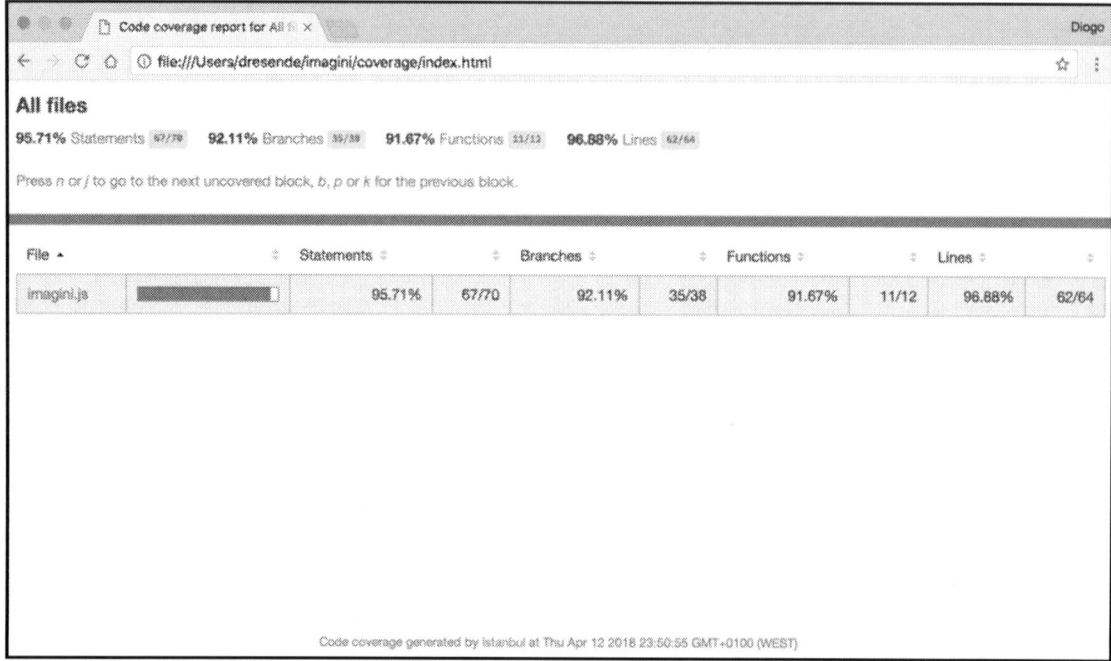

This is rewarding; we have almost *100%* coverage. There's only one function not covered, which is our timer. And, there are only tree statements, which also represent the three branches, that aren't covered, but those aren't actually that important.

What is important is to keep this high coverage mark during the course of our development.

Mocking our services

It's not at all uncommon to have parts of your service that are harder to test. Some, or most, of those parts are error-related conditions, where it's hard to make an external service such as a database engine return an error that will rarely occur during normal execution.

To be able to test, or at least simulate these kinds of events, we need to mock our services. There are a couple of options around, and Sinon is the most commonly used one in the Node.js ecosystem. This framework provides more than mocking; it also provides the following:

- **Spies**: Which monitor function calls and record arguments passed, the returned value and other properties
- **Stubs**: Which are enhanced spies with a pre-programmed behavior, helping us drive the execution into a pre-determined path (allowing us to mock a behavior)

Sinon also allows us to bend time, by virtually changing the service perception of time, and to be able to test timed interval calls (remember our interval timer?). With this in mind, let's see if we can make our microservice reach *100%* test coverage.

Let's start by installing the framework, as we did with `chai`:

```
npm install --save-dev sinon
```

Now, let's add a test for the image deletion. This method is tested through the other tests and that's why we didn't need to add it before, but now that we want to fully test it, let's add a basic test file called `image-delete.js`, with the following content:

```javascript
const chai = require("chai");
const sinon = require("sinon");
const http = require("chai-http");
const tools = require("../tools");

chai.use(http);

describe.only("Deleting image", () => {
    beforeEach((done) => {
        chai
        .request(tools.service)
        .delete("/uploads/test_image_delete.png")
        .end(() => {
            return done();
        });
    });

    it("should return 200 if it exists", (done) => {
        chai
        .request(tools.service)
        .post("/uploads/test_image_delete.png")
        .set("Content-Type", "image/png")
        .send(tools.sample)
        .end((err, res) => {
```

```
                chai.expect(res).to.have.status(200);
                chai.expect(res.body).to.have.status("ok");

                chai
                .request(tools.service)
                .delete("/uploads/test_image_delete.png")
                .end((err, res) => {
                    chai.expect(res).to.have.status(200);

                    return done();
                });
            });
        });
    });
});
```

Notice that I added the Sinon dependency on top, although I'm not using it just yet. You may run the tests again, but you shouldn't notice any difference.

We'll need to change the database behavior, so let's export a reference to it, so as to be able to access it from the tests. Add the following line in our microservice file before connecting to the database:

```
app.db = db;
```

Now, add another test to that file:

```
it("should return 500 if a database error happens", (done) => {
    chai
    .request(tools.service)
    .post("/uploads/test_image_delete.png")
    .set("Content-Type", "image/png")
    .send(tools.sample)
    .end((err, res) => {
        chai.expect(res).to.have.status(200);
        chai.expect(res.body).to.have.status("ok");

        let query = sinon.stub(tools.service.db, "query");

        query
        .withArgs("DELETE FROM images WHERE id = ?")
        .callsArgWithAsync(2, new Error("Fake"));

        query
        .callThrough();

        chai
        .request(tools.service)
        .delete("/uploads/test_image_delete.png")
```

```
        .end((err, res) => {
            chai.expect(res).to.have.status(500);

            query.restore();

            return done();
        });
    });
});
```

What we're doing is uploading an image, but, before requesting to delete it, we create a stub on the db.query method. We then inform Sinon that when the stub is called with the first argument with DELETE, we want it to asynchronously call the third argument (counting starts at 0) with a fake error. For any other call, we want it to just pass through.

Then, after deleting the image, we check that we received an HTTP 500 error code and restore the stub to the original function, ensuring that the other tests pass.

We're able to test this because mocha runs tests in serial; otherwise, we would need to do some gymnastics to ensure that we wouldn't interfere with the other tests.

Now, open the previously created test file, image-stats.js, include Sinon on the top, and add the following test:

```
it("should return 500 if a database error happens", (done) => {
    let query = sinon.stub(tools.service.db, "query");

    query
    .withArgs("SELECT COUNT(*) total, SUM(size) size, MAX(date_used)
    last_used FROM images")
    .callsArgWithAsync(1, new Error("Fake"));

    query
    .callThrough();

    chai
    .request(tools.service)
    .get("/stats")
    .end((err, res) => {
        chai.expect(res).to.have.status(500);

        query.restore();

        return done();
    });
});
```

We're now over 97% coverage. Let's bend time and test our timer. Create a new test file called `image-delete-old.js`, and add the following content:

```
const chai = require("chai");
const sinon = require("sinon");
const http = require("chai-http");
const tools = require("../tools");

chai.use(http);

describe("Deleting older images", () => {
    let clock = sinon.useFakeTimers({ shouldAdvanceTime : true });

    it("should run every hour", (done) => {
        chai
        .request(tools.service)
        .get("/stats")
        .end((err, res) => {
            chai.expect(res).to.have.status(200);

            clock.tick(3600 * 1000);
            clock.restore();

            return done();
        });
    });
});
```

In this test, we're replacing the global timer functions (`setTimeout` and `setInterval`) with fake timers. We then make a simple call to statistics, and then advance time by one hour (the tick call), and then finish.

Now, run the tests and see the results:

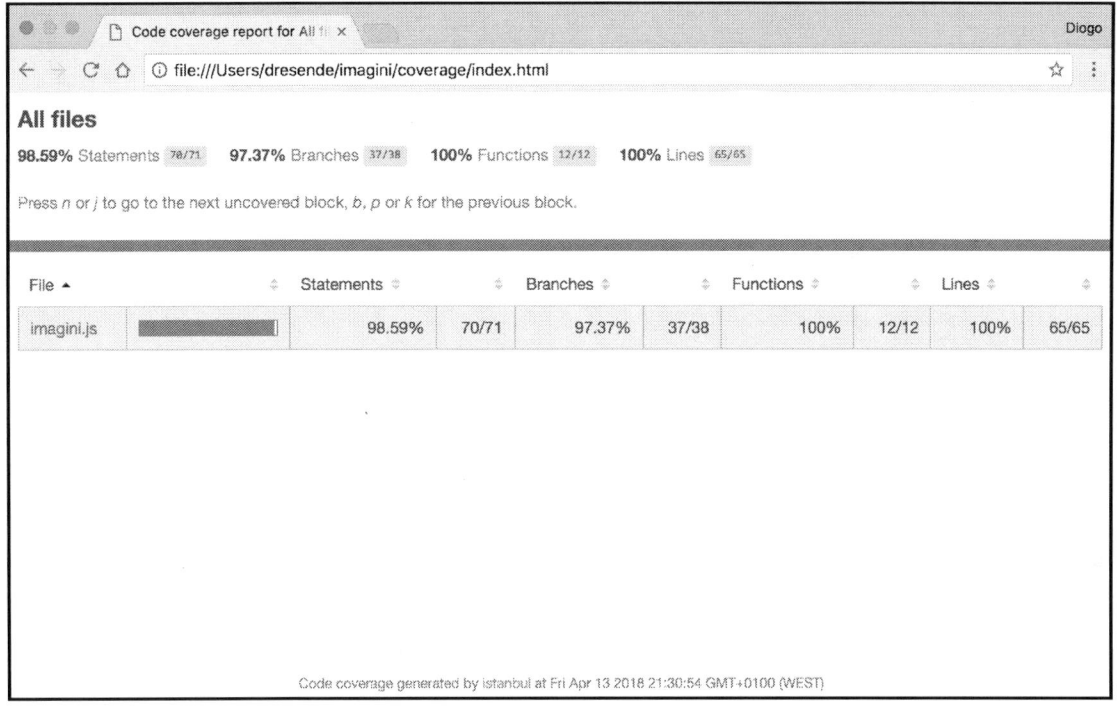

We now reach *100% coverage* on functions and lines. There's only one branch, with one statement missing. It's the possibility of a connection error:

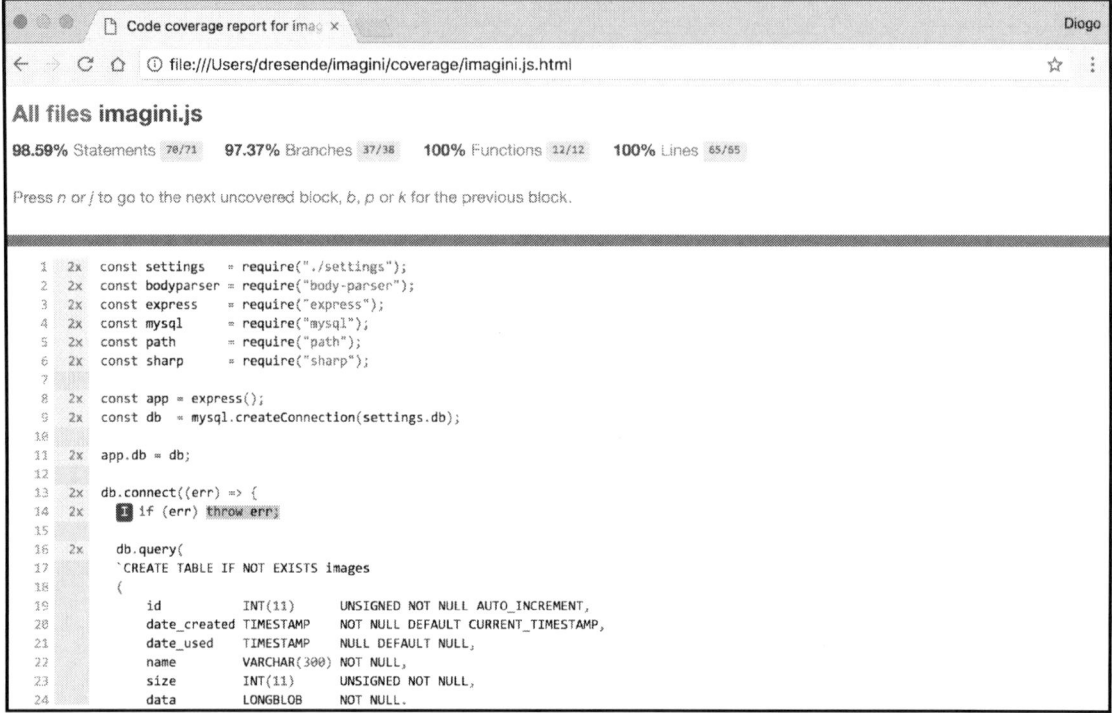

I'll leave it to you to figure it out how to mock that.

Remember that if you successfully mock the `connect` method, you'll also need to handle the throw.

Summary

Tests allow us to ensure a certain code quality level. It's very important to include tests from the very beginning, while the code is simple, to ensure that we keep tests updated and avoid regressions to the expected behavior.

It's very rewarding when we see that our code has a very high test coverage. This feeling forces you to keep that high mark and indirectly maintains good code quality.

Following on from this methodology of test coverage and continuous expected behavior, let's now look in the next chapter at how to deploy your code, be it for testing, staging, or production, while retaining the same expected behavior, no matter where you're deploying.

8
Deploying Microservices

Now that we're able to test out our microservice, we can go a step further and test it in a controlled environment -- an environment that could, and should, be very similar to a production one.

Being able to develop and test a piece of code in an environment that is a replica of production ensures that you won't find yourself in a situation where your service works in your development environment, but not in production, and you don't know why.

This happens because your development environment is usually your laptop and you certainly use it for other activities. You eventually install tools and applications that change your environment. These tools may introduce you to libraries or interfaces that you then use in your microservice and forget to include those in production.

To ensure your different environments are the same, there are several alternative paths. Let's look at two of them, which are going to be virtual machines and containers. We'll then take the container path and deploy our microservice using Docker.

Using virtual machines

One option is to use a virtual machine, a replica of production, that ensures that the environments are the same. There are a couple of drawbacks to this option:

- It's slow, as there's a complete virtualization guest operative system that you have to boot every time you want to develop
- It's resource consuming, as you need to store a complete base layout in your disk and you need to reserve RAM memory to start it

To make things worse, having a read-only machine with read-write code is not simple and will eventually make you frustrated. Virtual machines are the only option when you need an environment that you cannot have unless the entire machine is virtualized, for example, when you have a macOS laptop and you need a Windows environment.

Other than that, like when you're developing a microservice, the environment should be common to most operative systems. Node.js runs across platforms and, in this case, you're just exposing an HTTP interface.

Using containers

Another option is to use a container. A container is an operative system-level virtualization mechanism, where you isolate an environment inside your operative system. You still need the space for a base layout, but there are container layouts under 5 MB.

The most common and widely used container environment is Docker, which uses Linux containers and cgroups to create a secure and isolated environment to run applications. What boosted Docker actually was was the centralized repository of base layouts, called Docker images, where people could define, build, and then share these images with others, so people wouldn't have to build them themselves. There are pre-built images for all major database services and programming languages, so it's easy to just choose one and run your microservice inside it in a couple of minutes.

To make things even better, there's a description file, called `Dockerfile`, which has all the instructions you need to build an image locally. This is a text file that you can store in your code repository that allows developers to build an image to run the environment.

Even more interesting is the fact that images can be built on top of other images. You can pick one, add your specifications, and publish it. This is one of the major advantages that drove Docker to be the most used container technology.

There are a couple of Docker idiosyncrasies that you must understand before using it:

- Docker images are like a read-only template for running your application. There are ways of saving changes to images, but usually you pick an image and run your application inside an environment that will get lost when the container is removed. This is actually great because it ensures that when you restart your environment, everything is back to a common environment and nothing is left over.
- A container should run only one command and nothing more. This command can, of course, spawn other commands, but the purpose of a container is not to run multiple commands in parallel. If you have a complex environment, each service should run in its own container. For example, if you have a database, the database service could run in one container and your application should run on another.
- Because an image is supposed to be read-only, you can mount or link folders from the outside of the container. These are called volumes and allow you to, for example, run a read-only MySQL image with the data folder mapped to a folder on your laptop, allowing you to avoid losing your data when you stop the container. Volumes can either be folders or files and they can also be mounted read-only from the inside of the container.
- A container runs in an isolated environment and you need to create network links from your interface ports to the container ports. There's also an option to create virtualized networks that work across hosts and give you the power to deploy more complex environments.

Deploying using Docker

Before we start using Docker, you obviously need to install it. There are several installation channels to choose from. For many Linux distributions, there are packages available in their package manager. For Windows and macOS, you need to go to the Docker website and download the installer. This is actually the preferred one as the versions available from the package managers may not be up to date.

There are several graphical interfaces to manage Docker, but we'll keep it simple and just use the command-line interface. This gives you greater control and you get to know more of the internals of how everything is glued together.

So, let's open a console and type `docker info` to check whether everything is correct:

```
1. nazgul-2.local: /Users/dresende (bash)
~ > docker info
Containers: 0
 Running: 0
 Paused: 0
 Stopped: 0
Images: 0
Server Version: 18.03.0-ce
Storage Driver: overlay2
 Backing Filesystem: extfs
 Supports d_type: true
 Native Overlay Diff: true
Logging Driver: json-file
Cgroup Driver: cgroupfs
Plugins:
 Volume: local
 Network: bridge host macvlan null overlay
 Log: awslogs fluentd gcplogs gelf journald json-file logentries splunk syslog
Swarm: inactive
Runtimes: runc
Default Runtime: runc
Init Binary: docker-init
containerd version: cfd04396dc68220d1cecbe686a6cc3aa5ce3667c
runc version: 4fc53a81fb7c994640722ac585fa9ca548971871
init version: 949e6fa
Security Options:
 seccomp
  Profile: default
Kernel Version: 4.9.87-linuxkit-aufs
Operating System: Docker for Mac
OSType: linux
Architecture: x86_64
CPUs: 2
Total Memory: 1.952GiB
Name: linuxkit-025000000001
ID: E7DQ:TPVL:MPZ5:HT7R:7AOP:ZAR2:NV24:QXHJ:BAJN:ISDO:LCDZ:NRLV
Docker Root Dir: /var/lib/docker
Debug Mode (client): false
Debug Mode (server): false
HTTP Proxy: docker.for.mac.http.internal:3128
HTTPS Proxy: docker.for.mac.http.internal:3129
Registry: https://index.docker.io/v1/
Labels:
Experimental: false
Insecure Registries:
 127.0.0.0/8
Live Restore Enabled: false

~ >
```

You can see that there are no containers or images running. There is other information, such as storage and network information. You may also figure out that Docker for Mac uses a virtual machine to enable Docker on a macOS laptop.

This means that the `docker` command is actually a proxy to the `docker` command inside that virtual machine. You don't have to worry about it, it will work just fine; you'll probably only notice some lag from time to time.

Creating images

Before we deploy, we need to create an image for our service to run inside. Our service has no dependencies other than the ones defined on the top:

- `express` and `body-parser`: To handle our HTTP requests
- `mysql`: It enables us to use a MySQL database
- `sharp`: It enables us to manipulate images
- `path`: It is a core module to help working with directory paths

The core module is not a problem, and the first three are also not a problem since they're built completely in JavaScript. On the other hand, `sharp` is compiled, so our image needs to have at least a compiler.

To keep our image as slim as possible, we'll be using the Node.js Alpine version, which is a Node.js image based on Alpine Linux and it has a much smaller size than other distributions. You'll see what I mean in a moment. Let's download the image. Run the following:

```
docker pull node:alpine
```

If everything goes well, you should then have a new container image available, as the following screenshot shows:

```
● ● ●                                          1. nazgul-2.local: /Users/dresende (bash)
~ > docker images
REPOSITORY          TAG              IMAGE ID          CREATED          SIZE
~ > docker pull node:alpine
alpine: Pulling from library/node
605ce1bd3f31: Pull complete
f10758dcda1f: Pull complete
4cbe43d669e5: Pull complete
Digest: sha256:5149aec8f508d48998e6230cdc8e6832cba192088b442c8ef7e23df3c6892cd3
Status: Downloaded newer image for node:alpine
~ > docker images
REPOSITORY          TAG              IMAGE ID          CREATED          SIZE
node                alpine           7af437a39ec2      2 weeks ago      68.4MB
~ > _
```

First, I just checked that we had no local images. Then, I requested that Docker pull the Alpine version of the Node.js official repository. Notice that I didn't specify the version, as I'm targeting the latest stable one. If you want a specific version, head to Docker Hub and search for Node official images.

We now have our image, but there are a couple of things to do before being able to start our microservice. First, we need to create our own image. What we downloaded is just a base image, which doesn't have our code. We need to add our code and dependencies. To do that, we need to create a `Dockerfile`.

Defining a Dockerfile

This is a file specification with instructions for Docker to create an image. The instructions are clear and allow you to share that file on several servers so that Docker builds the image.

Our `Dockerfile` will have three parts:

- The header, which indicates the base image and author
- The instructions to build the image
- The instructions to run the image

There are many more instructions that we'll probably not cover. To get to know `Dockerfile` better, head over and read the documentation. This is an introduction that will actually help you go a long way. Here's our first `Dockerfile`:

```
FROM node:alpine
MAINTAINER Diogo Resende

ADD imagini /opt/app

WORKDIR /opt/app
RUN npm i

CMD [ "node", "/opt/app/imagini" ]
```

The empty lines were added for clarity only. The first two instructions define the base image (`FROM`) and the author (`MAINTAINER`). The next three add our `imagini` folder to the `/opt/app` folder inside the image. Then, we change directory to that folder and run `npm i` to install the required dependencies. Finally, the last instruction indicates how to run the image later on.

Save this to a file called `Dockerfile` and place it in an empty folder. Then, grab our microservice and place it inside a folder called `imagini`, inside this newly created folder:

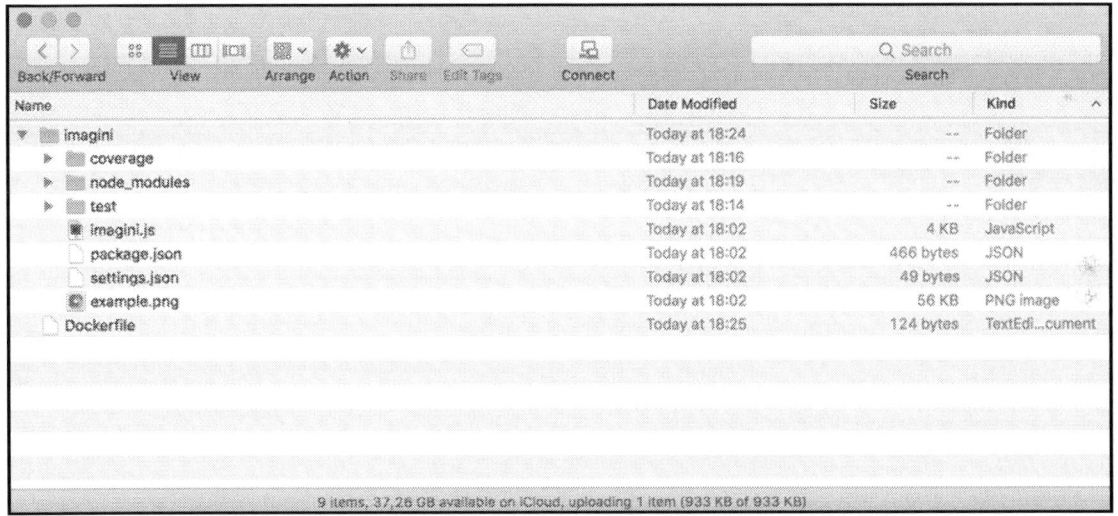

We can now try to build our image using the `docker build` command. Let's create the image, assign the name of our service, and indicate an initial version:

```
> docker build -t imagini:0.0.1 .
Sending build context to Docker daemon   43.4MB
Step 1/6 : FROM node:alpine
 ---> 7af437a39ec2
Step 2/6 : MAINTAINER Diogo Resende
 ---> Running in 009093d8c9d4
Removing intermediate container 009093d8c9d4
 ---> cdbe5185faf4
Step 3/6 : ADD imagini /opt/app
 ---> 9c062473535a
Step 4/6 : WORKDIR /opt/app
Removing intermediate container d734af3adba8
 ---> e39bdbfaf5ae
Step 5/6 : RUN npm i
 ---> Running in 3437fc2f74c9
npm notice created a lockfile as package-lock.json. You should commit this file.
npm WARN imagini@1.0.0 No description
npm WARN imagini@1.0.0 No repository field.

up to date in 0.613s
Removing intermediate container 3437fc2f74c9
 ---> 0b50046161f3
Step 6/6 : CMD [ "node", "/opt/app/imagini" ]
 ---> Running in 8d5786ea6ecf
Removing intermediate container 8d5786ea6ecf
 ---> a3e21d6fd379
Successfully built a3e21d6fd379
Successfully tagged imagini:0.0.1
> _
```

Let's check the list of images available:

```
> docker images
REPOSITORY          TAG               IMAGE ID            CREATED             SIZE
imagini             0.0.1             a3e21d6fd379        22 seconds ago      110MB
node                alpine            7af437a39ec2        2 weeks ago         68.4MB
>
```

Let's just start a container and see what happens. To do that, we use the `docker run` command and pass our image name and version. We don't need to specify what to run inside the image since we defined that on the `Dockerfile`, but we could change that:

```
                                    1. base (bash)
> docker run imagini:0.0.1
internal/modules/cjs/loader.js:683
    return process.dlopen(module, path.toNamespacedPath(filename));
                  ^

Error: Error loading shared library /opt/app/node_modules/sharp/build/Release/sharp.node: Exec format error
    at Object.Module._extensions..node (internal/modules/cjs/loader.js:683:18)
    at Module.load (internal/modules/cjs/loader.js:566:32)
    at tryModuleLoad (internal/modules/cjs/loader.js:506:12)
    at Function.Module._load (internal/modules/cjs/loader.js:498:3)
    at Module.require (internal/modules/cjs/loader.js:598:17)
    at require (internal/modules/cjs/helpers.js:11:18)
    at Object.<anonymous> (/opt/app/node_modules/sharp/lib/constructor.js:10:15)
    at Module._compile (internal/modules/cjs/loader.js:654:30)
    at Object.Module._extensions..js (internal/modules/cjs/loader.js:665:10)
    at Module.load (internal/modules/cjs/loader.js:566:32)
>
```

Well, I expected that to happen. I did this deliberately so that you never forget that dependencies should be held carefully. Just as you don't push dependencies to a git repository, you don't push dependencies to an image. Instead, you should install them inside the image. That's one of the reasons the image built so quickly because NPM assumed that everything was all right.

Let's change our `Dockerfile` and create a new image, but before that, let's go inside the image and look at it. To do that, let's run the container specifying another command to execute. We also need to specify a few more parameters, namely `-i` and `-t` for an interactive terminal. Let's run a console (we don't have bash in Alpine, so we'll stick with `sh`):

```
                                    1. base (docker)
> docker run -i -t imagini:0.0.1 sh
/opt/app # ls -l
total 120
drwxr-xr-x    2 root     root          4096 Apr 25 17:16 coverage
-rw-r--r--    1 root     root         55543 Apr 25 17:02 example.png
-rw-r--r--    1 root     root          3662 Apr 25 17:02 imagini.js
drwxr-xr-x  135 root     root          4096 Apr 25 17:19 node_modules
-rw-r--r--    1 root     root         38813 Apr 25 17:43 package-lock.json
-rw-r--r--    1 root     root           466 Apr 25 17:02 package.json
-rw-r--r--    1 root     root            49 Apr 25 17:02 settings.json
drwxr-xr-x    3 root     root          4096 Apr 25 17:14 test
/opt/app # _
```

This is what's inside the `/opt/app` folder inside the image. There are a couple of things we don't need to add to, like the test and coverage folders. We can just stick to the microservice, the dependencies file, and the settings file:

```
FROM node:alpine
MAINTAINER Diogo Resende

ADD imagini/imagini.js /opt/app/imagini.js
ADD imagini/package.json /opt/app/package.json
ADD imagini/settings.json /opt/app/settings.json

WORKDIR /opt/app
RUN npm i

CMD [ "node", "/opt/app/imagini" ]
```

The `ADD` instruction can be used with files, not just folders. This will keep our image as slim as possible. Let's run it and assign a new version:

That looks better, despite the error. NPM tried to install `sharp` but our image is so slim it doesn't have Python installed. Actually, it's not only Python that will be missing; you'll find there are no build tools for you to compile anything. If you really need a very slim image, you can this way and see what other dependencies you'll need.

For demonstration purposes, let's switch our base image to the standard version:

```
FROM node
MAINTAINER Diogo Resende

ADD imagini/imagini.js /opt/app/imagini.js
ADD imagini/package.json /opt/app/package.json
ADD imagini/settings.json /opt/app/settings.json
```

```
WORKDIR /opt/app
RUN npm i

CMD [ "node", "/opt/app/imagini" ]
```

See how we change the first line to just node. If you now run the docker build command, Docker will download the standard image and build our image in a single operation:

```
●  ●  ●                          1. base (bash)

> sharp@0.19.1 install /opt/app/node_modules/sharp
> node-gyp rebuild

make: Entering directory '/opt/app/node_modules/sharp/build'
  TOUCH Release/obj.target/libvips-cpp.stamp
  CXX(target) Release/obj.target/sharp/src/common.o
  CXX(target) Release/obj.target/sharp/src/metadata.o
  CXX(target) Release/obj.target/sharp/src/stats.o
  CXX(target) Release/obj.target/sharp/src/operations.o
  CXX(target) Release/obj.target/sharp/src/pipeline.o
  CXX(target) Release/obj.target/sharp/src/sharp.o
  CXX(target) Release/obj.target/sharp/src/utilities.o
  SOLINK_MODULE(target) Release/obj.target/sharp.node
  COPY Release/sharp.node
  TOUCH Release/obj.target/win_copy_dlls.stamp
make: Leaving directory '/opt/app/node_modules/sharp/build'

> sinon@4.5.0 postinstall /opt/app/node_modules/sinon
> node scripts/support-sinon.js

Have some ♥for Sinon? You can support the project via Open Collective:
 > https://opencollective.com/sinon/donate

npm notice created a lockfile as package-lock.json. You should commit this file.
npm WARN imagini@1.0.0 No description
npm WARN imagini@1.0.0 No repository field.

added 143 packages in 47.126s
Removing intermediate container 6671b4f2ce7b
 ---> ec99ff9189bd
Step 8/8 : CMD [ "node", "/opt/app/imagini" ]
 ---> Running in 0ed375501f97
Removing intermediate container 0ed375501f97
 ---> 304c4e53de6d
Successfully built 304c4e53de6d
Successfully tagged imagini:0.0.2
> _
```

As we can see, NPM now compiled our sharp dependency.

> Note that if you only rely on simple dependencies, you can stick with the Alpine version.

Let's try to run our container again:

```
                        1. nazgul-2.local: /Users/dresende (bash)
~ > docker run imagini:0.0.2
/opt/app/imagini.js:14
        if (err) throw err;
                 ^

Error: connect ECONNREFUSED 127.0.0.1:3306
    at TCPConnectWrap.afterConnect [as oncomplete] (net.js:1174:14)
    ---------------------
    at Protocol._enqueue (/opt/app/node_modules/mysql/lib/protocol/Protocol.js:145:48)
    at Protocol.handshake (/opt/app/node_modules/mysql/lib/protocol/Protocol.js:52:23)
    at Connection.connect (/opt/app/node_modules/mysql/lib/Connection.js:130:18)
    at Object.<anonymous> (/opt/app/imagini.js:13:4)
    at Module._compile (internal/modules/cjs/loader.js:654:30)
    at Object.Module._extensions..js (internal/modules/cjs/loader.js:665:10)
    at Module.load (internal/modules/cjs/loader.js:566:32)
    at tryModuleLoad (internal/modules/cjs/loader.js:506:12)
    at Function.Module._load (internal/modules/cjs/loader.js:498:3)
    at Function.Module.runMain (internal/modules/cjs/loader.js:695:10)
~ > _
```

Well, we forgot our settings file inside the container. That settings file points to the MySQL server on the local address, which is actually wrong because the container has its own interface.

To make our image free of passwords and a little bit usable, we need to have our `settings` file outside the image, and every time we want to run the image, we indicate the `settings` file we want to use. This enables you to have different deployments with different settings sharing the same base image.

But, because of how Docker mounts, we need to have the file there already, even if it's empty, to avoid Docker mounting as a directory. So, let's move the `settings` file to the parent folder, and create an empty `settings` file where it was before. You should end up with a structure similar to the following screenshot:

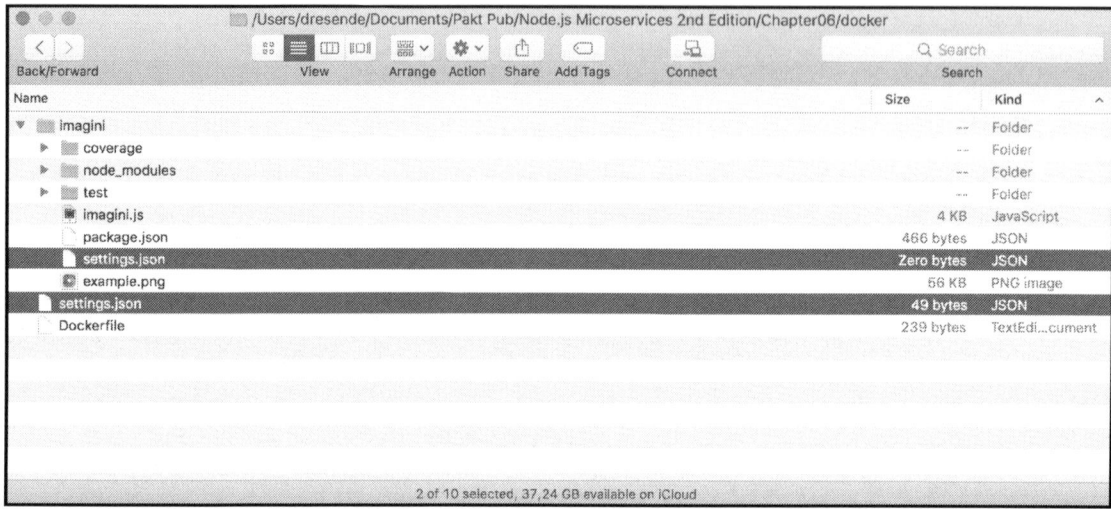

So, we should keep the same image instructions, but now with an empty settings file:

```
FROM node
MAINTAINER Diogo Resende

ADD imagini/imagini.js /opt/app/imagini.js
ADD imagini/package.json /opt/app/package.json
ADD imagini/settings.json /opt/app/settings.json

WORKDIR /opt/app
RUN npm i

CMD [ "node", "/opt/app/imagini" ]
```

Now, let's create a new version:

```
●  ●  ●                           1. base (bash)
  SOLINK_MODULE(target) Release/obj.target/sharp.node
  COPY Release/sharp.node
  TOUCH Release/obj.target/win_copy_dlls.stamp
make: Leaving directory '/opt/app/node_modules/sharp/build'

> sinon@4.5.0 postinstall /opt/app/node_modules/sinon
> node scripts/support-sinon.js

Have some ♥for Sinon? You can support the project via Open Collective:
 > https://opencollective.com/sinon/donate

npm notice created a lockfile as package-lock.json. You should commit this file.
npm WARN imagini@1.0.0 No description
npm WARN imagini@1.0.0 No repository field.

added 143 packages in 24.702s
Removing intermediate container bb501b1ac40f
 ---> bc86b031df5c
Step 7/7 : CMD [ "node", "/opt/app/imagini" ]
 ---> Running in fdc2b732ecd2
Removing intermediate container fdc2b732ecd2
 ---> d8878770bc0b
Successfully built d8878770bc0b
Successfully tagged imagini:0.0.3
> _
```

There are two things you should know about building an image:

- Since we haven't published the image to the public, and we're still testing, we could overwrite our image version and avoid incrementing the revision value. We're doing so just for you to see how the community usually adds new versions.
- If you read the log lines of the build, you'll notice some lines that contain Using cache, which indicate that Docker found that instruction step in a previous build and is using that instead of rebuilding. If we had the ADD instructions after the dependency installation, you would probably see that installation using cache and taking much less time to build.

To run our container with our image and our settings attached, we need to use the -v, which stands for volume, and allows us to mount a folder or a file from our local filesystem to the container filesystem. Assuming we're in a console on our root folder from the preceding screenshot, we should run the following command:

```
docker run -v $(pwd)/settings.json:/opt/app/settings.json imagini:0.0.3
```

Docker enforces us to use full paths, so I just added another bash interpolation to get the current working directory (pwd). Let's run it:

```
● ● ●                          1. base (bash)
> docker run -v $(pwd)/settings.json:/opt/app/settings.json imagini:0.0.3
/opt/app/imagini.js:14
        if (err) throw err;
            ^

Error: connect ECONNREFUSED 127.0.0.1:3306
    at TCPConnectWrap.afterConnect [as oncomplete] (net.js:1174:14)
    --------------------
    at Protocol._enqueue (/opt/app/node_modules/mysql/lib/protocol/Protocol.js:145:48)
    at Protocol.handshake (/opt/app/node_modules/mysql/lib/protocol/Protocol.js:52:23)
    at Connection.connect (/opt/app/node_modules/mysql/lib/Connection.js:130:18)
    at Object.<anonymous> (/opt/app/imagini.js:13:4)
    at Module._compile (internal/modules/cjs/loader.js:654:30)
    at Object.Module._extensions..js (internal/modules/cjs/loader.js:665:10)
    at Module.load (internal/modules/cjs/loader.js:566:32)
    at tryModuleLoad (internal/modules/cjs/loader.js:506:12)
    at Function.Module._load (internal/modules/cjs/loader.js:498:3)
    at Function.Module.runMain (internal/modules/cjs/loader.js:695:10)
> _
```

Well, that's another property of containers; they run isolated and have their own network interface. That interface is attached to a virtual switch created by Docker, which has no outside connectivity unless you say so.

We're using localhost as the database server hostname, which, in this case, points to the container itself. We need to change this to the local address of our system. Since our local system may have a changing IP address, Docker has a special DNS address, which is host.docker.internal, that points to our host.

I'm changing my settings file to something like the following lines. Change it according to your previous configuration:

```
{
    "db": "mysql://root:root@host.docker.internal/imagini"
}
```

If we run it again, we should be able to finally start our container:

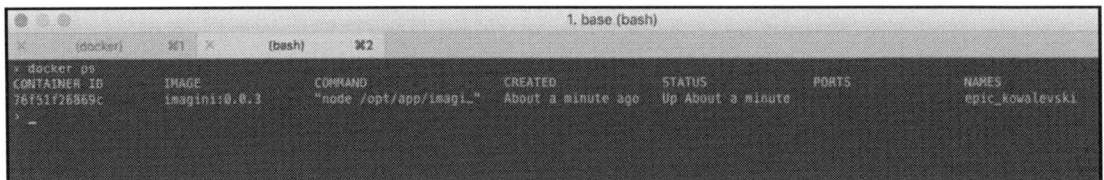

Managing containers

You may notice that the container is running in the foreground, which is not very useful because your console will be blocked until the service ends. Because our service is supposed to never stop, we should try running the service in the background. If you open another console and list the running container processes, you'll see that it's running:

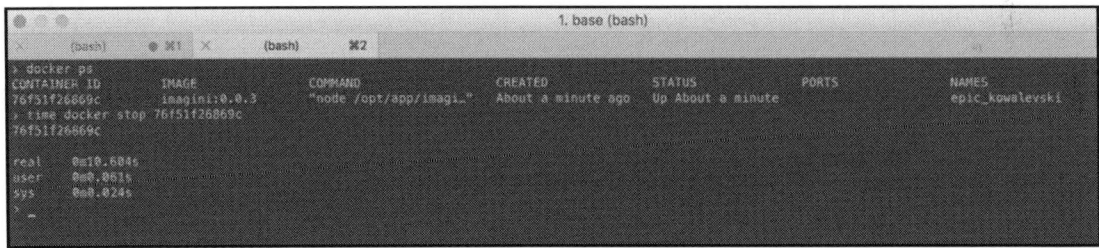

You can see the CONTAINER ID, which, along with the container name, can be used to perform several actions such as restarting and removing containers, as well as the image, and its status and uptime.

Let's stop our container and measure the time to stop it. You'll notice that it won't stop immediately:

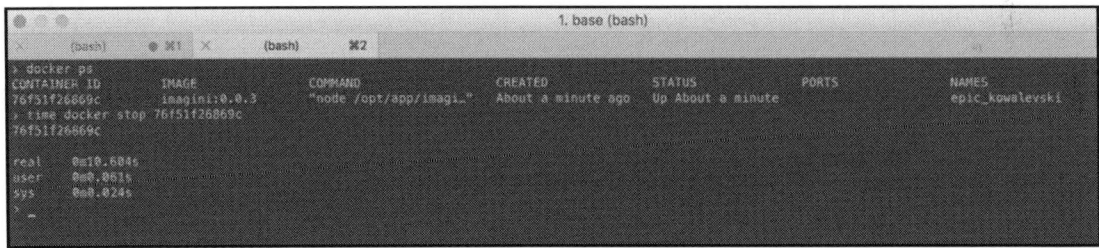

It took *10* seconds, which is a lot if you just made a change and want to restart it. This is because our service is ignoring any environment signals.

When trying to stop a container, Docker sends a SIGTERM signal and waits *10* seconds for it to stop. If it doesn't, Docker then sends a SIGKILL, which will escalate to the kernel and which, in turn, will immediately stop our service and the container will stop.

We can change this behavior and try to stop gracefully. Change our app.listen line to something along the following lines:

```
app.listen(3000, () => {
    console.log("ready");
});

process.on("SIGTERM", () => {
    db.end(() => {
        process.exit(0);
    });
});
```

This adds a ready line when starting the container and tries to close both the database connection and the HTTP server when receiving a SIGTERM. Let's build our image again (because we changed our service), this time as version 0.0.4, and run it again:

```
                                1. base (docker)
 X      (docker)     ⌘1   X       (bash)      ⌘2

   TOUCH Release/obj.target/win_copy_dlls.stamp
make: Leaving directory '/opt/app/node_modules/sharp/build'

> sinon@4.5.0 postinstall /opt/app/node_modules/sinon
> node scripts/support-sinon.js

Have some ♥for Sinon? You can support the project via Open Collective:
 > https://opencollective.com/sinon/donate

npm notice created a lockfile as package-lock.json. You should commit this file.
npm WARN imagini@1.0.0 No description
npm WARN imagini@1.0.0 No repository field.

added 143 packages in 35.654s
Removing intermediate container 624a74adf6f6
 ---> 486fd81d8803
Step 8/8 : CMD [ "node", "/opt/app/imagini" ]
 ---> Running in 24e18c31fcc4
Removing intermediate container 24e18c31fcc4
 ---> 86e9f7e5b606
Successfully built 86e9f7e5b606
Successfully tagged imagini:0.0.4
> docker run -v $(pwd)/settings.json:/opt/app/settings.json imagini:0.0.4
ready
```

Head to the other console and try to stop the container again:

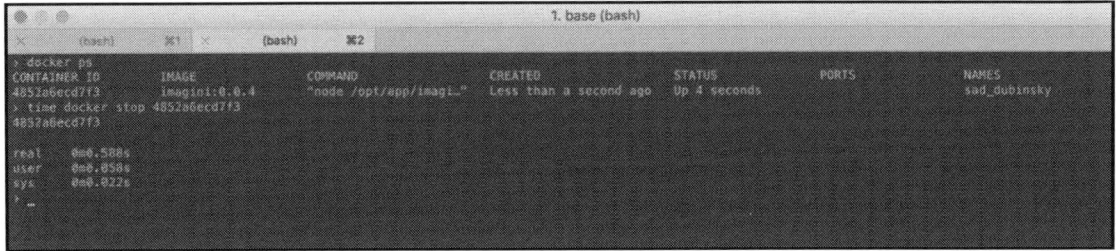

That was way faster. It could be even faster, but it's better to stop gracefully. We're just stopping the database connection, but you could also stop Express from accepting more connections and then wait some seconds while it handles the active connections before closing gracefully.

We can now continue to improve on our deployment by changing our container to run in the background instead of just blocking our console. This way, we don't need two consoles to deploy and manage our container. To run this in the background, we use the -d options, which enables detached mode.

Our updated command is now:

```
docker run -d -v $(pwd)/settings.json:/opt/app/settings.json imagini:0.0.4
```

If you try it out, Docker will inform you of the full CONTAINER ID and turn you back to the console:

If you check the running containers, you'll see our container, with the short ID (which corresponds to the first *12* characters) and some more information. Something that is actually important and is empty is the PORTS column, which indicates the container ports that are linked to ports on our host.

That column being empty means you have no access to the container other than through Docker itself, which is actually useless. We can't access our HTTP interface.

We need to change our image again and expose a port. To do that, we must use the EXPOSE instruction and pass the port we want to expose. Our service listens on port 3000, so we need to expose it:

```
FROM node
MAINTAINER Diogo Resende

ADD imagini/imagini.js /opt/app/imagini.js
ADD imagini/package.json /opt/app/package.json
ADD imagini/settings.json /opt/app/settings.json

WORKDIR /opt/app
RUN npm i

EXPOSE 3000

CMD [ "node", "/opt/app/imagini" ]
```

You can now build the image, but before using our new version, we need to change our run command. Just because we're exposing a port does not mean the person using our image wants those ports exposed. We need to specify what host ports we want to connect to the container ports. To accomplish that, we're going to use −p, which allows us to configure incoming ports. The syntax is similar to the previous −v but for ports:

```
docker run −d −p 80:3000 −v $(pwd)/settings.json:/opt/app/settings.json
imagini:0.0.5
```

In this case, we're exposing local port 80 to port 3000 of the container:

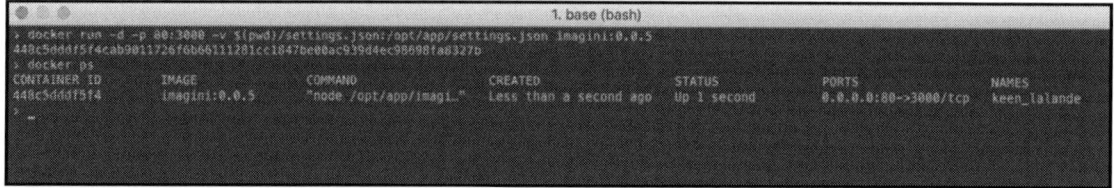

You can see that the container is running and that the address 0.0.0.0:80 (all our addresses at port 80) point to the container port 3000. We should be able to try it out and see if it's running correctly. Open a web browser and point it to the stats path:

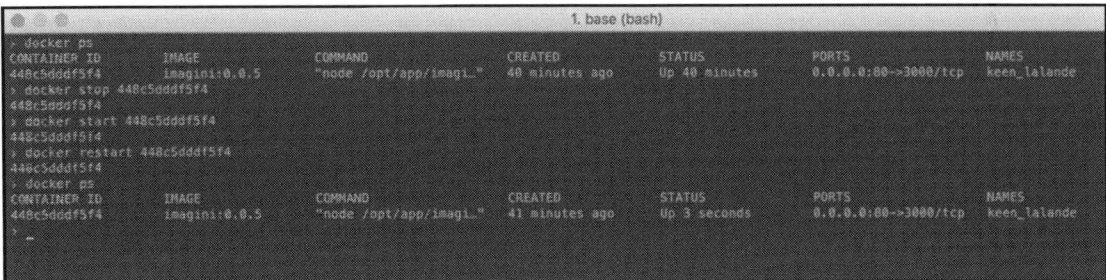

```
{
    "total": 5,
    "size": 277715,
    "last_used": "2018-04-13T20:30:53.000Z",
    "uptime": 259.215
}
```

We can now manage our container in a similar fashion to the service management on the current operative systems. You can start, stop, and restart it:

```
> docker ps
CONTAINER ID     IMAGE            COMMAND                CREATED          STATUS           PORTS                    NAMES
448c5dddf5f4     imagini:0.0.5    "node /opt/app/imagi…" 40 minutes ago   Up 40 minutes    0.0.0.0:80->3000/tcp     keen_lalande
> docker stop 448c5dddf5f4
448c5dddf5f4
> docker start 448c5dddf5f4
448c5dddf5f4
> docker restart 448c5dddf5f4
448c5dddf5f4
> docker ps
CONTAINER ID     IMAGE            COMMAND                CREATED          STATUS           PORTS                    NAMES
448c5dddf5f4     imagini:0.0.5    "node /opt/app/imagi…" 41 minutes ago   Up 3 seconds     0.0.0.0:80->3000/tcp     keen_lalande
> _
```

Every time you change one or more container's states, Docker returns the container IDs that have changed state. This allows you to, for example, to script actions and pipe the output of one command to the next.

Cleaning containers

Containers, when stopped, are not removed by default. Let's stop our container and list the currently running containers:

```
> docker ps
CONTAINER ID     IMAGE            COMMAND                CREATED          STATUS           PORTS                    NAMES
448c5dddf5f4     imagini:0.0.5    "node /opt/app/imagi…" About an hour ago Up 5 minutes    0.0.0.0:80->3000/tcp     keen_lalande
> docker stop 448c5dddf5f4
448c5dddf5f4
> docker ps
CONTAINER ID     IMAGE            COMMAND                CREATED          STATUS           PORTS          NAMES
> _
```

Nothing running now. So, where are they? Well, the container is stopped and, while it's not using your processor and memory right now, it's using space. And it's not just that container, either; it's all the containers we ran before.

To see all containers, use the `docker ps -a` command:

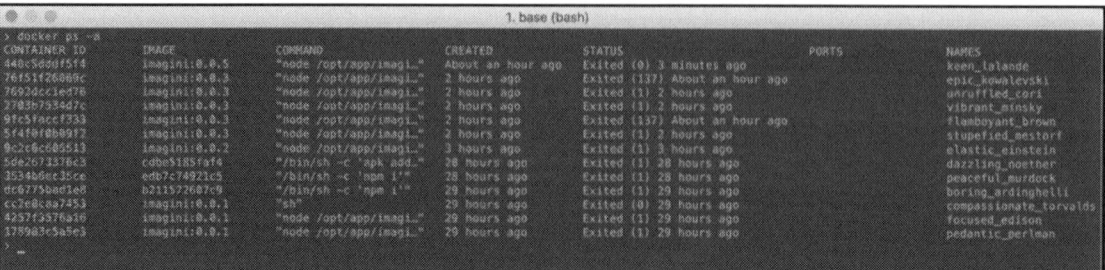

Wow, that's a lot of containers. We can see that we have containers for practically all the images we built, and that means the images are also available and using our disk space:

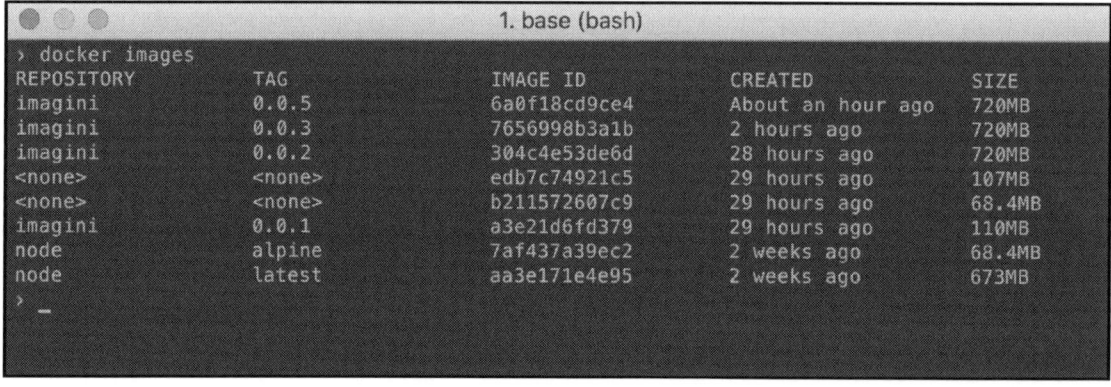

In the case of images, we can see the size they are occupying. Since we don't need them any more, as they were non-functioning experiences, we can remove them. To do that, we need to use the `rmi` command and pass the image IDs, or the name and version (the TAG column), as parameters.

But before removing the images, we need to remove the containers, or Docker will deny removing them as they're being used. As a dirty workaround, we can use a useful parameter from `docker ps`, which returns only the container IDs and passes those to the remove command. Docker won't remove any running containers, so it's safe to run.

Start our latest container (`docker start`) and then list the containers (`docker ps`):

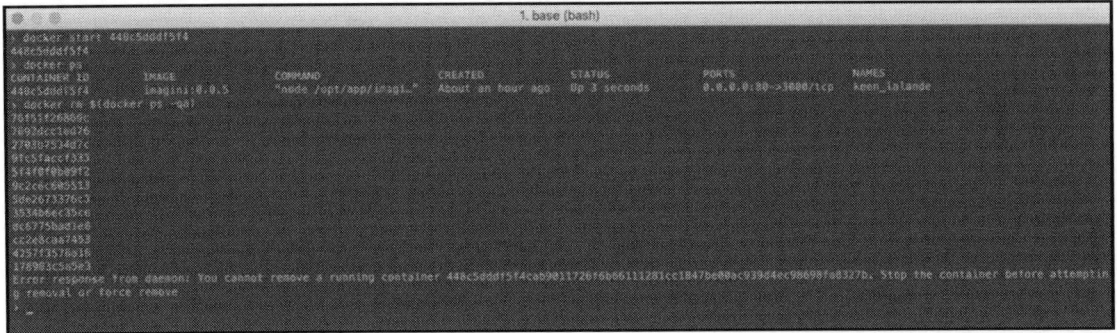

As described earlier, Docker will indicate each of the container IDs as it changes state (in this case, it removes them). The final error is our running container, which, as I explained earlier, Docker won't allow to be removed as it's running.

We can now do the exact same thing with the images. Those quickly occupy a lot of space and, when developing, it's easy to make changes to images and forget about non-functional images that we left behind:

```
                                            1. base (bash)
> docker rmi $(docker images -q)
Untagged: imagini:0.0.3
Deleted: sha256:7656998b3a1bfa82f2b69c8476be73c62a56e59e7207fc96f14098d36ced8876
Deleted: sha256:c1ec0df9147e6d194e1187d04088734b8ff690ebb2a6fe36eba7b6fe73e299f7
Deleted: sha256:3b4bde5dc6df574258f66c6a9d1c8a68aefd7c3e2c22b538fd5de4415bbb7e4e
Deleted: sha256:9ee05c9ef166a388cc4d7a4d9a4ee931ad49bb95d270ba45efa26e3d05622e98
Deleted: sha256:3781e1eaaaf2e9876c8d64ba400eaa87a86eae7f0e3056cc496d530f47747536
Deleted: sha256:7fa40a3ef4ad4eefa9d88b7f264a4d9baf1441d60518b3f8621e74286cc08a1b
Untagged: imagini:0.0.2
Deleted: sha256:3d4c4e53de6d35046d713cac1315b884e29ae3219aaeaed0f30109f6e7a35dce
Deleted: sha256:ec99ff9189bd57bbf989294526a6cbcddbe94fdb5833260b4852fb120f6e4a92
Deleted: sha256:7239b1f73f308858618ceb88d020944e7c970576c9c0bd513a9dc862b83fc0fe
Deleted: sha256:a6e1d10270a146d561ecdf53783c1407d00cf276b52e8c240285c2ddd64049c5
Deleted: sha256:c9e587d1db0197113b160d91e694286705343c6b9ecbb29d8922db8410ce3456
Deleted: sha256:1713f0f9b632e1a83a7ca855e174a22c274af9b3aa34ce71ebde372f1890da8f
Deleted: sha256:f42c28b46424ca7593c41b8d59a4bd78ee788a61a357e762213ce512332c2c0
Deleted: sha256:4819a1fe7f1ab618a7ba13da5d7b1107d008c75b419e8517310cf7433b2bd45d
Deleted: sha256:996b81fae81f3ea3b2a5d7ddab52a42e291cf2a69c46dd89ca1bcdf861ea6007
Deleted: sha256:c8558e17b75791658262020268e5c369674f8ab29f8cc44d56f0if0faaf834789a
Deleted: sha256:edb7c74921c5500a613277f5422c537c8f33f5383f7e1d42c37b3b0c422bad08
Deleted: sha256:91fb995cc465b32ccb85690a6819b104eed2dade40811d1e15bfa8fe9a80f135
Deleted: sha256:0b7a4d4c5b95e7b66b85a417d86376ad2275e50007bf0812fe821d975071268b
Deleted: sha256:6afd08765d3d4903d9846258b63e166ae043859ad0d6f96a195f86eceb949c1
Deleted: sha256:a1dd125976f9434e42c9a9164ab1b13dc74913fdb6b212863d20ff039ba78c27
Deleted: sha256:9ba68db9fbba4f811cf3f111e4353b9863973a482d793130750b8869aa9dd1e6
Deleted: sha256:cbd5c29a4453427941fc3c1502b1d0f562bce7f46ec0ddee44e4e87dba5c13d9
Deleted: sha256:0db53cbbeb1fb2320ebb4887a26ed7abce432b541ea5fe00bc9d28c0fd71036c8
Deleted: sha256:5c4e1ebc50b64379efb37e6e59e4564fe50125143ada86ab07177cf82dff27fe
Deleted: sha256:b211572607c9e2da241de8d9ccb2838ebc981f1518caba14a8263e90b8f1c1c0
Deleted: sha256:9fbe4cd1baca52c782dd93ebf75a4697e552b2fa8ad8e66d8d9d4ac48ae9c993
Deleted: sha256:3c9688faa361eaf51ca93aeldc2a3d0e21328c174c6ff023b42e48a0e4a29148
Deleted: sha256:10b36c1eb29eafff45410c546543d380adad3e6098623d325ed267f2263a1e84
Deleted: sha256:2ed142e00533dc1dd93f49f31c39c4537103102966c8461620b6b57e38d6a678
Deleted: sha256:11d933ee38b8cedf88c9934575254961dc2153b5b5a6fbc8f0e8f79c25d2ac5f
Deleted: sha256:cab1931964429883a748c0a64a331bce472a7db0a7382c8ecfb802243f744ca8
Untagged: imagini:0.0.1
Deleted: sha256:a3e21d6fd3796cf5dc475cf6a7c938c023ebd893f72f504aad85adb6370a9cafa
Deleted: sha256:0b50046161f3f4ba12ab10fb24c75f953454dad9756e38d9501f8070efbcf7e5
Deleted: sha256:9a41633e305aad6f2702a00458e5b30abe8ce5ee0bd42b92bd095591262ad709
Deleted: sha256:e39bdhfaf5ae5b9d8ff0b031fb0810046f11efe2e5818e728e96e27ae3f5698b
Deleted: sha256:9c062473535ae2675492394e5e9f810d9e313dc926e140ee9b299df709900fdd
Deleted: sha256:6c7374ffe0cc1521e56a0e2dc93bb4955a703e51c8881239bd0ce7d5f97993c9
Deleted: sha256:cdbe5185faf433675e240b57b476f67f56236df7fd6ae5abbdbdfde17583bde2
Untagged: node:alpine
Untagged: node@sha256:5149aec8f508d48990e6230cdc8e6832cba192088b442c8ef7e23df3c6892cd3
Deleted: sha256:7af437a39ec2ef08f9b5cd9bb766402b31e702544835de18d9263cea18bc7539
Deleted: sha256:69fb43723ced8f16e32d5b665d78f039b09917546c6a8f9ad00788ffc5e62adc
Deleted: sha256:59e899e684afbc3de017cd57e5f869a493ef1e78b7b1a1bd1bdaa5b94eb64d0a
Deleted: sha256:9dfa40a0da3b1a8a7c34abc596d81ede2dba4ecd5c0a7211086d6685da1ce6ef
Error response from daemon: conflict: unable to delete 6a0f18cd9ce4 (cannot be forced) - image is being used by running container 448c5ddd5f4
Error response from daemon: conflict: unable to delete aa3e171e4e95 (cannot be forced) - image has dependent child images
>
```

The last two errors are expected. First, one of the images is from our running container. Second, the other image is the base image of our image.

You may also notice that there are way more lines than images from the previous list. They're not images; they're the layers of each image (remember the cached steps when building?). Docker stores images in layers, which means that a similar image may have layers in common, and, in turn, some disk space may be saved.

You should now have something like this:

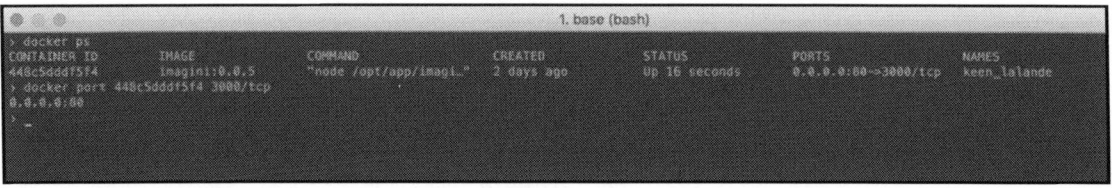

```
> docker images
REPOSITORY          TAG             IMAGE ID        CREATED             SIZE
imagini             0.0.5           6a0f18cd9ce4    About an hour ago   720MB
node                latest          aa3e171e4e95    2 weeks ago         673MB
>
```

That looks much better; no more garbage from our previous development iterations. We can now move on and focus on another dependency of our service that we still rely on and is not on a container yet.

Deploying MySQL

We now have our service running inside a container, with all its dependencies properly defined and installed inside. But we still need a database server and we're still relying on MySQL, which is on our host.

A single container was not meant to run many services at once. Similar to microservices, a container should do only one job. But containers can communicate with the outside, so this means they can communicate with each other.

We can deploy an additional container to run our database server. There are official MySQL container images, so it's as easy as a simple command to start running a database. But first, we need to take care of two things:

- The database server needs to store the database content on the host, or we'll lose the data when we remove our deployment
- Our initial container needs to know where the database server is, and this changes dynamically on each deploy, so we need to have a way of knowing this

Docker has a way of knowing what host port was associated to a container port. This is by using Docker port, and its syntax is simple; you indicate the container to get all port assignments or you indicate a specific port to get only that one:

```
> docker ps
CONTAINER ID    IMAGE           COMMAND                 CREATED     STATUS          PORTS                       NAMES
448c5dddf5f4    imagini:0.0.5   "node /opt/app/imagi…"  2 days ago  Up 16 seconds   0.0.0.0:80->3000/tcp        keen_lalande
> docker port 448c5dddf5f4 3000/tcp
0.0.0.0:80
>
```

In the case of our original container, we know that we are associated with port 80, and that's what the command indicates. In a production environment, you'll have several containers competing for the same ports. Docker has networks to help us isolate container groups easily and allow us to create custom networks of containers.

Let's just dive in and create a network for our service using `docker network`:

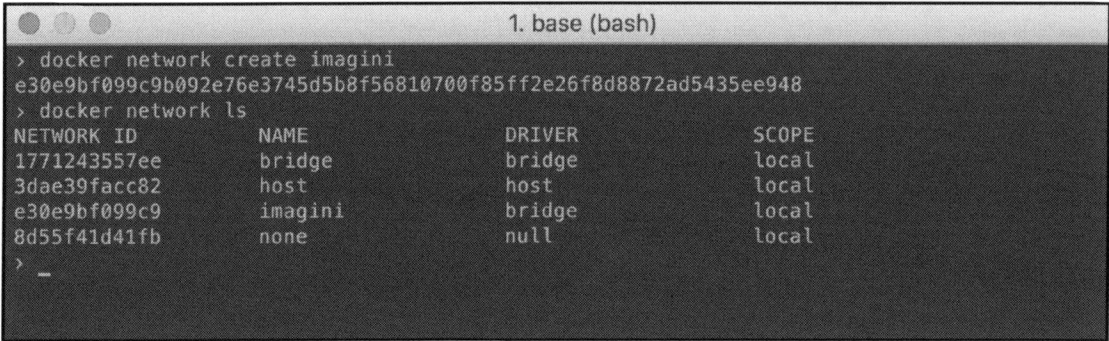

That's it. We have a network named imagini with the ID returned by the command. We can get a list of current Docker networks with the given command:

```
●  ○  ●                           1. base (bash)
> docker network create imagini
e30e9bf099c9b092e76e3745d5b8f56810700f85ff2e26f8d8872ad5435ee948
> docker network ls
NETWORK ID          NAME                DRIVER              SCOPE
1771243557ee        bridge              bridge              local
3dae39facc82        host                host                local
e30e9bf099c9        imagini             bridge              local
8d55f41d41fb        none                null                local
>  _
```

There are now four networks, one of which is the one we created. The other three are:

- **Bridge**: The default one for new containers
- **Host**: If you want to attach a container directly to the host network
- **None**: If you don't want a container to have a network at all

Now, let's remove our current deployment and make a few changes. First, let's remove and stop the container:

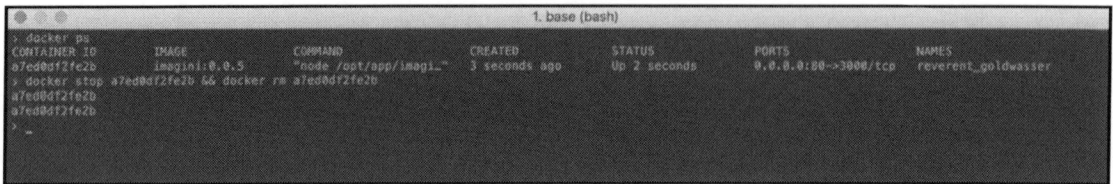

Second, let's deploy our new database server container on our new network. We'll use the official container image. We'll also create a `mysql` folder to store the database and anything else the server needs to operate between deployments without losing information.

I'll also introduce another option from Docker, which enables us to name a container. You might have noticed some funny names when you previously listed containers. We can avoid those random names and use our own:

```
1. base (bash)
> docker run \
> --name imagini-database \
> --network imagini \
> -v $(pwd)/mysql:/var/lib/mysql \
> -e MYSQL_DATABASE=imagini \
> -e MYSQL_ROOT_PASSWORD=secret \
> -d \
> mysql:5.7
Unable to find image 'mysql:5.7' locally
5.7: Pulling from library/mysql
2a72cbf407d6: Pull complete
38680a9b47a8: Pull complete
4c732aa0eb1b: Pull complete
c5317a34eddd: Pull complete
f92be680366c: Pull complete
e8ecd8bec5ab: Pull complete
2a650284a6a8: Pull complete
1c55ce706eb7: Pull complete
d19001513ac1: Pull complete
a338105fc636: Pull complete
9420aceee4b: Pull complete
Digest: sha256:e7b486e5548a3f1ef90c6571a44a0e9371a449a4b45e6f7f0e765842c10560f6
Status: Downloaded newer image for mysql:5.7
284b3e9f88f771a1a37d7a5ba791a99553af68ce9f3c670afec485d70ecd2cd1
> docker ps
CONTAINER ID    IMAGE       COMMAND              CREATED              STATUS       PORTS       NAMES
284b3e9f88f7    mysql:5.7   "docker-entrypoint.s…"   Less than a second ago   Up 2 seconds   3306/tcp    imagini-database
>
```

Docker automatically downloaded the latest MySQL version. We now have a database server called imagini-database running on our imagini network. Notice we didn't assign any of its ports to the host because we actually don't need to access it outside our custom network.

You can also see that I defined the database to be created initially, as well as the root password. We're specifying image `mysql:5.7`, which points to the latest revision of MySQL version 5.7.

> Always remember to use specific versions with containers. Never use the latest version as this may change between development and production, and you need to be certain of the versions you're running.

This is specific to this image and you can read more about it on the official Docker Hub page. We can confirm that the server is up and running using our local folder by just looking at its content:

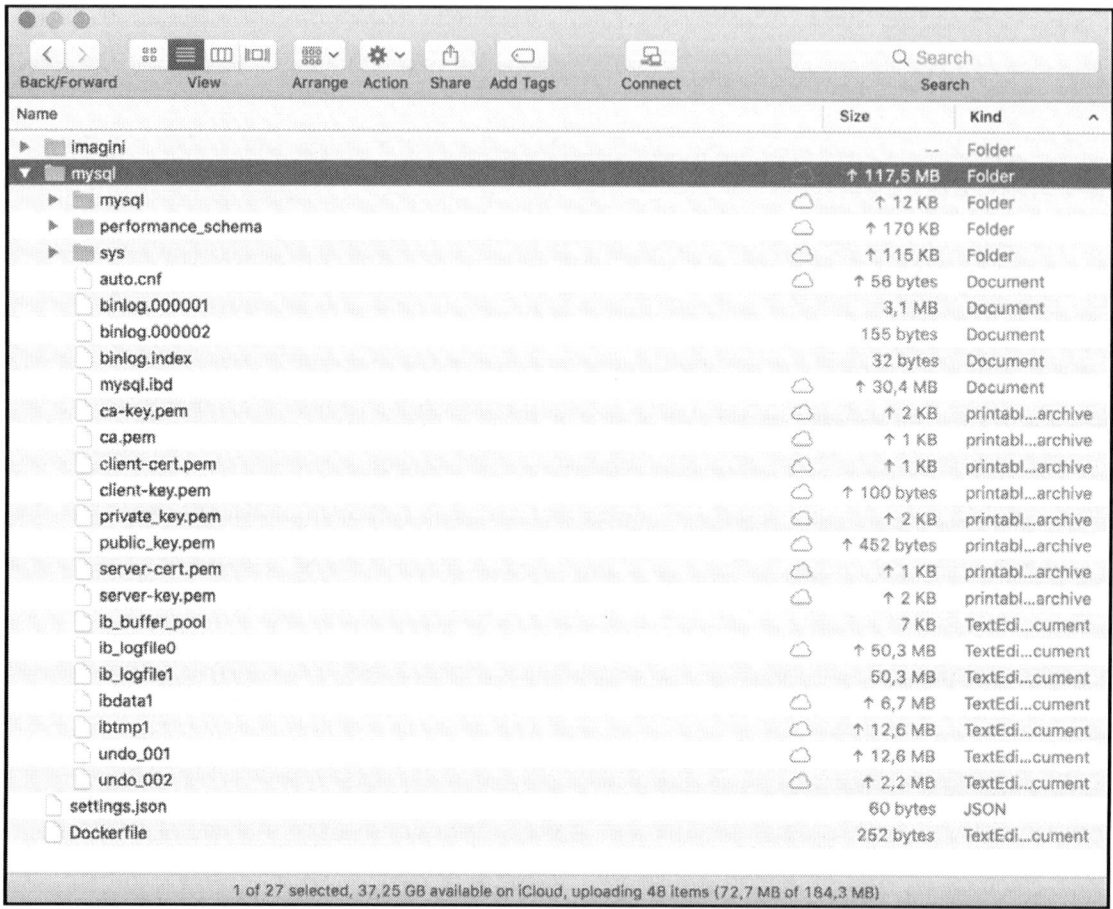

Before starting our main service container, we need to make just a few more changes. First, we need to change the `settings` file to point the configuration to our new database location.

One advantage of using a proper name for a container is that you can use that name just like it was a DNS name. We can confirm that our database server is reachable from another container we created on the same network.

Let's create a container to test this:

```
1. base (bash)
> docker ps
CONTAINER ID    IMAGE         COMMAND                  CREATED         STATUS          PORTS      NAMES
73ab6a588196    mysql         "docker-entrypoint.s…"   19 minutes ago  Up 19 minutes   3306/tcp   imagini-database
> docker run --rm -t -i --network imagini node:latest bash
root@3af1d1cbebd1:/# ping imagini-database -c 5
PING imagini-database (172.18.0.2): 56 data bytes
64 bytes from 172.18.0.2: icmp_seq=0 ttl=64 time=0.093 ms
64 bytes from 172.18.0.2: icmp_seq=1 ttl=64 time=0.132 ms
64 bytes from 172.18.0.2: icmp_seq=2 ttl=64 time=0.133 ms
64 bytes from 172.18.0.2: icmp_seq=3 ttl=64 time=0.128 ms
64 bytes from 172.18.0.2: icmp_seq=4 ttl=64 time=0.132 ms
--- imagini-database ping statistics ---
5 packets transmitted, 5 packets received, 0% packet loss
round-trip min/avg/max/stddev = 0.093/0.124/0.133/0.000 ms
root@3af1d1cbebd1:/# exit
> ▁
```

We just used an image that's already available and started the container with a bash console. We tried to ping our database server and it works. We then exited the container. Because we used the --rm command, the container is removed after the first stop.

Now, let's remove the settings file to point to the new location and to also change the root password:

```
{
    "db": "mysql://root:secret@imagini-database/imagini"
}
```

We can now deploy our container again. We'll just give this container a name, too:

```
1. base (bash)
> docker run \
>  --name imagini-service \
>  --network imagini \
>  -p 80:3000 \
>  -d \
>  -v $(pwd)/settings.json:/opt/app/settings.json \
>  imagini:0.0.5
1ae78ec2e4bbd6ca6e763a3e5241f55898e9afe2a4aebf3a97ded9fd9dd31644
> docker ps
CONTAINER ID    IMAGE           COMMAND                  CREATED              STATUS            PORTS                  NAMES
1ae78ec2e4bb    imagini:0.0.5   "node /opt/app/imagi…"   Less than a second ago  Up 3 seconds      0.0.0.0:80->3000/tcp   imagini-service
284b3e9f8877    mysql:5.7       "docker-entrypoint.s…"   About a minute ago   Up About a minute 3306/tcp              imagini-database
> ▁
```

We can see that our service is running correctly, with connections to the new database server by just hitting the stats address and seeing that there are no images there, contrary to our previous version that we used to test this:

```
{
    "total": 0,
    "size": null,
    "last_used": null,
    "uptime": 4.682
}
```

Using Docker Compose

Wouldn't it be great if we could define all the containers we need for our service to work in a simple interface? Welcome to Docker Compose. This is an orchestration tool that enables us to do what we just did in a simpler way and, most importantly, in a distributed way.

We can define how our containers interact with each other and what they need in a simple file structure, and then we can transfer that to another host and just run Docker Compose, where it will deploy it all for us.

Docker Compose uses a YAML file, which is a human-readable data serialization language. It's easier to read and understand and at the same time, allows us to make complex configurations.

Let's migrate our two containers to this layout. The only step we need right now is to create a file called `docker-compose.yml`. Inside, we define our two containers, the network, the ports, and the volumes. Here's an example:

```yaml
version: "3"
networks:
    imagini:
services:
    database:
        image: mysql:5.7
        networks:
```

```
    - imagini
    volumes:
    - ${PWD}/mysql:/var/lib/mysql
    environment:
        MYSQL_DATABASE: imagini
        MYSQL_ROOT_PASSWORD: secret
service:
    image: imagini:0.0.5
    networks:
    - imagini
    volumes:
    - ${PWD}/settings.json:/opt/app/settings.json
    ports:
    - "80:3000"
    restart: on-failure
```

Let's do this step by step:

```
version: "3"
```

First, we indicate that we're defining our services in Docker Compose version 3 syntax and features:

```
services:
    database:
        image: mysql:5.7
        networks:
        - imagini
        volumes:
        - ${PWD}/mysql:/var/lib/mysql
        environment:
            MYSQL_DATABASE: imagini
            MYSQL_ROOT_PASSWORD: secret
```

Then, we define our database using image `mysql:5.7`, attach it to the `imagini` network, and then use the host `mysql` folder to store the database and define the two environment variables. This is exactly what we did in the previous command:

```
service:
    image: imagini:0.0.5
    networks:
    - imagini
    volumes:
    - ${PWD}/settings.json:/opt/app/settings.json
    ports:
    - "80:3000"
    restart: on-failure
```

Finally, we do the same for our service, indicating the name, the `imagini:0.0.5` image, the network, the local `settings` file, and the port assignment. But there's something more, which is very important, and this is the restart policy. Because our database service does not load instantly, our service will most probably fail at first and stop. Docker will then lift it up again and then the database server will be ready, and everything will be up and running.

As we're composing a Docker Compose project, we can avoid using `imagini` on the service names, and so we need to once again change our `settings` file to something like this:

```
{
    "db": "mysql://root:secret@database/imagini"
}
```

We can now try it out by running `docker-compose up`. This will deploy our containers under the `imagini` project, which is the folder name:

This will start the containers, but you'll notice that they didn't start detached. To do that, hit *Ctrl* + *C* to stop the containers:

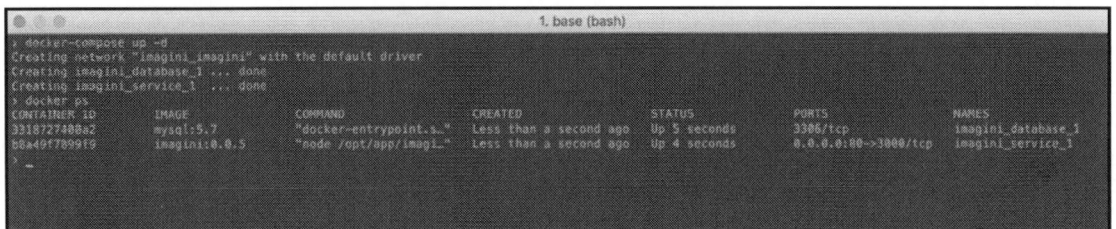

Now, let's run this again properly by using the −d parameter:

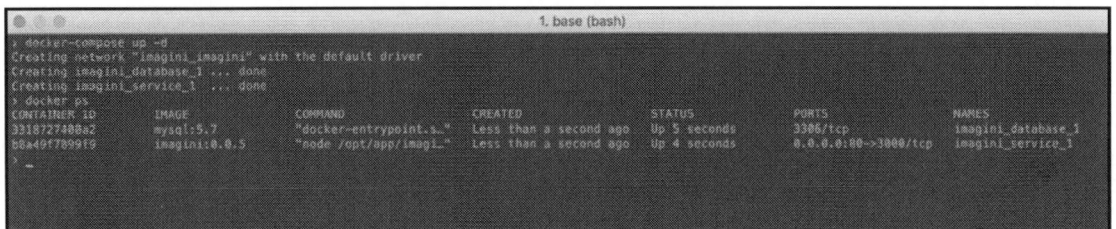

Great! We can start our service with everything it needs in a single command. You could just share this folder with a co-worker and he or she could have the service up and running in a matter of seconds.

Mastering Docker Compose

Now that we have our services up and running, we need some more information to manage these services together, and more specifically, to control and monitor its state.

To look at a specific service, you just need its original name. In our case, there's only the service and database to choose from. Let's look at our service:

```
●  ●  ●                                1. base (bash)
> docker-compose logs service
Attaching to imagini_service_1
service_1  |  /opt/app/imagini.js:14
service_1  |      if (err) throw err;
service_1  |      ^
service_1  |
service_1  |  Error: connect ECONNREFUSED 172.19.0.3:3306
service_1  |      at TCPConnectWrap.afterConnect [as oncomplete] (net.js:1174:14)
service_1  |      ---------------------
service_1  |      at Protocol._enqueue (/opt/app/node_modules/mysql/lib/protocol/Protocol.js:145:48)
service_1  |      at Protocol.handshake (/opt/app/node_modules/mysql/lib/protocol/Protocol.js:52:23)
service_1  |      at Connection.connect (/opt/app/node_modules/mysql/lib/Connection.js:130:18)
service_1  |      at Object.<anonymous> (/opt/app/imagini.js:13:4)
service_1  |      at Module._compile (internal/modules/cjs/loader.js:654:30)
service_1  |      at Object.Module._extensions..js (internal/modules/cjs/loader.js:665:10)
service_1  |      at Module.load (internal/modules/cjs/loader.js:566:32)
service_1  |      at tryModuleLoad (internal/modules/cjs/loader.js:506:12)
service_1  |      at Function.Module._load (internal/modules/cjs/loader.js:498:3)
service_1  |      at Function.Module.runMain (internal/modules/cjs/loader.js:695:10)
service_1  |  ready
> _
```

As I told you previously, the service will probably fail at first and then Docker will restart it before it finally becomes ready. We can see that in this log. If you want to see the logs of all of the services mixed together by date, you can just omit the service name.

Another important command to memorize is used to list the services that are running. This is the same as for Docker, but it only lists the ones from our configuration:

```
● ● ●                                                    1. base (bash)
> docker-compose ps
      Name                    Command           State         Ports
---------------------------------------------------------------------------
imagini_database_1    docker-entrypoint.sh mysqld   Up      3306/tcp
imagini_service_1     node /opt/app/imagini         Up      0.0.0.0:80->3000/tcp
> _
```

Finally, to stop and remove everything from our deployment, we can run `docker-compose` down. This will first stop the containers and then remove them completely. This ensures that we don't leave any garbage behind:

```
● ● ●                                                    1. base (bash)
> docker-compose ps
      Name                    Command           State         Ports
---------------------------------------------------------------------------
imagini_database_1    docker-entrypoint.sh mysqld   Up      3306/tcp
imagini_service_1     node /opt/app/imagini         Up      0.0.0.0:80->3000/tcp
> docker-compose down
Stopping imagini_database_1 ... done
Stopping imagini_service_1  ... done
Removing imagini_database_1 ... done
Removing imagini_service_1  ... done
Removing network imagini_imagini
> _
```

Summary

We now have a tool to deploy our service in a consistent way across hosts. We're now able to orchestrate other services, like we did with the database server, in order to have as many dependencies as possible in a controllable state. This ensures that the transition from development to deployment is as smooth as possible.

Let's follow this path and see what else Docker and other tools can do to help us deploy our service. In the following chapter, we'll see how we can take advantage of Docker tools to scale our service by creating replicas. We will see how to distribute our service parts and monitor its state.

9
Scaling, Sharding, and Replicating

We're now able to deploy our microservice almost anywhere with minimal effort. Let's take a look at how we can leverage this and scale our microservice to handle an intensive usage environment.

Before starting, let's see what each of the topics covered in this chapter mean. We'll start from the end. Replicating is the easiest one, and it means to replicate, or copy, your service. Basically, replicating a microservice means it is running multiple instances at the same time, usually on different locations.

Sharding is similar, but with a different purpose. When replicating, each replica can do the full service job. When sharing, each shard can do only part of the service and you need all shards to have your service online. This is a common practice on very large database servers.

Scaling is a common meaning to both replicating and sharding, as both of them allow you to scale your service. Scaling is the process of growing your microservice to handle more load or failure events.

Being able to deploy consistently is important. This gives you better confidence when developing and testing because you have a consistent base layout for your service to run on. Not just that, it also allows you to deploy to multiple locations faster.

This enables you to replicate your service across multiple locations. Replicating a microservice not only allows you to develop in parallel, enabling every developer to have an instance running on its own computer, but it also gives you several advantages in a production environment, such as:

- **Distribution**: When your service is spread across geographic locations, being closer to every customer, reducing latency from every location
- **Fault tolerance**: When your service has an outage or usage peak on specific instances and you're able to route customers to instances being less used
- **Zero downtime**: When your service has enough replicas that even if a substantial part of your infrastructure is affected by an external incident, your service is still generally available

Distributing your service geographically puts it near your customers. Usually, you want to distribute it in different continents to avoid inter-continental latency. If your service is broadly used, you may need to have several instances per continent, perhaps one in every country.

Fault tolerance and zero downtime are related to each other. Being able to operate when instances of your service are faulty gives users the perception of no downtime. This is also very important when you want to make an upgrade to your service without bringing all the instances down. You may phase-in each instance to upgrade while routing your customers to other instances, keeping your global service online in a virtual sense.

In this chapter, we'll see how we can use Docker tools to replicate our service using Swarm. Later on, we'll see how easy it is to migrate our microservice to Kubernetes locally.

Scaling your network

Scaling a service by itself is not sufficient. Just because you create instances of your service doesn't mean they'll just work together. There are two important steps to enable a service scale:

- Making instances work together
- Making instances reachable

Instances don't need to communicate with each other, but an instance must be able to work without interfering with the others. An instance should be able to handle a request from a client that was previously served by another instance. In our case, this means an instance must be able to manipulate an image that was uploaded by another instance. This ensures that if an instance goes offline, others can take over its clients.

Instances need to be reachable, which means you need to be able to point your customers to the nearest instances that are live and operating normally. This means you need to be able to monitor your instances and distribute your customers to the online instances.

Services are usually reachable by a DNS address. You need to be able to control address name resolution, preferably by geography, to point your customers to the best instances. You can point directly to instances or have proxies monitor a couple of nearby instances and proxy the traffic based on policies.

There are many different kinds of policies. For example, if the proxy is able to monitor how busy an instance is, it can direct new requests to the less busier instances. Or, it can just distribute requests using a round-robin approach.

There's also another common policy that routes traffic according to the IP address. For example, if you have three instances, you use the remainder of the remainder of the devision of the IP address (as a 4-byte integer) by three to choose the instance (possible values would be *0*, *1*, and *2*).

Replicating our microservice

Picking up from the previous chapter, we ended with a Docker Compose configuration that starts our two containers, one with our microservice and the other with the database server that stores our data:

```
                                              1. nazgul-2.local: /Users/dresende/imagini (bash)
~/imagini > docker-compose ps
        Name                   Command            State         Ports
-------------------------------------------------------------------------------------
imagini_database_1    docker-entrypoint.sh mysqld   Up     3306/tcp
imagini_service_1     node /opt/app/imagini         Up     0.0.0.0:80->3000/tcp
~/imagini > _
```

You may have noticed when deploying with Docker Compose that our two containers have a _1 suffix on the name. This is because Docker Compose supports replicating our instance using Docker swarm.

Docker swarm is another component of the Docker engine that enables you to create a cluster of hosts to run your microservice instances while orchestrating all of this using a simple tool from any of the hosts in your cluster.

Swarm is the name Docker uses to reference a cluster of nodes. Let's create a new Swarm using our host as the manager of the swarm. Since I'm using Docker for Mac, I need to create another Docker virtual machine to be able to simulate a couple of hosts. If you're using a Linux machine, you can just test this with two different hosts.

If you're using macOS like me, follow these steps. We'll use Docker machine to create two virtual machines to run as Docker hosts. First, let's see what machines we have created by typing:

```
docker-machine ls
```

You should see an output as follows:

```
1. nazgul-2.local: /Users/dresende/imagini (bash)
~/imagini > docker-machine ls
NAME    ACTIVE   DRIVER   STATE   URL   SWARM   DOCKER   ERRORS
~/imagini >
```

No machines. Let's create a manager node. To do that, run:

```
docker-machine create manager
```

Docker will create the new machine, assign a new IP address, and prepare the Docker engine inside the machine:

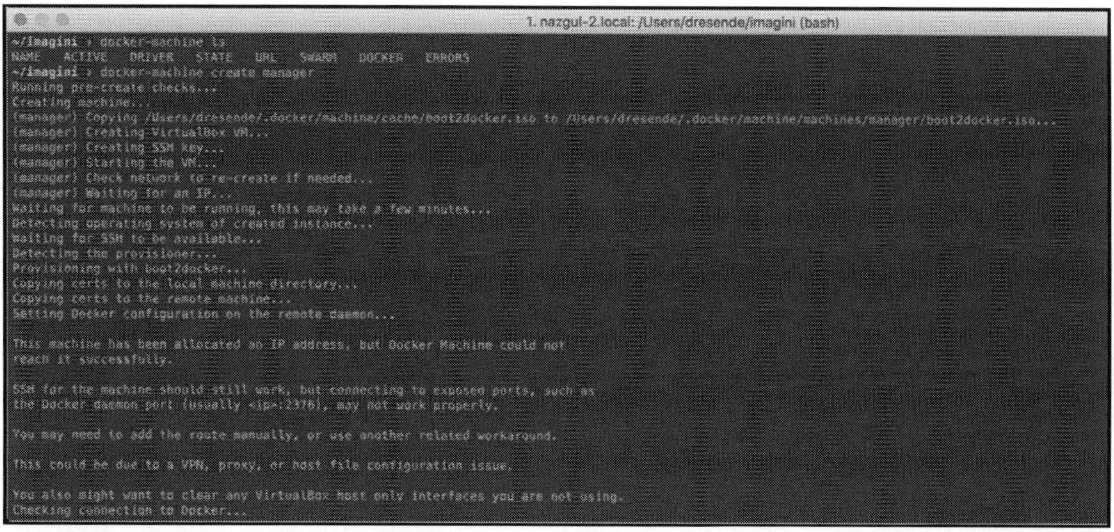

Now, run the following command:

```
docker-machine ls
```

You'll see that our new machine is ready to be used. You can see the IP address of the machine in the URL column:

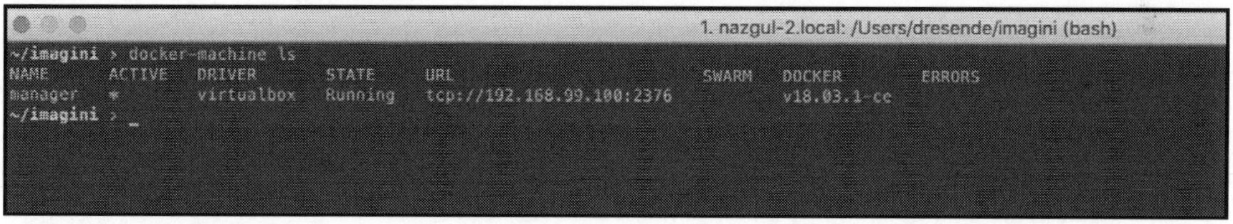

The Docker engine has an exposed API that enables you to manage a Docker host using the Docker commands from another host. The URL column indicates the API address to manage that specific host.

We can use a little helper command to configure our Docker command to manage this new host. Just type the following command:

```
docker-machine env manager
```

And follow the instructions:

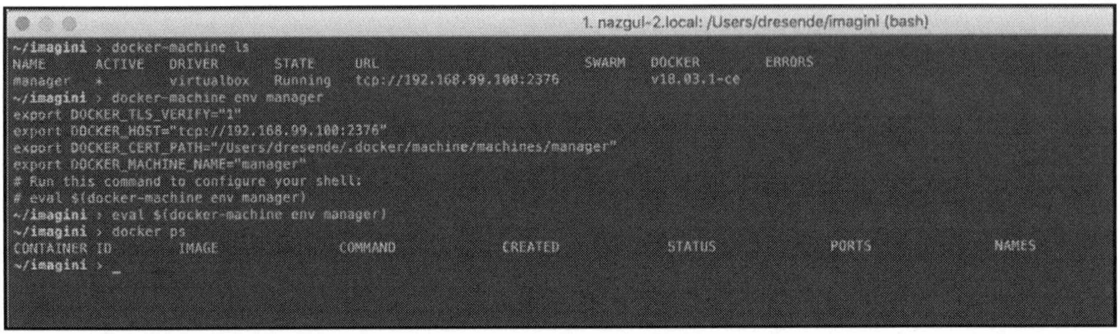

Now, let's keeps this Terminal untouched and open a new tab so that we can create a second machine. Let's call it replica, which will hold a second instance of our microservice:

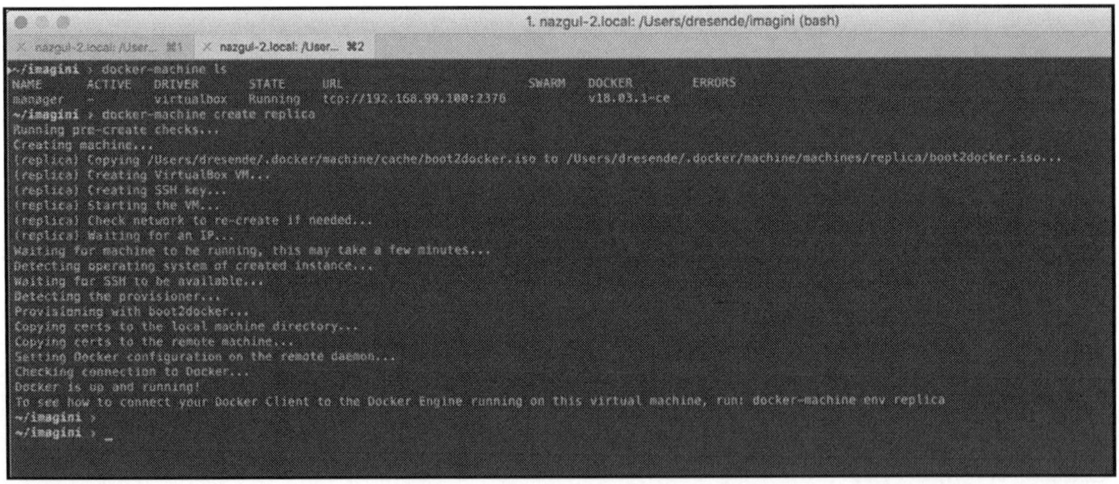

We can check that our new virtual machine is ready and running by checking the following output once more:

```
docker-machine ls
```

Both of our machines should be ready and running:

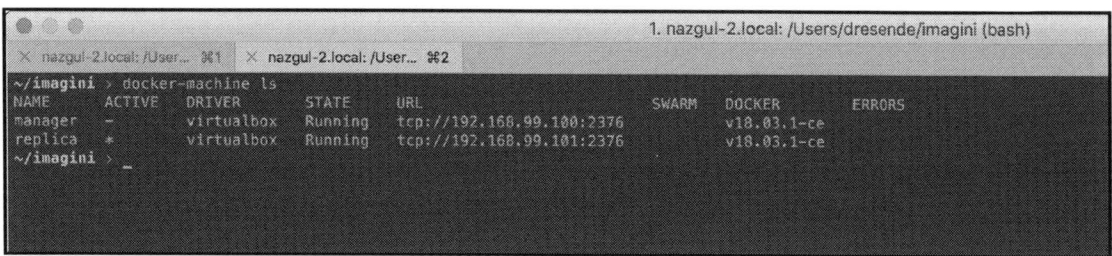

Using our initial tab, where we have the manager host, let's create a swarm. We're indicating the advertisement address because our virtual machines have more addresses, but we want the advertisement to be done on the network shown previously, so we're pointing out a specific IP address at the end:

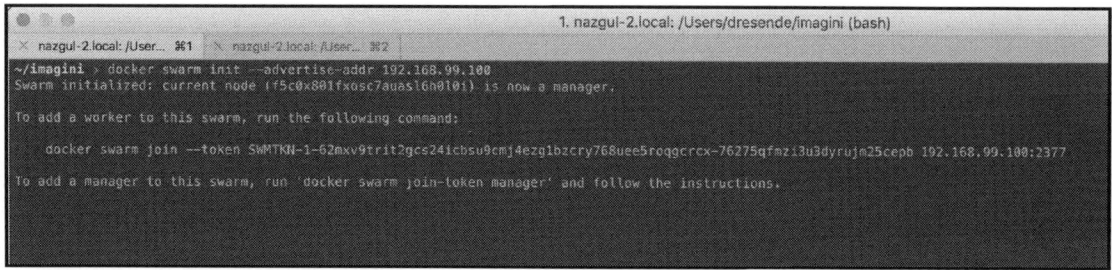

Docker created our swarm and gave us instructions on how to make other hosts join the swarm using a kind of secret token. If you want to add more nodes later on, save that command.

Now, head to the second tab and let's change our Docker command to manage our replica host and then join the swarm:

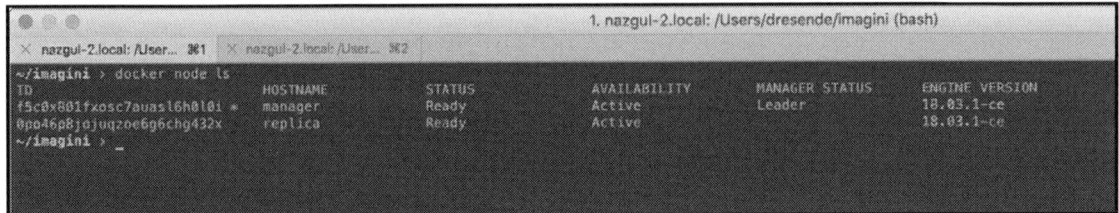

We now have two nodes on our swarm. From this point forward, assume that the first tab of our console is the manager host and that the second tab is our replica host.

We can check that the swarm has our two active nodes by using the `docker node ls` command from our manager:

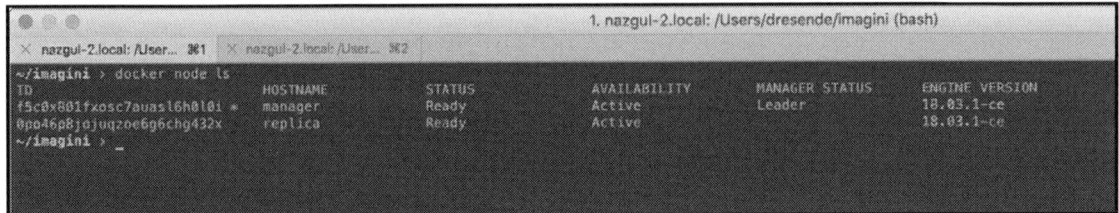

Deploying to swarm

We have two clean nodes in our swarm. We need to go back a little bit and prepare our hosts for our service. More specifically, we need to create our image again.

Because we have our `Dockerfile`, this is an easy task. Just run:

```
docker build —t imagini:0.0.5 .
```

Do this on both hosts:

```
~/imagini > docker build -t imagini:0.0.5 .
Sending build context to Docker daemon  263.2MB
Step 1/9 : FROM node
latest: Pulling from library/node
3d77ce4481b1: Pull complete
534514c83d69: Pull complete
d562b1c3ac3f: Pull complete
4b85e68dc01d: Pull complete
f6a66c5de9db: Pull complete
7a4e7d9a081d: Pull complete
d5019a4c5f9e: Pull complete
dbeca1767f60: Pull complete
Digest: sha256:4013aa6c297808defd01234fce4a42e1ca0518a5bd0260752a86a46542b38206
Status: Downloaded newer image for node:latest
 ---> 1c1272350058
Step 2/9 : MAINTAINER Diogo Resende
 ---> Running in 6be7ab8d4a6e
Removing intermediate container 6be7ab8d4a6e
 ---> 786fc6948ca1
Step 3/9 : ADD imagini/imagini.js /opt/app/imagini.js
 ---> d6fa93607a44
Step 4/9 : ADD imagini/package.json /opt/app/package.json
 ---> 268bf7981419
Step 5/9 : ADD imagini/settings.json /opt/app/settings.json
 ---> b018fac1a990
Step 6/9 : WORKDIR /opt/app
Removing intermediate container e2706db3eeaf
 ---> 6490c040a94f
Step 7/9 : RUN npm i
 ---> Running in dfe91a3f095c
```

Finally, we'll have our image available on both nodes. Our database container also needs an image, but since that's an official, published image, we don't need to build it, as Docker will download it when it needs it.

We can now use the Docker stack tool to deploy our instances. It uses our previous Docker Compose configuration to know how to deploy our service. But before we do this, we need to make a couple of adjustments to the configuration.

For now, we'll enforce our database to only have one replica, as we're not yet prepared to distribute our database server just yet. We can do that by having this section on the configuration:

```
deploy:
    replicas: 1
    placement:
        constraints: [node.role == manager]
```

It indicates that we only want one replica and that the container should be placed (should run) in the manager node.

Another change we need to do is change the database volume because our containers are running on a virtual machine that is no longer local. Let's change the volume section to this:

```
volumes:
- /var/lib/mysql:/var/lib/mysql
```

We need to create the folder on the manager machine. To do that, run:

```
docker-machine ssh manager 'mkdir /var/lib/mysql'
```

To sum up, you should have a configuration as follows:

```
version: "3"
networks:
    imagini:
services:
    database:
        image: mysql:5.7
        networks:
        - imagini
        volumes:
        - /var/lib/mysql:/var/lib/mysql
        ports:
        - "3306:3306"
        environment:
            MYSQL_DATABASE: imagini
            MYSQL_ROOT_PASSWORD: secret
        deploy:
            replicas: 1
            placement:
                constraints: [node.role == manager]
    service:
        image: imagini:0.0.5
        networks:
        - imagini
        volumes:
```

```
  - ${PWD}/settings.json:/opt/app/settings.json
ports:
  - "80:3000"
```

Head to the first tab, the one that controls the manager node, and run the following:

```
docker stack deploy --compose-file docker-compose.yml imagini
```

This should start the deployment. It will create the network on the swarm and then deploy the two services:

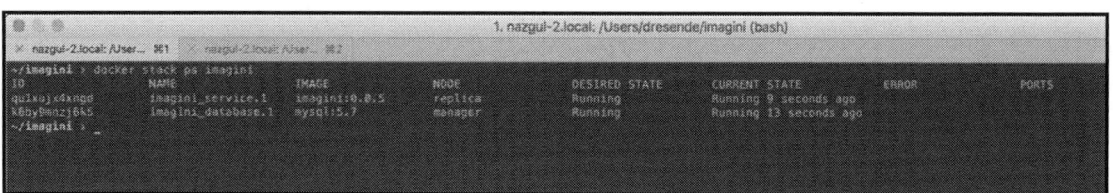

Wait a little bit and then run the following command:

```
docker stack ps imagini
```

This will do the same as `docker ps`, but just for our stack:

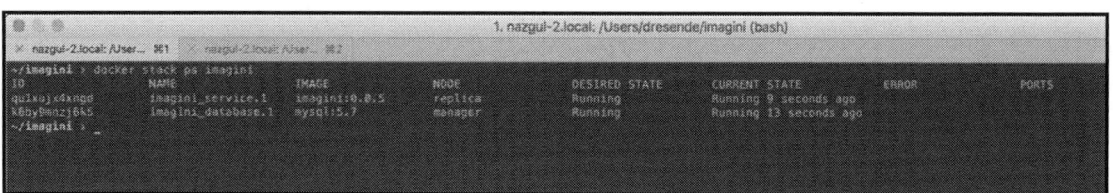

The only difference you may notice is that the name of the containers have a .1 on the end of them and that a new NODE column indicates where it's running inside our swarm.

Because our containers are running in a swarm inside two virtual machines, we need to use the IP address of the node that has the service running on it. Looking at the previous screenshot, we can see that it's in the replica machine:

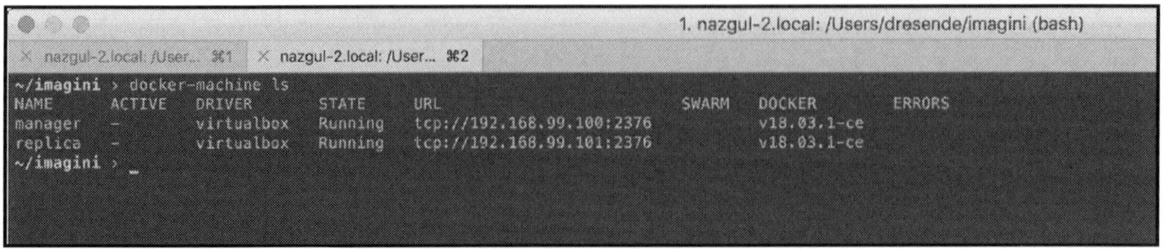

Its address is 192.168.99.101. Head to the browser and see if our service is available or not:

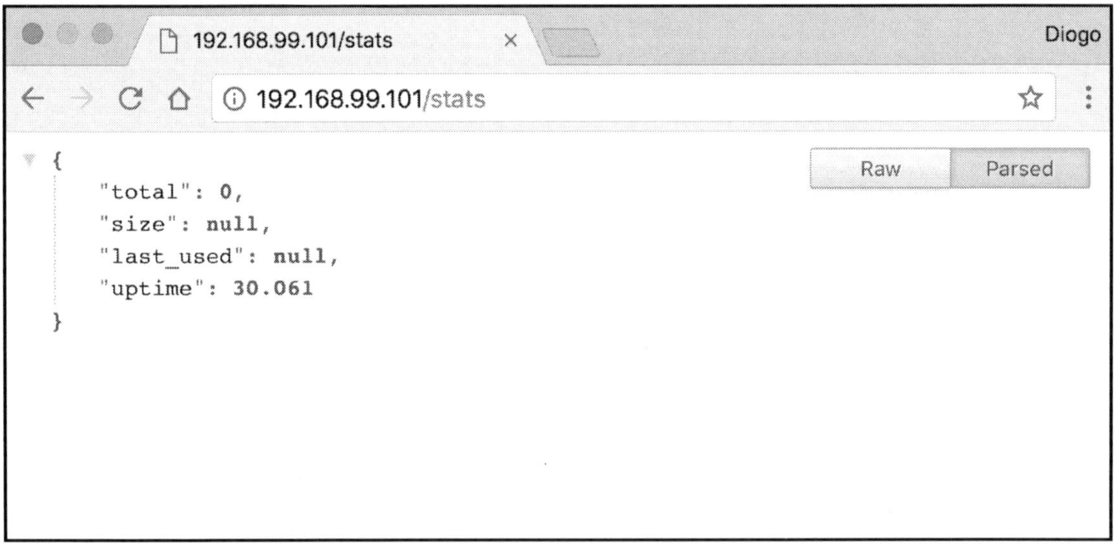

Great! It's working. But, if you think about it, if this is a swarm, shouldn't it be available from anywhere in the network? You're right, yes, it should be available. Let's check the other node address:

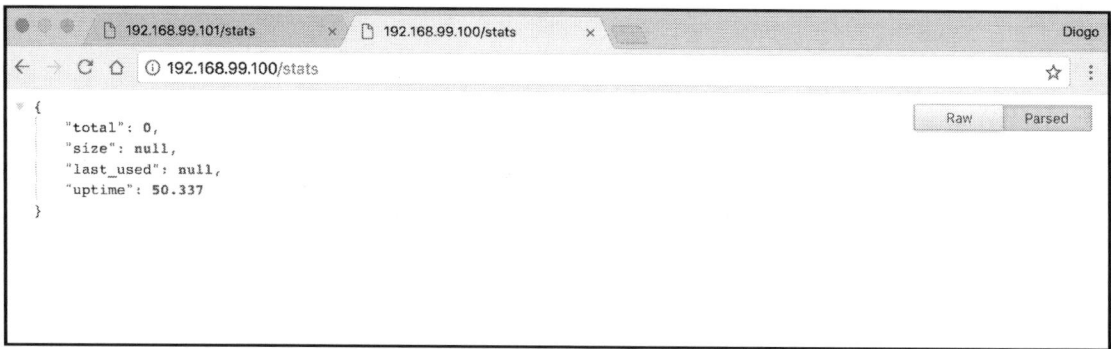

Now, this is something awesome. Notice that we only had one instance of each of our two services, and our `imagini` service was on the replica node. Although it's available from any of the swarm node addresses, if, for some reason, it fails, you wouldn't be able to reach it.

We can change this by scaling the number of instances, or replicas, in our swarm. To do that, just issue the following command to change the scale to two instances:

```
docker service scale imagini_service=2
```

Docker will handle the deployment and check if everything goes as planned:

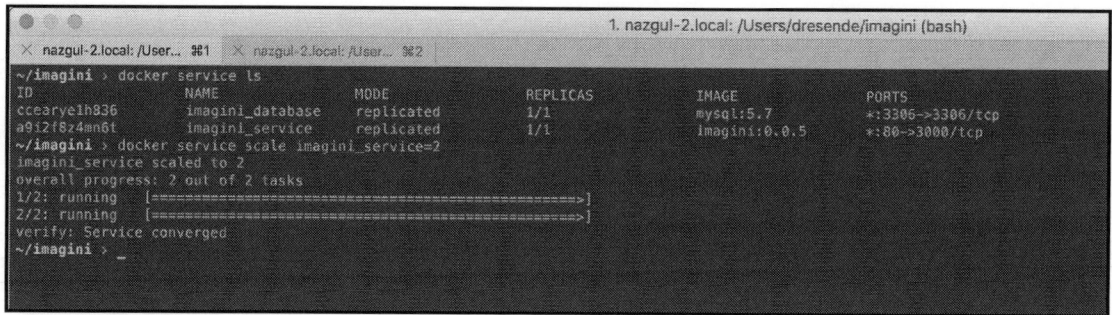

You can check the status of the services at any time using the following command:

```
docker service ls
```

Notice how our service 2 / 2 replicas are running:

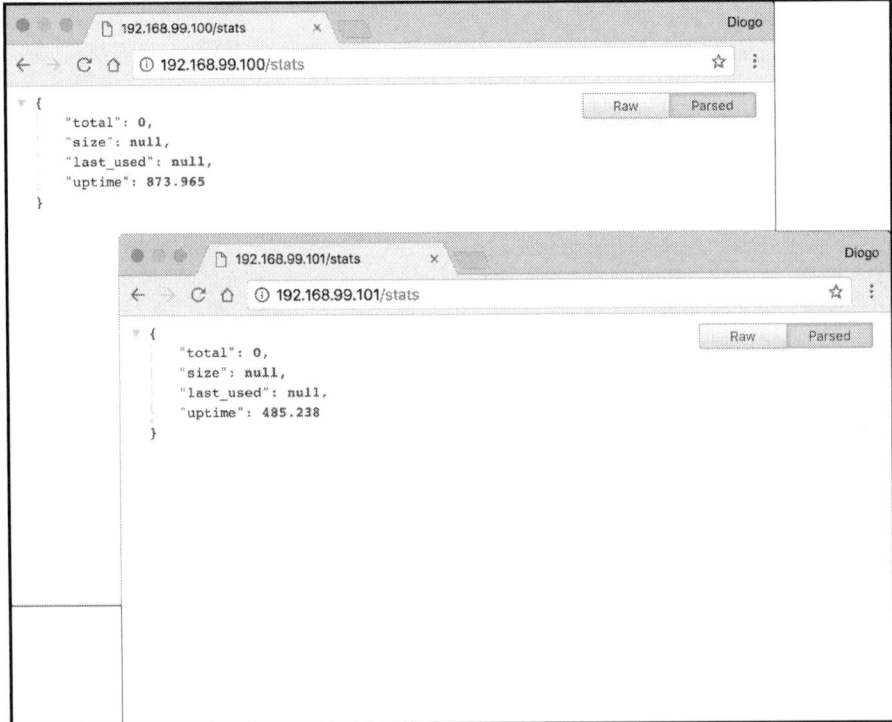

If you head to the browser, both addresses still work as expected, but in the background, we have two services running. You can notice this by looking at the uptime property.

If you run a little test, such as refreshing both addresses repeatedly, you'll notice that the uptime changes up and down. This is because we deployed both of the instances at different times, and although the statistics come from the database server, which is the same, the uptime is the process uptime:

Notice how the swarm is not constant and does not give you the same instance for the same address. It keeps rotating it.

The swarm also monitors our container instances. For example, let's imagine you're working on a host and, by accident, stop a container:

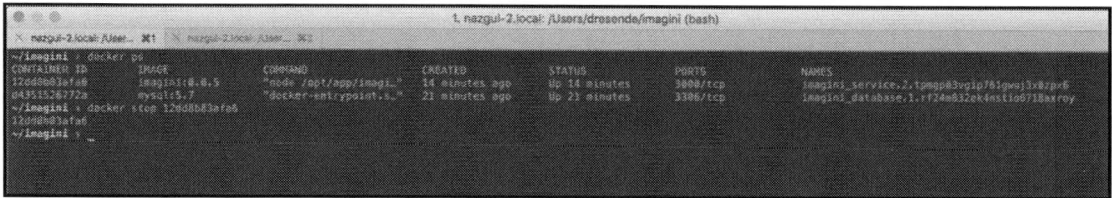

It's not very critical since we have two replicas running. But if you head to the browser and hit refresh, you may see something odd:

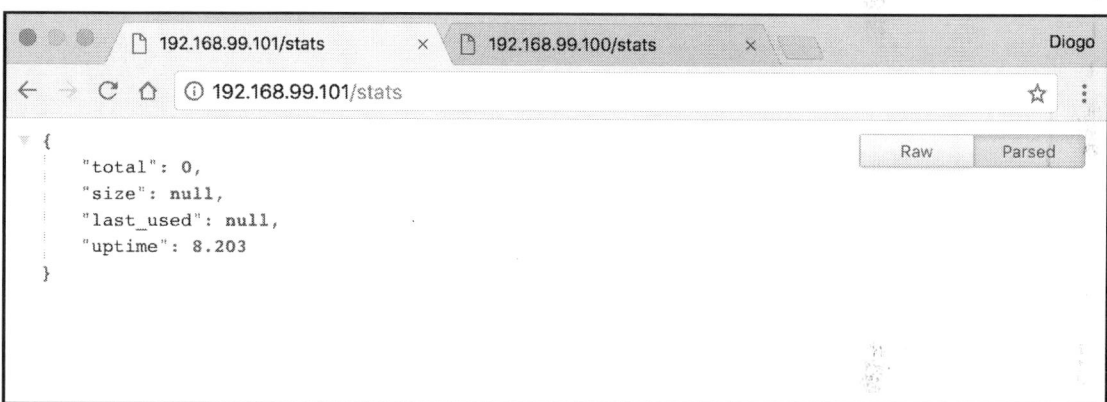

What happened to our `uptime`? It just went down to a few seconds. This is because the swarm just noticed our container stopping and restarted it. If you look at the Docker containers again, it's still running. Well, actually it restarted:

If you want to scale to more instances, you don't need to have more swarm nodes. There's no limitation on the number of instances of the same containers running on the same node. This is actually a good practice.

It enables you to test if your service is ready to be used in a scaled environment and also allows you to test a phased upgrade by stopping a container and upgrading one by one, while at least one other container is still serving your customers.

Let's just scale our service to five instances:

Notice how we have two of the five services running on this node, and also the database instance. The other three are in the replica node. This is known as swarm balancing the instances.

Creating services

You may have noticed how we're using the Docker service command to scale our instances. This is a command that is similar to the basic Docker command, but with services and scaling in mind. We can use this command to create containers and scale them easily.

MySQL has no simple replication mechanism. There are only two ways of doing it and both have disadvantages:

- Creating a set of nodes as masters of each other, creating a complex mesh of connections that will eventually lead to chaos
- Creating a cluster, which involves more nodes and still leads to a complex deployment, which is easier to manage but resource-intensive to maintain

Looking back at our examples from previous chapters, we could change our service to use another database server. More specifically, RethinkDB has a much friendlier cluster mechanism.

So, just replace our `imagini` service with the one we used with RethinkDB. This time, let's use the Docker Service commands manually and deploy our microservice step by step.

To begin with, let's prepare a RethinkDB cluster. To make it resilient, we will do the following:

1. Create an instance called `db-primary`.
2. Create another instance called `db-secondary` and instruct it to join `db-primary`.
3. Scale `db-secondary` to two instances so that we have a proper three-node cluster.
4. Remove and recreate `db-primary` to instruct it to join `db-secondary` this time.
5. Scale `db-primary` to two instances.

This will give you four nodes, two of each kind, that are formatted to join the other kind when they fail, and swarm restarts them. This is the definition of *no single point of failure*.

Because we're doing everything manually, we need to start by creating a network. Let's create the network `imagini`:

```
docker network create --driver overlay imagini
```

Then, create `db-primary` with only 1 replica as we're removing it later on:

```
docker service create --name db-primary \
                      --network imagini \
                      --replicas 1 \
                      rethinkdb:latest \
                      rethinkdb --bind all --no-http-admin
```

Then, create the first `db-secondary` with only 1 replica and tell it to join `db-primary`:

```
docker service create --name db-secondary \
                      --network imagini \
                      --replicas 1 \
                      rethinkdb:latest \
                      rethinkdb --bind all --no-http-admin --join db-
primary
```

You should now have something like this:

Similar to what we did before, let's scale db-secondary to two instances:

```
docker service scale db-secondary=2
```

Then, remove the db-primary and recreate it:

```
docker service create --name db-primary \
                --network imagini \
                --replicas 1 \
                rethinkdb:latest \
                rethinkdb --bind all --no-http-admin --join db-
secondary
```

Then, scale it to two instances:

```
docker service scale db-primary=2
```

You should now have four instances. List the services and you should see something like the following screenshot:

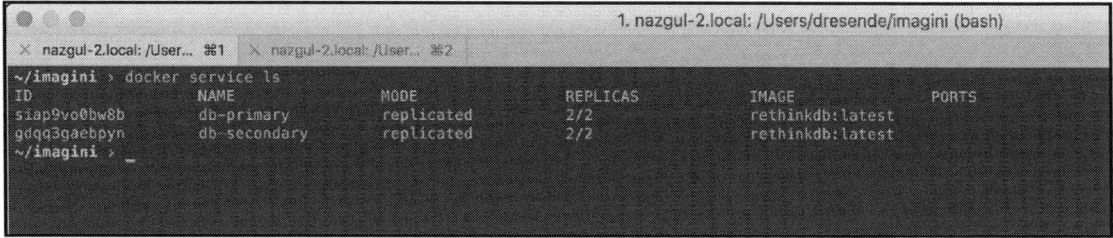

If you try to stop the containers, you'll notice that they will restart without you doing anything. Just give it a little time and they'll be up and running again:

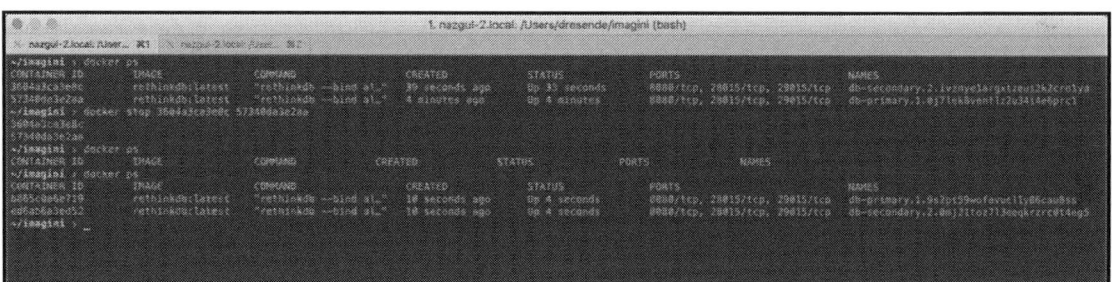

Now that we have our database cluster ready, we just need a proxy to be able to access the cluster:

```
docker service create --name database \
                --network imagini \
                --publish 8080:8080 \
                --publish 28015:28015 \
                rethinkdb:latest \
                rethinkdb proxy --bind all --join db-primary
```

If we look at the services, we can now see that we have our four cluster nodes and a proxy called database, which we'll use to manage and access the data:

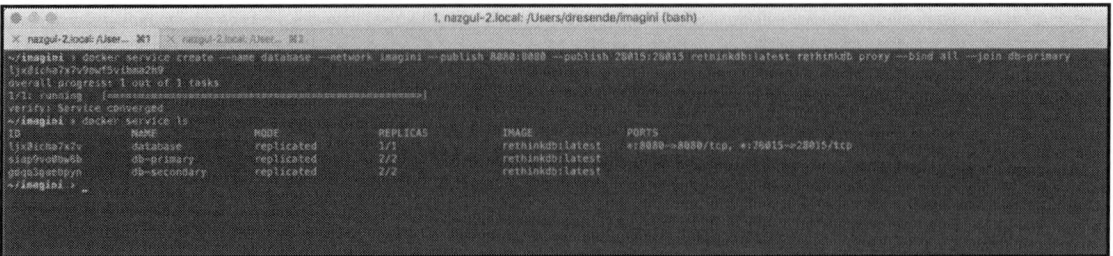

We can also see that we have the management port exposed, 8080. Head to the browser at any of the swarm addresses on that port and see if you can see the RethinkDB management interface:

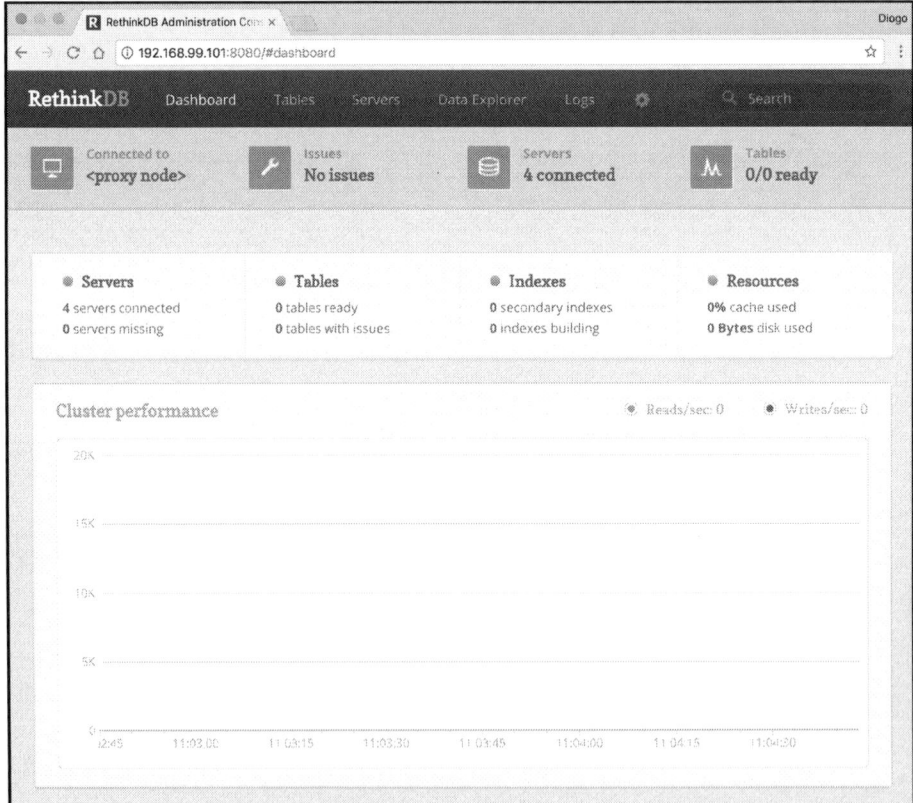

Great! We can see that there's a **4 servers connected** under the **Servers** label. On top, there's also a **Servers** section that you can look into and see that our instances are all there:

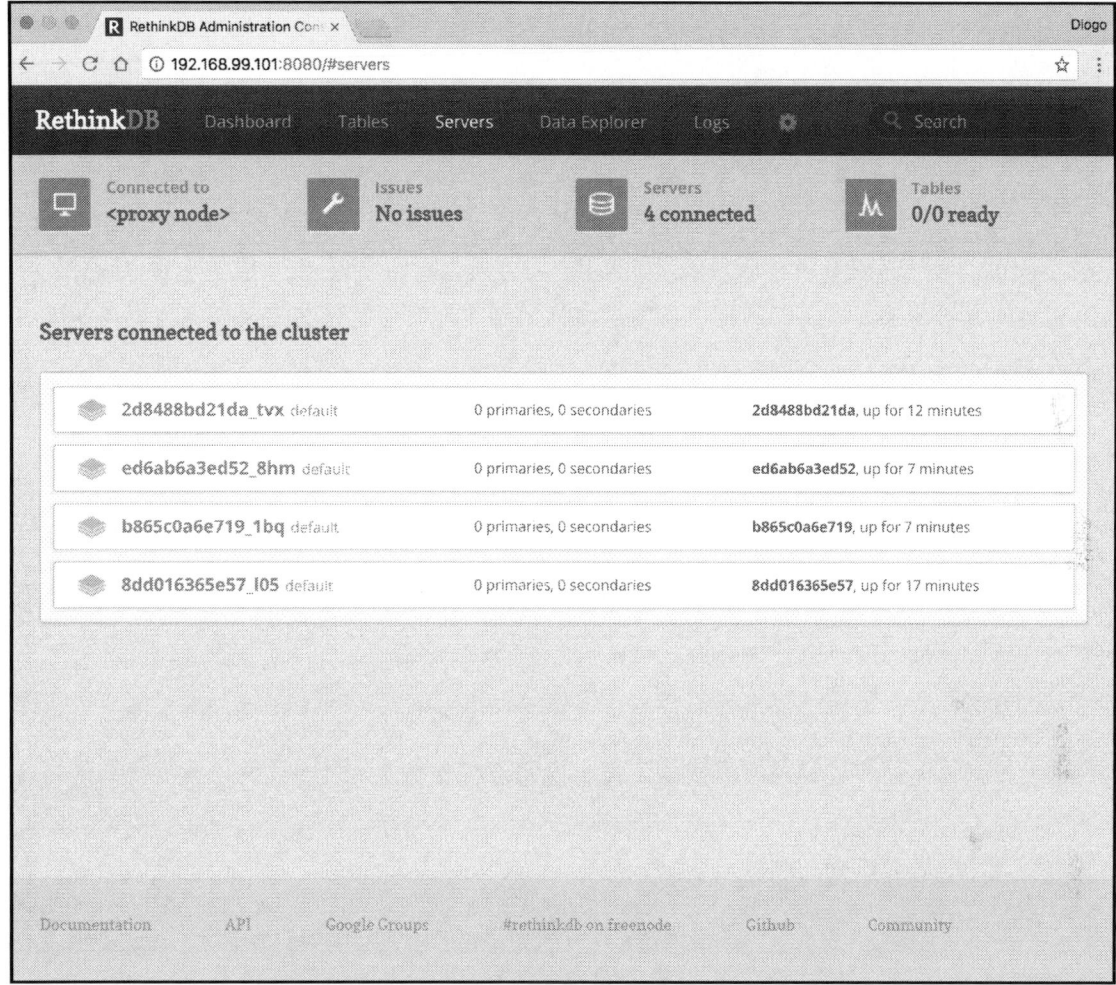

Use this interface and create a database called `imagini` in the **Tables** section.

Running our service

The only part missing is our main service. We need to rebuild it again. If you change the source code to use RethinkDB again, you have to change the `package.json` file in order to have different dependencies. We need to rebuild this using our `Dockerfile`. To avoid introducing another theme, which is Docker Volumes, let's change our RethinkDB connection to not depend on the `settings` file:

```
rethinkdb.connect({ host: "database", db: "imagini" }, (err, db) => {
```

This way, we can avoid mounting a settings file altogether. Now, let's just increment the version and build it on both tabs:

```
docker build -t imagini:0.0.6 .
```

Now, the only thing missing is creating our service:

```
docker service create --name imagini --network imagini --publish 80:3000
imagini:0.0.6
```

In just a few seconds, we have our service running:

We can even scale it right away and have three instances:

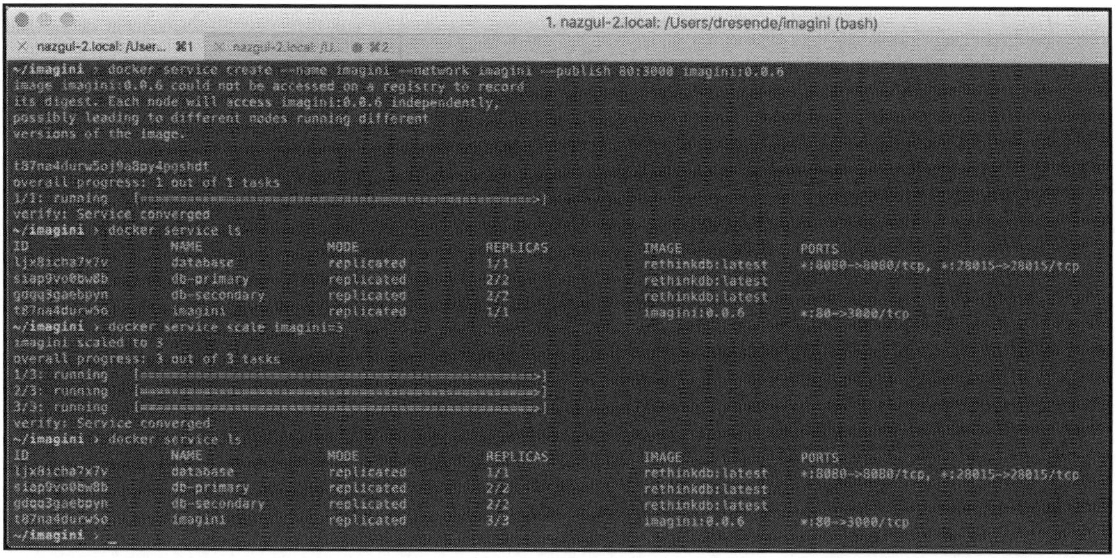

We can see that it's exposed on port `80`. As we did previously, we can see that the service is up and running. I'll just upload the example image again as this is a clean service and it has no images yet:

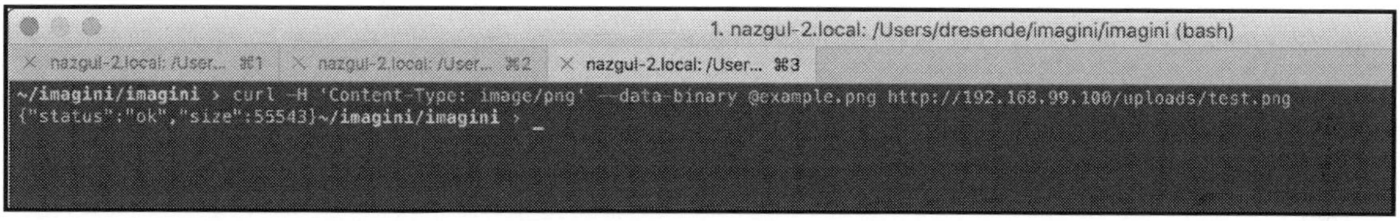

You can see it on the RethinkDB administration interface. And even if we use the other swarm address, we see that the image is now available to download:

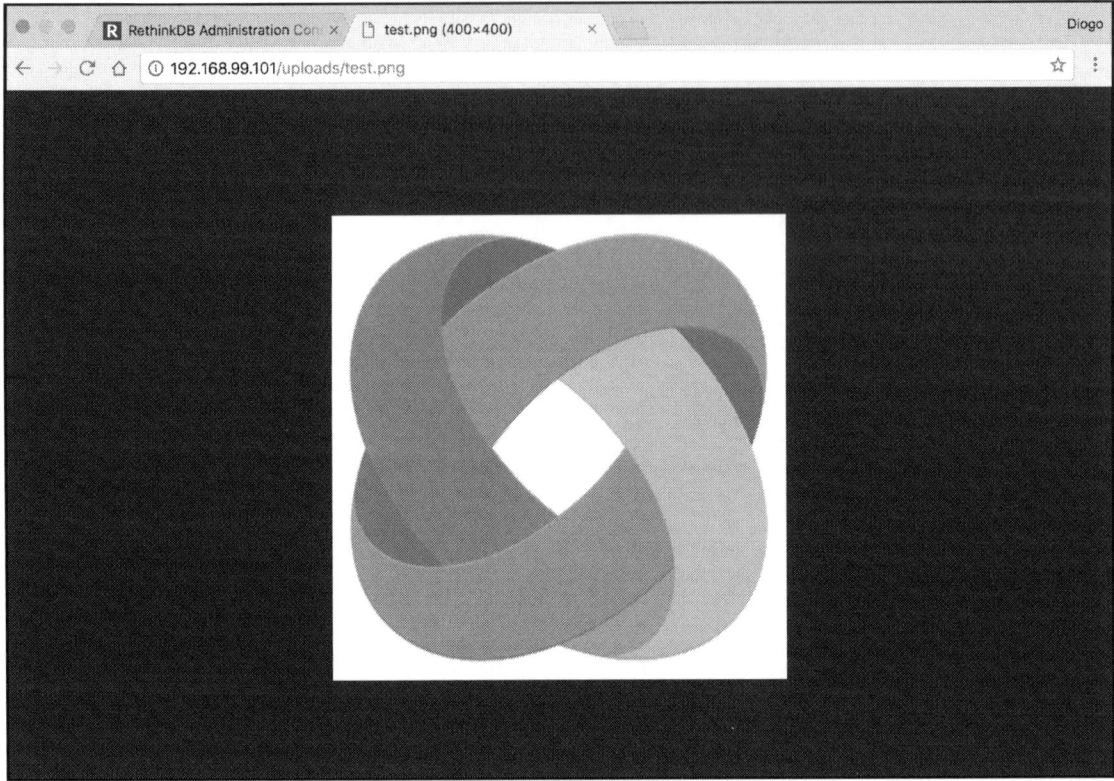

Sharding approach

Sharding is the process of fragmenting the data across different locations. This enables us to split a large dataset into different servers, each one with a smaller set. This is comparable to a RAID 0 configuration, where, for example, you may need a 10 TB disk and do this by combining two 5 TB disks:

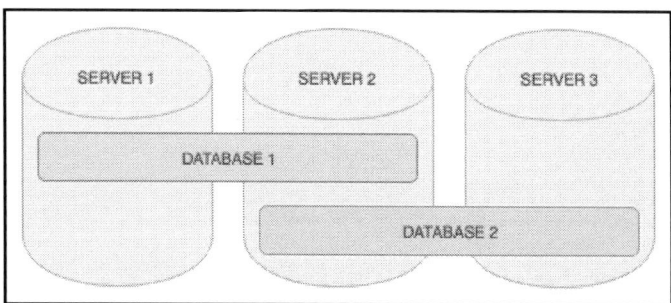

Doing so is considered scaling, but it comes at a cost. Each piece of data is important; it's not a copy, it's a fundamental part. Sharding adds complexity to your deployment but sometimes is inevitable if you have a very large dataset.

Replicating approach

Replicating is the process of having copies of the data across different locations. This enables us to have a bigger throughput as we can have different services serving the same data. It also brings complexity, at least for the database servers, as they need to keep everything synchronized:

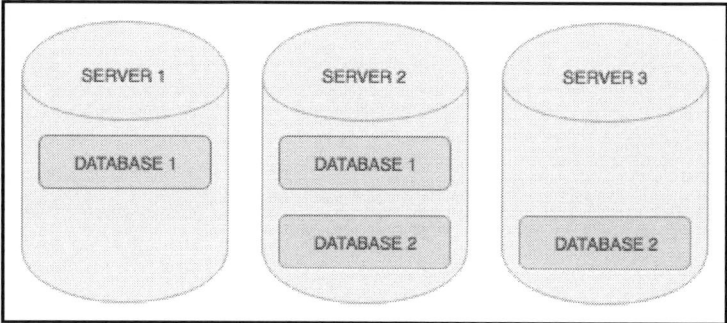

Doing replicas also gives you redundancy in case of any failures in regards to parts of the server nodes, depending on your configuration. If you use a database cluster for more than one application, you don't need to have replicas of a database in all cluster nodes; it all depends on your needs.

Sharding and replicating

Looking at our service, now that it's using RethinkDB, we can have the best of both worlds and enable sharding and replication at the same time. Head to the Administration Console and click on the **Tables** tab at the top:

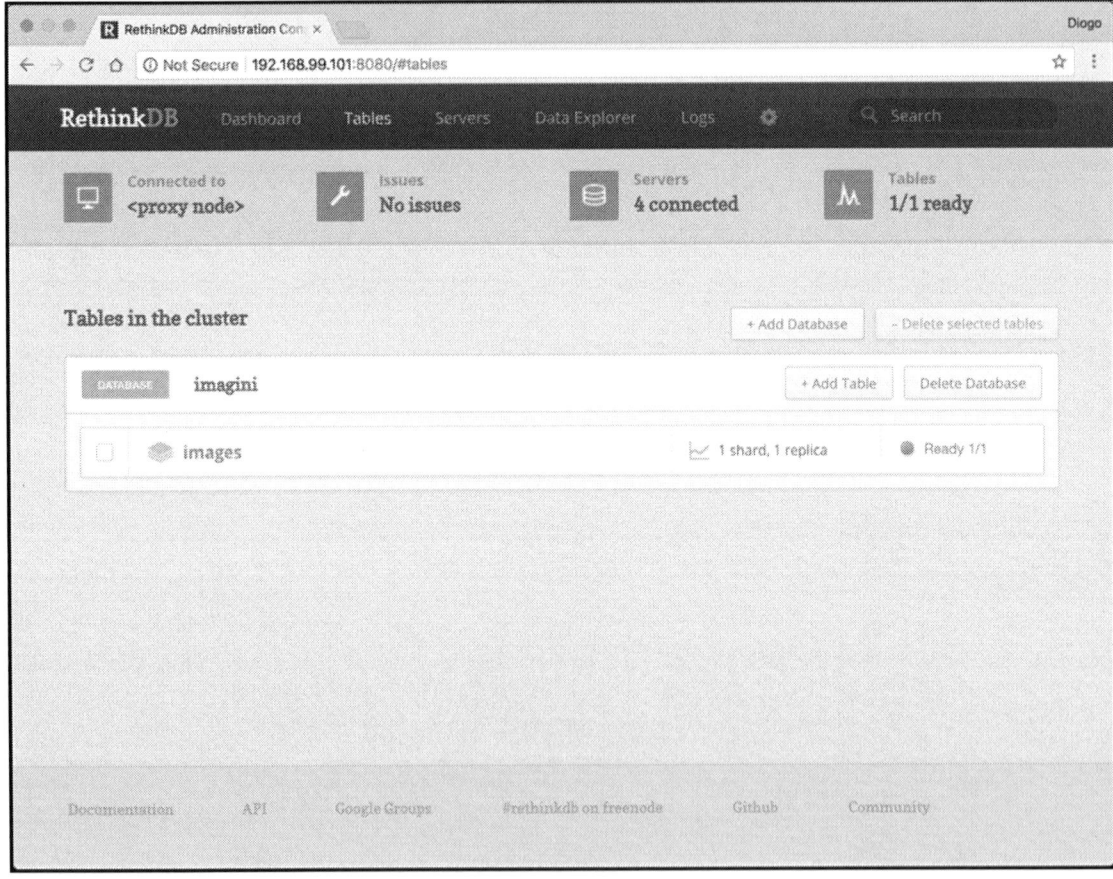

Click on our **images** table and scroll down:

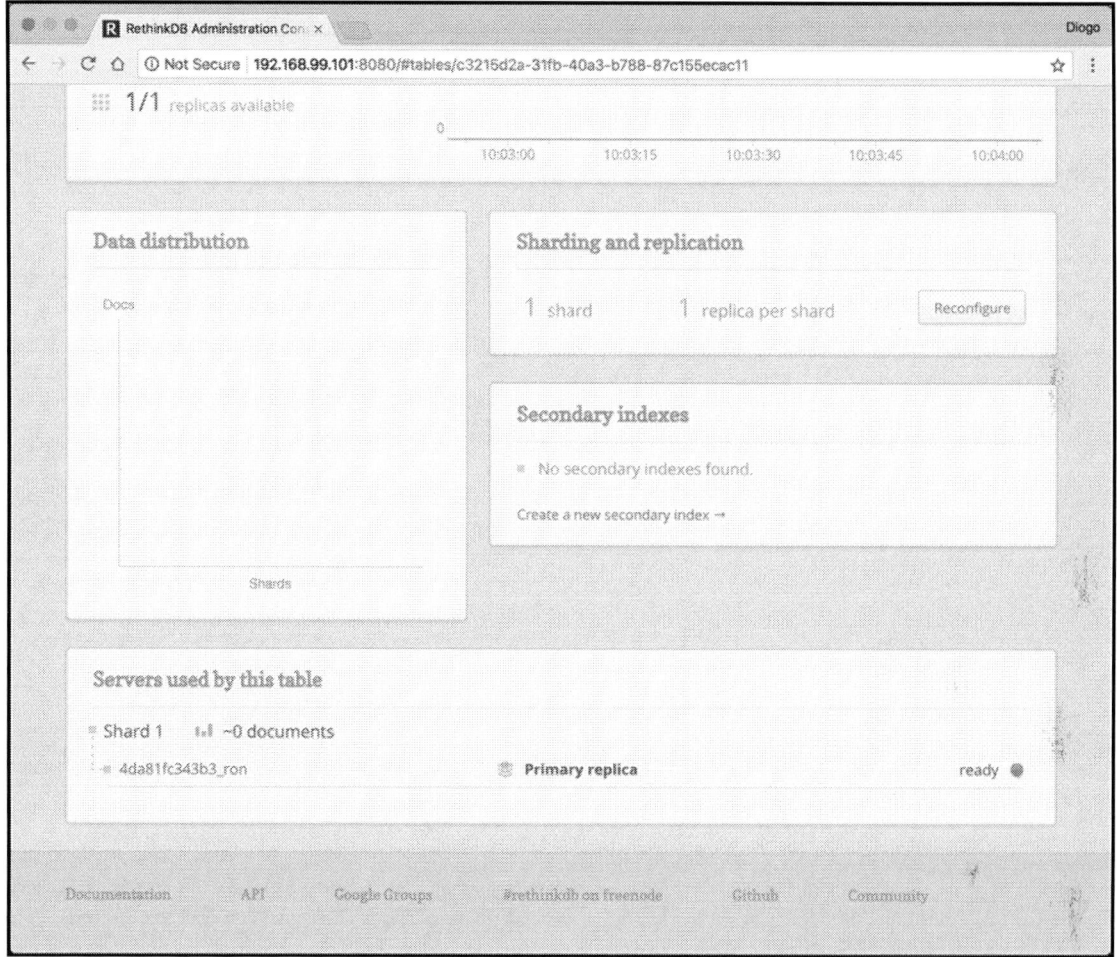

You can see that our table is on one shard (the default), with only one replica per shard. Down the bottom, you can see the server (blue link) on our cluster that is holding the table. Click on **Apply configuration**:

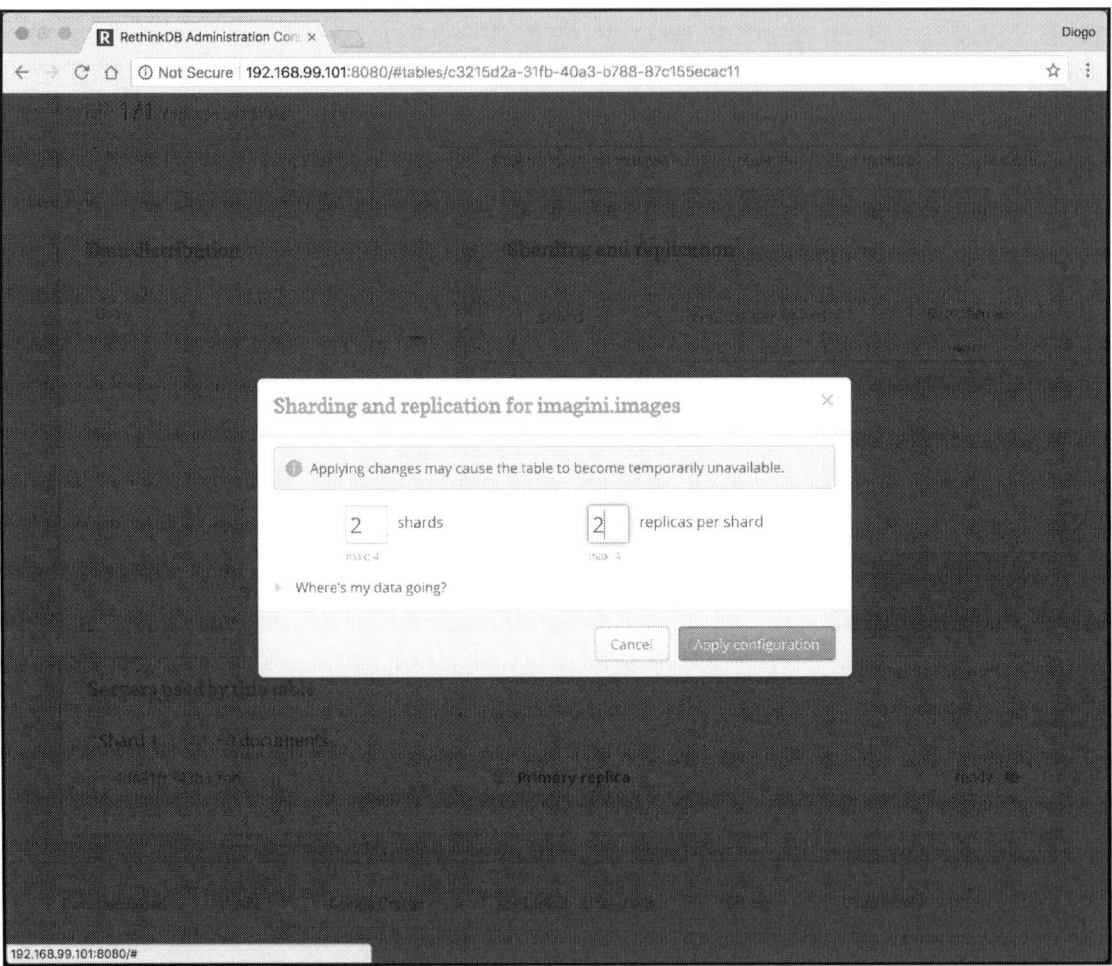

You can configure the number of shards and the number of replicas of every shard. The limitation on four shards and four replicas is because our cluster has only four nodes. Any number above that would not make sense.

Let's configure our table with two shards and two replicas per shard and apply the configuration. Wait a couple of seconds and look at how our table is distributed:

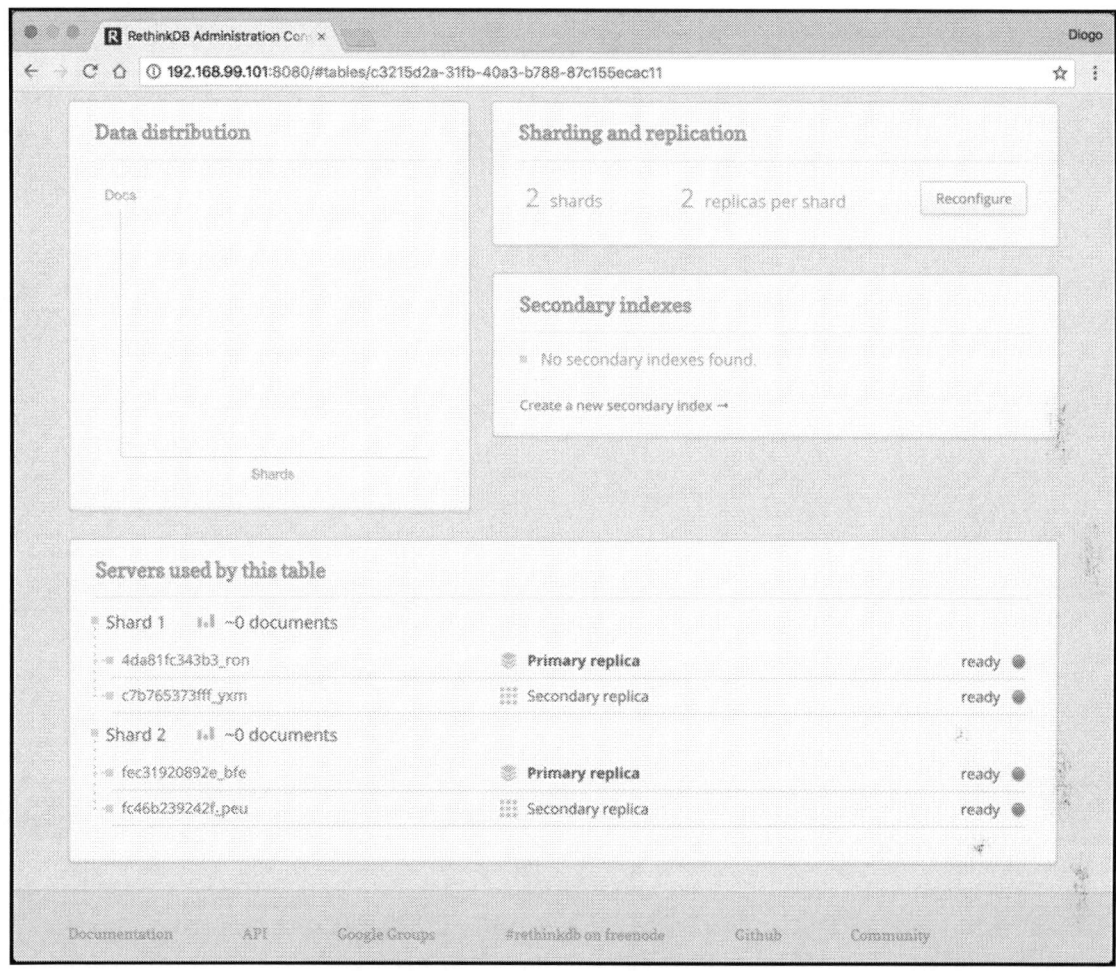

If one node restarts, the database keeps running without a problem. It will recover and synchronize everything when the node comes online again. Let's just try that. Head to a console of one of the Docker machines and restart one of the database containers.

If you keep the administration console open, you should see something like the following screenshot for just a few seconds:

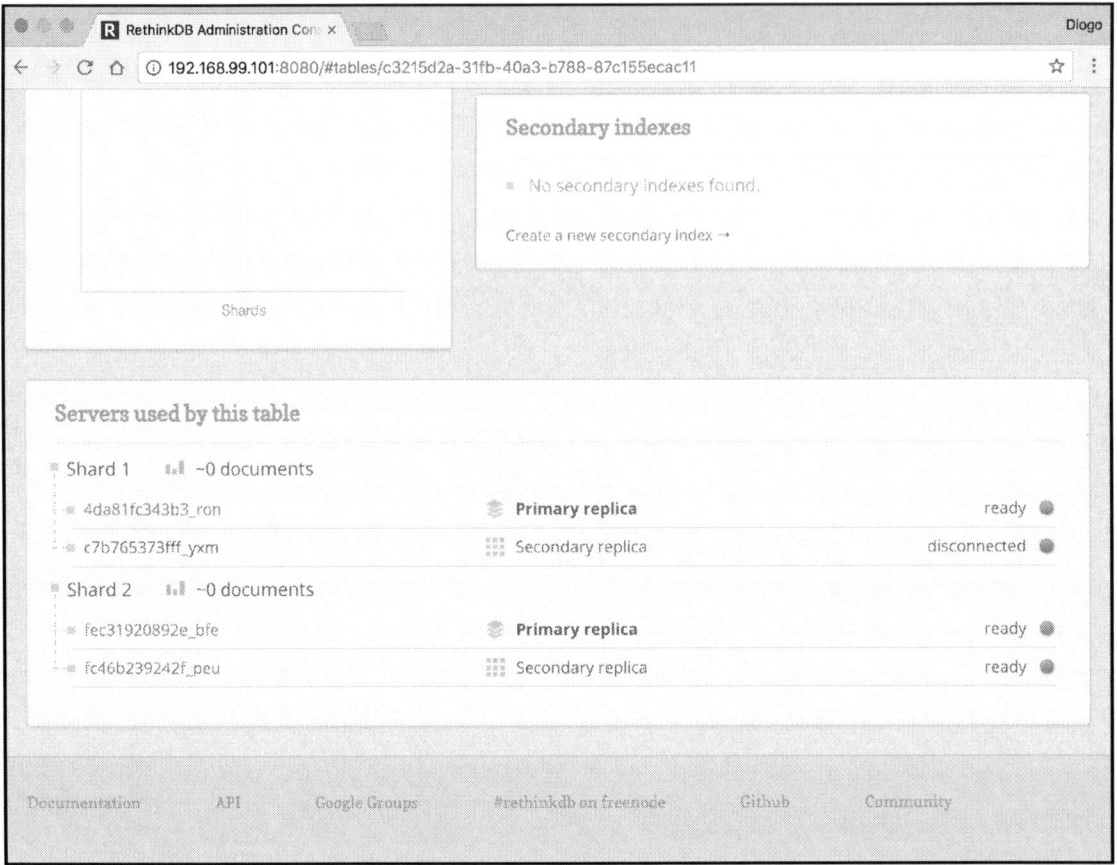

The server then reconnects, and everything recovers immediately. But this is a specific feature that will vary according to the database server and cluster type. Your operations' team should be comfortable with the database server chosen to run in production.

We now have a production-ready environment that we can tweak and scale to our needs.

Moving to Kubernetes

Kubernetes began with a group of Google developers from a previous Google system called Borg. Its goal was, and is, to help in the deployment, scaling, and maintenance of applications. When it was first announced in 2014, there was no open source alternative. At the time, there was no Docker swarm, Docker networks, or Docker services.

Let's see what changes we need to make to our microservice in order to successfully run it using Kubernetes. But first, we need to clarify some of the concepts that are used in Kubernetes:

- **Pods**: A Pod consists of one or more containers that share some resources, and because of that, need to be located on the same host. A Pod is assigned a unique network address to avoid port collision. Note that several Pods of your deployment may be created, each with a different address.
- **Labels**: Kubernetes allows us to assign several labels to Pods in order to create groups of different kinds of components, such as frontend and backend, production and staging.
- **Services**: A Service is a group of Pods that work together, like our microservice and the database server. You can create a Service by defining a Label of Pods.

Deploying with Kubernetes

That's not all of the concepts needed, but you may see some similarities and differences between Docker and Kubernetes. Actually, Kubernetes uses Docker and adds a few tools to enhance the deployment, scaling, and monitoring of containers.

The best way to start with Kubernetes is to install `minikube`. This is a tool to run Kubernetes locally on a single virtual machine:

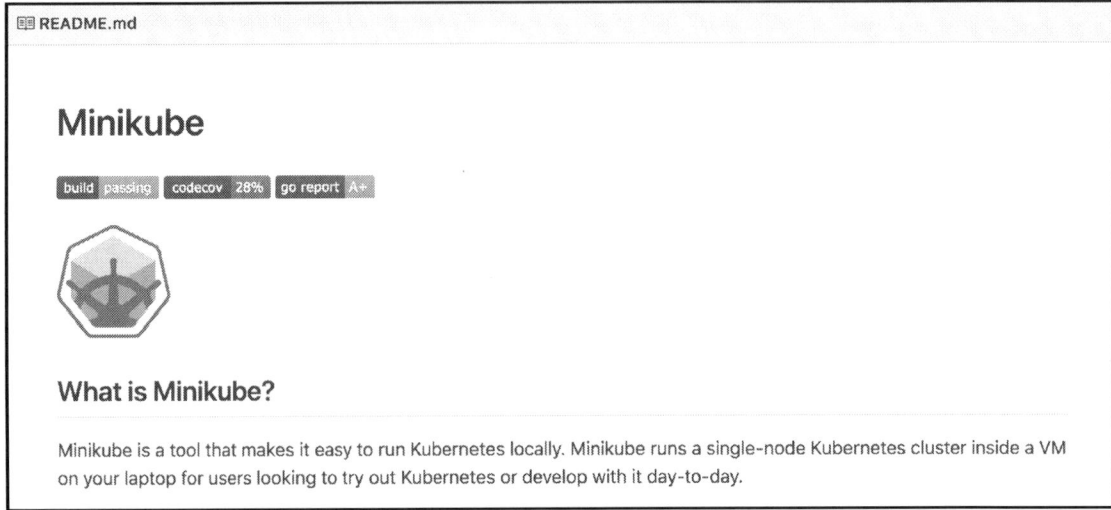

Follow the installation instructions. If you're on macOS and have `homebrew` installed, you just need to run:

```
brew cask install minikube
```

After installing `minikube`, you have to start it by running:

```
minikube start
```

You have to wait a minute or two before everything is set up:

```
●  ●  ●                    1. nazgul-2.local: /Users/dresende (bash)
~ > minikube start
Starting local Kubernetes v1.10.0 cluster...
Starting VM...
Downloading Minikube ISO
 150.53 MB / 150.53 MB [===============================================] 100.00% 0s
Getting VM IP address...
Moving files into cluster...
Downloading kubeadm v1.10.0
Downloading kubelet v1.10.0
Finished Downloading kubeadm v1.10.0
Finished Downloading kubelet v1.10.0
Setting up certs...
Connecting to cluster...
Setting up kubeconfig...
Starting cluster components...
Kubectl is now configured to use the cluster.
Loading cached images from config file.
~ > _
```

We can see that our Kubernetes cluster is up and running by running:

```
kubectl cluster-info
```

This is a cluster of nodes that run containers, similar to Docker swarm. You should get a positive response as follows:

```
●  ●  ●                    1. nazgul-2.local: /Users/dresende (bash)
~ > kubectl cluster-info
Kubernetes master is running at https://192.168.99.100:8443
KubeDNS is running at https://192.168.99.100:8443/api/v1/namespaces/kube-system/services/kube-dns:dns/proxy

To further debug and diagnose cluster problems, use 'kubectl cluster-info dump'.
~ > _
```

You're now able to access the Kubernetes dashboard by running:

```
minikube dashboard
```

Your browser should open something along the following lines:

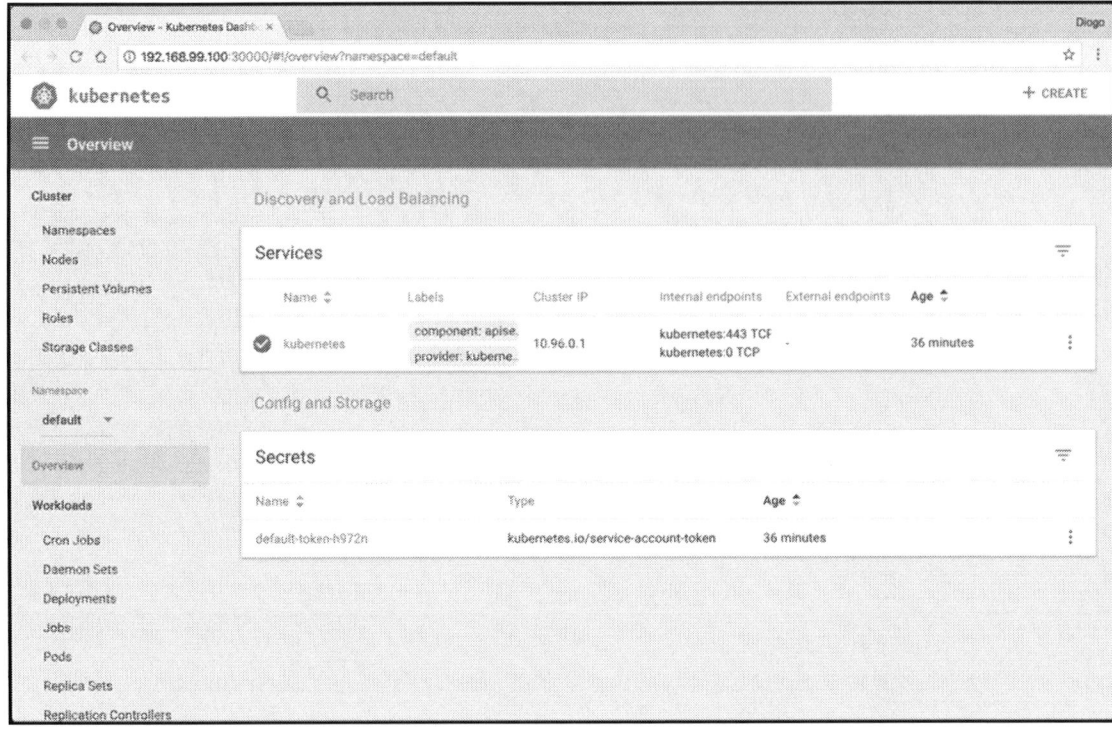

You can use the interface to monitor all of Kubernetes, but also to create services and deployments. Since our service depends on RethinkDB right now, we first need to ensure we have that up and running.

To begin, hit the **Create** button in the top right-hand corner of the page. On the text input that shows appears, write the following YAML configuration:

```
apiVersion: apps/v1beta1
kind: StatefulSet
metadata:
  name: rethinkdb-master
spec:
  serviceName: rethinkdb-master
  replicas: 1
  template:
    metadata:
      labels:
        app: rethinkdb-master
    spec:
```

```
          hostname: rethinkdb-master
          containers:
          - name: rethinkdb
            image: rethinkdb:2.3.6
            command: ["rethinkdb"]
            args:
            - --bind
            - "all"
            - --canonical-address
            - "rethinkdb-master:29015"
            - --canonical-address
            - "$(MY_POD_IP):29015"
            volumeMounts:
            - name: rdb-local-data
              mountPath: /data
            env:
            - name: MY_POD_NAME
              valueFrom:
                fieldRef:
                  fieldPath: metadata.name
            - name: MY_POD_IP
              valueFrom:
                fieldRef:
                  fieldPath: status.podIP
        volumes:
        - name: rdb-local-data
          hostPath:
            path: /var/data/rethinkdb


---
apiVersion: v1
kind: Service
metadata:
  name: rethinkdb-master
  labels:
    app: rethinkdb-master
spec:
  ports:
  - port: 28015
    name: rdb-api
  - port: 29015
    name: rdb-cluster-api
  selector:
    app: rethinkdb-master
```

Hit **Upload** and wait a few seconds. You should have a running RethinkDB database in no time:

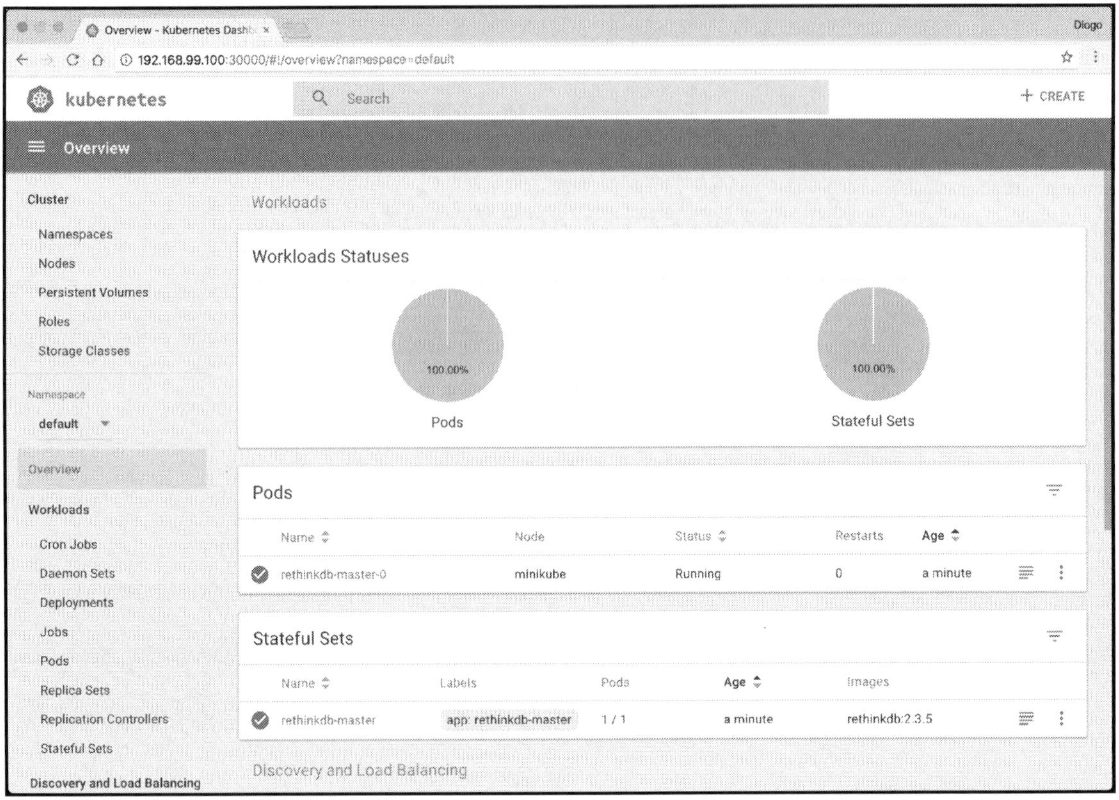

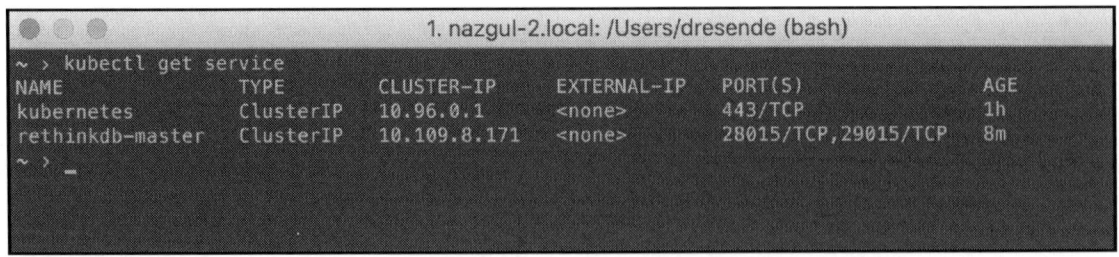

To check that our RethinkDB server is running correctly, we can add port forwarding from the outside of the cluster. First, let's list our services:

```
●  ●  ●                          1. nazgul-2.local: /Users/dresende (bash)
~ > kubectl get service
NAME               TYPE        CLUSTER-IP     EXTERNAL-IP   PORT(S)              AGE
kubernetes         ClusterIP   10.96.0.1      <none>        443/TCP              1h
rethinkdb-master   ClusterIP   10.109.8.171   <none>        28015/TCP,29015/TCP  8m
~ > _
```

Our service is there. There are some endpoints, but the Administration Console isn't actually there. Let's forward that local port, which is 5000, to port `8080`:

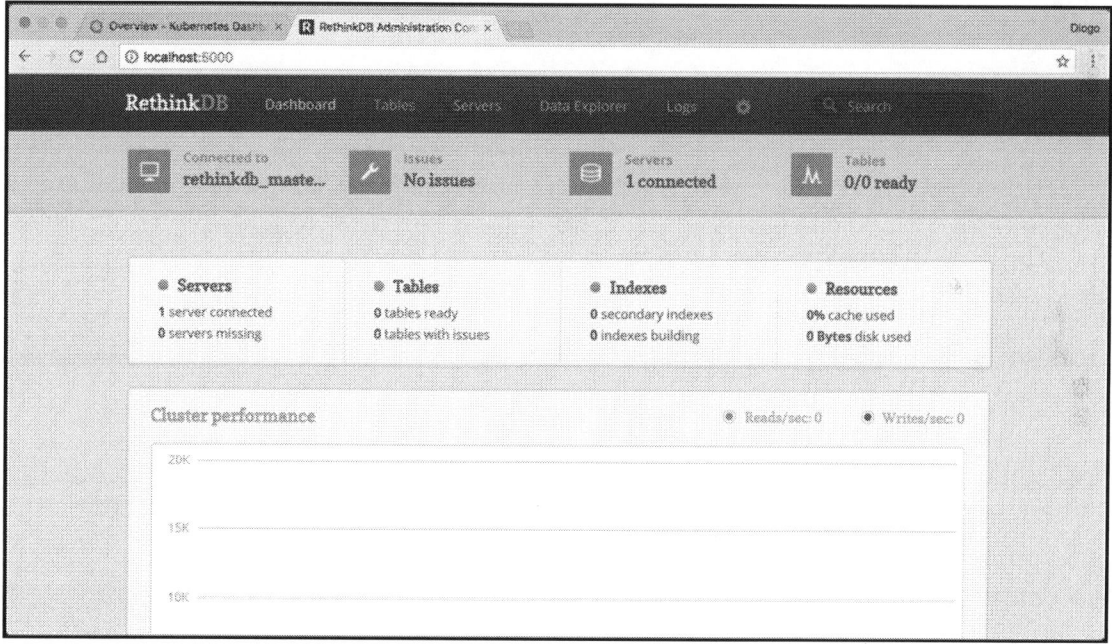

While keeping the command running, open a new browser tab and head to port `5000` of the localhost. You should see the RethinkDB Administration Console:

We can now head to our microservice and try to deploy it, similar to what we did previously with Docker. First, create the `imagini` database on the Administration Console:

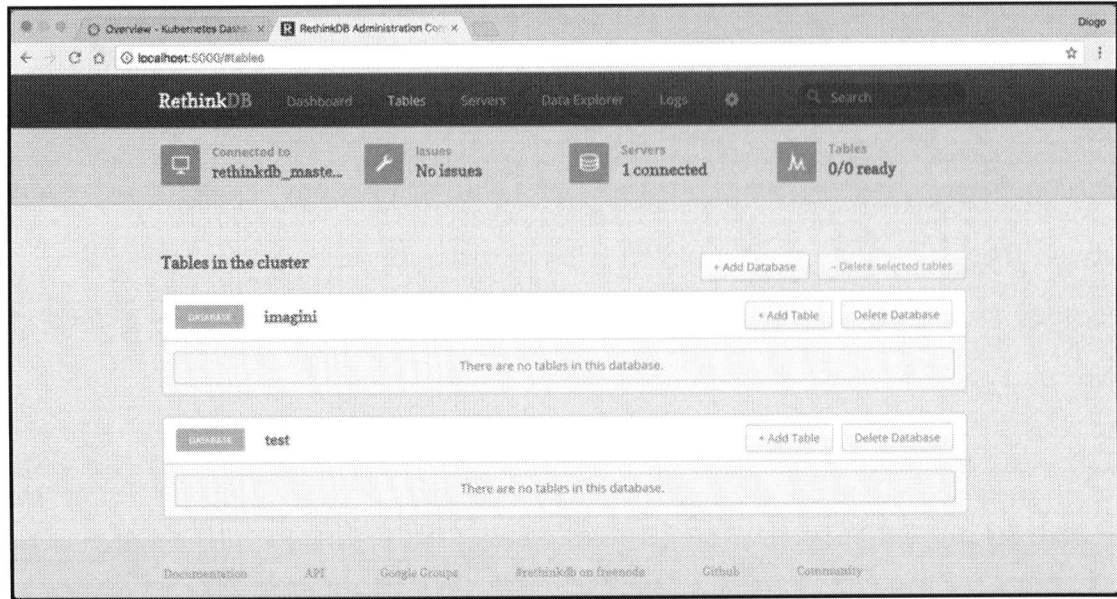

To keep it simple, we're keeping the RethinkDB connection hardcoded on our code. I'll leave it up to you to try it out later on with Kubernetes to see how you can have a persistent volume, have your settings there, and the database.

We just have to change our line to:

```
rethinkdb.connect({ host: "rethinkdb-master", db: "imagini" }, (err, db) =>
{
```

Since we have a local image, we need to build it just like we did before. Let's build it inside our `minikube`. First, let's make sure that we're going to push our commands to `minikube` and not our Docker base:

```
● ● ●                    1. nazgul-2.local: /Users/dresende (bash)

 ✕  ...s/dresende (kubectl)  ⌘1    ✕  ...ers/dresende (bash)  ⌘2

~ > minikube docker-env
export DOCKER_TLS_VERIFY="1"
export DOCKER_HOST="tcp://192.168.99.100:2376"
export DOCKER_CERT_PATH="/Users/dresende/.minikube/certs"
export DOCKER_API_VERSION="1.23"
# Run this command to configure your shell:
# eval $(minikube docker-env)
~ > eval $(minikube docker-env)
~ > _
```

Then, let's build our image using the same Docker command:

```
docker build -t imagini:0.0.6 .
```

After building it, let's begin the deployment:

```
kubectl run imagini --image=imagini:0.0.6 --port=3000
```

If everything runs smoothly, you should see a message like the following:

```
●  ●  ●                    1. nazgul-2.local: /Users/dresende/imagini (bash)

✕ ...resende (kubectl)  ● ⌘1   ✕ ...sende/imagini (bash)  ⌘2

Have some ♥for Sinon? You can support the project via Open Collective:
 > https://opencollective.com/sinon/donate

npm notice created a lockfile as package-lock.json. You should commit this file.
npm WARN imagini@1.0.0 No description
npm WARN imagini@1.0.0 No repository field.

added 143 packages in 32.328s
Removing intermediate container 89a11cc686b8
 ---> 147459a8a142
Step 8/9 : EXPOSE 3000
 ---> Running in 4bdd42b1bfdb
Removing intermediate container 4bdd42b1bfdb
 ---> 634585d0a22e
Step 9/9 : CMD [ "node", "/opt/app/imagini" ]
 ---> Running in f59883a53fe5
Removing intermediate container f59883a53fe5
 ---> 4f9fc82fbbf7
Successfully built 4f9fc82fbbf7
Successfully tagged imagini:0.0.6
~/imagini > kubectl run imagini --image=imagini:0.0.6 --port=3000
deployment.apps "imagini" created
~/imagini > _
```

If you refresh the Administration Console, you now have **Deployments** and a new Pod:

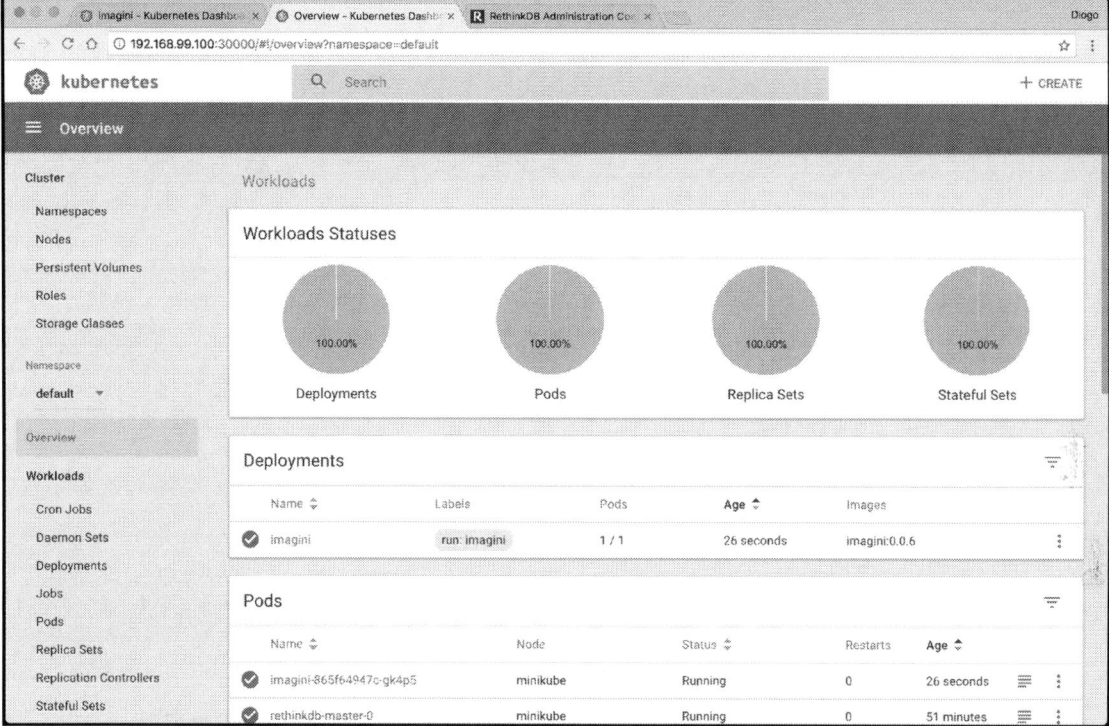

But Pods are, by default, only visible on the internal network. We need to expose our `imagini` to the exterior. Do this by running:

```
kubectl expose deployment imagini --type=LoadBalancer
```

If you check the services, you'll see that our service will expose on port `3000`, but it's currently pending. This is because we're using `minikube` and it has no `LoadBalancer`. For example, on a cloud provider, this would launch a real load balancer with an external address and would route traffic to the inside:

```
                                               1. nazgul-2.local: /Users/dresende/imagini (bash)
  X ...resende (kubectl) ● ⌘1    X ...sende/imagini (bash) ⌘2

~/imagini › kubectl expose deployment imagini --type=LoadBalancer
service "imagini" exposed
~/imagini › kubectl get services
NAME               TYPE           CLUSTER-IP      EXTERNAL-IP    PORT(S)                  AGE
imagini            LoadBalancer   10.98.43.23     <pending>      3000:30025/TCP           54s
kubernetes         ClusterIP      10.96.0.1       <none>         443/TCP                  2h
rethinkdb-master   ClusterIP      10.109.8.171    <none>         28015/TCP,29015/TCP      57m
~/imagini › minikube service imagini_
```

In our case, we can use the direct port, `30025`, which was assigned randomly. We can use the last command you see in the preceding screenshot in order to launch a browser window and point to our service.

You could do all of this using the administration tools from the browser or from the console. Some may be easier on the console, but it's up to you.

This is not an extensive introduction to Kubernetes. The objective was actually to see how easy it was to just make a few changes to our service and get it up and running on a new environment. That's one of the powers of containers.

Summary

Scaling an application used to be hard and complex. Today, with more information passing through our applications, and with a constantly increasing number of connected users, scaling is now imperative.

Thankfully, containers showed up a couple of years ago and helped solve this problem in a simpler way. There are still obstacles, but with the tools provided by Docker, Kubernetes, and others, replicating our applications and microservices became something that you can do almost without changing your code.

In the next chapter, we'll see what we need to do to have our service be cloud native while deploying our microservice to the **Google Cloud Platform (GCP)**.

10
Cloud-Native Microservices

Let's recap what we have done so far. We started by looking at the advantages of building applications based on microservices. Then, we looked at several tools that can help us start building our microservices. We stood with Express and embarked on building a simple microservice.

We learned the basics of state and security by interconnecting our microservice and a database server. We've chosen a test suite and added tests until we had a very good code coverage.

Finally, we learned how to deploy our microservice using containers. We then explored how we could scale our microservice using replicas across different sites.

When we deploy our microservice inside a container, we're opening a new world of possibilities. There are plenty of cloud providers that support containers. This means that as soon as we have our microservice running on a local container, we can replicate and do the same on many of these providers in no time.

You might have found that developing using containers gives you consistent and predictable behavior with the application. This also extends to the operations when they need to deploy.

Containers give them a much simpler and faster method to deploy any application. It's almost like your application is already native to the cloud environment, and they just need to specify a few details and that's it, it's deployed.

In this chapter, to make our microservice cloud-native, we're going to use the **Google Cloud Platform (GCP)**, and:

- Create a new project
- Deploy a database service
- Create a Kubernetes cluster
- Create our microservice files on the cluster
- Deploy our microservice to the cluster

Preparing for cloud-native

But what is cloud-native? What makes an application cloud-native? We say an application runs in the cloud when it's running outside our premises. More than that, it denotes when an application is supposedly running and spread across different locations and is resilient to failures.

A cloud-native application or microservice is designed from scratch to run in the cloud and take advantage of that computing model. It is able to scale and operate even if parts of its infrastructure fail. Being cloud-native is about how we deploy our microservice, not where.

And, we're already doing that! Since we first deployed using Docker, we have already started and restarted our microservice, and rebuilt new images and replicated without the worry of where, but instead, how.

Thinking generically, there are a few points to take into account when designing our microservice, or anything that will be cloud-native, for that matter:

- Understand what data your microservice will handle, and what kind of structures and relations will there be. Does a relational database such as MySQL or PostgreSQL suffice? Do you need a more loose database server that can handle documents with different information structures, such as MongoDB or RethinkDB?
  These questions must be answered to narrow the options. There are plenty of other types of databases. After narrowing your choices, you should pick the one that gives you more resilience and that can be replicated the same way as your microservice, to handle some degree of failure.
- Find out what other dependencies you might need. If you have choices, go for the ones that are not dependent on a specific operative system. Below the cloud servers, there are different operative systems and you don't want to be forced to choose any type.
- Avoid going non-standard. More specifically, try to take the most out of current standard protocols. Because you can deploy to geographically distant hosts, connectivity and policy rules may introduce restrictions to traffic, so keep with standards such as HTTP in order to communicate between microservices.
- Design your microservices to be able to scale horizontally. It's not uncommon for microservices to not scale linearly just by adding replicas, but try to design them to be able to distribute loads more evenly. One easy path is to have a layer of proxies on top.

Going cloud-native

Now that we're able to deploy using containers, and we have used Kubernetes already on a local virtual machine, let's see how we can do the same on a cloud environment. You can choose any type of cloud provider, as long as you follow the considerations we just discussed in the previous section.

We're going to use GCP. There's a one-year trial with free credit available, so you can try it out while you read this. Head to the website and register if you haven't done it before. You'll probably be asked to enter a payment method, but don't worry, they won't charge unless you exceed the free credit:

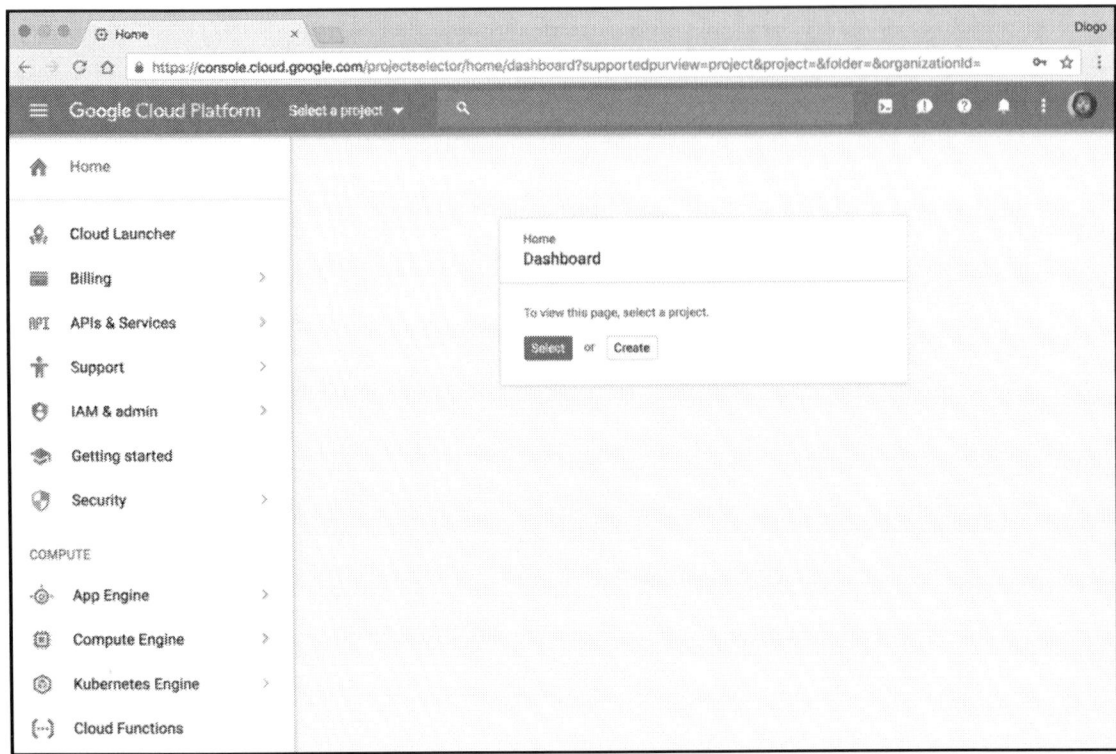

Creating a new project

You now need to create a project. Just follow the instructions, set a name, and hit the **Create** button:

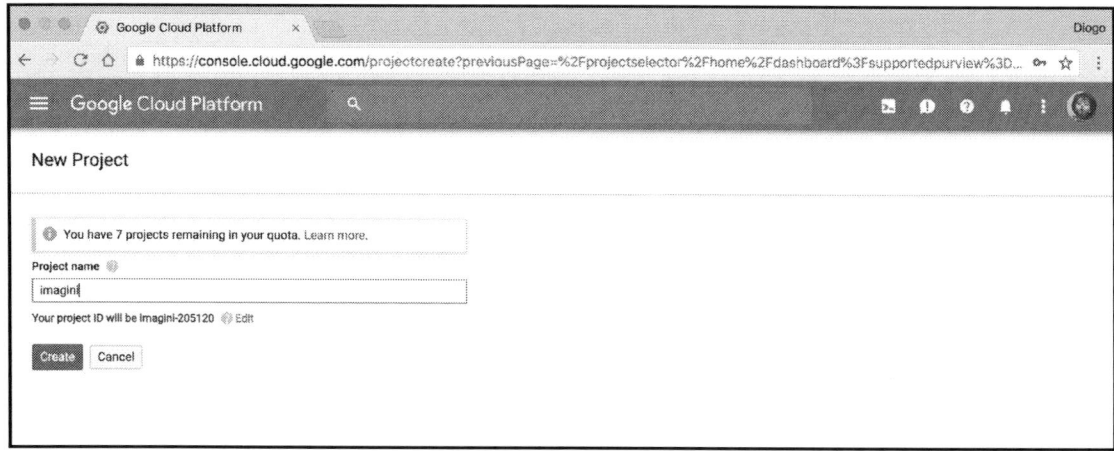

You'll then have access to the project dashboard. You can check resource usage and project status, as well as billing information:

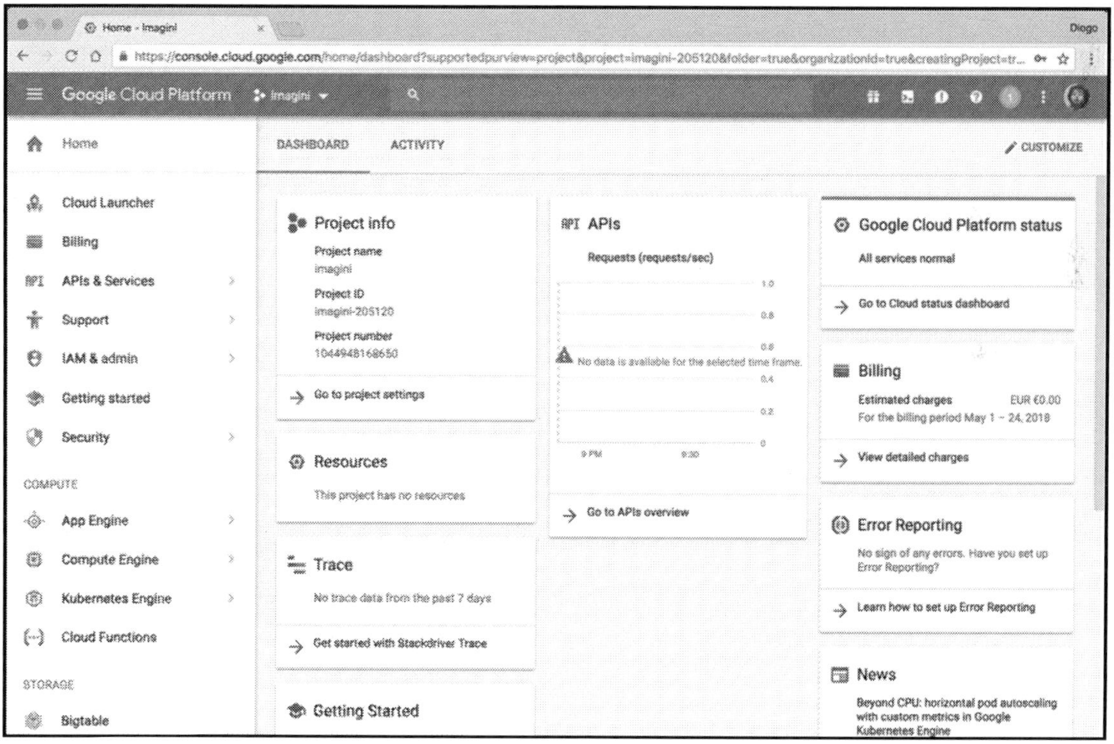

Deploying a database service

On the left-hand side, there are the main navigation options, one of which, Cloud Launcher, lets us easily set up services that we need. Since we used RethinkDB in the previous chapter, let's now try MySQL again. We need a database server, so let's head to Cloud Launcher:

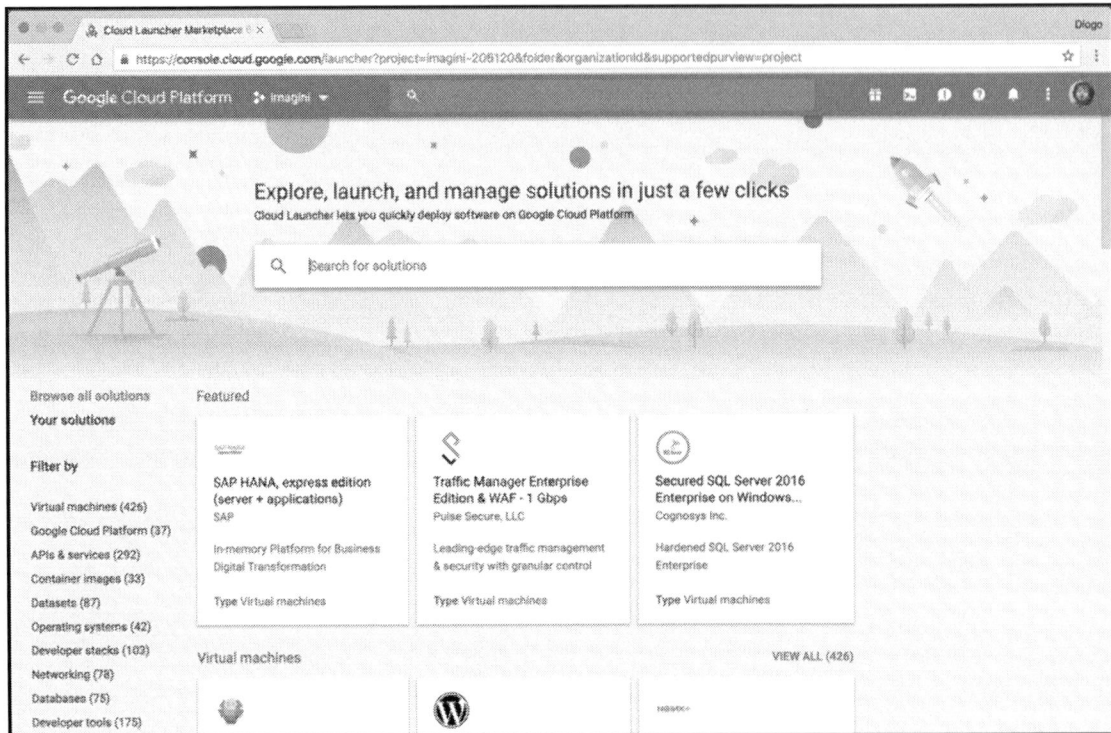

On the sidebar, there are a couple of service categories to choose from. Let's use the filter on top to search for **mysql**:

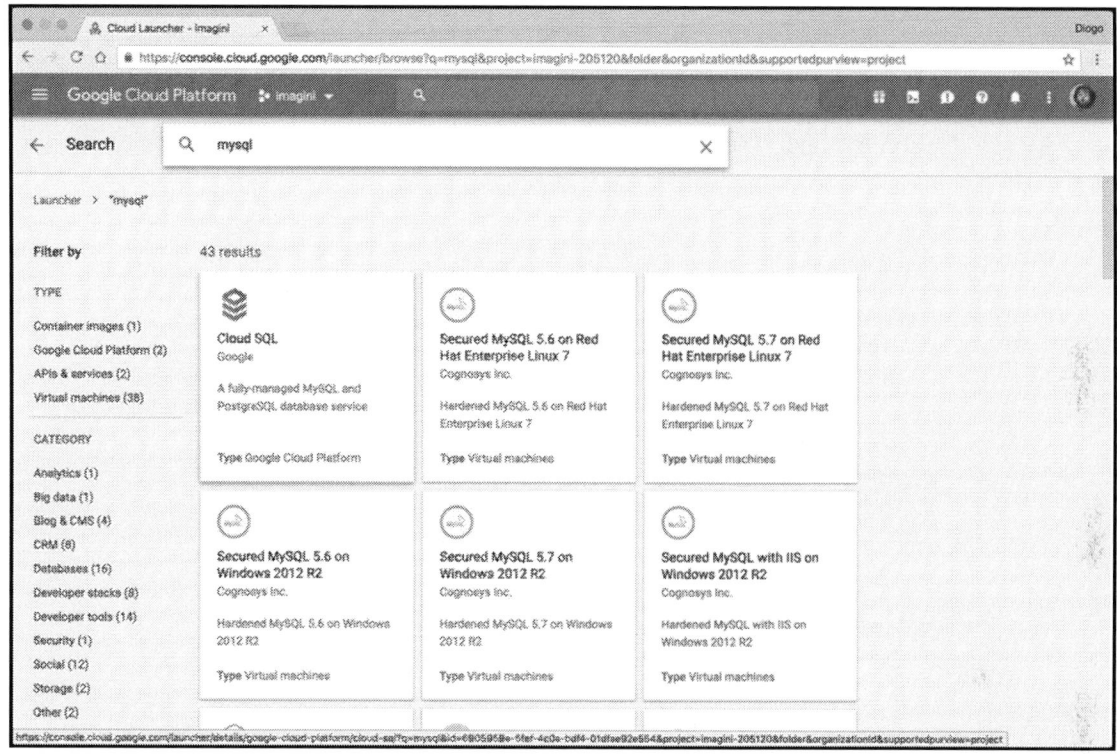

One of the options, in my case the first, is **Cloud SQL**, which is a Google service used to run a fully-managed MySQL or PostgreSQL database service. It alleviates the burden of configuration and maintenance. Click on that option:

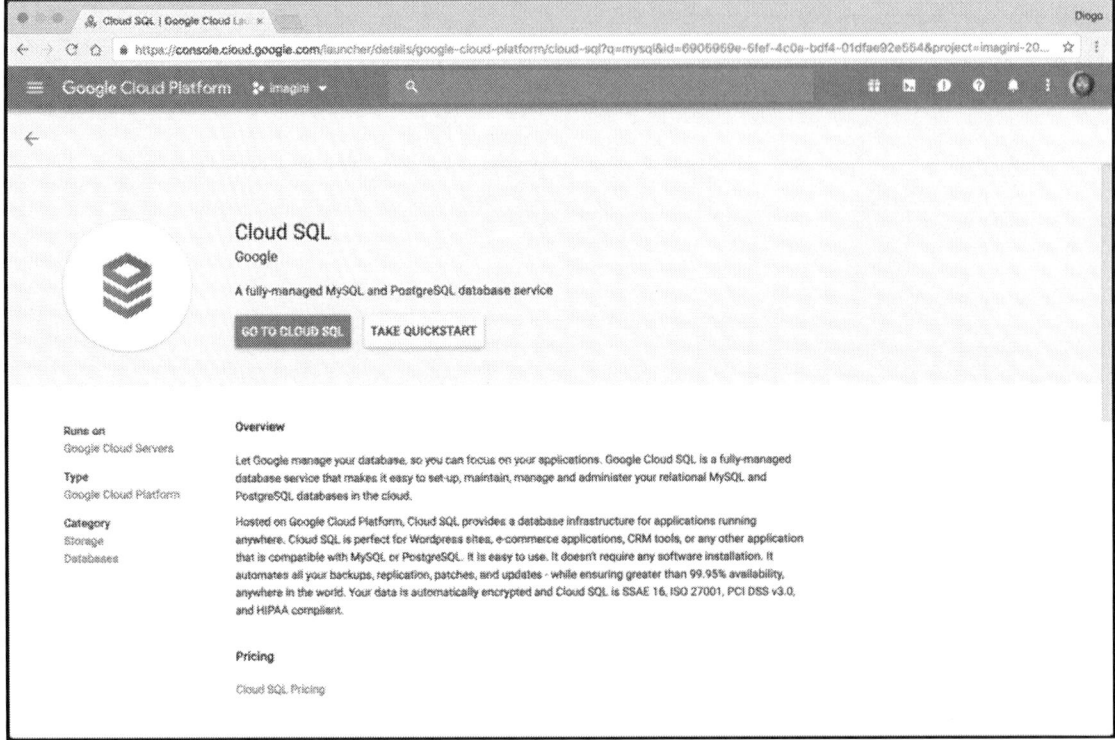

There's an overview with an explanation of the service, as well as pricing if you want to consult it. Because we're using free credit, that is not a concern for now. Click on **GO TO CLOUD SQL**:

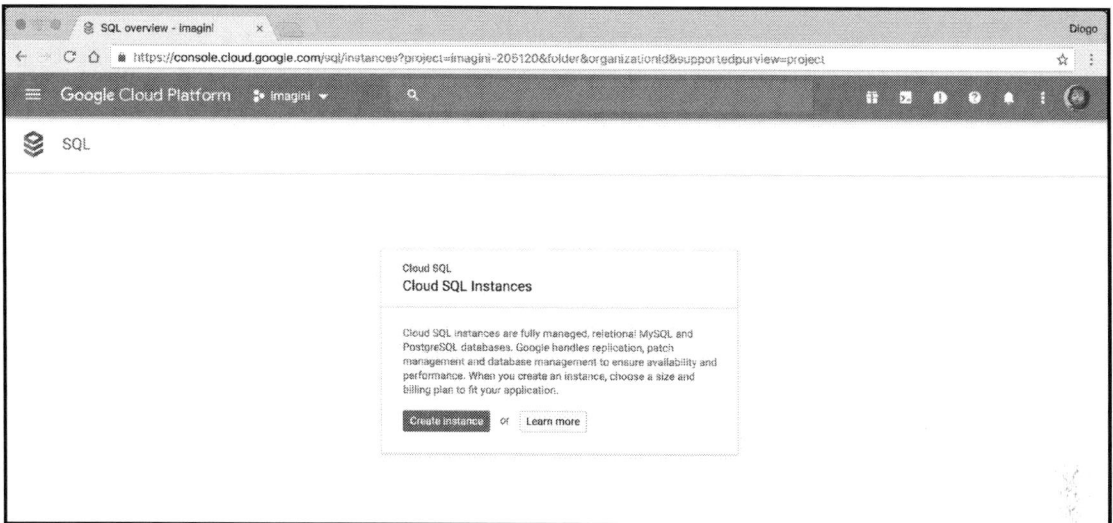

Because we're using the service for the first time, there's no service instance. Click on "Create Instance" to create a new one, follow the instructions, and create the instance. You'll be asked for a password for the default root account; don't forget it. At the end, you should see an instance list. Wait until your instance is fully up and running:

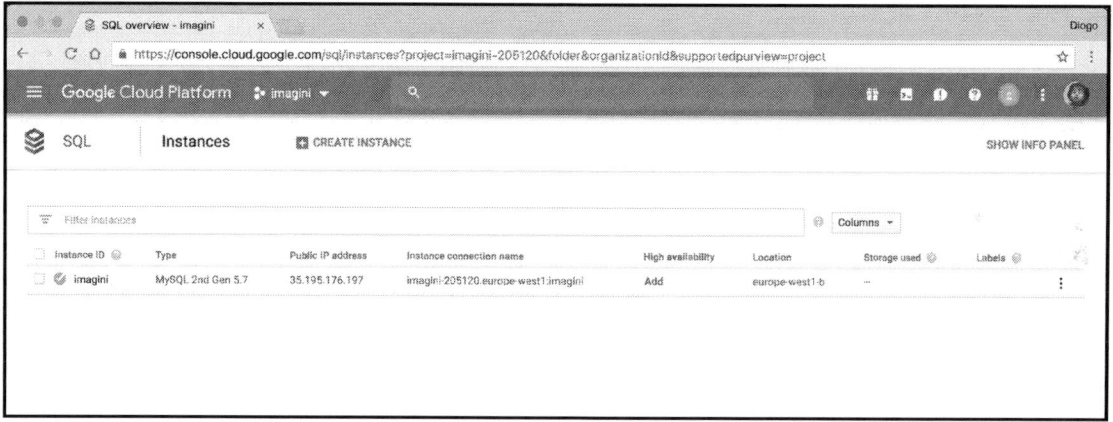

You can click on the instance ID and see more information about it. You'll have access to a service dashboard, as well as be able to import and export:

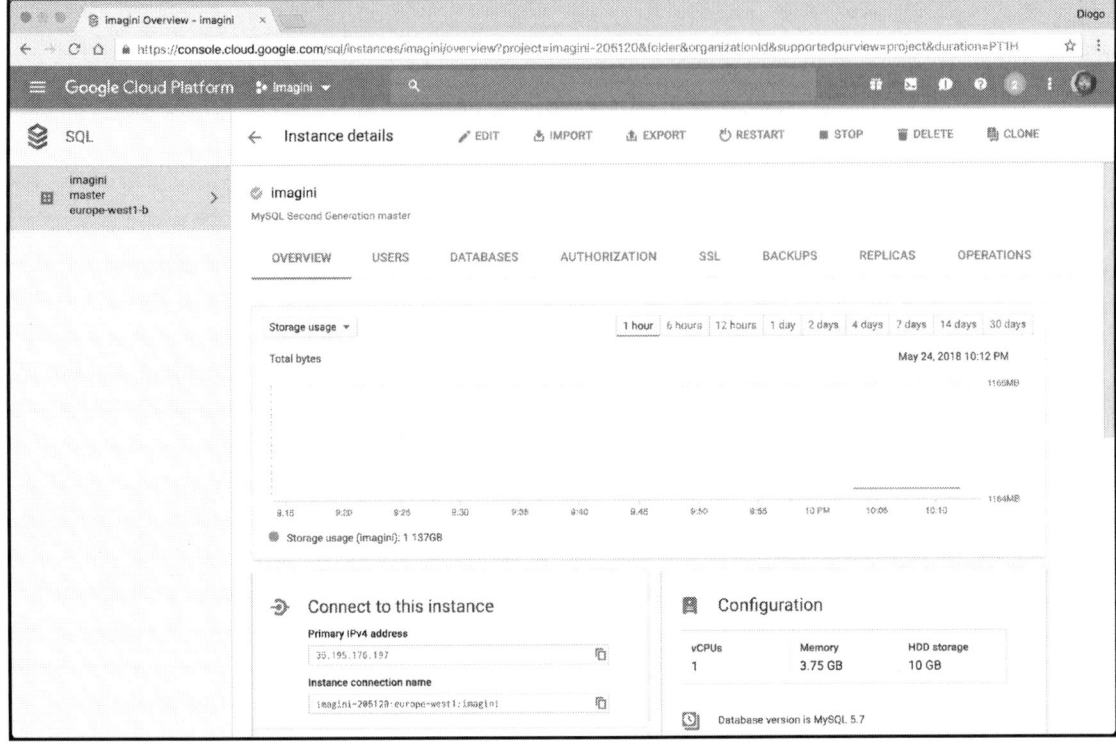

There's a **DATABASES** tab where we can create our microservice database. Head there and create it. Retain defaults on the character set and collation:

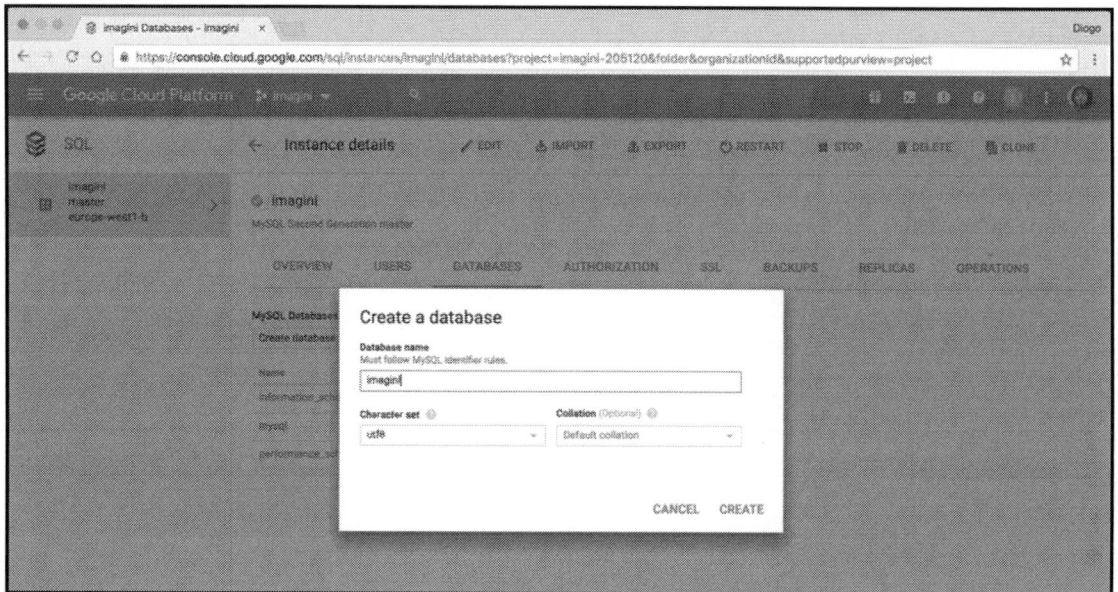

Our database is now ready. Let's head back to the project dashboard. Click on **Google Cloud Platform** in the top-left corner of the screen:

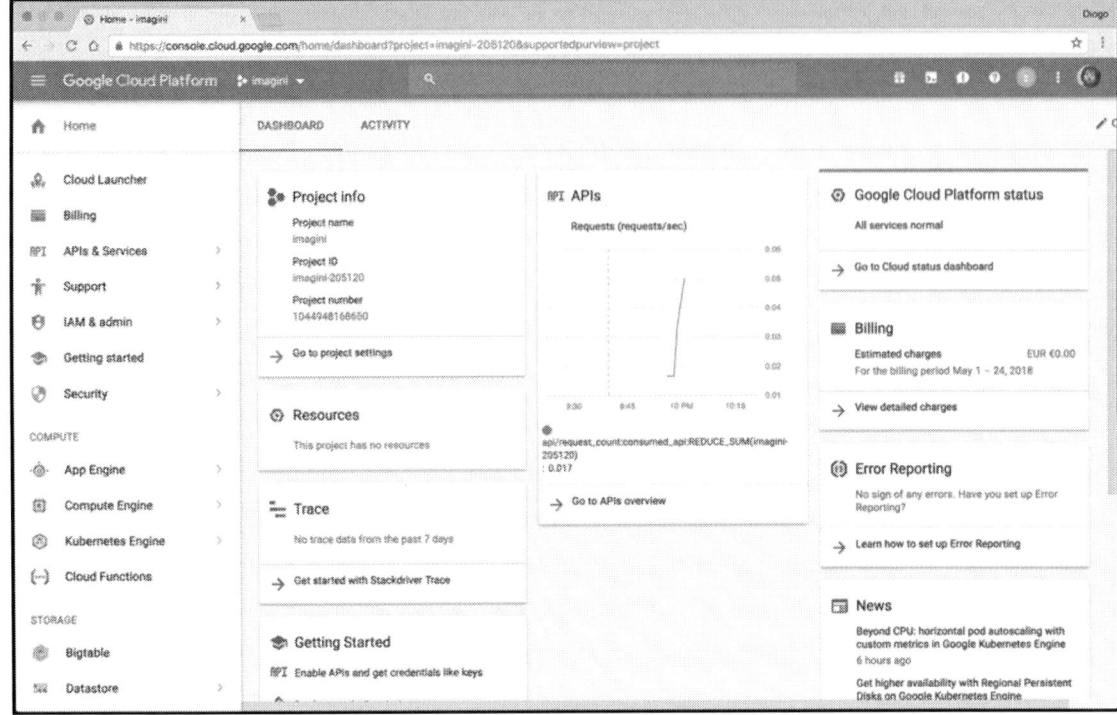

You'll notice that the **APIs** block on the middle column now has a line showing some activity. APIs are part of the infrastructure and, since we just created a service instance, there's some activity going on. Click on **Go to APIs overview**:

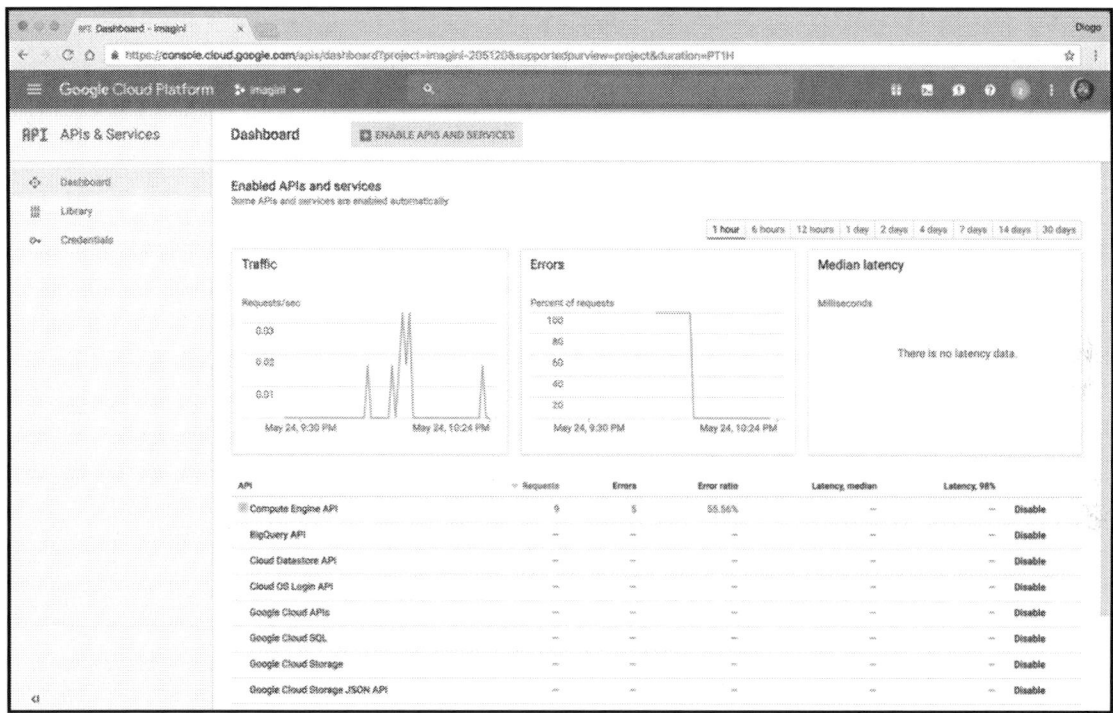

Here, you can monitor activity, traffic, and errors of all enabled and used APIs. Heading back to our project dashboard, and looking at the sidebar, you'll notice there are plenty of options available.

Scrolling down a bit, you'll find an **SQL** section, where you can find our previously created instance. If you need to go there in the future, this is how you find it:

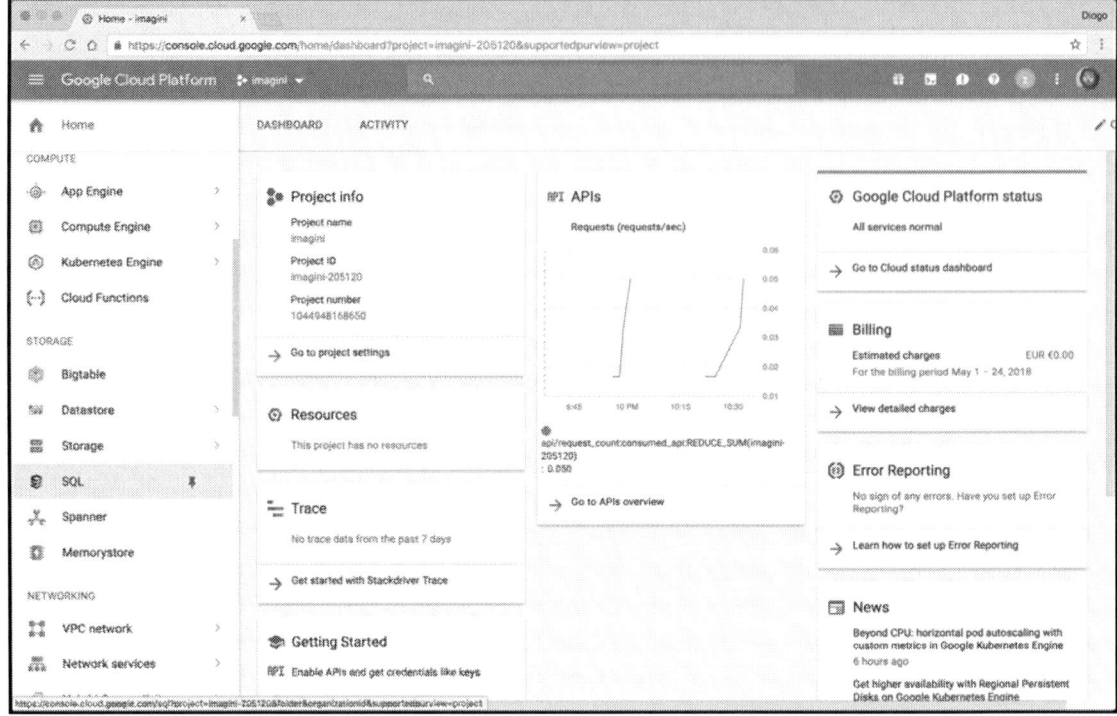

Creating a Kubernetes cluster

Previously, for a few items, you may have noticed the **Kubernetes Engine** option. That's where we're heading to prepare our cluster:

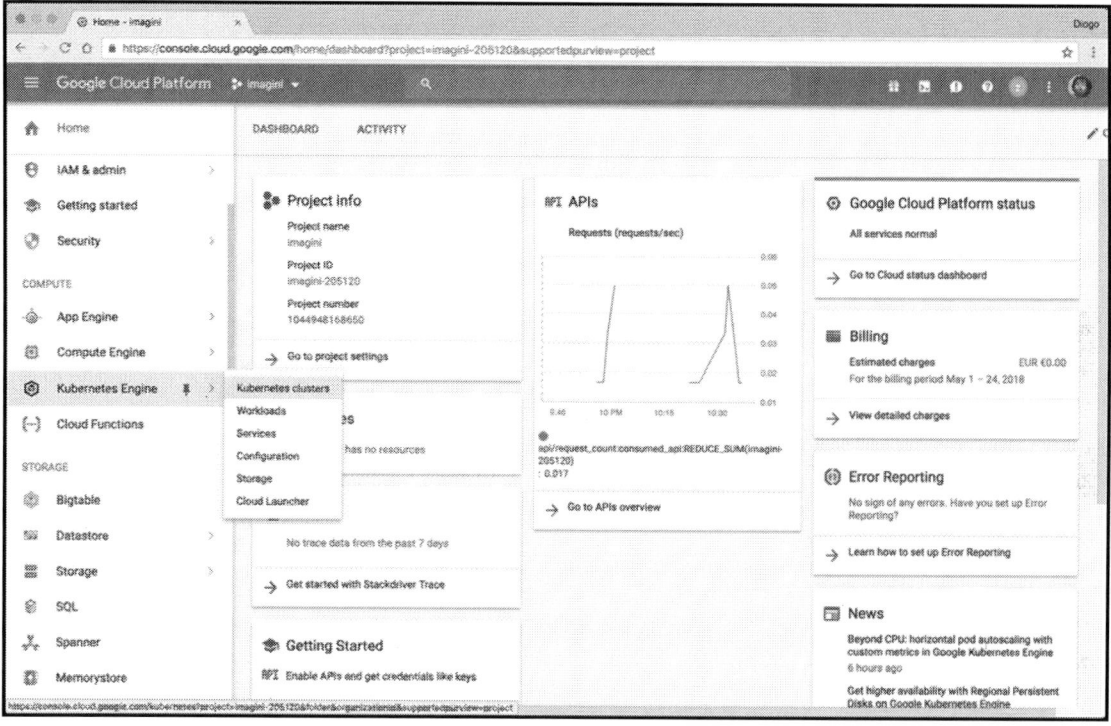

You'll be asked to create a new cluster. Choose the default options, or change the ones you want to try out, and create a cluster for our microservice to run on:

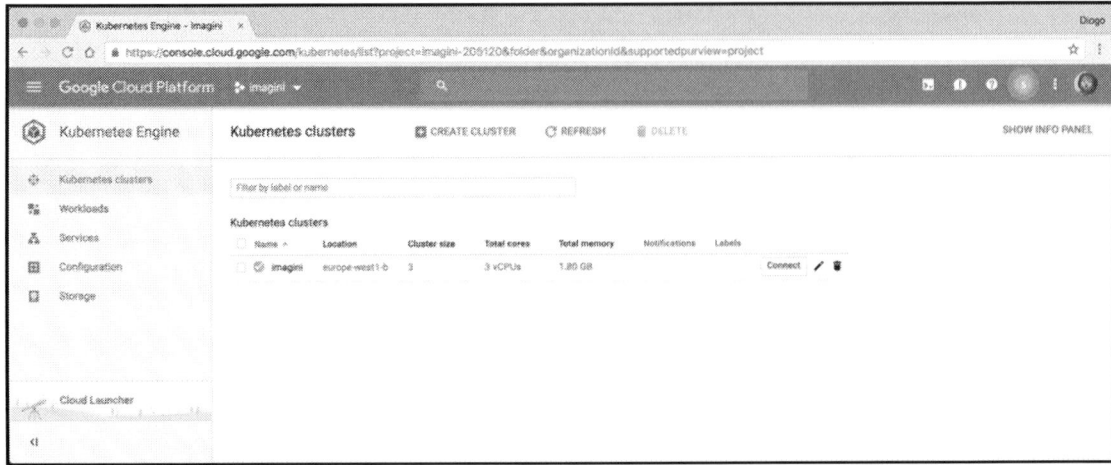

We now have a Kubernetes cluster of three nodes to run our microservice. In the top-right corner of the screen, you'll find one important icon, which is the **Google Cloud Shell icon**:

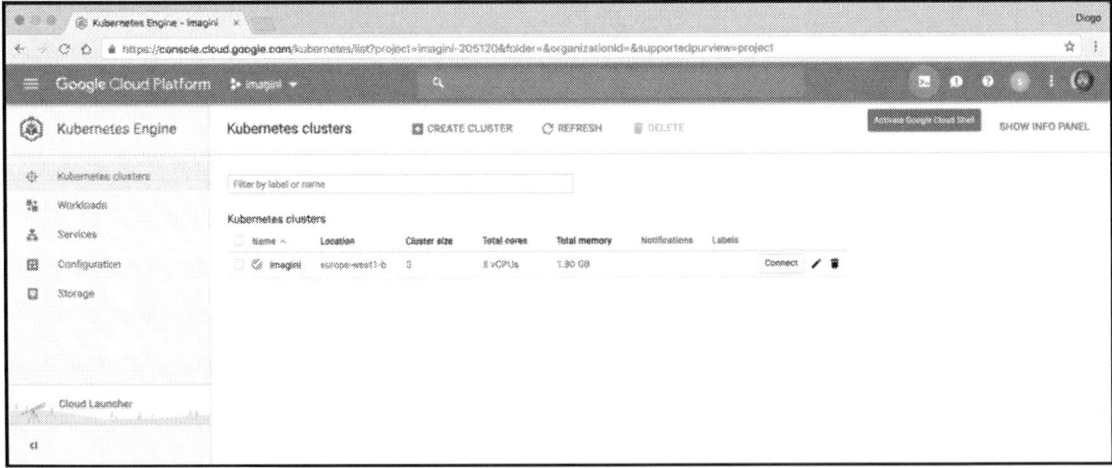

If you click on it, a console will open that gives you access to your platform using a terminal. You can do all kinds of stuff, such as monitoring containers, and checking connectivity:

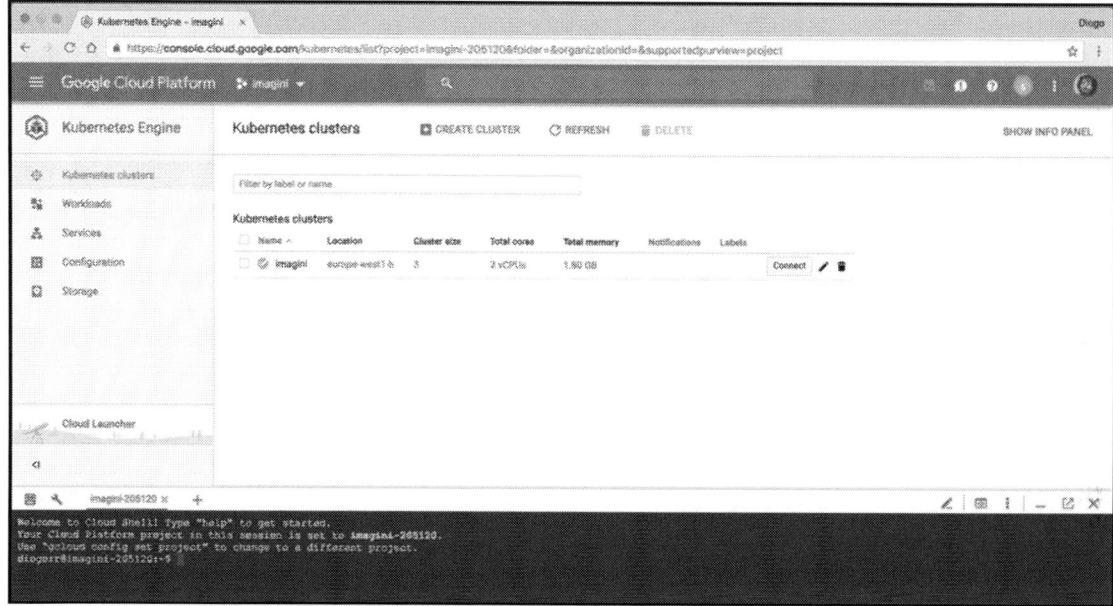

This is a normal console, but with the `gcloud` and `kubectl` commands already installed. You can have those installed locally and manage your clusters remotely, or just access this console to make a quick change or checkup.

Creating our microservice

Similar to what we did before, these are the steps we need to perform before successfully deploying to our new cluster:

1. Create our docker image that will use our MySQL instance.
2. Create credentials to access the instance.
3. Create the configuration for our service.
4. Deploy it.

First, notice the pencil icon in the top-right corner of the console. It's an online editor we can use to create the files we need:

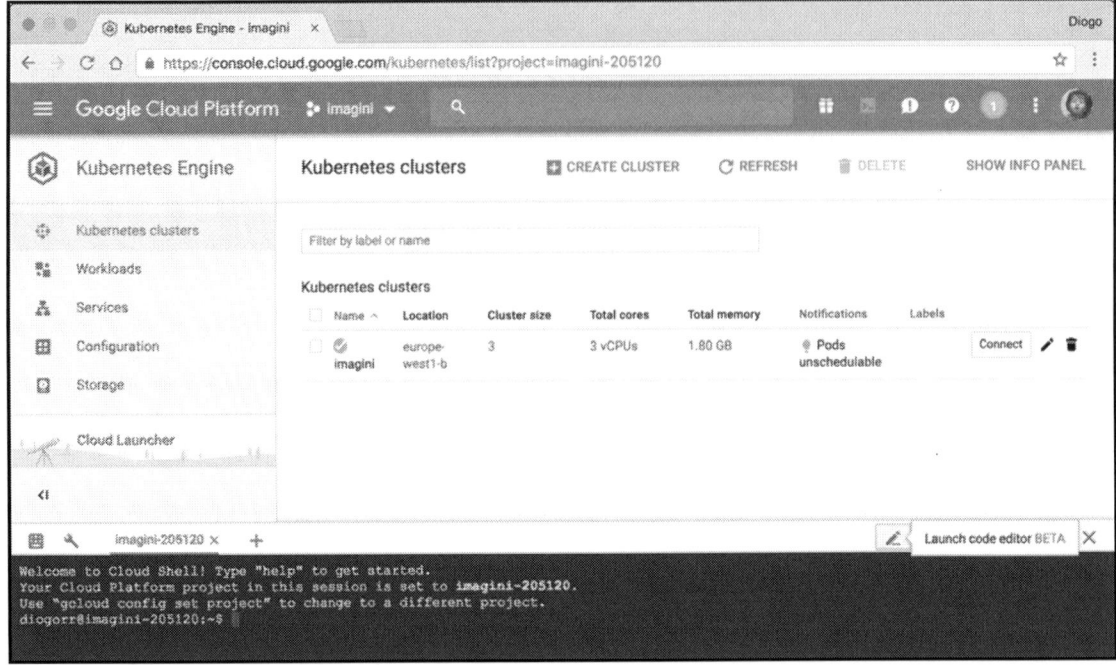

Click on it. It should open a new tab with an empty editor. This represents the root folder of the console you have on the bottom:

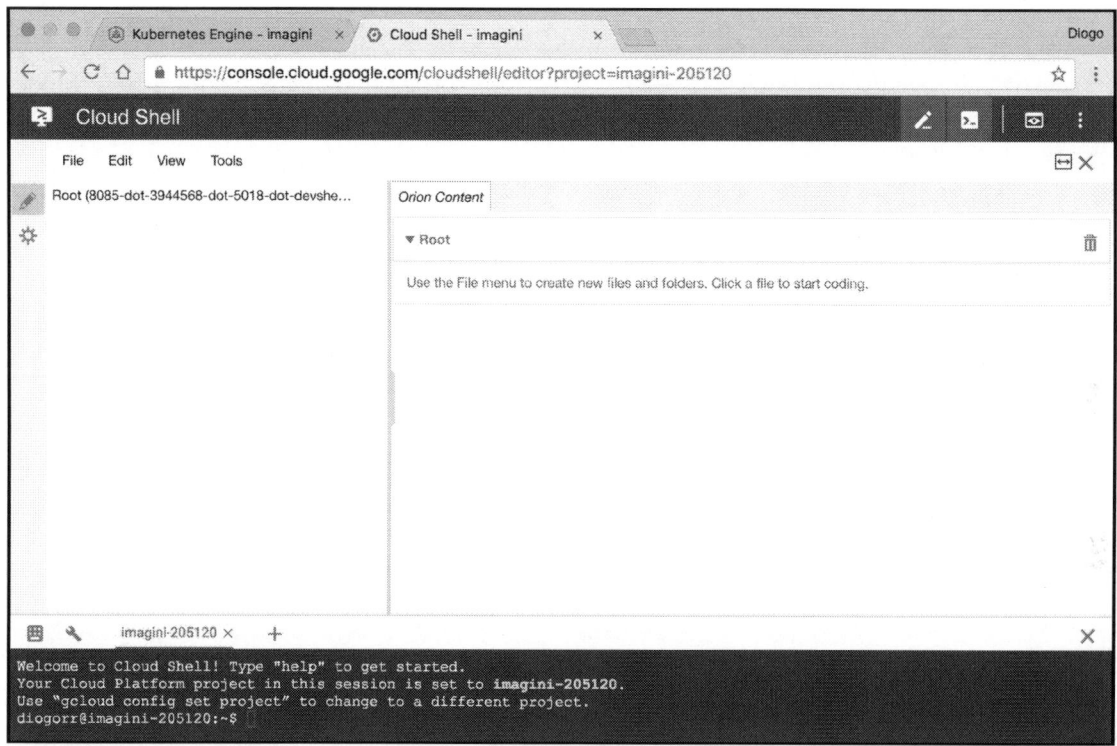

Let's start by creating our `package.json` file. Go to **File** and click **New**, and then **File**. Type `package.json` and insert our dependencies. Remember, we're using MySQL this time:

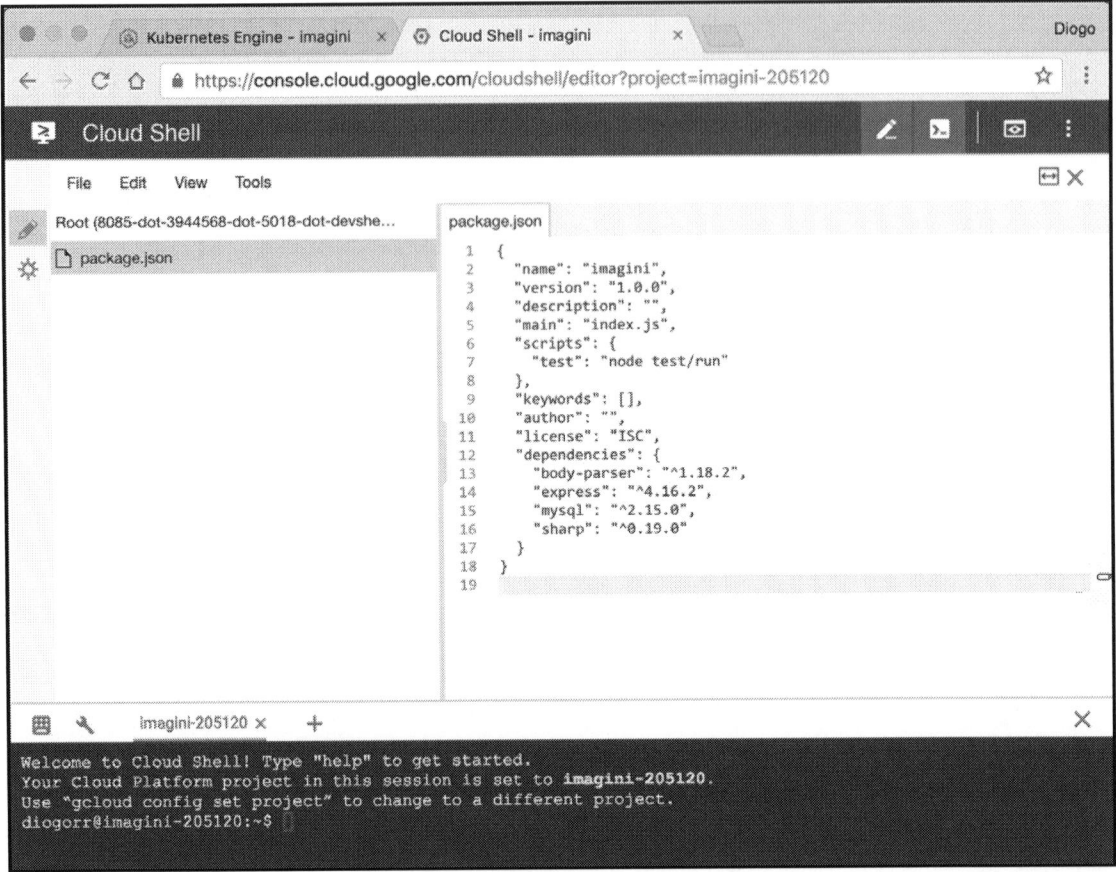

Then, create our service file. We're not using a `settings.json` file; we're going to use credentials passed to the container using an environment variable:

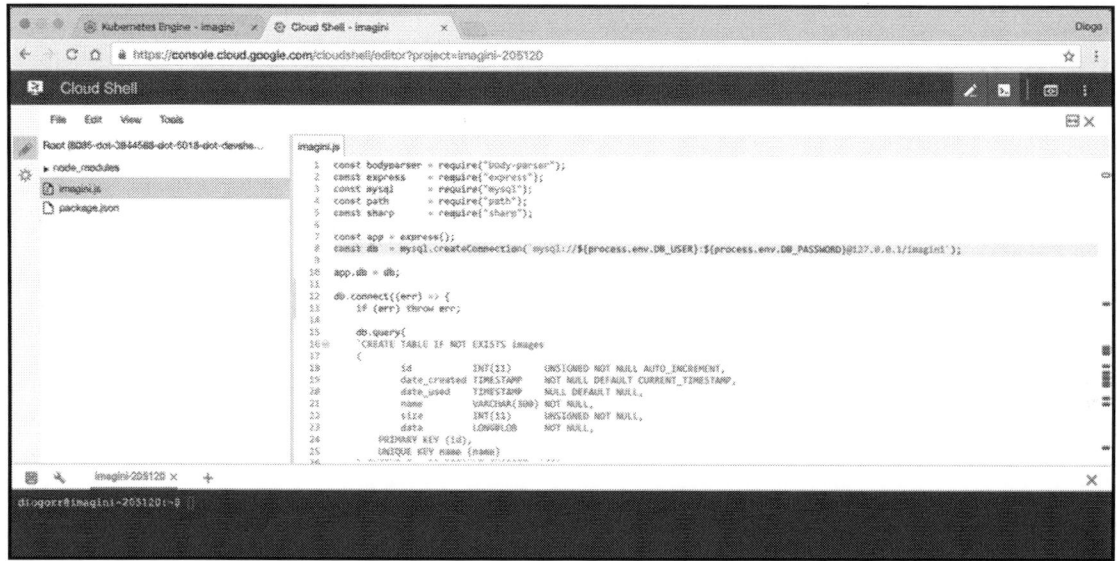

Then, create the `Dockerfile` for our service:

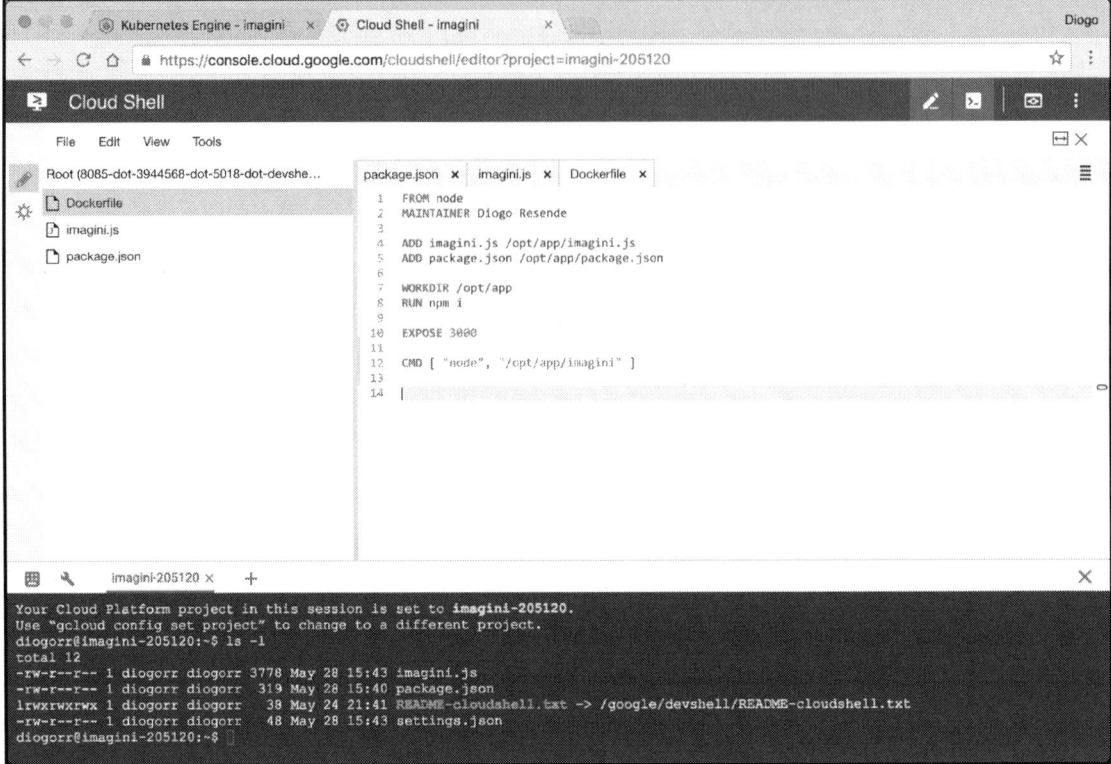

You can see on the bottom console that we're creating the files in the root folder. We're now going to use the console to create our container image. Type the following command:

```
docker build . -t gcr.io/imagini-205120/imagini
```

We're using a more composed name because we're publishing to the **Google Container Registry (GCR)**, and so it's good practice to use the project ID (as I did) and then the name of the service:

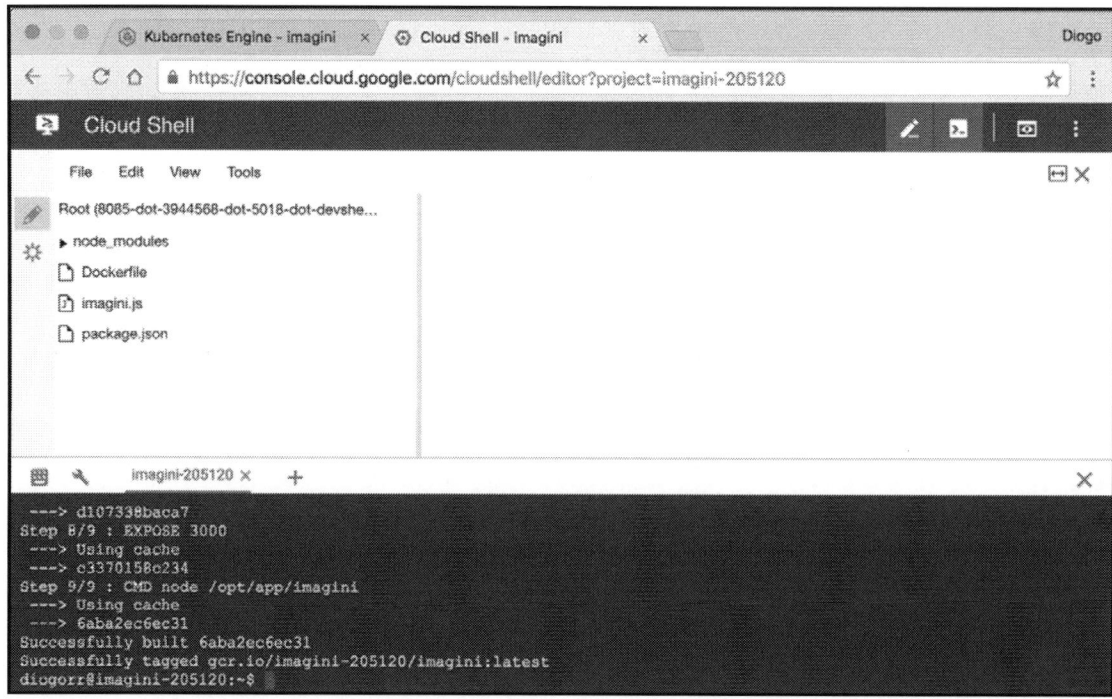

Then, let's push it to the registry using the following command:

```
gcloud docker -- push gcr.io/imagini-205120/imagini
```

If everything goes right, you should see a list of layers of the image being pushed (published to the registry) and, in the end, a digest and the size of the image, as shown here:

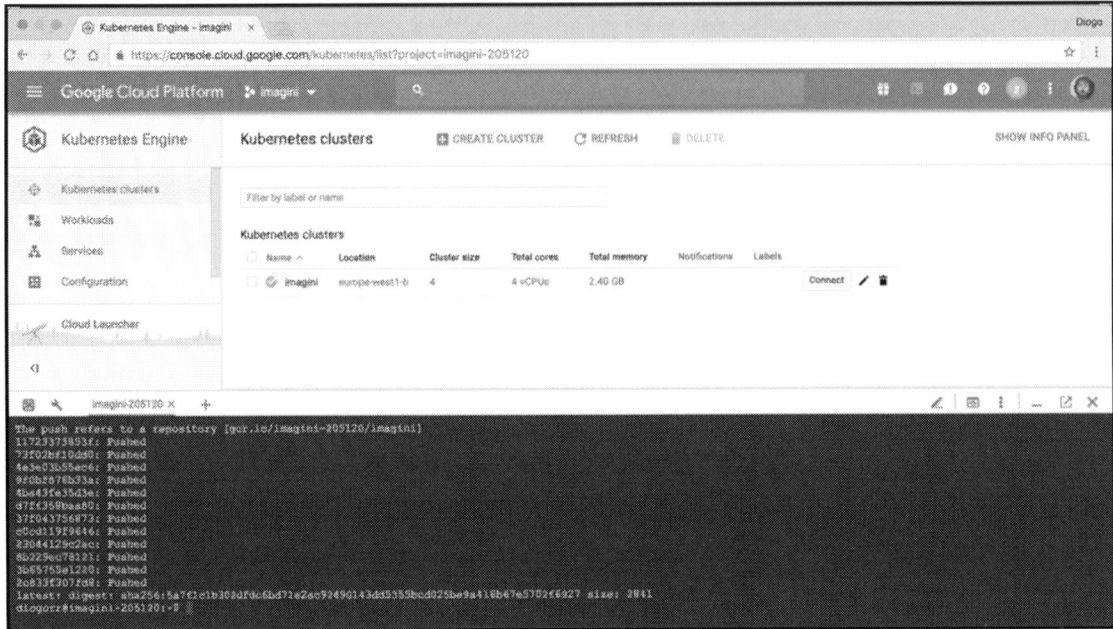

You may notice that I closed the editor between commands. You can use any console, and can even have more than one open.

We now need to create the credentials. We're not going to have passwords on text files. We're going to use an SQL proxy, and we'll expose credentials when the containers are executed, using an environment variable.

First, close the console and click the **Connect** button that is located on the right-hand side of the cluster name:

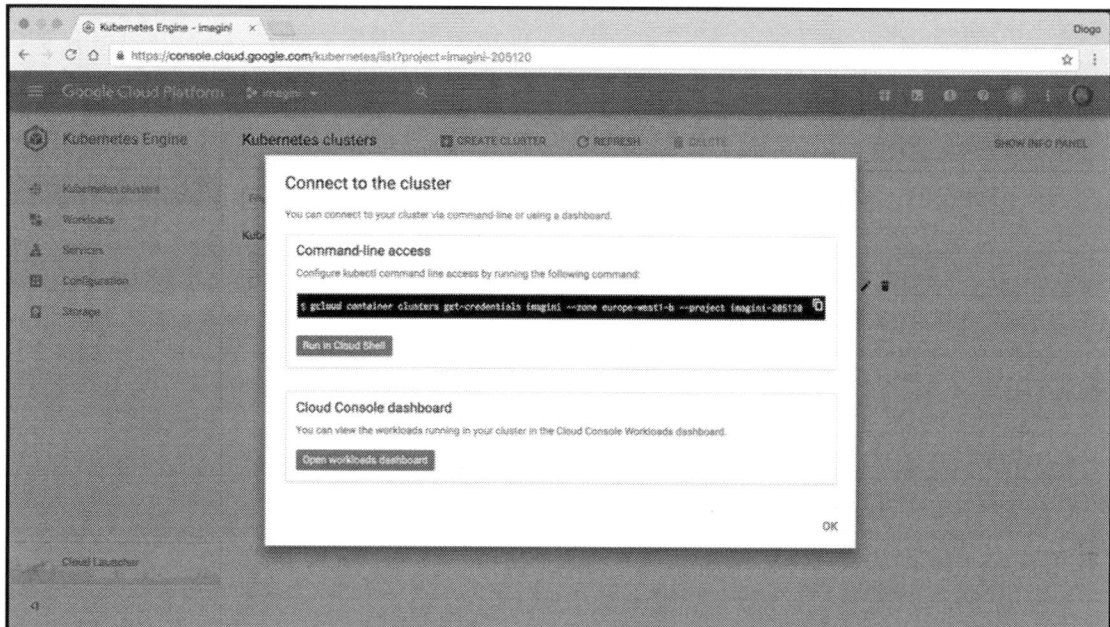

Click **Run in Cloud Shell**. This will reopen the console, but will type in the command to connect to our cluster:

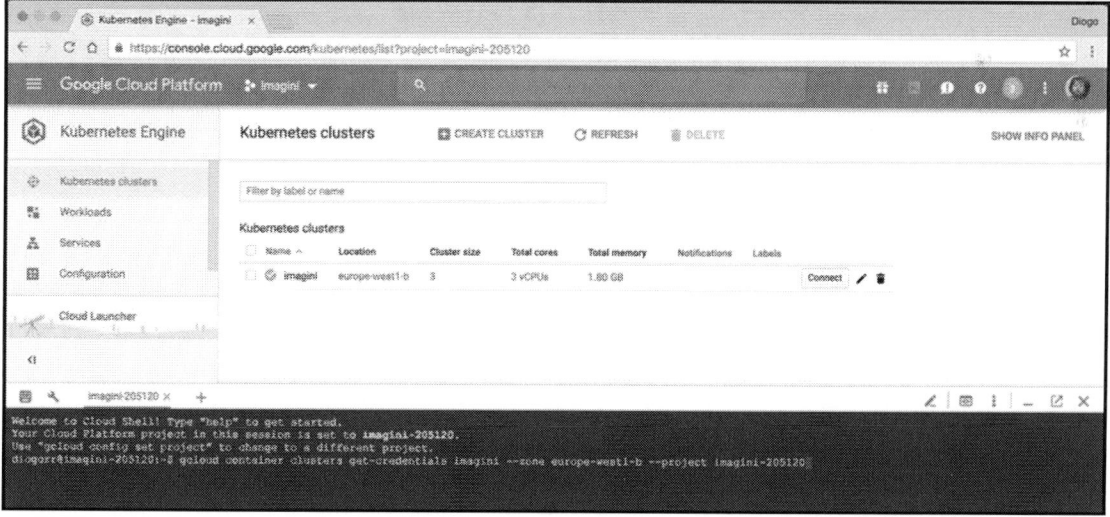

Just hit the *Enter* key in order to have access to the cluster:

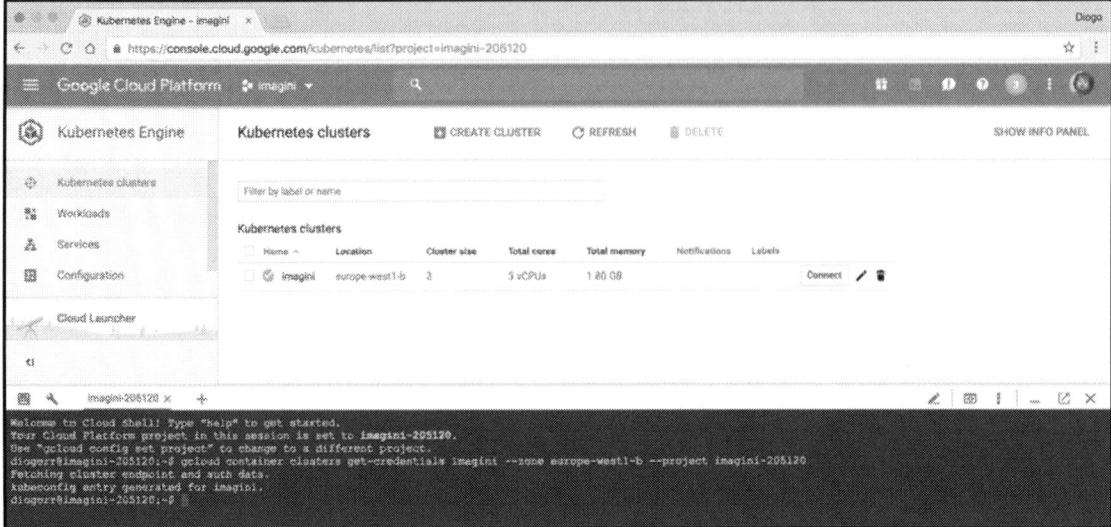

Then, we'll use the `gcloud` command to create the proxy user account that will be used by the SQL proxy to access our Cloud SQL instance:

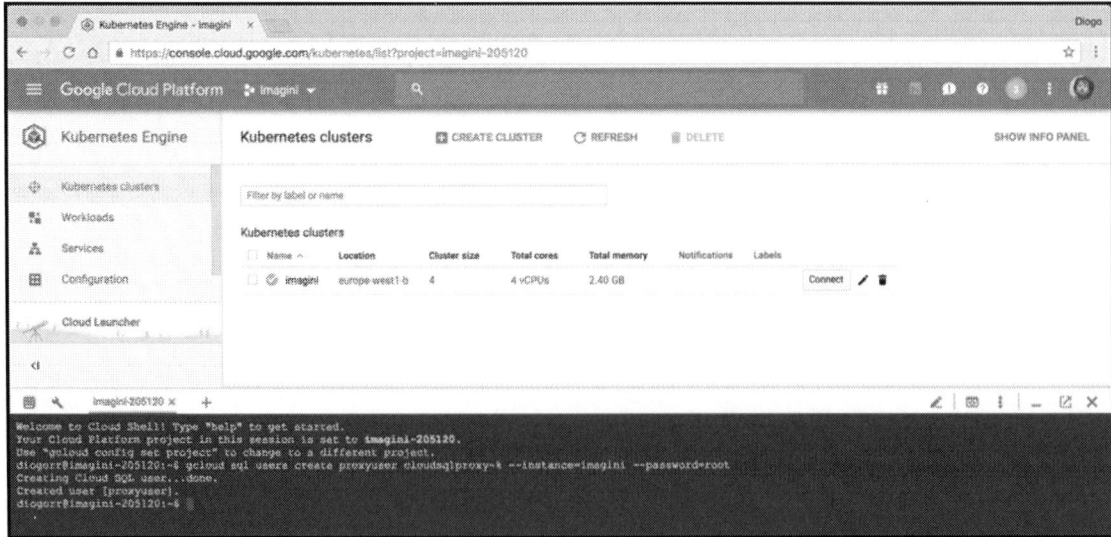

Now, type the following command:

```
gcloud sql instances describe imagini
```

Scroll up the console log until you see a line that starts with **connectionName**:. Take a look at the following screenshot and note the highlighted text in the console.

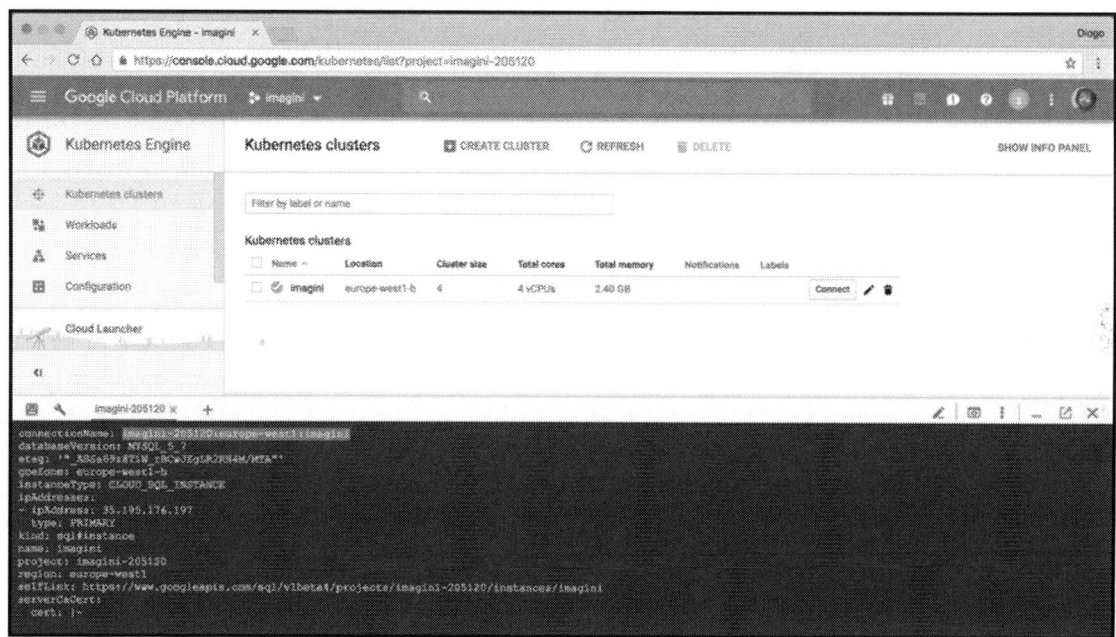

Copy the name down and save it for later. We'll need it when we create our deployment configuration.

Now, let's create a service account that is able to access our Cloud SQL instance. Head to **IAM & admin** and click **Service accounts**:

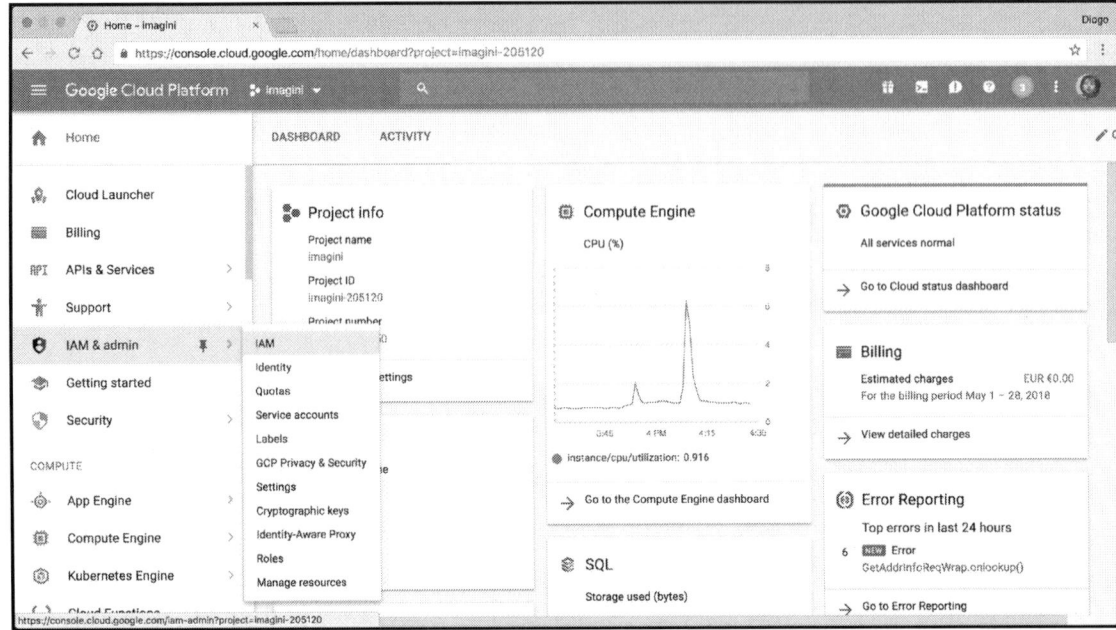

Create a service account with the **Cloud SQL Client** role, and check **Furnish a new private key**:

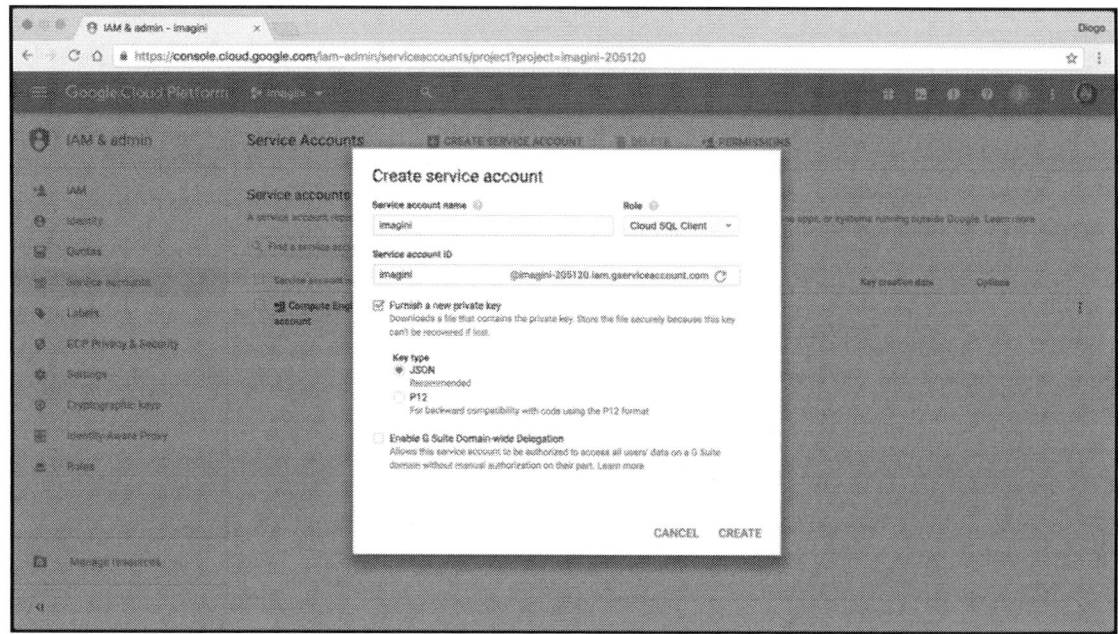

After hitting **Create**, the account will be created and a JSON file will be given to you to save in your local disk. Head back to the cluster, open the console, and then click to open the editor again.

You'll notice that there's a menu with several options in the top-right corner, one of which is **Upload file**:

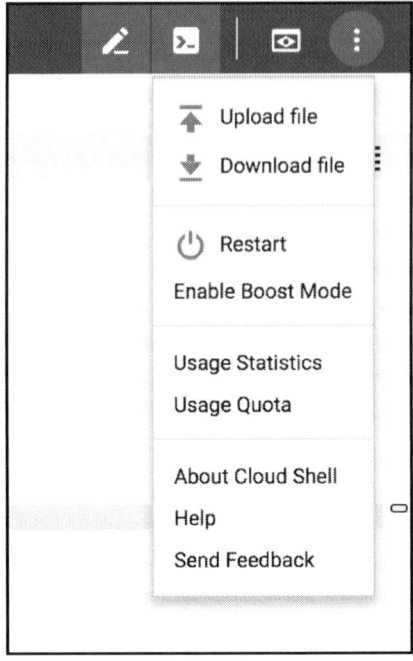

Pick the JSON file you just saved and upload it using that option:

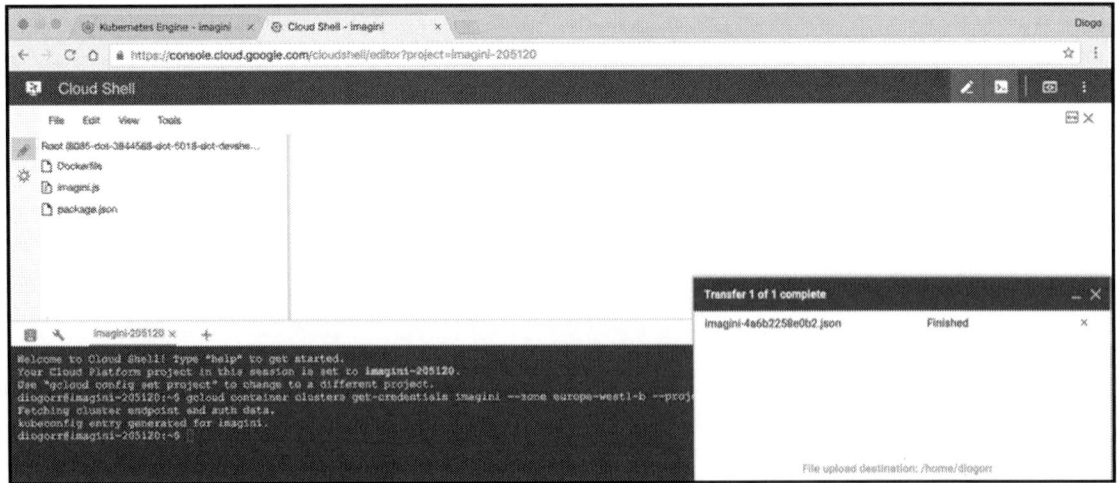

Now, let's use the console to create the instance secret using that credentials file. Use the following command (change the name to your JSON file):

```
kubectl create secret generic cloudsql-instance-credentials --from-file=credentials.json=imagini-4a6b2258e0b2.json
```

The following screenshot shows the result of the preceding command executed in the console. You should see something like **secret "cloudsql-instance-credentials" created**.

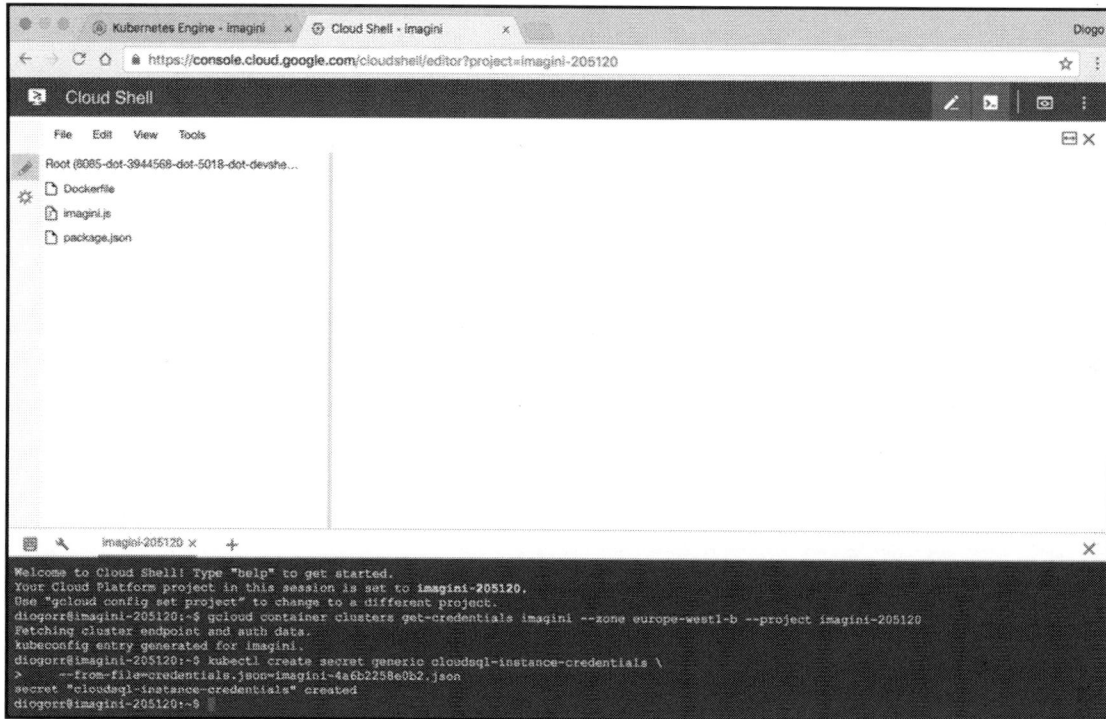

Now, let's create the database credentials secret:

```
kubectl create secret generic cloudsql-db-credentials --from-literal=username=proxyuser --from-literal=password=root
```

The following screenshot shows the result of the preceding command executed in the console. You should see something like **secret "cloudsql-db-credentials" created**.

We now have everything ready to deploy our service. This is the configuration we'll be using:

```
apiVersion: extensions/v1beta1
kind: Deployment
metadata:
  name: imagini-frontend
  labels:
    app: imagini
spec:
  replicas: 3
  template:
    metadata:
      labels:
        app: imagini
        tier: frontend
    spec:
      containers:
      - name: imagini-app
        image: gcr.io/imagini-205120/imagini
        imagePullPolicy: Always
        ports:
        - name: http-server
```

```
          containerPort: 3000
        env:
          - name: DB_USER
            valueFrom:
              secretKeyRef:
                name: cloudsql-db-credentials
                key: username
          - name: DB_PASSWORD
            valueFrom:
              secretKeyRef:
                name: cloudsql-db-credentials
                key: password
      - name: cloudsql-proxy
        image: gcr.io/cloudsql-docker/gce-proxy:1.11
        command: ["/cloud_sql_proxy",
                  "-instances=imagini-205120:europe-
                  west1:imagini=tcp:3306",
                  "-credential_file=/secrets/cloudsql/credentials.json"]
        volumeMounts:
          - name: cloudsql-instance-credentials
            mountPath: /secrets/cloudsql
            readOnly: true
      volumes:
        - name: cloudsql-instance-credentials
          secret:
            secretName: cloudsql-instance-credentials
```

Summing up, we're defining the following:

- The service name and same meta information
- The number of replicas we want
- The service, using our container image that we published earlier
- Two environment variables, based on the secrets we created earlier
- The SQL proxy that will enable our service to securely connect to our Cloud SQL

The secrets ensure that we have no confidential information spread on clear text files. Notice the instance name there. Replace it with the instance in **connectionName** that we saw before.

```
-instances=INSTANCE_ID=tcp:3306
```

Deploying our microservice

We can now create our deployment. Head to the editor and create a deployment file called `imagini.yml` with the content I just described:

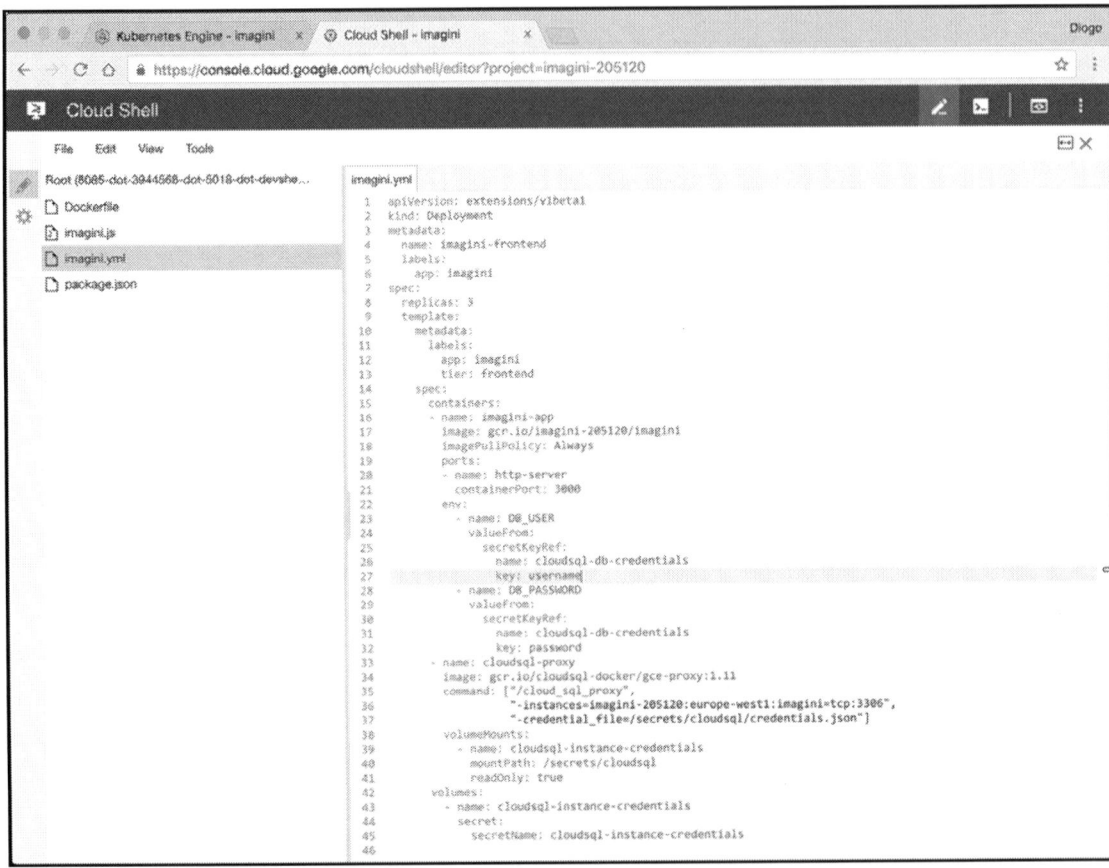

Then, use the console and type the following:

```
kubectl create -f imagini.yml
```

If nothing wrong happens, you should see a line along the lines of **deployment "imagini-frontend" created**, as shown in the console in the following screenshot:

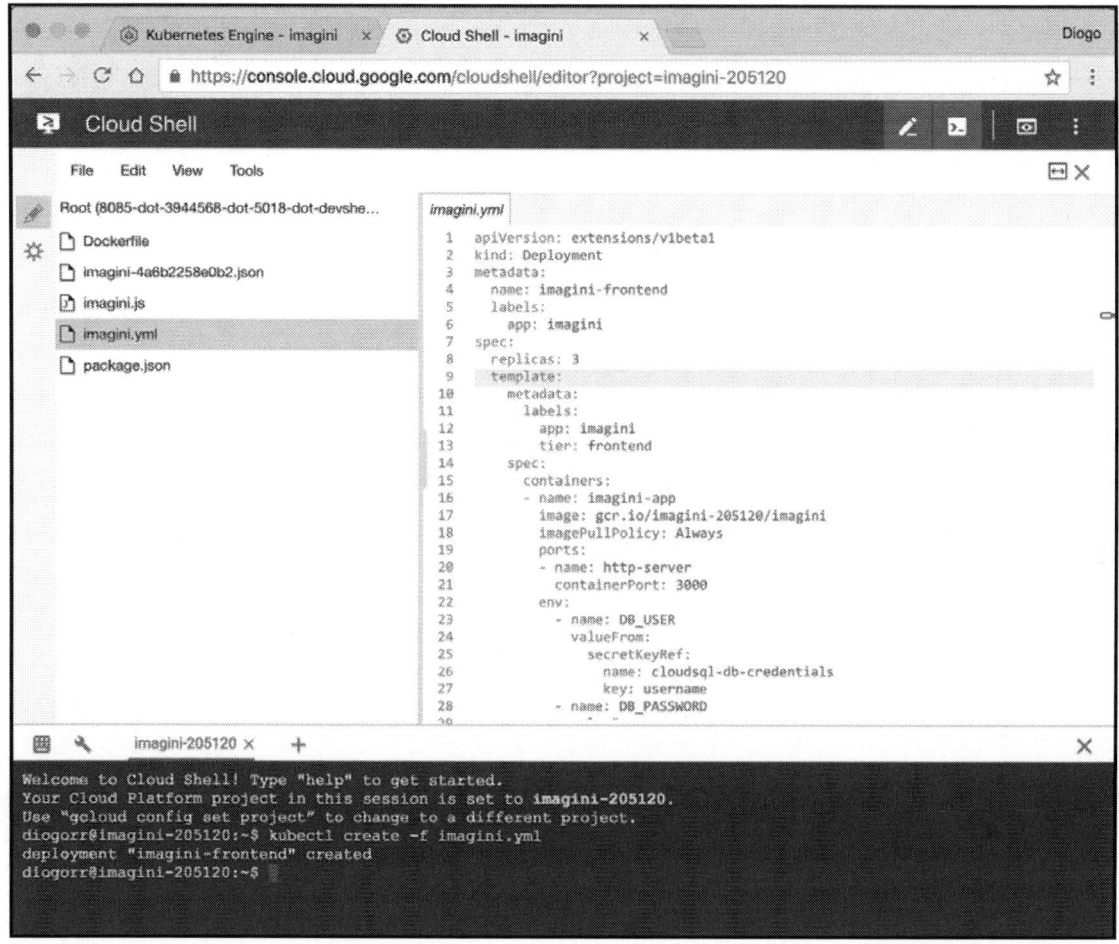

Our service is now deployed. It will take some time until it is fully running. Go back to the **Kubernetes Engine** and click on **Workloads**:

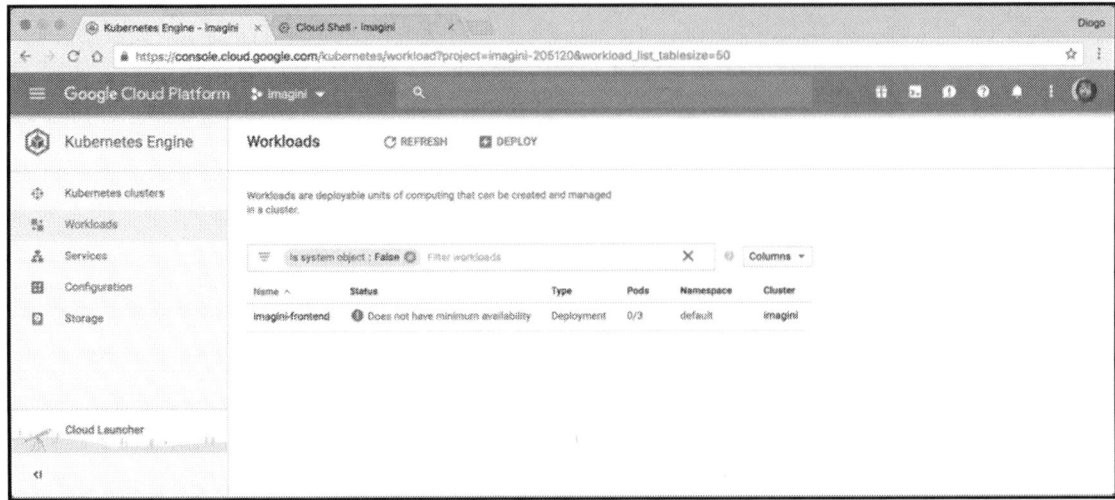

Click on **imagini-frontend** to see how deployment is proceeding:

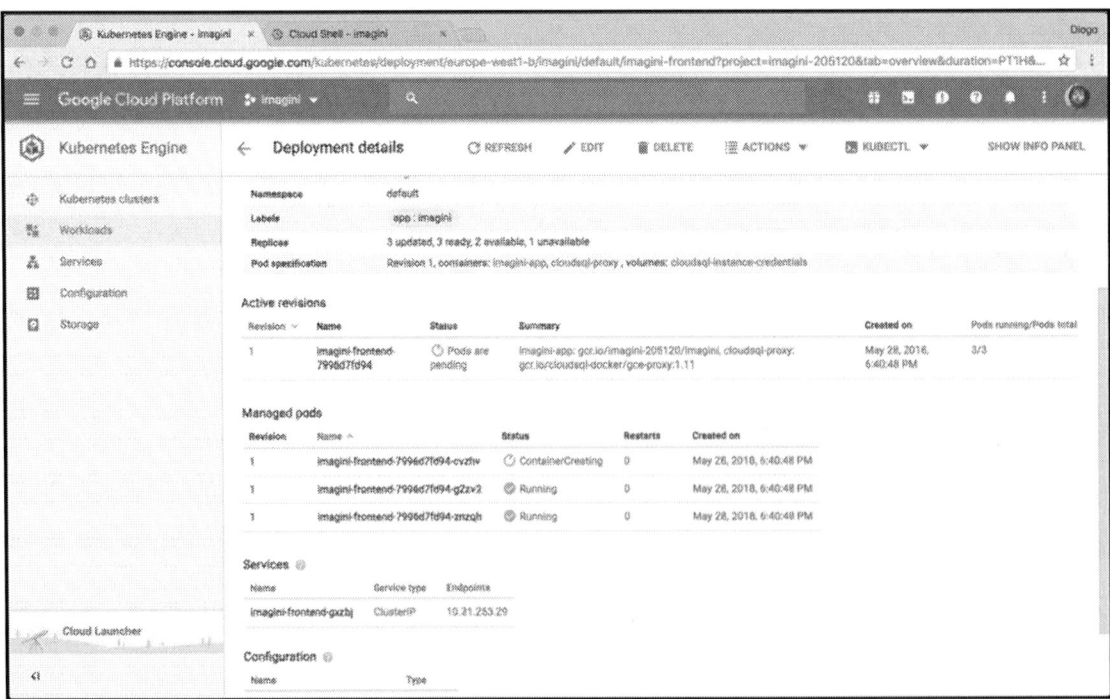

We see that some of the replicas are not running yet. You can hit **REFRESH** at the top to find out when all are ready. When they are, you'll see an **OK** on the previous page:

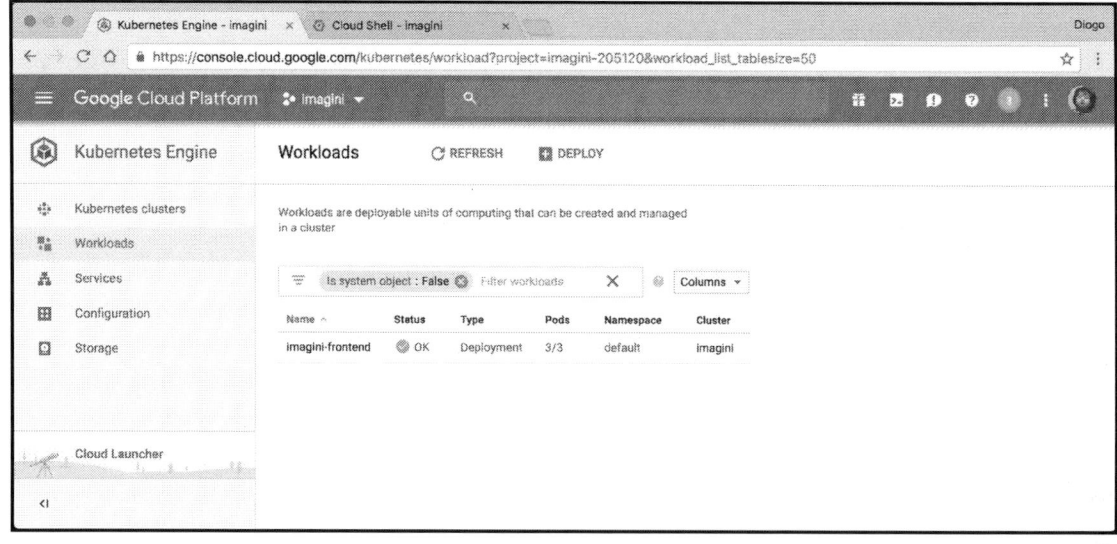

Inside the workload, you can change or destroy it, as well as scale it:

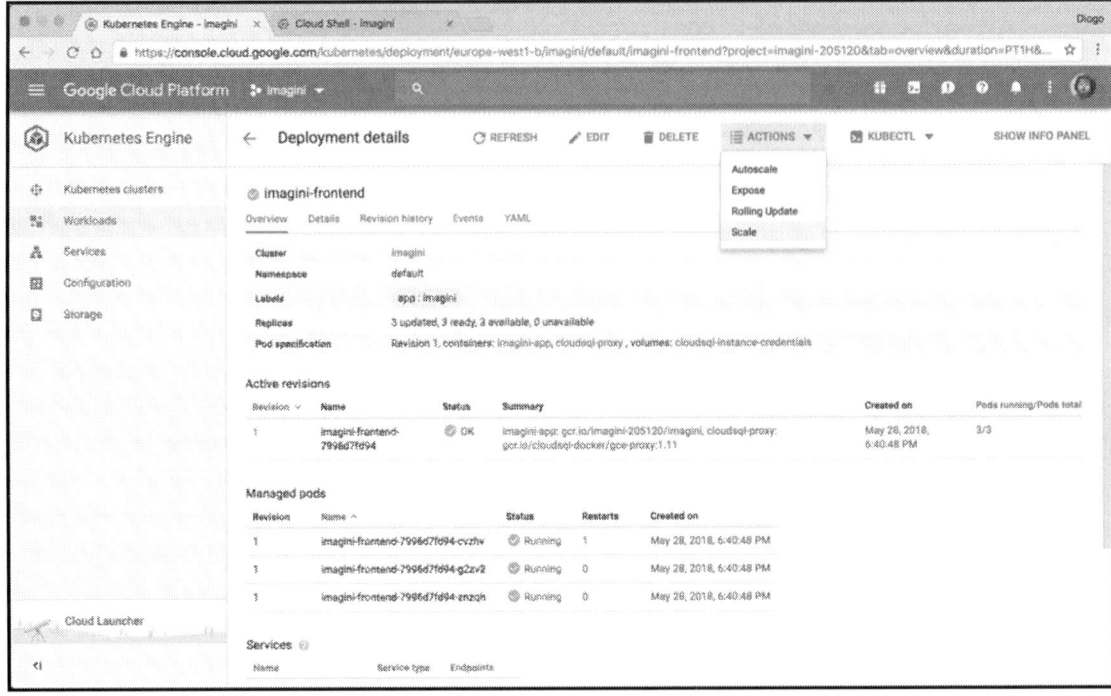

Try changing to five replicas. After a few seconds, you should now have five instances running:

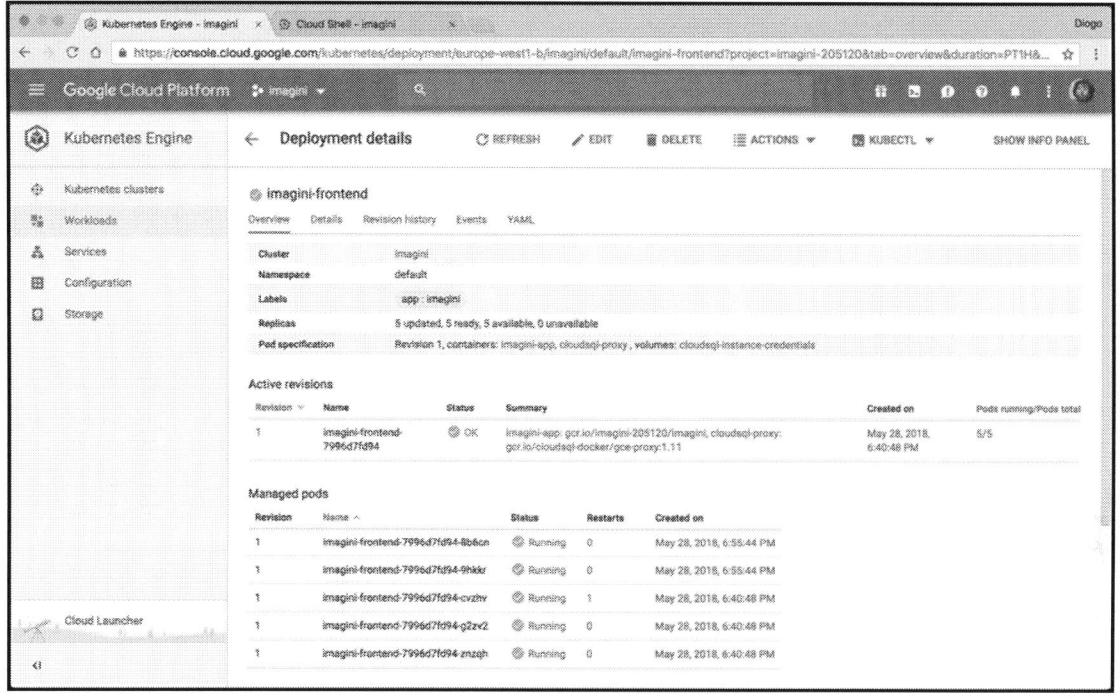

On the left sidebar, click on **Services**:

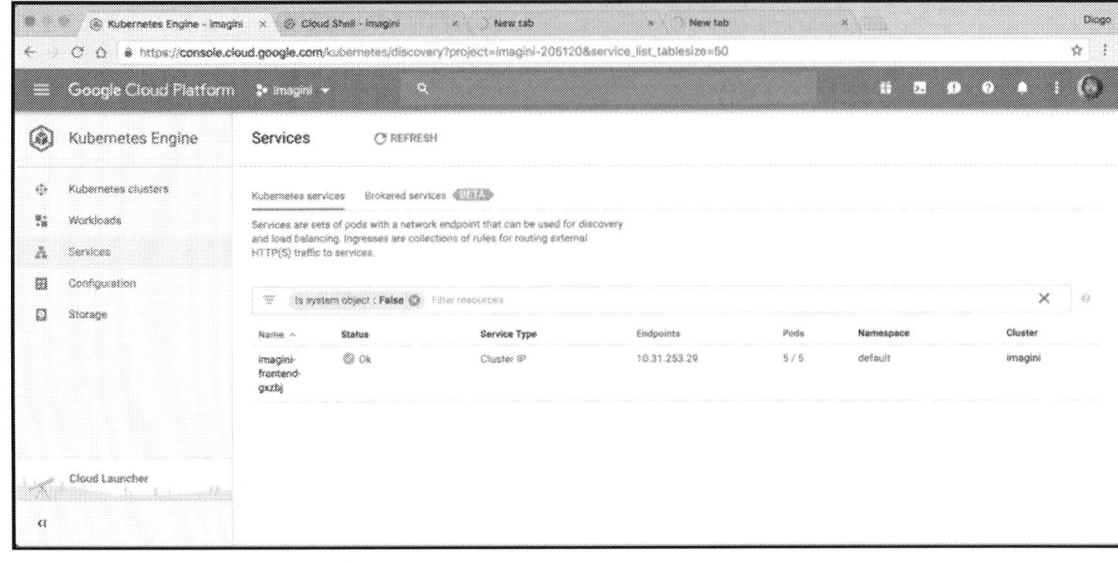

Our service is listed, using the cluster IP endpoint. You can click on the name for more details:

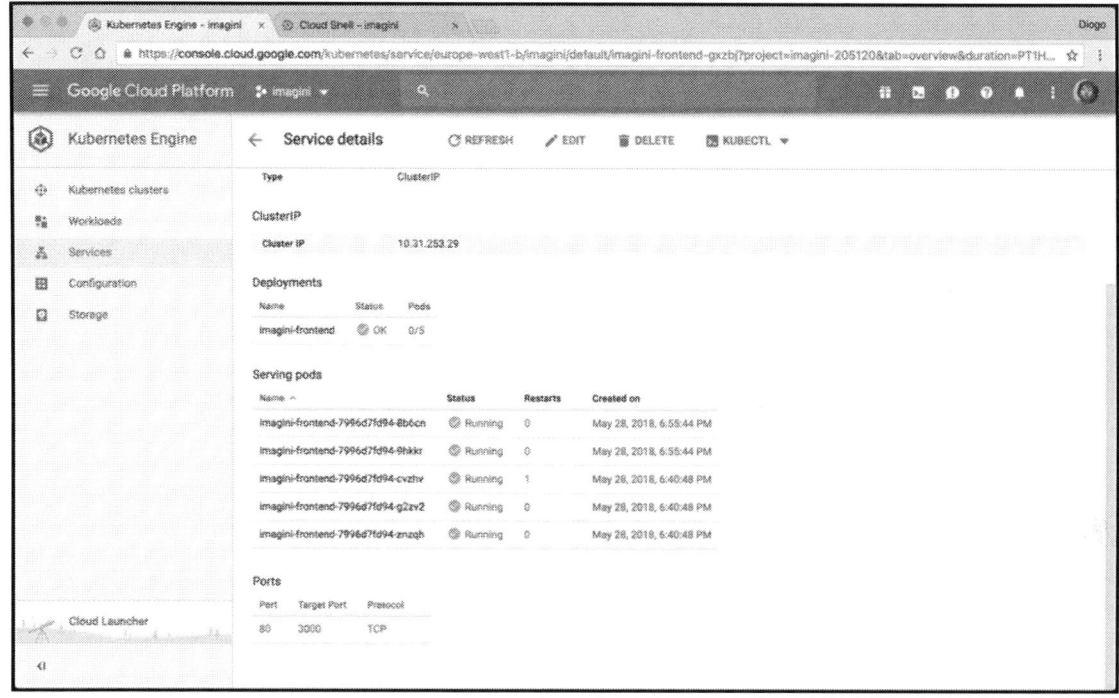

Scrolling down, you'll see the service port **3000** was exported to port **80**. And that's it!

Summary

As I mentioned earlier, being cloud-native is about how we deploy our microservice, not where. If you design it from scratch to not depend on where it's deployed, moving it to the cloud is as simple as getting around any cloud provider.

If you keep yourself out of provider lock-ins, you'll be able to migrate your microservice from provider to provider, or even deploy to multiple providers with little to no effort. We will look at some design patterns and best practices in the next chapter.

11
Design Patterns

In the previous chapter, we successfully deployed our service to a cloud provider without having to fundamentally change our code. We used a database to store our data, and the only thing we needed to do was to point to the new location.

It's common, during the specification and development process, to have challenging problems with one or more ways of solving them. The ways, or paths, you choose throughout the development are called design patterns, as they're part of your design.

Some design patterns are more common than others. Some are well-known, others, not so much. Some are good design patterns and you should follow them. Others are bad because of the disadvantages they bring in the short or long term.

In this chapter, we're going to take a look at the importance of choosing good patterns; we will look at some common architectural patterns and review the continuous integration we followed through the entire book until we successfully deployed to the cloud.

Choosing patterns

Patterns are not libraries or classes, they're concepts, reusable solutions to common programming problems, tested and optimized for specific use cases. As they're just concepts to solve specific problems, they have to be implemented in every language.

Every pattern has its advantages and disadvantages, and choosing a wrong pattern for a problem can cause you a big headache.

Patterns can speed up the development process because they provide well-tested and well-proven development paradigms. Reusing patterns helps prevent issues and improves code readability between developers that are familiar with the patterns.

Patterns have major importance in high-performance applications. Sometimes, in order to achieve some flexibility, patterns introduce a new level of indirection in the code, which may reduce performance. You should choose when to introduce a pattern or when that introduction will hurt the performance metric you're targeting.

Knowing good patterns is essential for avoiding the opposite: anti-patterns. An anti-pattern is something that looks good in the beginning but later on turns out to look like the worst decision you ever made. Anti-patterns are not specific patterns but are more like common errors, seen by the majority as strategies you shouldn't use. Some of the most common and frequent anti-patterns seen out there are:

- **Repeating yourself**: Don't repeat excessive parts of the code. Lean back, look at the big picture and refactor it. Some developers tend to look at this refactoring as a complexity of the application, but it can actually turn your application simpler. If you think you won't be able to understand the simplicity of your refactoring, don't forget to add a couple of introductory comments to the code.
- **Golden hammer or silver bullet**: Don't think your favorite language or framework is universally applicable. Most of the languages can actually do practically anything, at least the mature ones, and with a huge community. That doesn't mean a language performs some tasks well. If your goal is performance, try to have a couple of hammers in your belt.
- **Coding by exception**: Don't add new code to handle new cases as they appear. By new cases, I don't mean new features; I mean behavior your code was not expecting. For example, when you're making a file upload feature of some kind, remember an error might happen during transfer, the file can be empty, have weird content, be huge, and so on.
- **Programming by accident**: Don't program by trial and error until you succeed. This is something you should really avoid. Programming by accident can sometimes make your code work in some cases (by accident) and produce erroneous behaviors in others.

Architectural patterns

When developing microservices and, more specifically, an ecosystem of microservices, some patterns become very obvious, and you'll use them without knowing. Just looking at the architectural patterns, here are some that you might find interesting. Perhaps you have already used them before.

Front Controller

The **Front Controller** pattern is when all requests go for a single point in your architecture, called the handler, which then processes and dispatches the requests to other handlers. This is the pattern used by, for example, load balancers and reverses proxies:

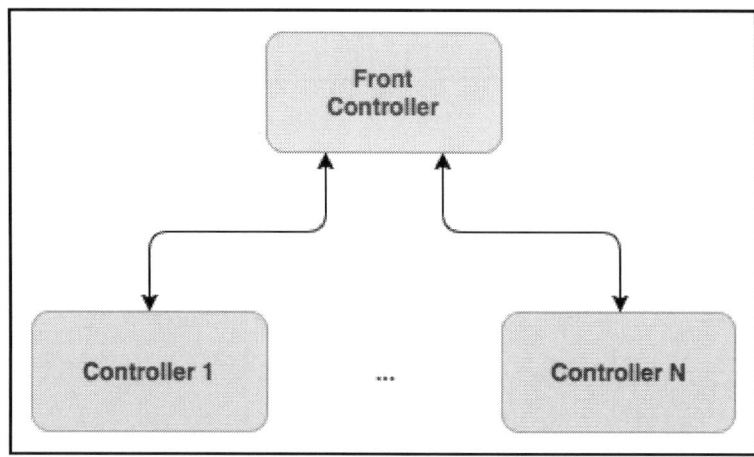

It's useful to scale horizontally, especially when the **Front Controller** is just routing requests, so it can handle a lot more requests than each separate controller, which need, some time to actually process each request.

This pattern is also very useful in helping other services not having to know where the controllers are and choosing the one with the lowest load that should handle the request faster.

Layered

The layered pattern is common in filesystems and operative systems (and virtual machines for that matter). This pattern consists of creating different layers that go from the raw data through to the data seen by a user:

The idea is to separate the complexity of the different layers, each one not having to know how the others do their tasks:

- Handling the data structures and storing them in a fast and secure way
- Manipulating the data structures and adding business logic to them
- Handling user requests and showing the data in a localised format

Service Locator

The **Service Locator** pattern is actually an anti-pattern. It's not considered a good practice because it adds much more complexity to an ecosystem. The pattern consists of a central registry, called a **Service Locator**, where services register their abilities, and other services can consult the registry and know where the services they need are located:

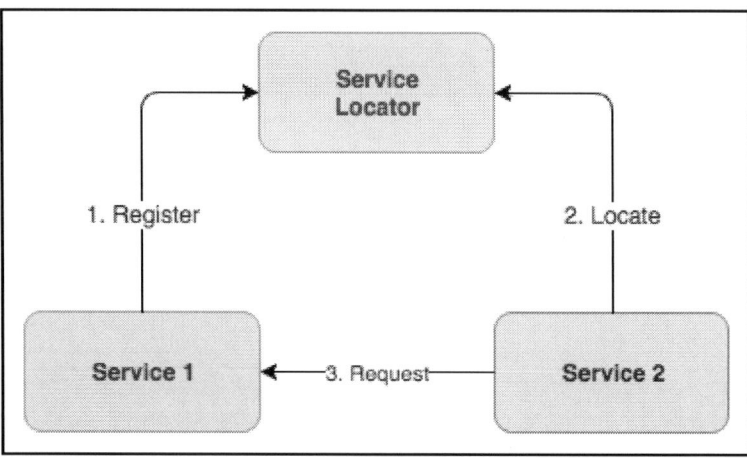

The **Service Locator** is similar to the Front Controller, but with added complexity, as you need to contact the Service Locator and the service you need, instead of just making a simple request to a Front Controller.

Observer

The Observer pattern is used every day in Node.js. It consists of a **Subject**, which maintains a list of dependents, called Observers, which get notified of any state change happening on the **Subject**:

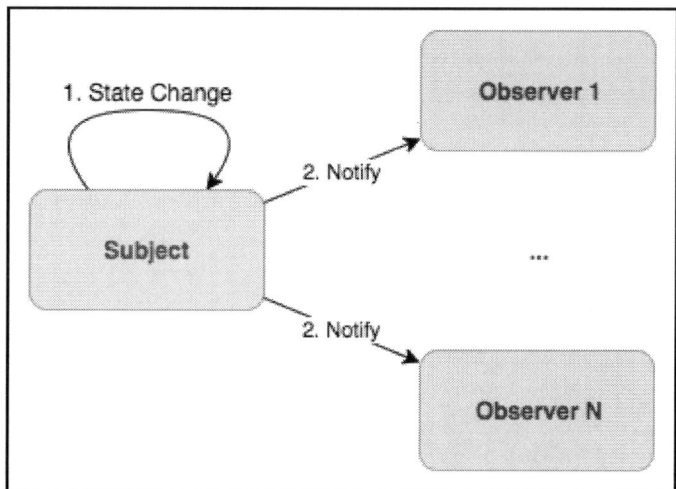

You can see this happening every time in your web browser when some code (**Observer**) attaches an event listener to an object or interface element (**Subject**).

Publish-Subscribe

Another very similar pattern is the Publish-Subscribe pattern, usually abbreviated as **Pub-Sub**. This pattern is almost exactly the same as the previous one. You have Subscribers that, as the name implies, subscribe to a specific event, or topic, or whatever you want to call it, and then you have Publishers that emit those events or send information to those topics:

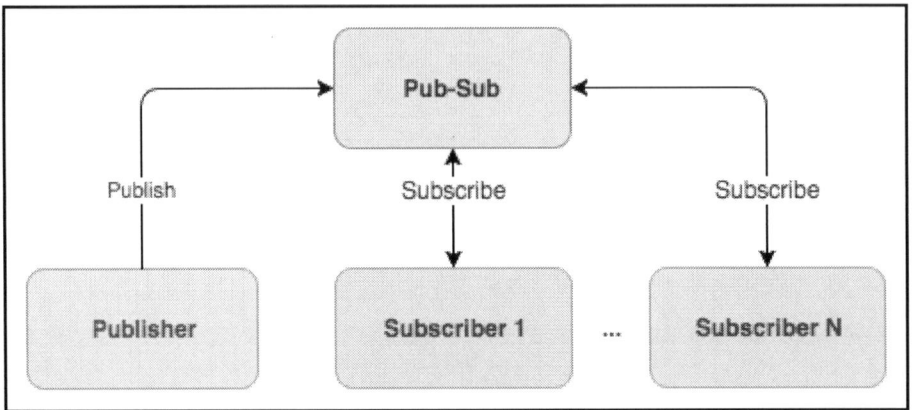

The difference to the previous pattern may look very thin but is actually very important. The **Pub-Sub** pattern involves a third-party service and, unlike the Observer pattern, the Publishers have no knowledge of the Subscribers. This removes the need to handle and directly notify the Subscribers, thereby simplifying your code.

This pattern is quite useful for microservice communication. It involves a third party that abstracts the state change notification. Also, Publishers and Subscribers have no knowledge of each other.

Using patterns

Choosing good design patterns is essentially choosing best practices. Not all design patterns fit every purpose, but for many scenarios, they'll make your life easier. Perhaps you may not notice any difference in the beginning, but you should in the long-term.

Good design patterns also have indirect advantages. You'll find more documentation and examples online, as well as a broader set of options to choose from, for example, when using the Publish-Subscribe pattern, where you'll find many types of implementations to integrate with your services.

Choosing the pattern that fits your needs also involves planning and knowing what you need and what you'll need in the future. Think of the edge cases and see if the pattern is capable of handling them.

Planning your microservice

Developing a microservice may look like a simple task. As the name implies, it is a micro service. But that is not necessarily true, as sometimes we tend to complexify something that should be simple.

This does not mean a service should be simple, it can be quite complex. What should be simple is the goal and the properties of the service. There shouldn't be any doubt regarding what it does and what it shouldn't do.

Before writing any line of code, you should start by knowing a couple of what I call characteristics of the service, such as:

- What is it for? What tasks will it do?
- What other services will use it? What protocol will it speak?
- Will it replace another service? Will it cover the same tasks?

This can be summed in one word—purpose. If you don't clearly define its purpose and just start developing tasks it can handle, you'll end up having a mixed service that deviates from the main goal of a microservice.

After having a proper purpose, you can then choose the best pattern and plan the individual tasks. The first task will probably take longer to develop, as you're creating the base layout for the service.

Don't forget to add tests, coverage, and documentation as soon as possible. I know this is something most developers tend to ignore, but it will bite you later. It's easier to add a simple test for a first simple task. Code coverage is easier at this point. Adding documentation should also be easier if you're planning the individual tasks.

After having your first task, with a proper test, you should set your first deploy. This will end your first development cycle and bring you back to planning. If you keep this loop going, with small tasks, you'll develop faster, and deploy faster:

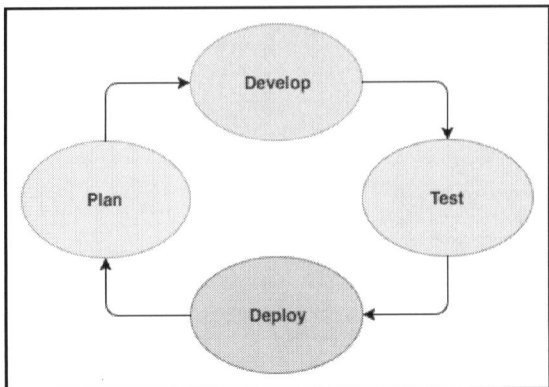

This type of simple loop with small tasks will allow you to do what is called **continuous integration** and **continuous deployment**, where you're able to develop and deploy to a testing cluster. The change can be automatically tested and deployed if everything passes the tests.

Obstacles when developing

As we saw previously, a microservice architecture has many advantages, such as splitting code into smaller isolated projects, where it becomes easier to develop or even delegate responsibility.

These advantages come at a cost, which is the build of a more complex system or application. Because of how microservices are supposed to work, an information barrier is intrinsic. A microservice responsible for a type of information should be the only one manipulating it, forcing any other service to communicate with it to have access to information.

This gives you a finer control over the information because you know the service responsible for it, and you can force service or user authentication, with authorization or even rate-access limits. But, this means that a complex application will tend to penalize the network as there will be significant inter-service messaging.

Inter-service messaging means network traffic and latency. If the services are not on the same local network, this will eventually create noticeable latency. Adding some kind of cache service to accelerate access will also add more complexity.

Although testing and development for each microservice should be easier than a monolith application, looking at the microservice test frameworks all together, and having two or more services test together, is more complicated.

Finally, avoid something called a nanoservice. This is considered an anti-pattern, and it's when you exaggerate on fine-graining your architecture and create overly small services, complexifying your development to the extreme.

Find a good balance between the number of microservices and what each will do. Think of them as a person that will handle a specific task. Is the task too simple to have one person allocated to do just that? Shouldn't the person have a broader set of tasks from the same context?

Summary

Today's applications have space for microservices. Applications are no longer monolith and left the traditional computer architecture long ago. Users constantly demand integrations and interoperability between applications.

Microservices help developers to reduce the complexity of applications by separating different contexts, such as frontend, backend, mobile, or a simple API. They're a concept, or a pattern, that, when used well, can give you great power, and split complexity and responsibility.

But, microservices are more than that. Microservices help you scale horizontally by just replicating the services you need and not a complete monolith application, saving resources and, ultimately, money.

There's a lot to explore out there; we have just scratched the surface. There are plenty of cloud providers and tools for you to experiment with and choose what fits you best.

Inter-service Communication 12

In this chapter, we will cover the following recipes:

- Service-to-service communication
- Making concurrent asynchronous requests
- Finding services using service discovery
- Server-side load balancing
- Client-side load balancing
- Building event-driven microservices
- Evolving APIs

Introduction

In a real-world microservice architecture, services will frequently need to invoke other services in order to fulfill a user's request. A typical user request will commonly create dozens of requests to services in your system.

Managing the communication between services presents a number of challenges. Before a service can speak to another service, it will need to locate it through some kind of service-discovery mechanism. When generating requests to a downstream service, we also need a way to distribute traffic across the various instances of the service that minimizes latency and distributes the load evenly without compromising data integrity. We'll need to consider how to handle service failures and prevent them from cascading throughout our system.

Sometimes a service will need to communicate with other services asynchronously, in these cases, we can use event-driven architectural patterns to create reactive workflows. Breaking our system up into multiple services also means that different services will evolve their APIs independently, so we'll need ways to handle changes that won't break upstream services.

In this chapter, we'll discuss recipes designed to address each of these challenges. By the end of this chapter, you'll be able to confidently handle the various kinds of interactions we're bound to require in a microservice architecture.

Service-to-service communication

In large-scale systems, problems arise less often in services themselves and more often in the communication between services. For this reason, we need to carefully consider all of the various challenges in service-to-service communication. When discussing service-to-service communication, it's useful to visualize the flow of information in our system. Data flows in both directions–from the client (upstream) to the database, or event bus (downstream) in the form of requests, and back again in the form of responses. When we refer to upstream services, we are describing components of the system that are closer to the user in the flow of information. When we refer to downstream services, we are describing components of the system that are further away from the user–in other words, the user makes a request that is routed to a service that then makes requests to other, downstream services, as shown in the following diagram:

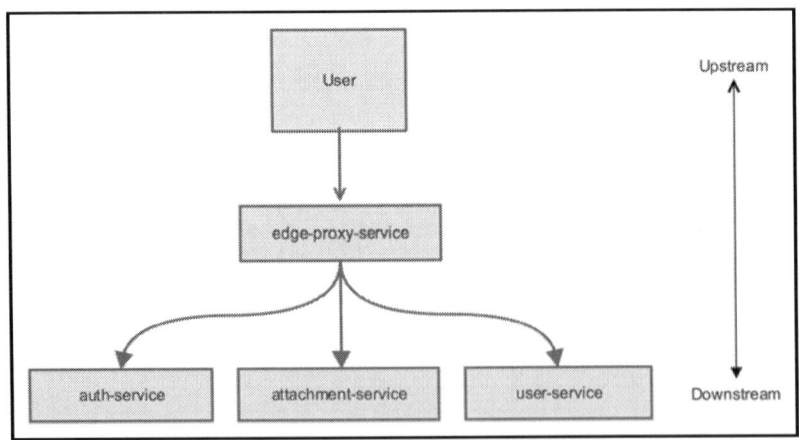

In the preceding diagram, the originating **User** is upstream from the **edge-proxy-service**, which is upstream from the **auth-service**, **attachment-service**, and **user-service**.

In order to demonstrate the service-to-service communication, we'll create a simple service that calls another service synchronously using the Spring Boot Java framework. Keeping with the example of our fictional messaging application, we'll create a message service that is responsible for sending messages. The message service has to invoke the social graph service in order to determine whether the sender and recipient of a message are friends before allowing a message to be sent. The following simplified diagram illustrates the relationship between services:

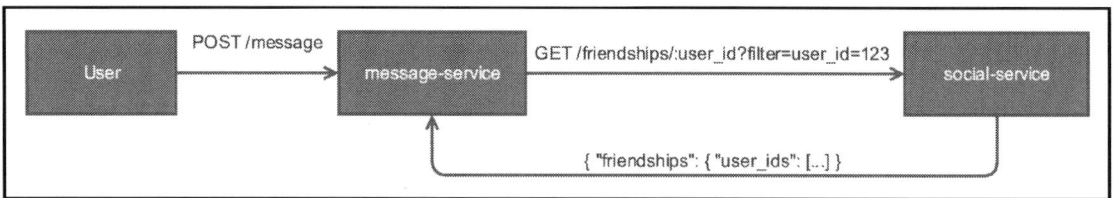

As you can see, a **POST** request comes in from the user to the **/message** endpoint, which is routed to **message-service**. The **message-service** service then makes an HTTP **GET** request to the **social-service** service using the **/friendships/:id** endpoint. The **social-service** service returns a JSON representation of friendships for a user.

How to do it...

1. Create a new Java/Gradle project called `message-service` and add the following content to the `build.gradle` file:

```
group 'com.packtpub.microservices'
version '1.0-SNAPSHOT'

buildscript {
    repositories {
        mavenCentral()
    }
    dependencies {
        classpath group: 'org.springframework.boot', name: 'spring-
boot-gradle-plugin', version: '1.5.9.RELEASE'
    }
}

apply plugin: 'java'
apply plugin: 'org.springframework.boot'

sourceCompatibility = 1.8
```

```
repositories {
    mavenCentral()
}

dependencies {
    compile group: 'org.springframework.boot', name: 'spring-boot-
starter-web'
    testCompile group: 'junit', name: 'junit', version: '4.12'
}
```

2. Create a new package called `com.packtpub.microservices.ch03.message` and a new class called `Application`. This will be our service's entry point:

```
package com.packtpub.microservices.ch03.message;

import org.springframework.boot.SpringApplication;
import
org.springframework.boot.autoconfigure.SpringBootApplication;

@SpringBootApplication
public class Application {
    public static void main(String[] args) {
        SpringApplication.run(Application.class, args);
    }
}
```

3. Create the model. Create a package called `com.packtpub.microservices.ch03.message.models` and a class called `Message`. This is the internal representation of the message. There's a lot missing here. We're not actually persisting the message in this code, as it's best to keep this example simple:

```
package com.packtpub.microservices.ch03.message.models;

public class Message {

    private String toUser;
    private String fromUser;
    private String body;

    public Message() {}

    public Message(String toUser, String fromUser, String body) {
        this.toUser = toUser;
        this.fromUser = fromUser;
        this.body = body;
    }
```

```
    public String getToUser() {
        return toUser;
    }

    public String getFromUser() {
        return fromUser;
    }

    public String getBody() {
        return body;
    }
}
```

4. Create a new package called
   com.packtpub.microservices.ch03.message.controllers and a new
   class called MessageController. At the moment, our controller doesn't do
   much except accept the request, parse the JSON, and return the message instance,
   as you can see from this code:

```
package com.packtpub.microservices.ch03.message.controllers;

import com.packtpub.microservices.models.Message;
import org.springframework.web.bind.annotation.*;

@RestController
public class MessageController {

    @RequestMapping(
            path="/messages",
            method=RequestMethod.POST,
            produces="application/json")
    public Message create(@RequestBody Message message) {
        return message;
    }
}
```

5. Test this basic service by running it and trying to send a simple request:

```
$ ./gradlew bootRun
Starting a Gradle Daemon, 1 busy Daemon could not be reused, use --
status for details

> Task :bootRun

  .   ____          _            __ _ _
 /\\ / ___'_ __ _ _(_)_ __  __ _ \ \ \ \
( ( )\___ | '_ | '_| | '_ \/ _` | \ \ \ \
 \\/  ___)| |_)| | | | | || (_| |  ) ) ) )
  '  |____| .__|_| |_|_| |_\__, | / / / /
 =========|_|==============|___/=/_/_/_/
 :: Spring Boot ::        (v1.5.9.RELEASE)

...
```

Take a look at the following command line:

```
$ curl -H "Content-Type: application/json" -X POST
http://localhost:8080/messages -d'{"toUser": "reader", "fromUser":
"paulosman", "body": "Hello, World"}'

{"toUser":"reader","fromUser":"paulosman","body":"Hello, World"}
```

Now we have a basic service working, but it's pretty dumb and not doing much. We won't go into persistence in this chapter, but let's add some intelligence by checking with the social service to verify that our two users have a friendship before allowing the message to be sent. For the purposes of our example, imagine we have a working social service that allows us to check for relationships between users with requests, like so:

```
GET /friendships?username=paulosman&filter=reader

{
  "username": "paulosman",
  "friendships": [
    "reader"
  ]
}
```

6. Before we can consume this service, let's create a model to store its response. In the `com.packtpub.microservices.ch03.message.models` package, create a class called `UserFriendships`:

```
package com.packtpub.microservices.ch03.message.models;

import com.fasterxml.jackson.annotation.JsonIgnoreProperties;

import java.util.List;

@JsonIgnoreProperties(ignoreUnknown = true)
public class UserFriendships {
    private String username;
    private List<String> friendships;

    public UserFriendships() {}

    public String getUsername() {
        return username;
    }

    public void setUsername(String username) {
        this.username = username;
    }

    public List<String> getFriendships() {
        return friendships;
    }

    public void setFriendships(List<String> friendships) {
        this.friendships = friendships;
    }
}
```

7. Modify `MessageController`, adding a method to get a list of friendships for a user, optionally filtering by a username. Note that we're hardcoding the URL in this example, which is a bad practice. We'll discuss alternatives to this in the next recipe. Take a look at the following code:

```
private List<String> getFriendsForUser(String username, String
filter) {
    String url = "http://localhost:4567/friendships?username=" +
username + "&filter=" + filter;
    RestTemplate template = new RestTemplate();
```

```
        UserFriendships friendships = template.getForObject(url,
    UserFriendships.class);
        return friendships.getFriendships();
    }
```

8. Modify the `create` method we wrote earlier. If the users are friends, we'll continue and return the message as before; if the users are not friends, the service will respond with a `403` indicating that the request is forbidden:

```
@RequestMapping(
            path="/messages",
            method=RequestMethod.POST,
            produces="application/json")
    public ResponseEntity<Message> create(@RequestBody Message
message) {
        List<String> friendships =
getFriendsForUser(message.getFromUser(), message.getToUser());

        if (friendships.isEmpty())
            return
ResponseEntity.status(HttpStatus.FORBIDDEN).build();

        URI location = ServletUriComponentsBuilder
                .fromCurrentRequest().path("/{id}")
                .buildAndExpand(message.getFromUser()).toUri();
        return ResponseEntity.created(location).build();
    }
```

Asynchronous requests

Previously we were making a single service invocation per request, from the message service to the social service. This has the benefit of being incredibly simple to implement and, when using single-threaded languages, such as Python, Ruby, or JavaScript, is often the only choice. Performing a network call synchronously in this manner is acceptable when you're only doing it once per request—it doesn't matter that the call blocks the thread since you can't respond to the user until the invocation is complete anyway. When you're making multiple requests, however, blocking network calls will severely impact the performance and scalability of your application. What we need is an easy way to make use of Java's concurrency features.

If you're writing your microservices in Scala, you can take advantage of the `Future` type, which is used to represent an asynchronous computation. The **Finagle** RPC framework even uses futures as one of its base abstractions for modeling dependent RPCs. Java also has futures and the Spring Boot framework has some useful utilities that make it easy to wrap network calls, making them asynchronous and therefore non-blocking.

In this recipe, we'll retool the message service we introduced in the previous recipe. Instead of checking to see whether the sender and recipient of a message are friends, we'll now imagine that our app uses an asymmetric following model. For a user to message another user, the two users will have to follow each other. This requires the message service to make two network calls to the social service, checking that the sender follows the recipient and simultaneously checking that the recipient follows the sender. The following simplified diagram represents the relationship between services:

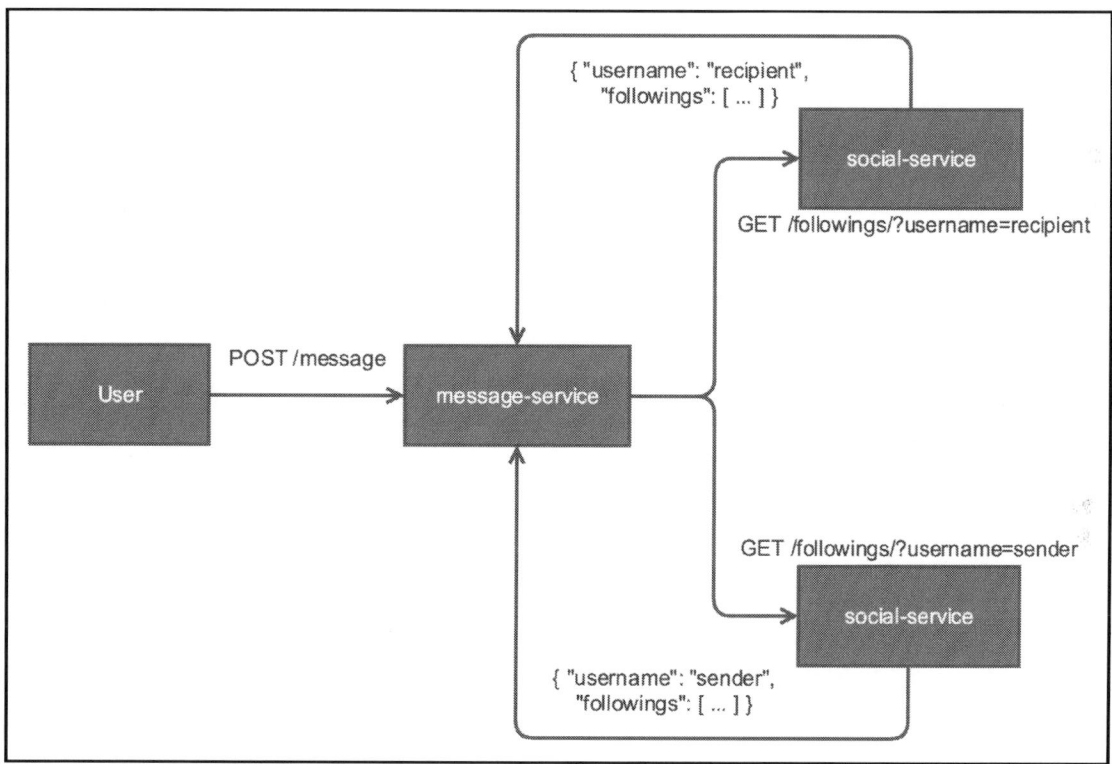

Spring Boot has useful tools that we can use to make methods asynchronous using Java's `CompletableFuture` type. We'll modify our previous message service to make two concurrent calls to the search service.

How to do it...

1. Open the `MessageController` file and insert the following content:

```
package com.packtpub.microservices.ch03.message.controllers;

import com.packtpub.microservices.models.Message;
import com.packtpub.microservices.models.UserFriendships;
import org.springframework.http.HttpStatus;
import org.springframework.http.ResponseEntity;
import org.springframework.web.bind.annotation.*;
import org.springframework.web.client.RestTemplate;
import
org.springframework.web.servlet.support.ServletUriComponentsBuilder
;

import java.net.URI;
import java.util.List;

@RestController
public class MessageController {

    @RequestMapping(
            path="/messages",
            method=RequestMethod.POST,
            produces="application/json")
    public ResponseEntity<Message> create(@RequestBody Message
message) {
        List<String> friendships =
getFriendsForUser(message.getFromUser(), message.getToUser());

        if (friendships.isEmpty())
            return
ResponseEntity.status(HttpStatus.FORBIDDEN).build();

        URI location = ServletUriComponentsBuilder
                .fromCurrentRequest().path("/{id}")
                .buildAndExpand(message.getFromUser()).toUri();

        return ResponseEntity.created(location).build();
    }

    private List<String> getFriendsForUser(String username, String
filter) {
        String url = "http://localhost:4567/friendships?username="
+ username + "&filter=" + filter;
        RestTemplate template = new RestTemplate();
```

```
            UserFriendships friendships = template.getForObject(url,
     UserFriendships.class);
            return friendships.getFriendships();
        }
    }
```

2. Replace the getFriendsForUser method with a new method, called
   isFollowing. We give the new method an @Async annotation, which tells
   Spring Boot that this method will be run in a different thread:

```
import org.springframework.scheduling.annotation.Async;
import java.util.concurrent.CompletableFuture;

...

@Async
public CompletableFuture<Boolean> isFollowing(String fromUser,
String toUser) {

    String url = String.format(
      "http://localhost:4567/followings?user=%s&filter=%s",
      fromUser, toUser);

    RestTemplate template = new RestTemplate();
    UserFollowings followings = template.forObject(url,
UserFollowings.class);

    return CompletableFuture.completedFuture(
        followings.getFollowings().isEmpty()
    );
}
```

3. Modify the create method to make the two service invocations. We'll need to
   wait until they are both done before deciding how to proceed, but the two service
   calls will be made concurrently:

```
@RequestMapping(
            path="/messages",
            method=RequestMethod.POST,
            produces="application/json")
    public ResponseEntity<Message> create(@RequestBody Message
message) {

    CompletableFuture<Boolean> result1 =
isFollowing(message.getFromUser(), message.getToUser());
    CompletableFuture<Boolean> result2 =
isFollowing(message.getToUser(), message.getFromUser());
```

```
CompletableFuture.allOf(result1, result2).join();

// if both are not true, respond with a 403
if (!(result1.get() && result2.get()))
    ResponseEntity.status(HttpStatus.FORBIDDEN).build();

... // proceed

}
```

4. For the `@Async` annotation to schedule methods on separate threads, we need to configure an `Executor`. This is done in our `Application` class, as follows:

```
package com.packtpub.microservices;

import org.springframework.boot.SpringApplication;
import
org.springframework.boot.autoconfigure.SpringBootApplication;
import org.springframework.context.annotation.Bean;
import org.springframework.scheduling.annotation.EnableAsync;
import
org.springframework.scheduling.concurrent.ThreadPoolTaskExecutor;

import java.util.concurrent.Executor;

@SpringBootApplication
@EnableAsync
public class Application {

    public static void main(String[] args) {
        SpringApplication.run(Application.class, args).close();
    }

    @Bean
    public Executor asyncExecutor() {
        ThreadPoolTaskExecutor executor = new
ThreadPoolTaskExecutor();
        executor.setCorePoolSize(2);
        executor.setMaxPoolSize(2);
        executor.setQueueCapacity(500);
        executor.setThreadNamePrefix("SocialServiceCall-");
        executor.initialize();
        return executor;
    }

}
```

Our service now makes concurrent asynchronous calls to the social service in order to ensure that the sender and recipient of a message follow each other. We customize our `Async` scheduler with `Executor` defined as part of our application's configuration. We've configured our `ThreadPoolTaskExecutor` class to limit the number of threads to 2 and the queue size to 500. There are many factors to consider when configuring `Executor`, such as the amount of traffic you expect your service to receive and the average amount of time it takes for your service to serve a request. In this example, we'll leave it with these values.

Service discovery

Before services can invoke each other, they need to be able to find each other using some kind of service discovery mechanism. This means being able to translate a service name into a network location (IP address and port). Traditional applications maintained the network locations of services to send requests to, probably in a configuration file (or worse, hardcoded in the application code). This approach assumes that network locations are relatively static, which isn't going to be the case in modern, cloud-native applications. The topologies of microservice architectures are constantly changing. Nodes are being added and removed through auto-scaling, and we have to assume that some nodes will fail either completely or by serving requests with unacceptably high latency. As a microservice architecture grows, you'll need to consider a more feature-rich service-discovery mechanism.

When choosing a service-discovery mechanism, the datastore used to back your service registry is extremely important. You want a well-tested, battle-worn system. Apache **ZooKeeper** is an open source hierarchical key-value store commonly used for distributed locking, service discovery, maintaining configuration information, and other distributed coordination tasks. The development of ZooKeeper was in part motivated by a paper published by Google in 2006 that described **Chubby**, an internally-developed system for distributed lock storage. In this recipe, we'll use ZooKeeper to build a service-discovery mechanism.

Spring Cloud ZooKeeper is a project that provides easy ZooKeeper integration in Spring Boot applications.

How to do it...

For this recipe, there are two sets of steps, as shown in the next sections.

Registering with the service registry

This recipe requires a running ZooKeeper cluster. At a minimum, you will need a single ZooKeeper node running locally on your development machine. For instructions on installing and running ZooKeeper, please visit the excellent ZooKeeper documentation. Take a look at the following steps:

1. For this example, we'll create a service to handle the creation and retrieval of user accounts. Create a new Gradle Java application called `users-service` with the following `build.gradle` file:

```
group 'com.packtpub.microservices'
version '1.0-SNAPSHOT'

buildscript {
    repositories {
        mavenCentral()
    }
    dependencies {
        classpath group: 'io.spring.gradle', name: 'dependency-
management-plugin', version: '0.5.6.RELEASE'
        classpath group: 'org.springframework.boot', name: 'spring-
boot-gradle-plugin', version: '1.5.9.RELEASE'
    }
}

apply plugin: 'java'
apply plugin: 'org.springframework.boot'
apply plugin: "io.spring.dependency-management"

sourceCompatibility = 1.8

dependencyManagement {
    imports {
        mavenBom 'org.springframework.cloud:spring-cloud-zookeeper-
dependencies:1.1.1.RELEASE'
    }
}

repositories {
    mavenCentral()
```

```
    }

    dependencies {
        compile group: 'io.reactivex', name: 'rxjava', version: '1.1.5'
        compile group: 'org.springframework.boot', name: 'spring-boot-
    starter-web'
        compile group: 'org.springframework.cloud', name: 'spring-
    cloud-starter-zookeeper-discovery', version: '1.1.1.RELEASE'
        testCompile group: 'junit', name: 'junit', version: '4.12'
    }
```

2. Because we've declared `spring-boot-starter-zookeeper-discovery` as a dependency, we have access to the necessary annotations to tell our application to register itself with a ZooKeeper service registry on startup. Create a new class called `Application`, which will serve as our service's entry point:

```
    package com.packtpub.microservices.ch03.servicediscovery;

    import org.springframework.boot.SpringApplication;
    import
    org.springframework.boot.autoconfigure.SpringBootApplication;
    import
    org.springframework.cloud.client.discovery.EnableDiscoveryClient;

    @EnableDiscoveryClient
    @SpringBootApplication
    public class Application {
        public static void main(String[] args) {
            SpringApplication.run(Application.class, args);
        }
    }
```

3. The application now attempts to connect to a ZooKeeper node, by default running on port 2181 on localhost. This default will work for local development, but will need to be changed in a production environment anyway. Add a file `src/resources/application.yml` with the following contents:

```
    spring:
      cloud:
        zookeeper:
          connect-string: localhost:2181
```

4. To give your service a meaningful name in the service registry, modify the `application.yml` file and add the following content:

```
spring:
  cloud:
    zookeeper:
      connect-string: localhost:2181
    application:
      name: users-service
```

Finding services

Now that we have a service being registered with the service registry, we'll create another service to demonstrate using the Spring ZooKeeper `DiscoveryClient` to find a running instance of that service:

1. Open our previously created message-service client. Add the following lines to `build.gradle`:

```
group 'com.packtpub.microservices'
version '1.0-SNAPSHOT'

buildscript {
    repositories {
        mavenCentral()
    }
    dependencies {
        classpath group: 'io.spring.gradle', name: 'dependency-
management-plugin', version: '0.5.6.RELEASE'
        classpath group: 'org.springframework.boot', name: 'spring-
boot-gradle-plugin', version: '1.5.9.RELEASE'
    }
}

apply plugin: 'java'
apply plugin: 'org.springframework.boot'
apply plugin: 'io.spring.dependency-management'

sourceCompatibility = 1.8

dependencyManagement {
    imports {
        mavenBom 'org.springframework.cloud:spring-cloud-zookeeper-
dependencies:1.1.1.RELEASE'
    }
}
```

```
repositories {
    mavenCentral()
}

dependencies {
    compile 'io.reactivex:rxjava:1.3.4'
    compile group: 'org.springframework.cloud', name: 'spring-
cloud-starter-zookeeper-discovery', version: '1.1.1.RELEASE'
    compile group: 'org.springframework.cloud', name: 'spring-
cloud-starter-feign', version: '1.2.5.RELEASE'
    compile group: 'org.springframework.kafka', name: 'spring-
kafka', version: '2.1.1.RELEASE'
    compile group: 'org.springframework.boot', name: 'spring-boot-
starter-web'
    testCompile group: 'junit', name: 'junit', version: '4.12'
}
```

2. We're using an HTTP client developed by Netflix, called **Feign**. Feign allows you to declaratively build HTTP clients and supports service discovery by default. Create a new file called UsersClient.java with the following content:

```java
package com.packtpub.microservices.ch03.servicediscovery.clients;

import org.springframework.beans.factory.annotation.Autowired;
import
org.springframework.cloud.client.discovery.EnableDiscoveryClient;
import org.springframework.cloud.netflix.feign.EnableFeignClients;
import org.springframework.cloud.netflix.feign.FeignClient;
import org.springframework.context.annotation.Configuration;
import org.springframework.web.bind.annotation.PathVariable;
import org.springframework.web.bind.annotation.RequestMapping;
import org.springframework.web.bind.annotation.RequestMethod;
import org.springframework.web.bind.annotation.ResponseBody;

import java.util.List;

@Configuration
@EnableFeignClients
@EnableDiscoveryClient
public class UsersClient {

    @Autowired
    private Client client;

    @FeignClient("users-service")
    interface Client {
        @RequestMapping(path = "/followings/{userId}", method =
RequestMethod.GET)
```

```
        @ResponseBody
        List<String> getFollowings(@PathVariable("userId") String
userId);
    }

    public List<String> getFollowings(String userId) {
        return client.getFollowings(userId);
    }
}
```

3. Open the `MessageController.java` file, and add an instance of `UsersClient` as a field:

```
package com.packtpub.microservices;
...
@RestController
public class MessagesController {
    ...
    @Autowired
    private UsersClient usersClient;
    ...
}
```

4. Instead of manually building the URL in the `isFollowing` method, we can use the Feign client to automatically get a list of friendships for a user, as follows:

```
@Async
public CompletableFuture<Boolean> isFollowing(String fromUser,
String toUser) {
    List<String> friends = usersClient.getFollowings(fromUser)
            .stream()
            .filter(toUser::equals)
            .collect(Collectors.toList());

    return CompletableFuture.completedFuture(friends.isEmpty());
}
```

Because we're using a service registry, we no longer have to worry about clunky configs holding onto hostname values that can change. Furthermore, we're in a position to start deciding how we want to distribute the load among available instances of a service.

Server-side load balancing

When thinking about distributing load across a cluster of servers running instances of an application, it's interesting to consider a brief (and incomplete) history of web application architectures. Some of the earliest web applications were static HTML pages hosted by a web server, such as Apache or similar web server daemon software. Gradually, applications became more dynamic, using technologies such as server-side scripts executed through CGI. Even dynamic applications were still files hosted and served directly by a web server daemon. This simple architecture worked for a long time. Eventually, however, as the amount of traffic an application received grew, a way to distribute load among identical stateless instances of an application was needed.

There are a number of techniques for load balancing, including round-robin DNS or DNS geolocation. The simplest and most common form of load balancing for microservices is to use a software program that forwards requests to one of a cluster of backend servers. There are a number of different ways load can be distributed, based on the specific load-balancing algorithm used by the load balancer we choose. Simple load-balancing algorithms include round-robin and random choice. More often, in real-world production applications, we'll opt for a load-balancing algorithm that takes reported metrics, such as load or the number of active connections, into account when choosing a node in a cluster to forward a request to.

There are a number of popular open source applications that can perform effective load balancing for microservices. **HAProxy** is a popular open source load balancer that can do TCP and HTTP load balancing. NGINX is a popular open source web server that can be effectively used as a reverse proxy, application server, load balancer, or even HTTP cache. Nowadays, more organizations are in positions to develop microservices that are deployed on cloud platforms, such as Amazon Web Services or Google Cloud Platform, which each have solutions for server-side load balancing.

AWS provides a load-balancing solution called **Elastic Load Balancing** (**ELB**). ELB can be configured to forward traffic to a member of an **Auto Scaling Groups**. Auto Scaling Groups are collections of EC2 instances that are treated as a logical group. ELB use health checks (TCP or HTTP) that help the load balancer determine whether to forward traffic to a particular EC2 instance.

In this recipe, we'll use the AWS CLI tool to create an Auto Scaling Groups and attach an ELB to it. We won't cover configuration management or deployment in this recipe, so imagine that you have a microservice running on each of the EC2 instances in the Auto Scaling Groups.

How to do it...

1. We'll be using the AWS CLI in this recipe, a command-line utility written in Python, that makes interacting with the AWS API easy. We'll assume you have an AWS account and have installed and configured the AWS CLI application. Consult the AWS documentation (https://docs.aws.amazon.com/cli/latest/index.html#) for installation instructions.

2. Create a launch configuration. Launch configurations are templates that our Auto Scaling Groups will use for creating new EC2 instances. They contain information such as the instance type and size that we want to use when creating new instances. Give your launch configuration a unique name–in our case, we'll simply call it `users-service-launch-configuration`:

```
$ aws create-launch-configuration --launch-configuration-name
users-service-launch-configuration \
  --image-id ami-05355a6c --security-groups sg-8422d1eb \
  --instance-type m3.medium
```

3. Create an Auto Scaling Groups that uses our new launch configuration:

```
$ aws create-auto-scaling-group --auto-scaling-group-name users-
service-asg \
  --launch-configuration-name users-service-launch-configuration \
  --min-size 2 \
  --max-size 10
```

4. Create an ELB, as follows:

```
$ aws create-load-balancer --load-balancer-name users-service-elb \
  --listeners
"Protocol=HTTP,LoadBalancerPort=80,InstanceProtocol=HTTP,InstancePo
rt=8080"
```

5. Attach the ASG to our load balancer by running the following command line:

```
$ aws autoscaling attach-load-balancers --auto-scaling-group-name
users-service-asg --load-balancer-names users-service-elb
```

Client-side load balancing

Server-side load balancing is a well-established and battle-tested way to distribute load to an application. It has drawbacks, however, in that there is an upper limit to the amount of incoming connections that a single load balancer can handle. This can be at least partially solved with round-robin DNS, which would distribute load to a number of load balancers, but this configuration can quickly become cumbersome and costly. Load balancer applications can also become points of failure in an already-complex microservices architecture.

An increasingly popular alternative to server-side load balancing is client-side load balancing. In this convention, clients are responsible for distributing requests evenly to running instances of a service. Clients can keep track of latency and failure rates from nodes and opt to reduce the amount of traffic to nodes that are experiencing high latency or high failure rates. This method of load balancing can be extremely effective and simple, especially in large-scale applications.

Ribbon is an open source library developed by Netflix that, among other features, provides support for client-side load balancing. In this recipe, we'll modify our message service to use `ribbon` for client-side load balancing. Instead of sending our requests for a user's friendships to a single instance of the users service, we'll distribute load to a number of available instances.

How to do it...

1. Open the `message-service` project and add the following lines to `build.gradle`:

```
...
dependencies {
  ...
  compile group: 'org.springframework.cloud', name: 'spring-cloud-
starter-ribbon', version: '1.4.2.RELEASE'
}
...
```

2. Navigate to `src/main/resources/application.yml` and add the following configuration for `users-service`:

```
users-service:
  ribbon:
    eureka:
      enabled: false
    listOfServers: localhost:8090,localhost:9092,localhost:9999
    ServerListRefreshInterval: 15000
```

3. Create a new Java class called `UsersServiceConfiguration`. This class will configure the specific rules we want `ribbon` to follow when deciding how to distribute load:

```
package com.packtpub.microservices.ch03.clientsideloadbalancing;

import org.springframework.beans.factory.annotation.Autowired;
import org.springframework.context.annotation.Bean;

import com.netflix.client.config.IClientConfig;
import com.netflix.loadbalancer.IPing;
import com.netflix.loadbalancer.IRule;
import com.netflix.loadbalancer.PingUrl;
import com.netflix.loadbalancer.AvailabilityFilteringRule;

public class UsersServiceConfiguration {

  @Autowired
  IClientConfig ribbonClientConfig;

  @Bean
  public IPing ribbonPing(IClientConfig config) {
    return new PingUrl();
  }

  @Bean
  public IRule ribbonRule(IClientConfig config) {
    return new AvailabilityFilteringRule();
  }

}
```

4. Open `MessageController` and add the following annotation to the
   `MessageController` class:

```
@RibbonClient(name = "users-service", configuration =
UsersServiceConfiguration.class)
@RestClient
public class MessageController {

}
```

5. Annotate the `RestTemplate` class to indicate that we want it to use `ribbon`
   load-balancing support, and modify our URL to use the service name, not the
   hostname we had hardcoded previously:

```
@RibbonClient(name = "users-service", configuration =
UsersServiceConfiguration.class)
@RestClient
public class MessageController {
    ...
    @LoadBalanced
    @Bean
    RestTemplate restTemplate(){
      return new RestTemplate();
    }
    ...

    @Async
    public CompletableFuture<Boolean> isFollowing(String fromUser,
String toUser) {

        String url = String.format(
"http://localhost:4567/followings?user=%s&filter=%s",
                fromUser, toUser);

        RestTemplate template = new RestTemplate();
        UserFriendships followings = template.getForObject(url,
UserFriendships.class);

        return CompletableFuture.completedFuture(
                followings.getFriendships().isEmpty()
        );
    }
}
```

Building event-driven microservices

So far, all of our service-to-service communication recipes have involved having one service call one or more other services directly. This is necessary when the response from the downstream service is required to fulfill the user's request. This isn't always required however. In cases when you want to react to an event in the system, for example, when you want to send an email or notification or when you want to update an analytics store, using an event-driven architecture is preferable. In this design, one service produces a message to a broker and another application consumes that message and performs an action. This has the benefit of decoupling the publisher from the consumer (so your message service doesn't have to worry about sending email notifications, for instance) and also removing potentially expensive operations off the critical path of the user's request. The event-driven architecture also provide some level of fault tolerance as consumers can fail, and messages can be replayed to retry any failed operations.

Apache Kafka is an open source stream-processing platform. At its core, it is an event broker architected as a distributed transaction log. A full description of Apache Kafka is worthy of an entire book in itself—for a great introduction, I highly recommend reading the LinkedIn blog post that introduces Kafka (`https://engineering.linkedin.com/distributed-systems/log-what-every-software-engineer-should-know-about-real-time-datas-unifying`). The minimum you need to know to follow this recipe is that Kafka is a distributed event store that lets you publish messages to categories called **topics**. Another process can then consume messages from a topic and react to them.

Going back to our fictional messaging application, when a user sends a message to another user, we want to be able to notify the recipient in a number of ways. Depending on the recipient's preferences, we'll probably send an email or a push notification or both. In this recipe, we'll modify our message service from previous recipes to publish an event to a Kafka topic called **messages**. We'll then build a consumer application that listens for events in the message's topic and can react by sending the recipient notifications.

How to do it...

Spring for Apache Kafka (`spring-kafka`) is a project that makes it easy to integrate Spring applications with Apache Kafka. It provides useful abstractions for sending and receiving messages.

Note that to follow the steps in this recipe, you will need to have a version of Kafka and ZooKeeper running and accessible. Installing and configuring these two pieces of software is beyond the scope of this recipe, so please visit the respective project websites and follow their wonderfully written guides on getting started. In this recipe, we'll assume that you have Kafka running a single broker on port 9092 and a single instance of ZooKeeper running on port 2181.

Message producer

1. Open the `message-service` project from previous recipes. Modify the `build.gradle` file and add the `spring-kafka` project to the list of dependencies:

```
dependencies {
    compile group: 'org.springframework.kafka', name: 'spring-kafka', version: '2.1.1.RELEASE'
    compile group: 'org.springframework.boot', name: 'spring-boot-starter-web'
    testCompile group: 'junit', name: 'junit', version: '4.12'
}
```

2. The `spring-kafka` project provides a template for sending messages to a Kafka broker. To use the template in our project, we'll need to create a `ProducerFactory` interface and provide it to the constructor of the template.

3. Open the `Application.java` file and add the following content. Note that we're hardcoding the network location of the Kafka broker here—in a real application, you'd at least place this value in some kind of configuration (preferably respecting 12 factor conventions):

```
package com.packtpub.microservices.ch03.message;

import org.apache.kafka.clients.producer.ProducerConfig;
import org.apache.kafka.common.serialization.StringSerializer;
import org.springframework.boot.SpringApplication;
import org.springframework.boot.autoconfigure.SpringBootApplication;
import org.springframework.context.annotation.Bean;
import org.springframework.kafka.core.DefaultKafkaProducerFactory;
import org.springframework.kafka.core.KafkaTemplate;
import org.springframework.kafka.core.ProducerFactory;

import java.util.HashMap;
import java.util.Map;
```

```
@SpringBootApplication
@EnableAsync
public class Application {
    public static void main(String[] args) {
        SpringApplication.run(Application.class, args);
    }

    @Bean
    public Map<String, Object> producerConfigs() {
        Map<String, Object> props = new HashMap<>();
        props.put(ProducerConfig.BOOTSTRAP_SERVERS_CONFIG,
"localhost:9092");
        props.put(ProducerConfig.KEY_SERIALIZER_CLASS_CONFIG,
StringSerializer.class);
        props.put(ProducerConfig.VALUE_SERIALIZER_CLASS_CONFIG,
StringSerializer.class);
        return props;
    }

    @Bean
    public ProducerFactory<Integer, String> producerFactory() {
        return new
DefaultKafkaProducerFactory<>(producerConfigs());
    }

    @Bean
    public KafkaTemplate<Integer, String> kafkaTemplate() {
        return new KafkaTemplate<Integer,
String>(producerFactory());
    }
}
```

4. Now that we can use `KafkaTemplate` in our application, add one to the `MessageController` class. Also, use the Jackson `ObjectMapper` class to convert our `Message` instance into a JSON string that we'll publish to the Kafka topic. Open the `MessageController` class and add following fields:

```
...
import org.springframework.kafka.core.KafkaTemplate;
import com.fasterxml.jackson.databind.ObjectMapper;
...


@RestController
public class MessageController {

    @Autowired
```

```
    private KafkaTemplate kafkaTemplate;

    @Autowired
    private ObjectMapper objectMapper;

    ...
}
```

5. Now that we have access to the Jackson `ObjectMapper` and the `KafkaTemplate` classes, create a method for publishing events. In this example, we're printing out to standard error and standard output. In a real application, you'd configure a logger, such as log4j, and use the appropriate log levels:

```
@RestController
public class MessageController {

    ...


    private void publishMessageEvent(Message message) {
        try {
            String data = objectMapper.writeValueAsString(message);
            ListenableFuture<SendResult> result =
kafkaTemplate.send("messages", data);
            result.addCallback(new
ListenableFutureCallback<SendResult>() {
                @Override
                public void onFailure(Throwable ex) {
                    System.err.println("Failed to emit message
event: " + ex.getMessage());
                }

                @Override
                public void onSuccess(SendResult result) {
                    System.out.println("Successfully published
message event");
                }
            });
        } catch (JsonProcessingException e) {
            System.err.println("Error processing json: " +
e.getMessage());
        }
    }
}
```

6. Add the following line to the `create` method, calling the previously created the `publishMessageEvent` method:

```
@RequestMapping(
            path="/messages",
            method=RequestMethod.POST,
            produces="application/json")
public ResponseEntity<Message> create(@RequestBody Message message)
{

    . . .


    publishMessageEvent(message);
    return ResponseEntity.created(location).build();
}
```

7. To test this example, create a message topic using the `kafka-topics.sh` Kafka utility (packaged with the Kafka binary distribution), as follows:

```
bin/kafka-topics.sh --create \
  --zookeeper localhost:2181 \
  --replication-factor 1 --partitions 1 \
  --topic messages
```

Message consumer

Now that we're publishing message-send events, the next step is to build a small consumer application that can react to these events in our system. We'll discuss the scaffolding as it relates to Kafka in this recipe; implementing email and push notification functionality is left as an exercise for the reader:

1. Create a new Gradle Java project called `message-notifier` with the following `build.gradle` file:

```
group 'com.packtpub.microservices'
version '1.0-SNAPSHOT'

buildscript {
    repositories {
        mavenCentral()
    }
    dependencies {
        classpath group: 'org.springframework.boot', name: 'spring-
boot-gradle-plugin', version: '1.5.9.RELEASE'
    }
}
```

```
apply plugin: 'java'
apply plugin: 'org.springframework.boot'

sourceCompatibility = 1.8

repositories {
    mavenCentral()
}

dependencies {
    compile group: 'org.springframework.kafka', name: 'spring-
kafka', version: '2.1.1.RELEASE'
    compile group: 'org.springframework.boot', name: 'spring-boot-
starter'
    testCompile group: 'junit', name: 'junit', version: '4.12'
}
```

2. Create a new Java class called `Application` with the Spring Boot application boilerplate:

```
package com.packtpub.microservices.ch03.consumer;

import org.springframework.boot.SpringApplication;
import
org.springframework.boot.autoconfigure.SpringBootApplication;

@SpringBootApplication
public class Application {
    public static void main(String[] args) {
        SpringApplication.run(Application.class, args);
    }
}
```

Evolving APIs

APIs are contracts between clients and servers. Backward-incompatible changes to APIs can cause unexpected errors for clients of the service. In a microservices architecture, precautions have to be taken to ensure that changes to a service's API do not unintentionally cause cascading problems throughout the system.

A popular approach is to version your API, either through the URL or via content negotiation in request headers. Because they're generally easier to work with, and often easier to cache, URL prefixes or query strings tend to be more common—in this case, the API endpoint is either prefixed with a version string (that is, /v1/users) or called with a query string parameter specifying a version or even a date (that is, /v1/users?version=1.0 or /v1/users?version=20180122).

With edge proxies or service mesh configurations, it's even possible to run multiple versions of software in an environment and route requests based on the URL to older or newer versions of a service. This changes the traditional life cycle of a service–you can safely decommission a version when it is no longer receiving any traffic. This can be useful, especially in the case of a public API where you have little control over clients.

Microservices are different than public APIs. The contract between clients and the server in a public API is much more long-lived. In a microservices architecture, it's easier to track down clients who are using your service and convince them to upgrade their code! Nevertheless, API versioning is sometimes necessary. Because being able to respond successfully to multiple versions of an API is a maintenance burden, we'd like to avoid it for as long as possible. To do this, there are a few practices that can be used to avoid making backward-incompatible changes.

How to do it...

1. Using our example application, pichat, let's imagine that we want to change the name of the message body from body to message_text. This presents a problem because our message service is designed to accept the following requests:

```
GET /messages?user_id=123
GET /messages/123
POST /messages
DELETE /messages/123
```

2. In the case of the GET requests, the client will expect a JSON object with a field called body in the response. In the case of the POST request, clients will be sending payloads as the JSON objects with a field called body. We can't simply remove body because that would break existing clients, thus necessitating a change to the API version. Instead, we'll simply add the new field in addition to the old one, as follows:

```json
{
  "message": {
    "from_user": "sender",
    "to_user": "recipient",
    "body": "Hello, there",
    "message_text": "Hello, there"
  }
}
```

3. Now you can gradually track down clients using these responses; once they've all been upgraded, you can safely remove the deprecated field from the JSON response.

13
Client Patterns

In this chapter, we will cover the following recipes:

- Modeling concurrency with dependent futures
- Backend For Frontend
- Consistent RPC with HTTP and JSON
- Using gRPC
- Using Thrift

Introduction

When building a service-oriented architecture, it's easy to get stuck thinking about the most general way to represent the domain entities and behaviors that are controlled by a particular service. The truth is, we rarely use services in general ways—we usually combine calls to multiple services and use the responses to create a new, aggregate response body. We often make service calls in ways that resemble how we used to aggregate data from a database, so we have to think about relationships between disparate types in our system and how best to model data dependencies.

We also want to make client development easy. When designing general-purpose APIs, it's easy to get stuck thinking about the right way to do things (if you've ever heard someone critique an API design as not being RESTful, this might sound familiar) instead of thinking about the easy way to do things. A service isn't much good if a client needs to make dozens of calls to it in order to get the data they need. When designing systems that involve microservices, it's essential to think about data aggregation from the client's perspective.

Clients have to think about more than just the services they are invoking, but often they have to consider what instance of those services they want to configure themselves to invoke. It's common to have staging or testing environments, and these get much more complicated in the microservices architectures.

In this chapter, we'll discuss techniques for modeling dependent service calls and aggregating responses from various services to create client-specific APIs. We'll also discuss managing different microservices environments and making RPC consistent with JSON and HTTP, as well as the gRPC and Thrift binary protocols.

Modeling concurrency with dependent futures

We saw in a previous recipe that we can use asynchronous methods to make service calls that are handled in separate threads. This is essential because blocking on network I/O would severely limit the number of incoming requests our service would be able to handle. A service that blocks on the network I/O would only be able to handle a relatively small number of requests per process, requiring us to spend more resources on horizontal scaling. In the example we used, the message service needed to call the social graph service for two users, the sender, and the recipient of a message, and make sure that the two users followed each other before allowing a message to be sent. We modified our request methods to return the `CompletableFuture` instances that wrapped the response, and then waited on all of the results to finish before verifying that the sender and recipient of the message had a symmetric following relationship. This model works fine when you're making multiple requests that are not dependent (you do not need the response from one request to make the subsequent request). In this situation, where we have dependent service calls, we need a better way to model that dependency.

In our `pichat` application, we need to render a screen that lists information about users we follow. In order to do that, we need to call the social-graph service to get a list of users and then call the users service to get details such as the display name and avatar for each user. This use case involves making dependent service calls. We need an effective way of modeling this kind of service invocation while still scheduling asynchronous operations in ways that allow them to be run in separate threads of execution.

In this recipe, we'll demonstrate this by using composition of `CompletableFuture` as well as Java 8 streams to model dependent service invocations. We'll create a sample client application that calls a social service to get a list of users that the logged in user follows, and then calls the user service to get details for each user.

How to do it...

In order to model dependent asynchronous service calls, we'll take advantage of two features in Java 8. Streams are useful for processing data, so we'll use them in our example to extract usernames from a list of followings and map a function to each element. Java 8's `CompletableFuture` can be composed, which allows us to naturally express dependencies between futures.

In this recipe, we'll create a simple client application that calls the social service for a list of users that the current user follows. For each user returned, the application will get user details from the users service. We'll build this example as a command-line application for easy demonstration purposes, but it could just as well be another microservice, or a web or mobile client.

 In order to build a command-line application that has all of the capabilities of a Spring Boot application, we're going to cheat a little and just implement `CommandLineRunner` and call `System.exit(0);` in the `run()` method.

Before we start building our application, we'll outline the responses from our hypothetical social service and users service services. We can mimic these services by just hosting the appropriate JSON response on a local web server. We'll use ports `8000` and `8001` for the social service and users service, respectively. The social service has an endpoint, `/followings/:username`, that returns a JSON object with a list of followings for the specified username. The JSON response will look like the following snippet:

```
{
  "username": "paulosman",
  "followings": [
    "johnsmith",
    "janesmith",
    "petersmith"
  ]
}
```

The users service has an endpoint called `/users/:username`, which will return a JSON representation of the user's details, including the username, full name, and avatar URL:

```
{
  "username": "paulosman",
  "full_name": "Paul Osman",
  "avatar_url": "http://foo.com/pic.jpg"
}
```

Now that we have our services and we've outlined the responses we expect from each, let's go ahead and build our client application by performing the following steps:

1. Create a new Java/Gradle application called `UserDetailsClient` with the following `build.gradle` file:

```
group 'com.packtpub.microservices'
version '1.0-SNAPSHOT'

buildscript {
    repositories {
        mavenCentral()
    }
    dependencies {
        classpath group: 'org.springframework.boot', name: 'spring-
boot-gradle
        -plugin', version: '1.5.9.RELEASE'
    }
}

apply plugin: 'java'
apply plugin: 'org.springframework.boot'

sourceCompatibility = 1.8

repositories {
    mavenCentral()
}

dependencies {
    testCompile group: 'junit', name: 'junit', version: '4.12'
    compile group: 'org.springframework.boot',
    name: 'spring-boot-starter-web'
}
```

2. Create a package called `com.packtpub.microservices.ch04.user.models` and a new class called `UserDetails`. We'll use this class to model our response from the users service:

```
package com.packtpub.microservices.ch04.user.models;

import com.fasterxml.jackson.annotation.JsonProperty;

public class UserDetails {
    private String username;

    @JsonProperty("display_name")
```

```java
    private String displayName;

    @JsonProperty("avatar_url")
    private String avatarUrl;

    public UserDetails() {}

    public UserDetails(String username, String displayName,
    String avatarUrl) {
        this.username = username;
        this.displayName = displayName;
        this.avatarUrl = avatarUrl;
    }

    public String getUsername() {
        return username;
    }

    public void setUsername(String username) {
        this.username = username;
    }

    public String getDisplayName() {
        return displayName;
    }

    public void setDisplayName(String displayName) {
        this.displayName = displayName;
    }

    public String getAvatarUrl() {
        return avatarUrl;
    }

    public void setAvatarUrl(String avatarUrl) {
        this.avatarUrl = avatarUrl;
    }

    public String toString() {
        return String.format("[UserDetails: %s, %s, %s]", username,
        displayName, avatarUrl);
    }
}
```

3. Create another class in the
   com.packtpub.microservices.ch04.user.models package called
   Followings. This will be used to model the response from the social service:

```
package com.packtpub.microservices.ch04.user.models;

import java.util.List;

public class Followings {
    private String username;
    private List<String> followings;

    public Followings() {}

    public Followings(String username, List<String> followings) {
        this.username = username;
        this.followings = followings;
    }

    public String getUsername() {
        return username;
    }

    public void setUsername(String username) {
        this.username = username;
    }

    public List<String> getFollowings() {
        return followings;
    }

    public void setFollowings(List<String> followings) {
        this.followings = followings;
    }

    public String toString() {
        return String.format("[Followings for username: %s - %s]",
            username, followings);
    }
}
```

4. Create a service representation for calling our social service. Predictably enough, we'll call it `SocialService` and put it in the `com.packtpub.microservices.ch04.user.services` package:

```
package com.packtpub.microservices.ch04.user.services;

import com.packtpub.microservices.models.Followings;
import org.springframework.boot.web.client.RestTemplateBuilder;
import org.springframework.scheduling.annotation.Async;
import org.springframework.stereotype.Service;
import org.springframework.web.client.RestTemplate;

import java.util.concurrent.CompletableFuture;

@Service
public class SocialService {

    private final RestTemplate restTemplate;

    public SocialService(RestTemplateBuilder restTemplateBuilder) {
        this.restTemplate = restTemplateBuilder.build();
    }

    @Async
    public CompletableFuture<Followings>
    getFollowings(String username) {
        String url =
String.format("http://localhost:8000/followings/
        %s", username);
        Followings followings = restTemplate.getForObject(url,
        Followings.class);
        return CompletableFuture.completedFuture(followings);
    }
}
```

5. Create a service representation for our users service. Appropriately, we'll call the class `UserService` in the same package:

```
package com.packtpub.microservices.services;

import com.packtpub.microservices.models.Followings;
import com.packtpub.microservices.models.UserDetails;
import org.springframework.boot.web.client.RestTemplateBuilder;
import org.springframework.scheduling.annotation.Async;
import org.springframework.stereotype.Service;
import org.springframework.web.client.RestTemplate;
```

```
import java.util.concurrent.CompletableFuture;

@Service
public class UserService {
    private final RestTemplate restTemplate;

    public UserService(RestTemplateBuilder restTemplateBuilder) {
        this.restTemplate = restTemplateBuilder.build();
    }

    @Async
    public CompletableFuture<UserDetails>
    getUserDetails(String username) {
        String url = String.format("http://localhost:8001/users/
        %s", username);
        UserDetails userDetails = restTemplate.getForObject(url,
        UserDetails.class);
        return CompletableFuture.completedFuture(userDetails);
    }

}
```

6. We now have classes to model the responses from our services, and service objects to represent the services we're going to invoke. It's time to tie it all together by creating our main class, which will call these two services in a dependent manner, using the composability of futures to model the dependency. Create a new class called UserDetailsClient, as follows:

```
package com.packtpub.microservices.ch04.user;

import com.packtpub.microservices.models.Followings;
import com.packtpub.microservices.models.UserDetails;
import com.packtpub.microservices.services.SocialService;
import com.packtpub.microservices.services.UserService;
import org.springframework.beans.factory.annotation.Autowired;
import org.springframework.boot.CommandLineRunner;
import org.springframework.boot.SpringApplication;
import
org.springframework.boot.autoconfigure.SpringBootApplication;

import java.util.List;
import java.util.concurrent.CompletableFuture;
import java.util.concurrent.Future;
import java.util.stream.Collectors;

@SpringBootApplication
public class UserDetailsClient implements CommandLineRunner {
```

```
public UserDetailsClient() {}

@Autowired
private SocialService socialService;

@Autowired
private UserService userService;

public CompletableFuture<List<UserDetails>>
getFollowingDetails(String username) {
    return socialService.getFollowings(username).thenApply(f ->
            f.getFollowings().stream().map(u ->userService.
            getUserDetails(u)).map(CompletableFuture::join).
            collect(Collectors.toList()));
}

public static void main(String[] args) {
    SpringApplication.run(UserDetailsClient.class, args);
}

@Override
public void run(String... args) throws Exception {
    Future<List<UserDetails>> users = getFollowingDetails
    ("paulosman");
    System.out.println(users.get());
    System.out.println("Heyo");
    System.exit(0);
}
}
```

The magic really happens in the following method:

```
CompletableFuture<List<UserDetails>> getFollowingDetails(String
username)
{
  return socialService.getFollowings(username).thenApply(
    f -> f.getFollowings().stream().map(u ->
      userService.getUserDetails(u)).map(
        CompletableFuture::join).collect(Collectors.toList()));
}
```

Recall that the `getFollowings` method in `SocialService` returns `CompletableFuture<Followings>`. `CompletableFuture` has a method, called `thenApply`, that takes the eventual result of the future (`Followings`) and applies it to be passed in the Lambda. In this case, we're taking `Followings` and using the Java 8 Stream API to call map on the list of usernames returned by the social service. The map applies each username to a function that calls `getUserDetails` on `UserService`. The `CompletableFuture::join` method is used to turn `List<Future<T>>` into `Future<List<T>>`, which is a common operation when performing these kinds of dependent service invocations. Finally, we collect the results and return them as a list.

Backend for frontend

When software shifted from desktop and web-based applications to mobile applications, distributed architectures became much more prevalent. It became a focus for many organizations to build a platform instead of just a product. This approach places a much larger emphasis on APIs that a product can expose to clients as well as third-party partners. As APIs became a given for any web-based application, it became popular to try to build client applications (mobile or JavaScript) on the same API used to provide functionality to the third-party partners. The idea is that if you exposed one well-designed, general-purpose API, you would have everything you need to build any kind of application. The general architecture looked like this:

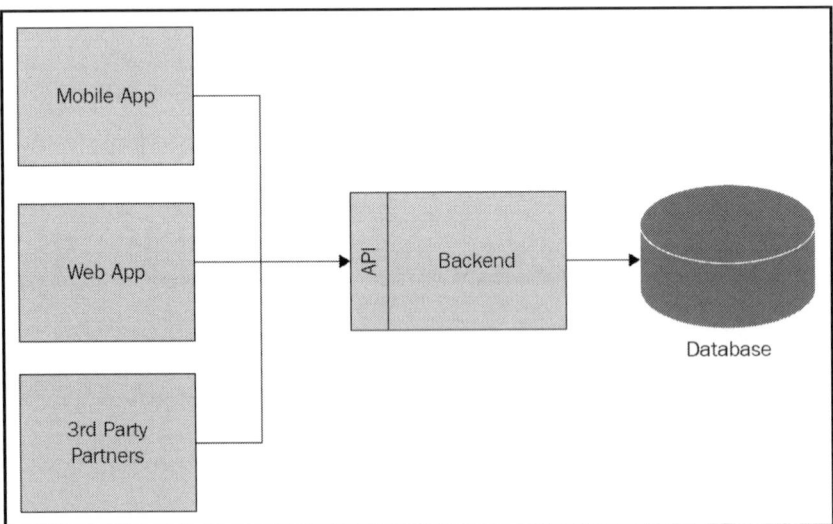

The flaw in this approach is that it assumes that the needs of your first-party (mobile and web) and third-party (partner) applications are always going to be aligned, and this is rarely the case. More often than not, you want to encourage certain kinds of functionality in the third-party integrations and a different set of functionality in first-party clients. Additionally, you want to be much more tolerant (encouraging, even) of changes in first-party clients—your client applications will evolve and constantly be changing their API requirements. Finally, you cannot anticipate all of the possible use cases third-party partners will have for your API, so a general-purpose design is beneficial, but you will be able to anticipate the needs of your mobile and web applications, and being too general in your API design can often hamper your product's needs. A good example of this is a server-side website that is rewritten as a single-page JavaScript application. With a general-purpose API, this kind of project can result in page views that require dozens of XMLHttpRequests to render a single page view.

Backend For Frontend (**BFF**) is an architectural pattern that involves creating separate, **bespoke APIs** for different classes of client applications. Instead of a single API layer in your architecture, separate BFF layers can be developed depending on how many categories of client applications you want to support. How you categorize clients is completely up to the needs of your business. You may decide to have a single BFF layer for all mobile clients, or you may divide them into an iOS BFF and an Android BFF. Similarly, you may choose to have a separate BFF layer for your web application and your third-party partners (what used to be the primary driver for your single API):

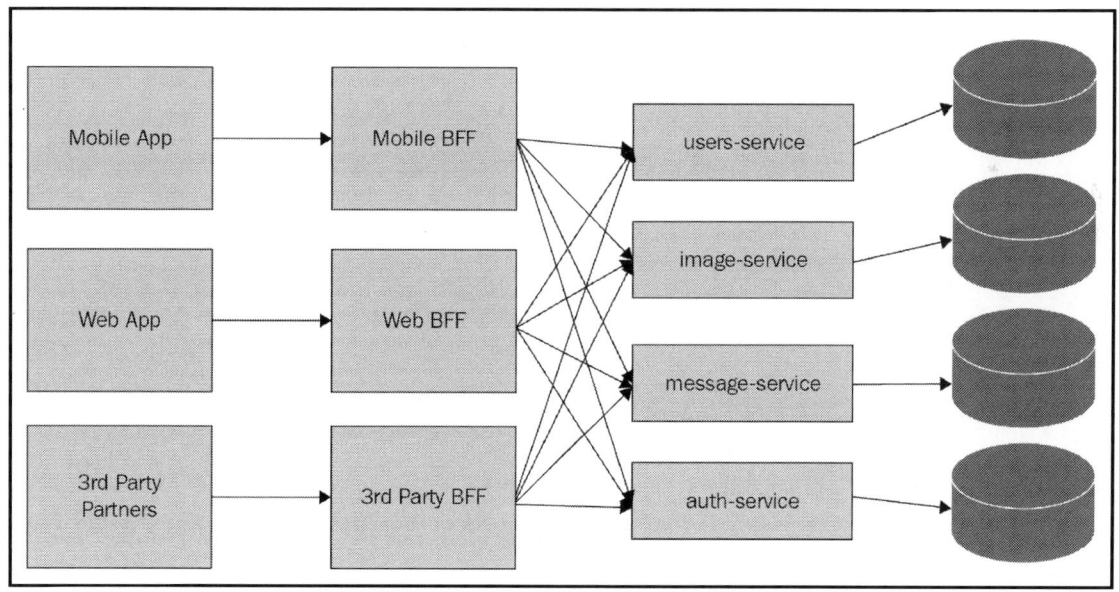

In this system, each category of client makes requests to its own BFF layer, which can then aggregate calls to downstream services and build a cohesive, bespoke API.

How to do it...

In order to design and build a BFF layer, we should first design the API. In fact, we've already done this. In the previous recipe, we demonstrated using `CompletableFuture` to asynchronously make a request to our systems, social service and then for each user returned, make asynchronous requests to the user-details-service to fetch certain user profile information. This is a great use case for a BFF layer for our mobile apps. Imagine that our mobile app has a screen that shows a list of users that the user follows, with basic information such as their avatar, username, and display name. Since the social graph information (the list of users the user is following) and the user profile information (avatar, username, and display name) are the responsibility of two separate services, it's cumbersome to require our mobile clients to aggregate calls to these services to render a following page. Instead, we can create a mobile BFF layer that handles this aggregation and returns a convenient response to the client. Our request endpoint would be as follows:

```
GET /users/:user_id/following
```

And the response body we expect to get back should be as follows:

```
{
  "username": "paulosman",
  "followings": [
    {
      "username": "friendlyuser",
      "display_name": "Friendly User",
      "avatar_url": "http://example.com/pic.jpg"
    },
    {
      ...
    }
  ]
}
```

As we can see, the BFF will return a response with all of the information we need to render a following screen in our mobile app:

1. Create a new Gradle/Java project called `bff-mobile` with the following `build.gradle` file:

```
group 'com.packtpub.microservices'
version '1.0-SNAPSHOT'

buildscript {
    repositories {
        mavenCentral()
    }
    dependencies {
        classpath group: 'org.springframework.boot',
        name: 'spring-boot-gradle-plugin',
        version: '1.5.9.RELEASE'
    }
}

apply plugin: 'java'
apply plugin: 'org.springframework.boot'

sourceCompatibility = 1.8

repositories {
    mavenCentral()
}

dependencies {
    testCompile group: 'junit', name: 'junit', version: '4.12'
    compile group: 'org.springframework.boot',
    name: 'spring-boot-starter-web'
}
```

2. Create a new package called `com.packtpub.microservices.mobilebff` and a new class called `Main`:

```
package com.packtpub.microservices.ch04.mobilebff;

import org.springframework.boot.SpringApplication;
import
org.springframework.boot.autoconfigure.SpringBootApplication;

@SpringBootApplication
public class Main {
    public static void main(String[] args) {
```

```
            SpringApplication.run(Main.class, args);
    }
}
```

3. Create a new package called
    com.packtpub.microservices.ch04.mobilebff.models and a new class
    called User:

```
package com.packtpub.microservices.ch04.mobilebff.models;

import com.fasterxml.jackson.annotation.JsonProperty;

public class User {
    private String username;

    @JsonProperty("display_name")
    private String displayName;

    @JsonProperty("avatar_url")
    private String avatarUrl;

    public User() {}

    public User(String username, String displayName,
    String avatarUrl) {
        this.username = username;
        this.displayName = displayName;
        this.avatarUrl = avatarUrl;
    }

    public String getUsername() {
        return username;
    }

    public void setUsername(String username) {
        this.username = username;
    }

    public String getDisplayName() {
        return displayName;
    }

    public void setDisplayName(String displayName) {
        this.displayName = displayName;
    }

    public String getAvatarUrl() {
        return avatarUrl;
```

```
    }

    public void setAvatarUrl(String avatarUrl) {
        this.avatarUrl = avatarUrl;
    }

    public String toString() {
        return String.format(
                "[User username:%s, displayName:%s, avatarUrl:%s]",
                username, displayName, avatarUrl);
    }
}
```

4. **Create another model, called** `Followings`:

```
package com.packtpub.microservices.ch04.mobilebff.models;

import java.util.List;

public class Followings {
    private String username;

    private List<String> followings;

    public Followings() {}

    public Followings(String username, List<String> followings) {
        this.username = username;
        this.followings = followings;
    }

    public String getUsername() {
        return username;
    }

    public void setUsername(String username) {
        this.username = username;
    }

    public List<String> getFollowings() {
        return followings;
    }

    public void setFollowings(List<String> followings) {
        this.followings = followings;
    }
}
```

5. The last model we'll create is called `HydratedFollowings`. This is similar to the `Followings` model, but instead of storing the list of users as a string, it contains a list of the `User` objects:

```java
package com.packtpub.microservices.ch04.mobilebff.models;

import java.util.List;

public class HydratedFollowings {
    private String username;

    private List<User> followings;

    public HydratedFollowings() {}

    public HydratedFollowings(String username, List<User>
    followings) {
        this.username = username;
        this.followings = followings;
    }

    public String getUsername() {
        return username;
    }

    public void setUsername(String username) {
        this.username = username;
    }

    public List<User> getFollowings() {
        return followings;
    }

    public void setFollowings(List<User> followings) {
        this.followings = followings;
    }
}
```

6. Create the service clients. Create a new package called `com.packtpub.microservices.ch04.mobilebff.services` and a new class called `SocialGraphService`:

```java
package com.packtpub.microservices.ch04.mobilebff.services;

import com.packtpub.microservices.ch04.mobilebff.models.Followings;
import org.springframework.boot.web.client.RestTemplateBuilder;
import org.springframework.scheduling.annotation.Async;
```

```
import org.springframework.stereotype.Service;
import org.springframework.web.client.RestTemplate;

import java.util.concurrent.CompletableFuture;

@Service
public class SocialGraphService {

    private final RestTemplate restTemplate;

    public SocialGraphService(RestTemplateBuilder
    restTemplateBuilder) {
        this.restTemplate = restTemplateBuilder.build();
    }

    @Async
    public CompletableFuture<Followings>
    getFollowing(String username) {
        String url =
String.format("http://localhost:4567/followings/
        %s", username);
        Followings followings = restTemplate.getForObject(url,
        Followings.class);
        return CompletableFuture.completedFuture(followings);
    }
}
```

7. Create a new class, called UsersService, that will serve as a client for our users service:

```
package com.packtpub.microservices.ch04.mobilebff.services;

import com.packtpub.microservices.ch04.mobilebff.models.User;
import org.springframework.boot.web.client.RestTemplateBuilder;
import org.springframework.scheduling.annotation.Async;
import org.springframework.stereotype.Service;
import org.springframework.web.client.RestTemplate;

import java.util.concurrent.CompletableFuture;

@Service
public class UsersService {

    private final RestTemplate restTemplate;

    public UsersService(RestTemplateBuilder restTemplateBuilder) {
        this.restTemplate = restTemplateBuilder.build();
    }
```

```
@Async
public CompletableFuture<User> getUserDetails(String username)
{
    String url = String.format("http://localhost:4568/users/
    %s", username);
    User user = restTemplate.getForObject(url, User.class);
    return CompletableFuture.completedFuture(user);
}
}
```

8. Let's tie it all together by creating our controller that exposes the endpoint. This code will look familiar if you completed the previous recipe, since we're using exactly the same pattern to model dependent asynchronous service invocations. Create a package called com.packtpub.microservices.ch04.mobilebff.controllers and a new class called UsersController:

```
package com.packtpub.microservices.ch04.mobilebff.controllers;

import
com.packtpub.microservices.ch04.mobilebff.models.HydratedFollowings
;
import com.packtpub.microservices.ch04.mobilebff.models.User;
import
com.packtpub.microservices.ch04.mobilebff.services.SocialGraphServi
ce;
import
com.packtpub.microservices.ch04.mobilebff.services.UsersService;
import org.springframework.beans.factory.annotation.Autowired;
import org.springframework.web.bind.annotation.*;

import java.util.List;
import java.util.concurrent.CompletableFuture;
import java.util.concurrent.ExecutionException;
import java.util.stream.Collectors;

@RestController
public class UsersController {

    @Autowired
    private SocialGraphService socialGraphService;

    @Autowired
    private UsersService userService;

    @RequestMapping(path = "/users/{username}/followings",
    method = RequestMethod.GET)
```

```
        public HydratedFollowings getFollowings(@PathVariable String
    username)
        throws ExecutionException, InterruptedException {
            CompletableFuture<List<User>> users =
    socialGraphService.getFollowing
            (username).thenApply(f -> f.getFollowings().stream().map(
                        u -> userService.getUserDetails(u)).map(
    CompletableFuture::join).collect(Collectors.toList()));
            return new HydratedFollowings(username, users.get());
        }
    }
```

9. That's it! Run the application and make a GET request to
   /users/username/followings. You should get back a fully-hydrated JSON
   response with the user's username and details for each of the users the user
   follows.

Consistent RPC with HTTP and JSON

When building multiple microservices, consistency and conventions between services start
to make a real impact. When problems arise in a microservice architecture, you can end up
spending time debugging many services—being able to make certain assumptions about
the nature of a particular service interface can save a lot of time and mental energy. Having
a consistent way of doing RPC also allows you to codify certain concerns into libraries that
can be easily shared between services. Things such as authentication, how headers should
be interpreted, what information is included in a response body, and how to request
paginated responses can be made simpler by having a consistent approach. Additionally,
the way that errors are reported should be made as consistent as possible.

Because the microservice architectures commonly consist of services written in different
programming languages by different teams, any efforts toward consistent RPC semantics
will have to be implemented, probably as libraries, in as many languages as you have used
to build services. This can be cumbersome, but is well worth the effort for the consistency
clients can assume when speaking to a variety of services.

In this recipe, we'll focus on services written in Java using Spring Boot. We'll write a custom
serializer to present resources and collections of resources in a consistent manner, including
pagination information. We'll then modify our message service to use our new serializer.

How to do it...

In this recipe, we'll create a wrapper class to represent collections of resources with pagination information. We'll also use the `JsonRootName` annotation from the `jackson` library to make single-resource representations consistent. The following code should be added to the message service, which was introduced in a previous recipe:

1. Create a new class called `ResourceCollection`. This class will be a regular POJO with fields to represent the page number, a list of items, and a URL that can be used to access the next page in a collection:

```
package com.packtpub.microservices.ch04.message.models;

import com.fasterxml.jackson.annotation.JsonProperty;
import com.fasterxml.jackson.annotation.JsonRootName;

import java.util.List;

@JsonRootName("result")
public class ResourceCollection<T> {

    private int page;

    @JsonProperty("next_url")
    private String nextUrl;

    private List<T> items;

    public ResourceCollection(List<T> items, int page, String
nextUrl) {
        this.items = items;
        this.page = page;
        this.nextUrl = nextUrl;
    }

    public int getPage() {
        return page;
    }

    public void setPage(int pageNumber) {
        this.page = page;
    }

    public String getNextUrl() {
        return nextUrl;
    }
```

```
        public void setNextUrl(String nextUrl) {
            this.nextUrl = nextUrl;
        }

        public List<T> getItems() {
            return items;
        }

        public void setItems(List<T> items) {
            this.items = items;
        }
    }
```

2. Create or modify the `Message` model. We're using the `JsonRootName` annotation here to wrap the `Message` representation in a single JSON object with the `item` key. In order to have consistent representations, we should add these to all models that our services expose as a resource:

```java
package com.packtpub.microservices.ch04.message.models;

import com.fasterxml.jackson.annotation.JsonRootName;

@JsonRootName("item")
public class Message {
    private String id;
    private String toUser;
    private String fromUser;
    private String body;

    public Message(String id, String toUser, String fromUser,
String body) {
        this.id = id;
        this.toUser = toUser;
        this.fromUser = fromUser;
        this.body = body;
    }

    public String getId() {
        return id;
    }

    public void setId(String id) {
        this.id = id;
    }

    public String getToUser() {
        return toUser;
```

```
        }

        public void setToUser(String toUser) {
            this.toUser = toUser;
        }

        public String getFromUser() {
            return fromUser;
        }

        public void setFromUser(String fromUser) {
            this.fromUser = fromUser;
        }

        public String getBody() {
            return body;
        }

        public void setBody(String body) {
            this.body = body;
        }
    }
```

3. The following controller returns a list of messages and a specific message. We wrap the list of messages in the ResourceCollection class that we created previously:

```
package com.packtpub.microservices.ch04.message.controllers;

import com.packtpub.microservices.ch04.message.models.Message;
import
com.packtpub.microservices.ch04.message.models.ResourceCollection;
import org.springframework.web.bind.annotation.*;

import javax.servlet.http.HttpServletRequest;
import java.util.List;
import java.util.stream.Collectors;
import java.util.stream.Stream;

@RestController
public class MessageController {

    @RequestMapping(value = "/messages", method =
RequestMethod.GET)
    public ResourceCollection<Message>
messages(@RequestParam(name="page", required=false,
defaultValue="1") int page,
                                    HttpServletRequest request)
```

```
{
        List<Message> messages = Stream.of(
                new Message("1234","paul", "veronica", "hello!"),
                new Message("5678","meghann", "paul", "hello!")
        ).collect(Collectors.toList());

        String nextUrl = String.format("%s?page=%d",
request.getRequestURI(), page + 1);

        return new ResourceCollection<>(messages, page, nextUrl);
    }

    @RequestMapping(value = "/messages/{id}", method =
RequestMethod.GET)
    public Message message(@PathVariable("id") String id) {
        return new Message(id, "paul", "veronica", "hi dad");
    }
}
```

4. If you test requesting a collection of items by making a request to /messages, the following JSON should now be returned:

```
{
    "result": {
        "page": 1,
        "items": [
            {
                "id": "1234",
                "toUser": "paul",
                "fromUser": "veronica",
                "body": "hello!"
            },
            {
                "id": "5678",
                "toUser": "meghann",
                "fromUser": "paul",
                "body": "hello!"
            }
        ],
        "next_url": "/messages?page=2"
    }
}
```

5. The following JSON should be returned for a single resource:

```
{
    "item": {
        "id": "123",
        "toUser": "paul",
        "fromUser": "veronica",
        "body": "hi dad"
    }
}
```

Having some standardization for how resources or lists of resources are represented can greatly simplify working with services in a microservices architecture. Doing this with JSON and HTTP involves a fair amount of manual work however, which can be abstracted away. In the next recipes, we'll explore using Thrift and gRPC, two alternatives to HTTP/JSON for RPC.

Using Thrift

JSON and HTTP are simple, straightforward solutions for data transportation and definition that should serve the purposes of many microservice architectures. If you want type safety and often better performance, however, it can be worthwhile to look at binary solutions such as Thrift or gRPC.

Apache Thrift is an **interface definition language** (**IDL**) and binary transport protocol invented at Facebook. It allows you to specify APIs by defining the structs (which are similar to objects in most languages) and exceptions that your service exposes. Thrift interfaces defined in the IDL are used to generate code in a supported language that is then used to manage the RPC calls. Supported languages include C, C++, Python, Ruby, and Java.

The benefits of a binary protocol such as Thrift are primarily improved performance and type safety. Depending on the JSON library used, serializing and deserializing large JSON payloads can be quite expensive and JSON does not have any type system that clients can use when handling responses. Additionally, because Thrift includes an IDL that can be used to generate code in any supported language, it's easy to let Thrift handle the generation of both client and server code, cutting down the amount of manual work needing to be done.

Because Apache Thrift doesn't use HTTP as the transport layer, services that export Thrift interfaces start their own Thrift server. In this recipe, we'll define the IDL for our message service and use Thrift to generate the handler code. We'll then create the server boilerplate that handles starting the service, listening on a specified port, and so on.

How to do it...

1. Create a new Gradle/Java project with the following `build.gradle` file:

```
group 'com.packtpub.microservices'
version '1.0-SNAPSHOT'

buildscript {
    repositories {
        maven {
            url "https://plugins.gradle.org/m2/"
        }
    }
    dependencies {
        classpath "gradle.plugin.org.jruyi.gradle:thrift-gradle-
plugin:0.4.0"
    }
}

apply plugin: 'java'
apply plugin: 'org.jruyi.thrift'
apply plugin: 'application'

mainClassName =
'com.packtpub.microservices.ch04.MessageServiceServer'

compileThrift {
    recurse true

    generator 'html'
    generator 'java', 'private-members'
}

sourceCompatibility = 1.8

repositories {
    mavenCentral()
}

dependencies {
```

```
    compile group: 'org.apache.thrift', name: 'libthrift', version:
'0.11.0'
    testCompile group: 'junit', name: 'junit', version: '4.12'
}
```

2. Create a directory called `src/main/thrift` and a file called `service.thrift`. This is the IDL file for our service. We'll define a `MessageException` exception, the actual `Message` object, and a `MessageService` interface. For more information on the specific syntax of Thrift IDL files, the Thrift project website has good documentation (`https://thrift.apache.org/docs/idl`). To keep things simple, we'll just define a single method in our service that returns a list of messages for a specific user:

```
namespace java com.packtpub.microservices.ch04.thrift

exception MessageException {
    1: i32 code,
    2: string description
}

struct Message {
    1: i32 id,
    2: string from_user,
    3: string to_user,
    4: string body
}

service MessageService {
    list<Message> inbox(1: string username) throws
(1:MessageException e)
}
```

3. Running the assembled Gradle task will generate the code for the preceding IDL. We'll now create the implementation of our `MessageService` class. This will extend the autogenerated interface from the preceding IDL. For simplicity's sake, our `MessageService` implementation will not connect to any database but instead will use a static, hardcoded representation of inboxes that will be built in the constructor:

```
package com.packtpub.microservices.ch04.thrift;

import com.packtpub.microservices.ch04.thrift.Message;
import com.packtpub.microservices.ch04.thrift.MessageException;
import com.packtpub.microservices.ch04.thrift.MessageService;
import org.apache.thrift.TException;
```

```
import java.util.HashMap;
import java.util.List;
import java.util.Map;
import java.util.stream.Collectors;
import java.util.stream.Stream;

public class MessageServiceImpl implements MessageService.Iface {

    private Map<String, List<Message>> messagesRepository;

    MessageServiceImpl() {
        // populate our mock repository with some sample messages
        messagesRepository = new HashMap<>();
        messagesRepository.put("usertwo", Stream.of(
            new Message(1234, "userone", "usertwo", "hi"),
            new Message(5678, "userthree", "usertwo", "hi")
        ).collect(Collectors.toList()));
        messagesRepository.put("userone", Stream.of(
            new Message(1122, "usertwo", "userone", "hi"),
            new Message(2233, "userthree", "userone", "hi")
        ).collect(Collectors.toList()));
    }

    @Override
    public List<Message> inbox(String username) throws TException {
        if (!messagesRepository.containsKey(username))
            throw new MessageException(100, "Inbox is empty");
        return messagesRepository.get(username);
    }
}
```

4. **Create the server.** Create a new class called `MessageServiceServer`, as follows:

```
package com.packtpub.microservices.ch04.thrift;

import com.packtpub.microservices.ch04.thrift.MessageService;
import org.apache.thrift.server.TServer;
import org.apache.thrift.server.TSimpleServer;
import org.apache.thrift.transport.TServerSocket;
import org.apache.thrift.transport.TServerTransport;
import org.apache.thrift.transport.TTransportException;

public class MessageServiceServer {

    private TSimpleServer server;

    private void start() throws TTransportException {
```

```
            TServerTransport serverTransport = new TServerSocket(9999);
            server = new TSimpleServer(new
    TServer.Args(serverTransport)
                    .processor(new MessageService.Processor<>(new
    MessageServiceImpl())));
            server.serve();
        }

        private void stop() {
            if (server != null && server.isServing())
                server.stop();
        }

        public static void main(String[] args) {
            MessageServiceServer service = new MessageServiceServer();
            try {
                if (args[1].equals("start"))
                    service.start();
                else if (args[2].equals("stop"))
                    service.stop();
            } catch (TTransportException e) {
                e.printStackTrace();
            }
        }
    }
```

Your service is now built and uses Apache Thrift for RPC. As a further exercise, you can experiment with using the same IDL to generate client code that can be used to call this service.

Using gRPC

gRPC is an RPC framework originally invented at Google. Unlike Thrift, gRPC makes use of existing technologies, specifically **protocol buffers**, for its IDL and HTTP/2 for its transport layer. After having completed the previous recipe, aspects of gRPC will feel similar to aspects of Thrift. Instead of the Thrift IDL, types and services are defined in a .proto file. The .proto file can then be used to generate code using the protocol buffer's compiler.

How to do it...

1. Create a new Gradle/Java project with the following `build.gradle` file. Of note here is that we're installing and configuring the `protobuf` Gradle plugin, which will allow us to generate code from `protobuf` files using Gradle, and we're listing the required `protobuf` libraries as dependencies. Finally, we have to tell our IDE where to look for generated classes:

```
group 'com.packtpub.microservices'
version '1.0-SNAPSHOT'

buildscript {
    repositories {
        mavenCentral()
    }
    dependencies {
        classpath 'com.google.protobuf:protobuf-gradle-
plugin:0.8.3'
    }
}

apply plugin: 'java'
apply plugin: 'com.google.protobuf'
apply plugin: 'application'

mainClassName =
'com.packtpub.microservices.ch04.grpc.MessageServer'

sourceCompatibility = 1.8

repositories {
    mavenCentral()
}

def grpcVersion = '1.10.0'

dependencies {
    compile group: 'com.google.api.grpc', name: 'proto-google-
common-protos', version: '1.0.0'
    compile group: 'io.grpc', name: 'grpc-netty', version:
grpcVersion
    compile group: 'io.grpc', name: 'grpc-protobuf', version:
grpcVersion
    compile group: 'io.grpc', name: 'grpc-stub', version:
grpcVersion
    testCompile group: 'junit', name: 'junit', version: '4.12'
```

```
    }

protobuf {
    protoc {
        artifact = 'com.google.protobuf:protoc:3.5.1-1'
    }
    plugins {
        grpc {
            artifact = "io.grpc:protoc-gen-grpc-
java:${grpcVersion}"
        }
    }
    generateProtoTasks {
        all()*.plugins {
            grpc {}
        }
    }
}

// Inform IDEs like IntelliJ IDEA, Eclipse or NetBeans about the
generated code.
sourceSets {
    main {
        java {
            srcDirs 'build/generated/source/proto/main/grpc'
            srcDirs 'build/generated/source/proto/main/java'
        }
    }
}
```

2. Create a new directory called `src/main/proto` and a new file called `message_service.proto`. This will be our definition of `protobuf` for our service. Like in the last recipe, we'll keep it simple by only exposing one method that returns a list of messages for a specified user:

```
option java_package = "com.packtpub.microservices.ch04.grpc";

message Username {
    required string username = 1;
}

message Message {
    required string id = 1;
    required string from_user = 2;
    required string to_user = 3;
    required string body = 4;
}
```

```
message InboxReply {
    repeated Message messages = 1;
}

service MessageService {
    rpc inbox(Username) returns (InboxReply) {}
}
```

3. Implement the actual service. In order to do this, we need to create a new class called `MessageServer` with all the necessary boilerplate for starting and stopping our server. We'll also create an inner class called `MessageService` that extends the generated `MessageServiceGrpc.MessageServiceImplBase` class:

```
package com.packtpub.microservices.ch04.grpc;

import io.grpc.Server;
import io.grpc.ServerBuilder;
import io.grpc.stub.StreamObserver;

import java.io.IOException;

public class MessageServer {

    private final int port;
    private final Server server;

    private MessageServer(int port) throws IOException {
        this(ServerBuilder.forPort(port), port);
    }

    private MessageServer(ServerBuilder<?> serverBuilder, int port)
{
        this.port = port;
        this.server = serverBuilder.addService(new
MessageService()).build();
    }

    public void start() throws IOException {
        server.start();
        Runtime.getRuntime().addShutdownHook(new Thread() {
            @Override
            public void run() {
                // Use stderr here since the logger may has been
reset by its JVM shutdown hook.
                System.err.println("*** shutting down gRPC server
since JVM is shutting down");
                MessageServer.this.stop();
```

```
                            System.err.println("*** server shut down");
                }
        });
    }

    public void stop() {
        if (server != null) {
            server.shutdown();
        }
    }

    private void blockUntilShutdown() throws InterruptedException {
        if (server != null) {
            server.awaitTermination();
        }
    }

    private static class MessageService extends
MessageServiceGrpc.MessageServiceImplBase {
        public void inbox(MessageServiceOuterClass.Username
request,
StreamObserver<MessageServiceOuterClass.InboxReply>
responseObserver) {
            MessageServiceOuterClass.InboxReply reply =
MessageServiceOuterClass.InboxReply.newBuilder().addMessages(
                MessageServiceOuterClass.Message.newBuilder()
                    .setId("1234")
                    .setFromUser("Paul")
                    .setToUser("Veronica")
                    .setBody("hi")
            ).addMessages(
                MessageServiceOuterClass.Message.newBuilder()
                    .setId("5678")
                    .setFromUser("FooBarUser")
                    .setToUser("Veronica")
                    .setBody("Hello again")
            ).build();
            responseObserver.onNext(reply);
            responseObserver.onCompleted();
        }
    }

    public static void main(String[] args) throws Exception {
        MessageServer server = new MessageServer(8989);
        server.start();
        server.blockUntilShutdown();
    }
}
```

14
Reliability Patterns

In this chapter, we will cover the following recipes:

- Using circuit breakers to implement backpressure
- Retrying requests with exponential backoff
- Improving performance with caching
- Fronting your services with a CDN
- Gracefully degrading the user experience
- Testing your failure scenarios with controlled game days
- Introducing automated chaos

Introduction

Reliability is becoming an increasingly popular topic in the world of distributed systems. Job postings for **Site Reliability Engineers (SRE)** or **chaos engineers** are becoming common, and as more and more organizations move toward cloud-native technologies, it's becoming impossible to ignore that system failure is always a reality. Networks will experience congestion, switches, other hardware components will fail, and a whole host of potential failure modes in systems will surprise us in production. It is impossible to completely prevent failures, so we should try to design our systems to be as tolerant of failure as possible.

Microservices provide interesting and useful opportunities to design for reliability. Because microservices encourage us to break our systems into services encapsulating single responsibilities, we can use a number of useful reliability patterns to isolate failures when they do occur. Microservice architectures also present a number of challenges when planning for reliability. Increased reliance on network requests, heterogeneous configurations, multiple data stores and connection pools, and different technical stacks all contribute to an inherently more complex environment where different styles of failure modes can surface.

Whether dealing with a microservice architecture or a monolith code base, we all find ourselves fundamentally surprised [1] (you can check this link for more information: `https://www.youtube.com/watch?v=tZ2wj2pxO6Q`) by the behavior of a system under some kind of failure state at one point or another. Building resiliency into our systems from the start allows us to optimize how we react in these situations. In this chapter, we'll discuss a number of useful reliability patterns that can be used when designing and building microservices to prepare for and reduce the impact of system failures, both expected and unexpected.

Using circuit breakers

Failures in distributed systems can be difficult to debug. A symptom (spikes in latency or a high error rate) can appear far away from the underlying cause (slow database query, garbage collection cycles causing a service to slow down the processing of requests). Sometimes a complete outage can be the result of a failure in a small part of the system, especially when components of the system are having difficulty handling increases in load.

Whenever possible, we want to prevent failures in one part of a system from cascading to other parts, causing widespread and hard-to-debug production issues. Furthermore, if a failure is temporary, we'd like our system to be able to self-repair when the failure is over. If a specific service is experiencing problems because of a temporary spike in load, we should design our system in such a way that it prevents requests to the unhealthy service, allowing it time to recover before beginning to send it traffic again.

Circuit breakers are used in houses to prevent the overuse of electricity from heating up the internal wiring and burning the house down. A circuit is tripped if the breaker detects that it is being overused and cannot handle the amount of current being drawn from it. After some time passes, the circuit can be closed again, allowing the system to function normally.

This same approach can be translated to software and applied to microservice architectures. When a service invokes another service, we should wrap the RPC call in a circuit breaker. If the request fails repeatedly, indicating that the service is unhealthy, the circuit breaker is opened, preventing any further requests from being attempted. The invoking service can then "fail fast" and decide how to handle the failure mode. After a configurable period of time, we can allow another request through, and if it succeeds, close the circuit again, allowing the system to resume normal operation. You can a look at the following related flowchart:

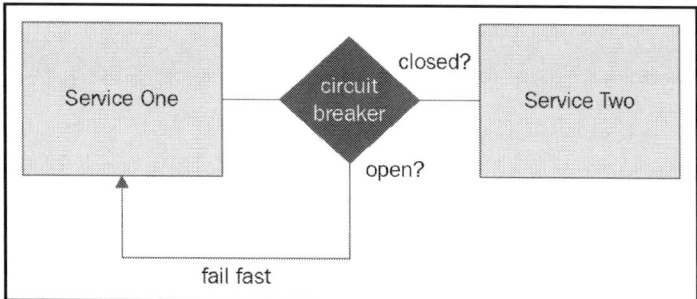

Libraries that implement circuit breakers are available for most popular programming languages. The Hystrix fault-tolerance library, built by Netflix and used in previous recipes is one such library. Some frameworks, such as Twitter's Finagle, automatically wrap RPCs in circuit breakers, keeping track of failures and automatically managing the state of the breaker. Open source service-mesh software, such as **Conduit** and **Linkerd**, automatically add circuit breakers to RPCs as well. In this recipe, we'll introduce a library called `resilience4j` and use its circuit breaker implementation to allow calls from one service to another to fail fast in the event of a failure threshold being reached. To make the example more concrete, we'll modify a message service, which calls a socialgraph service to determine whether two users follow each other, and wrap RPC calls in a circuit breaker.

How to do it...

To demonstrate wrapping service invocations in circuit breakers, we're going to create a version of the `pichat` message service that exposes endpoints for sending and retrieving messages. To send a message from a sender to a recipient, those two users must have a friendship. Friendships are handled by a social-graph-service. For the sake of simplicity, we'll code up a simple mock social-graph-service in Ruby, as we have done in previous recipes. The mock service will expose a single endpoint that lists friendships for a specified user. Here is the source code for the mock social-graph-service in Ruby:

```ruby
require 'sinatra'
require 'json'

get '/friendships/:username' do
  content_type :json
  {
    'username': params[:username],
    'friendships': [
      'pichat:users:johndoe',
      'pichat:users:janesmith',
      'pichat:users:anotheruser'
```

```
    ]
  }.to_json
end
```

 In our mock service, we're using strings in the `pichat:users:username` format to identify users in our system. These are pseudo-URIs, which uniquely identify users in our system. For now, just know that these are unique strings used to identify users in our system.

Our mock social-graph-service exposes the following single endpoint:

```
GET /friendships/paulosman
```

The preceding endpoint returns a JSON response body representing the friendships that the requested user has:

```
{
  "username": "fdsa",
  "friendships": [
    "pichat:users:foobar",
    "pichat:users:asomefdsa"
  ]
}
```

With our mock social-graph-service running on the localhost, port 4567 (the default port for Ruby Sinatra applications), we're ready to start writing our message service. As in previous recipes, we'll use Java and the Spring Boot framework. We'll also use the `resilience4j` circuit-breaker library to wrap calls from the message service to the social-graph-service. First, we'll develop our message-service code, then we'll add in the `resilience4j` circuit-breaker library to add a level of resilience to our service, as shown in the following steps:

1. Create a new Gradle Java project and add the following code to `build.gradle`:

```
group 'com.packtpub.microservices'
version '1.0-SNAPSHOT'

buildscript {
    repositories {
        mavenCentral()
    }
    dependencies {
        classpath group: 'org.springframework.boot', name: 'spring-
boot-gradle-plugin', version: '1.5.9.RELEASE'
    }
```

```
}

apply plugin: 'java'
apply plugin: 'org.springframework.boot'

sourceCompatibility = 1.8

repositories {
    mavenCentral()
}

dependencies {
    testCompile group: 'junit', name: 'junit', version: '4.12'
    compile group: 'org.springframework.boot', name: 'spring-boot-
starter-web'
}
```

2. Our message-service code will have two beans that get autowired into our controller. The first is an in-memory message repository (in a real-world example, this would be replaced with a more durable persistence layer), and the second is a client for the social-graph-service. Before we create those, let's create some supporting objects. Create a new package called com.packtpub.microservices.ch05.message.exceptions and a new class called MessageNotFoundException. This will be used to indicate that a message cannot be found, which will result in a 404 response from our service, as shown here:

```
package com.packtpub.microservices.ch05.exceptions;

import org.springframework.http.HttpStatus;
import org.springframework.web.bind.annotation.ResponseStatus;

@ResponseStatus(HttpStatus.NOT_FOUND)
public class MessageNotFoundException extends Exception {
    public MessageNotFoundException(String message) {
super(message); }
}
```

3. Create another class in the exceptions package called MessageSendForbiddenException. This will be used to indicate that a message cannot be sent because the sender and the recipient are not friends. The response code from our service will be 403 forbidden, as shown here:

```
package com.packtpub.microservices.ch05.message.exceptions;

import org.springframework.http.HttpStatus;
```

```
import org.springframework.web.bind.annotation.ResponseStatus;

@ResponseStatus(HttpStatus.FORBIDDEN)
public class MessageSendForbiddenException extends Exception {
    public MessageSendForbiddenException(String message) {
super(message); }
}
```

4. Create the `SocialGraphClient` class. Create a new package called `com.packtpub.microservices.ch05.message.clients` and a new class called `SocialGraphClient`, as shown here:

```
package com.packtpub.microservices.ch05.message.clients;

import com.packtpub.microservices.ch05.models.Friendships;
import org.springframework.web.client.RestTemplate;

import java.util.List;

public class SocialGraphClient {
    private String baseUrl;

    public SocialGraphClient(String baseUrl) {
        this.baseUrl = baseUrl;
    }

    public List<String> getFriendships(String username) {
        String requestUrl = baseUrl + "/friendships/" + username;
        RestTemplate template = new RestTemplate();
        UserFriendships friendships =
template.getForObject(requestUrl, UserFriendships.class);
        return friendships.getFriendships();
    }
}
```

5. Let's create our models. We'll need a model to represent `UserFriendships` that a specific user has as well as a model to represent `Messages`. Create a new package called `com.packtpub.microservices.ch05.models` and a new class called `Friendships` as shown here:

```
package com.packtpub.microservices.ch05.models;

import java.util.List;

public class Friendships {
    private String username;
    private List<String> friendships;
```

```
public Friendships() {
    this.friendships = new ArrayList<>();
}

public Friendships(String username) {
    this.username = username;
    this.friendships = new ArrayList<>();
}

public Friendships(String username, List<String> friendships) {
    this.username = username;
    this.friendships = friendships;
}

public String getUsername() {
    return username;
}

public void setUsername(String username) {
    this.username = username;
}

public List<String> getFriendships() {
    return friendships;
}

public void setFriendships(List<String> friendships) {
    this.friendships = friendships;
}
}
```

6. Create a new class, in the same package, called `Message` as shown here:

```
package com.packtpub.microservices.ch05.message.models;

import com.fasterxml.jackson.annotation.JsonProperty;

public class Message {
    private String id;
    private String sender;
    private String recipient;
    private String body;
    @JsonProperty("attachment_uri")
    private String attachmentUri;

    public Message() {}

    public Message(String sender, String recipient, String body,
```

```
                String attachmentUri) {
                    this.sender = sender;
                    this.recipient = recipient;
                    this.body = body;
                    this.attachmentUri = attachmentUri;
                }

            public Message(String id, String sender, String recipient,
            String body, String attachmentUri) {
                    this.id = id;
                    this.sender = sender;
                    this.recipient = recipient;
                    this.body = body;
                    this.attachmentUri = attachmentUri;
                }

            public String getId() {
                return id;
            }

            public String getSender() {
                return sender;
            }

            public void setSender(String sender) {
                this.sender = sender;
            }

            public String getRecipient() {
                return recipient;
            }

            public void setRecipient(String recipient) {
                this.recipient = recipient;
            }

            public String getBody() {
                return body;
            }

            public void setBody(String body) {
                this.body = body;
            }

            public String getAttachmentUri() {
                return attachmentUri;
            }
```

```
    public void setAttachmentUri(String attachmentUri) {
        this.attachmentUri = attachmentUri;
    }
}
```

7. With our models created, we can now move on to our in-memory message repository. This class simply uses `HashMap` to store messages keyed by `UUID`. These messages are not durable and will not survive a restart of the service, so this is not a recommended technique for a production service. The class has two methods: `saved`, which generates UUID and stores a message in the map, and `get`, which attempts to retrieve a message from the map. If no message is found, an exception is thrown, as shown here:

```
package com.packtpub.microservices.ch05.message;

import
com.packtpub.microservices.ch05.message.exceptions.MessageNotFoundE
xception;
import com.packtpub.microservices.ch05.message.models.Message;

import java.util.HashMap;
import java.util.Map;
import java.util.UUID;

public class MessageRepository {

    private Map<String, Message> messages;

    public MessageRepository() {
        messages = new HashMap<>();
    }

    public Message save(Message message) {
        UUID uuid = UUID.randomUUID();
        Message saved = new Message(uuid.toString(),
message.getSender(), message.getRecipient(),
                message.getBody(), message.getAttachmentUri());
        messages.put(uuid.toString(), saved);
        return saved;
    }

    public Message get(String id) throws MessageNotFoundException {
        if (messages.containsKey(id)) {
            Message message = messages.get(id);
            return message;
        } else {
            throw new MessageNotFoundException("Message " + id + "
```

```
could not be found");
            }
        }
    }
```

8. Our service has a single controller for messages. The controller has two endpoints, one that allows a caller to retrieve a message by ID (or a 404 response if the message is not found) and another that attempts to send a message (or a 403 response if the sender and recipient of the message are not friends):

```java
package com.packtpub.microservices.ch05.message;

import
com.packtpub.microservices.ch05.message.clients.SocialGraphClient;
import
com.packtpub.microservices.ch05.message.exceptions.MessageNotFoundE
xception;
import
com.packtpub.microservices.ch05.message.exceptions.MessageSendForbi
ddenException;
import com.packtpub.microservices.ch05.message.models.Message;
import org.springframework.beans.factory.annotation.Autowired;
import org.springframework.http.ResponseEntity;
import org.springframework.web.bind.annotation.*;
import
org.springframework.web.servlet.support.ServletUriComponentsBuilder
;

import java.net.URI;
import java.util.List;

@RestController
public class MessageController {

    @Autowired
    private MessageRepository messagesStore;

    @Autowired
    private SocialGraphClient socialGraphClient;

    @RequestMapping(path = "/messages/{id}", method =
RequestMethod.GET, produces = "application/json")
    public Message get(@PathVariable("id") String id) throws
MessageNotFoundException {
        return messagesStore.get(id);
    }

    @RequestMapping(path = "/messages", method =
```

```
RequestMethod.POST, produces = "application/json")
    public ResponseEntity<Message> send(@RequestBody Message
message) throws MessageSendForbiddenException {

        List<String> friendships =
socialGraphClient.getFriendships(message.getSender());
        if (!friendships.contains(message.getRecipient())) {
            throw new MessageSendForbiddenException("Must be
friends to send message");
        }

        Message saved = messagesStore.save(message);
        URI location = ServletUriComponentsBuilder
                .fromCurrentRequest().path("/{id}")
                .buildAndExpand(saved.getId()).toUri();
        return ResponseEntity.created(location).build();
    }
}
```

9. Create a `Application` class that simply runs our application and creates the necessary beans that get wired into our controller, as shown here:

```
package com.packtpub.microservices.ch05.message;

import
com.packtpub.microservices.ch05.message.clients.SocialGraphClient;
import org.springframework.boot.SpringApplication;
import
org.springframework.boot.autoconfigure.SpringBootApplication;
import org.springframework.context.annotation.Bean;

@SpringBootApplication
public class Application {
    @Bean
    public MessageRepository messageRepository() {
        return new MessageRepository();
    }

    @Bean
    public SocialGraphClient socialGraphClient() {
        return new SocialGraphClient("http://localhost:4567");
    }
```

```
        public static void main(String[] args) {
            SpringApplication.run(Main.class, args);
        }
    }
```

This service works, and meets our primary requirement that a message cannot be sent if the sender and recipient are not friends, but it is susceptible to all the problems we described. If the social-graph-service is experiencing problems, the message service will be dependent on timeouts in the `RestTemplate` client, which will impact the number of requests the message service is able to serve. Furthermore, if the social-graph-service is overwhelmed and starts returning `503` (an HTTP status code meant to indicate that a service is temporarily unavailable) the message service has no mechanism to allow the social-graph-service to recover. Let's now introduce the `resilience4j` circuit-breaker library and wrap calls to the social-graph-service:

1. Open `build.gradle` and add the `resilience4j` circuit-breaker library to the list of dependencies, as shown here:

   ```
   . . .
   dependencies {
       testCompile group: 'junit', name: 'junit', version: '4.12'
       compile group: 'io.github.resilience4j', name: 'resilience4j-
   circuitbreaker', version: '0.11.0'
       compile group: 'org.springframework.boot', name: 'spring-boot-
   starter-web'
   }
   . . .
   ```

2. Modify `SocialGraphClient` to use `CircuitBreaker` when invoking the social-graph-client. In the event that the `SocialGraphClient` returns a failure, we'll return an empty `Friendships` instance, which will cause our service to respond to the user request with a `403` forbidden (default closed). We'll use the default configuration for circuit breakers here, but you should consult the documentation for `resilience4j`, which contains plenty of information about configuring circuit breakers to suit the specific needs of your service. Take a look at this code:

   ```
   package com.packtpub.microservices.ch05.clients;

   import com.packtpub.microservices.ch05.models.Friendships;
   import io.github.resilience4j.circuitbreaker.CircuitBreaker;
   import
   io.github.resilience4j.circuitbreaker.CircuitBreakerRegistry;
   import io.vavr.CheckedFunction0;
   import io.vavr.control.Try;
   ```

```
import org.springframework.web.client.RestTemplate;

import java.util.List;

public class SocialGraphClient {
    private String baseUrl;

    private CircuitBreaker circuitBreaker;

    public SocialGraphClient(String baseUrl) {
        this.baseUrl = baseUrl;
        this.circuitBreaker =
CircuitBreaker.ofDefaults("socialGraphClient");
    }

    public List<String> getFriendships(String username) {

        CheckedFunction0<Friendships> decoratedSupplier =
CircuitBreaker.decorateCheckedSupplier(circuitBreaker, () -> {
            String requestUrl = baseUrl + "/friendships/" +
username;
            RestTemplate template = new RestTemplate();
            return template.getForObject(requestUrl,
Friendships.class);
        });

        Try<Friendships> result = Try.of(decoratedSupplier);

        return result.getOrElse(new
Friendships(username)).getFriendships();
    }
}
```

Now our service wraps dangerous network calls in a circuit breaker, preventing failures in the social-graph-service from cascading to the message service. In the event of a temporary failure in the social-graph-service, the message service will eventually fail fast and allow the social-graph-service time to recover. You can test this by forcing the mock-social-graph service to return an error code—that's left as a fun exercise for the reader!

Retrying requests with exponential backoff

Failure in distributed systems is inevitable. Instead of trying to prevent failure entirely, we want to design systems that are capable of self-repair. To accomplish this, it is essential to have a good strategy for clients to follow when initiating retries. A service may become temporarily unavailable or experience a problem that requires manual response from an on-call engineer. In either scenario, clients should be able to queue and then retry requests to be given the best chance of success.

Retrying endlessly in the event of an error is not an effective tactic. Imagine a service starts to experience a higher-than-normal failure rate, perhaps even failing 100% of requests. If clients all continuously enqueue retries without ever giving up, you'll end up with a thundering-herd problem—clients continuously retrying requests without limit. As the timeline of the failure progresses, more clients will experience failures, resulting in more retries. You'll end up with a traffic pattern, illustrated by the following diagram, which is a similar graph to the one you'll see during a denial-of-service attack. The end result will be the same—cascading failures due to overwhelmed services and a shedding of legitimate traffic. Your application will become unusable and the failing service will be harder to isolate and repair:

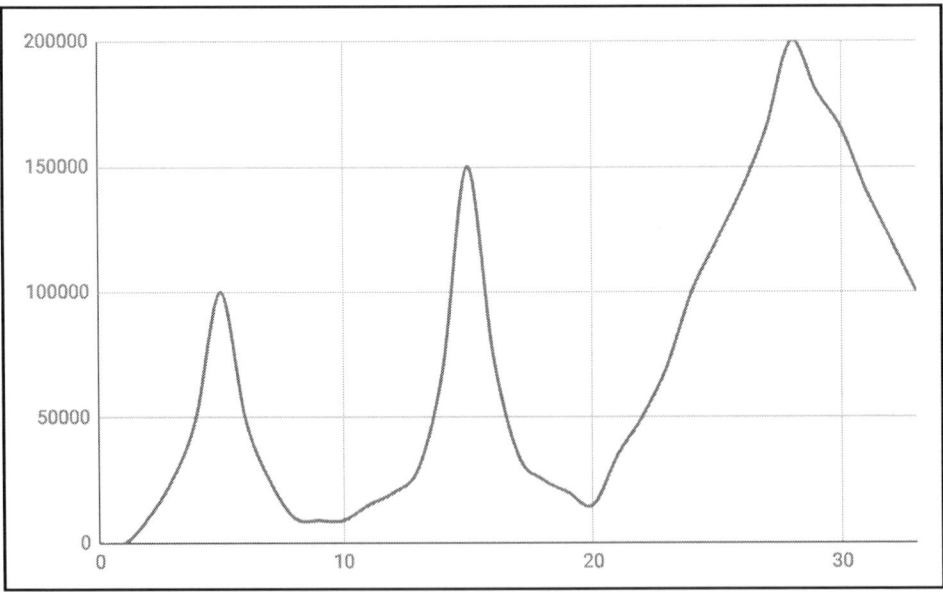

The solution to prevent thundering herds is to add a backoff algorithm that exponentially increases the wait period between retries and gives up after a certain number of failures. This approach is referred to as capped exponential backoff. Adding an exponentially-increasing sleep function between retries accomplishes half of what we're after—clients will slow down their retry attempts, distributing load over time. Unfortunately, client retries will still be clustered, resulting in periods of time where your service is being hammered by many concurrent requests. The second half of our strategy addresses this problem by adding a randomized value or jitter to our sleep function to distribute the retries over time. To summarize, our retry strategy has the following three requirements:

- Retries must be spaced out using an exponential backoff
- Retries must be randomized by adding jitter
- Retries must terminate after a specific amount of time

Most HTTP libraries will have support for a retry strategy that meets these requirements. In this recipe, we'll look at the HTTP `client` library for Java written by Google.

How to do it...

1. To demonstrate using exponential backoff and jitter, we're going to create a sample service in Ruby that has one simple job: to return an HTTP status that indicates a failure. In previous recipes, we've used the `sinatra` Ruby library to do this, so we'll continue with this, a service that simply returns a `503` HTTP status code for every request, as shown here:

```ruby
require 'sinatra'

get '/' do
  halt 503
end
```

2. Create an HTTP client using the Google HTTP `client` Library. First, create a new Gradle Java project with the following `build.gradle` file that imports the necessary libraries and plugins, as shown here:

```
group 'com.packtpub.microservices'
version '1.0-SNAPSHOT'

apply plugin: 'java'
apply plugin: 'application'

mainClassName = 'com.packtpub.microservices.ch05.retryclient.Main'
```

```
sourceCompatibility = 1.8

repositories {
    mavenCentral()
}

dependencies {
    compile group: 'com.google.http-client', name: 'google-http-
client', version: '1.23.0'
    testCompile group: 'junit', name: 'junit', version: '4.12'
}
```

3. Create a new package called
   com.packtpub.microservices.ch05.retryclient. Create a new class called
   Main. In the Main class, we're just going to create an HTTP request and execute
   it. If the request was successful, we'll just print its status code with a nice
   message. If the success fails, we'll still print its status code, but with a message
   indicating that something went wrong. The first version of our HTTP client will
   not attempt any retries. The purpose of this code is to write the simplest client
   possible, not to show off the features of the Google HTTP client library, but I
   encourage you to consult the documentation for the project to learn more about
   it. Let's take a look at the following code:

```java
package com.packtpub.microservices.ch05.retryclient;

import com.google.api.client.http.*;
import com.google.api.client.http.javanet.NetHttpTransport;
import com.google.api.client.util.ExponentialBackOff;

import java.io.IOException;

public class Main {

    static final HttpTransport transport = new NetHttpTransport();

    public static void main(String[] args) {
        HttpRequestFactory factory =
transport.createRequestFactory();
        GenericUrl url = new GenericUrl("http://localhost:4567/");

        try {
            HttpRequest request = factory.buildGetRequest(url);
            HttpResponse response = request.execute();
            System.out.println("Got a successful response: " +
response.getStatusCode());
        } catch (HttpResponseException e) {
```

```
            System.out.println("Got an unsuccessful response: " +
    e.getStatusCode());
        } catch (IOException e) {
            e.printStackTrace();
        }
    }
}
```

4. If you run the preceding code either with your IDE or by running `./gradlew`
   run from your command line, you'll see that the code tries to make a single
   HTTP request, receives 503 from our Ruby service, and then gives up. Let's now
   instrument it with a configurable backoff that has a randomization factor for
   adding jitter, as shown here:

```
package com.packtpub.microservices.ch05.retryclient;

import com.google.api.client.http.*;
import com.google.api.client.http.javanet.NetHttpTransport;
import com.google.api.client.util.ExponentialBackOff;

import java.io.IOException;

public class Main {

    static final HttpTransport transport = new NetHttpTransport();

    public static void main(String[] args) {
        HttpRequestFactory factory =
transport.createRequestFactory();
        GenericUrl url = new GenericUrl("http://localhost:4567/");

        try {
            HttpRequest request = factory.buildGetRequest(url);
            ExponentialBackOff backoff = new
ExponentialBackOff.Builder()
                    .setInitialIntervalMillis(500)
                    .setMaxElapsedTimeMillis(10000)
                    .setMaxIntervalMillis(6000)
                    .setMultiplier(1.5)
                    .setRandomizationFactor(0.5)
                    .build();

            request.setUnsuccessfulResponseHandler(
                new HttpBackOffUnsuccessfulResponseHandler(backoff));
            HttpResponse response = request.execute();
            System.out.println("Got a successful response: " +
response.getStatusCode());
```

```
        } catch (HttpResponseException e) {
            System.out.println("Got an unsuccessful response: " +
e.getStatusCode());
        } catch (IOException e) {
            e.printStackTrace();
        }
    }
}
```

5. If you run the program now and watch the logs of your Ruby service, you'll see that the code makes multiple attempts to make the request, increasing the amount of time it sleeps between retries, before eventually giving up after about 10 seconds. In a real-world setting, this could give the service enough time to possibly recover while not creating a thundering herd that would eliminate any possibility of repair.

Improving performance with caching

Microservices should be designed in such a way that a single service is usually the only thing that reads or writes to a particular data store. In this model, services have full ownership over the domain models involved in the business capability they provide. Having clean boundaries makes it easier to think about the life cycle of data in a system. Some models in our system will change frequently, but many will be read much more often than they are written. In these cases, we can use a cache to store infrequently changed data, saving us from having to make a request to the database every time the object is requested. Database queries are typically more expensive than cache lookups, so it's ideal to use a cache whenever possible.

In addition to help improve performance, having an effective caching layer can help improve the reliability of a service. It's impossible to guarantee 100% availability for a database, so in the event of a database failure, a service can revert to serving cached data. In most cases, it's preferable for a user to receive some data, even if it's old and potentially out of date, than to receive no data at all. Having a cache layer allows you to configure your service to use it as another source of available data to serve to users of your service.

In this recipe, we'll create a simple example service that serves information about users of your application. It will have two endpoints, the first will accept POST requests and will persist a properly formed user to a database. The second will retrieve a user representation by the ID specified. IDs are stored as UUIDs, which is preferable to autoincrementing IDs for many reasons, which we'll go into in later chapters. We'll start with the basic service, then add caching so we can see specifically what steps are required. In this recipe, we'll use Redis, a popular open source in-memory data-structure store that is particular useful for storing key-value pairs.

How to do it...

1. Create a Gradle Java project called caching-user-service with the following `build.gradle` file. Note that we're adding dependencies for **Java Persistence API (JPA)** and a Java MySQL `client` library:

    ```
    group 'com.packtpub.microservices.ch05'
    version '1.0-SNAPSHOT'

    buildscript {
        repositories {
            mavenCentral()
        }
        dependencies {
            classpath("org.springframework.boot:spring-boot-gradle-
    plugin:2.0.0.RELEASE")
        }
    }

    apply plugin: 'java'
    apply plugin: 'org.springframework.boot'

    sourceCompatibility = 1.8

    repositories {
        mavenCentral()
    }

    dependencies {
        compile group: 'org.springframework.boot', name: 'spring-boot-
    starter-web', version: '2.0.0.RELEASE'
    ```

```
    compile group: 'org.springframework.boot', name: 'spring-boot-
starter-data-jpa', version: '2.0.0.RELEASE'
    compile group: 'mysql', name: 'mysql-connector-java', version:
'6.0.6'
    testCompile group: 'junit', name: 'junit', version: '4.12'
}
```

2. Create the `Main` class. As usual, this is the main entry point to our application and is pretty simple:

```
package com.packtpub.microservices.ch05.userservice;

import org.springframework.boot.SpringApplication;
import
org.springframework.boot.autoconfigure.SpringBootApplication;

@SpringBootApplication
public class Main {
    public static void main(String[] args) {
        SpringApplication.run(Main.class, args);
    }
}
```

3. Create a `User` class in the `com.packtpub.microservices.ch05.userservice.models` package. This will serve as our entity representation and contains the fields that will be stored in the database and eventually in our Redis cache:

```
package com.packtpub.microservices.ch05.userservice.models;

import com.fasterxml.jackson.annotation.JsonProperty;
import org.hibernate.annotations.GenericGenerator;

import javax.persistence.Column;
import javax.persistence.Entity;
import javax.persistence.GeneratedValue;
import javax.persistence.Id;

@Entity
public class User {

    @Id
    @GeneratedValue(generator = "uuid")
    @GenericGenerator(name = "uuid", strategy = "uuid2")
    private String id;

    private String username;
```

```java
@JsonProperty("full_name")
private String fullName;

private String email;

public User() {}

public String getId() {
    return id;
}

public void setId(String id) {
    this.id = id;
}

public String getUsername() {
    return username;
}

public void setUsername(String username) {
    this.username = username;
}

public String getFullName() {
    return fullName;
}

public void setFullName(String fullName) {
    this.fullName = fullName;
}

public String getEmail() {
    return email;
}

public void setEmail(String email) {
    this.email = email;
}
}
```

4. To wire up our `User` entity to our MySQL database, create a `UserRepository` interface that extends the `CrudRepository` interface defined by the `springframework` data package, as shown here:

```
package com.packtpub.microservices.ch05.userservice.db;

import com.packtpub.microservices.ch05.userservice.models.User;
import org.springframework.data.repository.CrudRepository;

public interface UserRepository extends CrudRepository<User,
String> {}
```

5. Create the `UserController` class. This is `RestController`, which maps certain endpoints to the functionality discussed previously, namely creating and retrieving user records. Everything here should look familiar. Of note is that the `findById` method returns `Optional<T>`, so we use `map` and `orElseGet` to return either a `200 OK HTTP` response with the user in the response body or a `404` status, as shown in the following code:

```
package com.packtpub.microservices.ch05.userservice.controllers;

import
com.packtpub.microservices.ch05.userservice.db.UserRepository;
import com.packtpub.microservices.ch05.userservice.models.User;
import org.springframework.beans.factory.annotation.Autowired;
import org.springframework.http.HttpStatus;
import org.springframework.http.ResponseEntity;
import org.springframework.web.bind.annotation.*;

import java.util.Optional;

@RestController
public class UserController {

    @Autowired
    private UserRepository userRepository;

    @RequestMapping(path = "/users", method = RequestMethod.POST,
produces = "application/json")
    public User create(@RequestBody User user) {
        User savedUser = userRepository.save(user);
        return savedUser;
    }

    @RequestMapping(path = "/users/{id}", method =
RequestMethod.GET, produces = "application/json")
```

```
    public ResponseEntity<User> getById(@PathVariable("id") String
id) {
        Optional<User> user = userRepository.findById(id);

        return user.map(u -> new ResponseEntity<>(u,
HttpStatus.OK)).orElseGet(
                () -> new ResponseEntity<>(HttpStatus.NOT_FOUND));
    }
}
```

6. Add the following `application.properties` file to the `src/main/resources` directory. It contains the necessary configuration to connect to a local MySQL instance. It's assumed that you have installed MySQL and have it running locally. You should have also created a database called `users`, a user with the username `userservice`, and a password: `password`. Note that we're setting `ddl-auto` to `create`, which is a good practice for development, but should not be used for production:

```
spring.jpa.hibernate.ddl-auto=create
spring.datasource.url=jdbc:mysql://localhost:3306/users?serverTimez
one=UTC&&&useSSL=false
spring.datasource.username=userservice
spring.datasource.password=password
```

7. Let's add some caching! The first thing we'll do is open the `application.properties` file again and add some configuration for a `redis` instance running locally on port `6379` (the default), as shown here:

```
spring.jpa.hibernate.ddl-auto=create
spring.datasource.url=jdbc:mysql://localhost:3306/users?serverTimez
one=UTC&&&useSSL=false
spring.datasource.username=userservice
spring.datasource.password=password
spring.cache.type=redis
spring.redis.host=localhost
spring.redis.port=6379
```

8. With our application configured to use MySQL as a primary datasource and Redis as a cache, we can now override methods in the `CrudRepository<T, ID>` interface and add annotations instructing it to cache. We want to write to our cache every time we call the `save` method with a `User` object, and read from the cache every time we call `findById` with a valid user ID string:

```
package com.packtpub.microservices.ch05.userservice.db;

import com.packtpub.microservices.ch05.userservice.models.User;
import org.springframework.cache.annotation.CachePut;
import org.springframework.cache.annotation.Cacheable;
import org.springframework.data.repository.CrudRepository;
import org.springframework.stereotype.Repository;

import java.util.Optional;

@Repository
public interface UserRepository extends CrudRepository<User,
String> {
    @Override
    @Cacheable(value = "users", key = "#id")
    Optional<User> findById(String id);

    @Override
    @CachePut(value = "users", key = "#user.id")
    User save(User user);
}
```

9. That's it! You can test this by running the service, creating a user, verifying that the user is in both the MySQL database and Redis cache, and then deleting the user from the database. Requests to the `users/ID` endpoint will still return the user record. Before finishing this service, you'll want to make sure that the cache is invalidated if a user is ever deleted. Any other endpoints that mutate users should invalidate and/or rewrite the cache. This is left as an exercise for the reader!

Fronting your services with a CDN

The **Content Delivery Network (CDN)** improves performance and availability by delivering content through a globally distributed network of proxy servers. When a user (usually through their mobile device) makes a request to your API through a CDN, they will create a network connection with one of many **points of presence (PoPs)**, based on their geographic location. Instead of having to make roundtrips to the origin data center for every single request, content can be cached at the edge of a CDN, greatly reducing the response time for the user and reducing unnecessary, costly traffic to the origin.

CDNs are a requirement if you plan to have a global user base. If every request to your application's API has to perform a full roundtrip to a single origin, you'll create a subpar experience for users in parts of the world physically distant from the data center that you host your applications in. Even if you host your applications in multiple data centers, you'll never be able to create as high-performing an experience for as many users as you can using a CDN.

In addition to performance, CDNs can improve the availability of your application. As we discussed in the previous recipe, many entities in your system are read much more frequently than they are written. In these cases, you can configure your CDN to cache payloads from a service for a specific amount of time (commonly specified by a TTL or time-to-live). Caching responses from your service reduces the amount of traffic to your origin, making it harder to run out of capacity (compute, storage, or network). Additionally, if your service starts to experience high latency, or total or partial failure, the CDN can be configured to serve cached responses instead of continuing to send traffic to a failing service. This allows you to at least be able to serve content to users in the event of service downtime.

Some CDN providers have APIs that allow you to automatically invalidate a resource. In these cases, you can instrument your microservice to invalidate a resource just as you would using a Redis- or Memcached-based cache, as discussed in the previous recipe.

There are many different CDN providers out there. Some of the large ones include **Akamai** and **Edgecast**. Amazon Web Services provides a CDN offering, called CloudFront, that can be configured to serve requests to origin servers in AWS or static resources hosted in S3 buckets. One of the more developer-friendly offerings in the CDN market is from a company called **Fastly**. Fastly is built using **Varnish**, an open source web-application accelerator.

As a provider, Fastly allows you to upload your own **Varnish Configuration Language (VCL)** files, effectively allowing you to create caching rules based on any aspect of the request (incoming headers, path segments, query string parameters, and so on). Additionally, Fastly provide a **Fast Purge API** that allows you to invalidate resources based on a URI.

In this recipe, we'll go through the basic steps required to create an account with a CDN provider and start serving traffic through a CDN. We'll do this with a hypothetical service made accessible to the public internet with the hostname `api.pichat.me`. The service authenticates requests by inspecting the value of the Authorization header of the incoming request for a valid OAuth2 bearer token.

How to do it...

1. Create an account with Fastly, the CDN provider we'll be using in this example. As of this writing, the signup URL is `https://www.fastly.com/signup`.
2. Fastly will ask you to create a service. Enter a name for your service, along with the domain (`api.pichat.me`) and the hostname of the origin server the application is running on.
3. Using your DNS provider for the domain, create a CNAME for `api.pichat.me`, pointing your domain to Fastly's servers. Read the updated documentation to find out what hostnames to use.
4. Once that is set up and your service is created, requests to your hostname will now go through the Fastly CDN. Read the Fastly documentation (`https://docs.fastly.com/guides/basic-setup/`) to discover how to customize VCLs and other settings for your service.

Gracefully degrading the user experience

We understand by now that a certain amount of failure is inevitable. In a sufficiently complex system, some amount of failure will occur some of the time. By using the techniques in this chapter, we can try and reduce the likelihood that one of these failures will impact customers. Regardless of how much we try to prevent it from happening, some kind of failure will probably impact the customer experience at some point in your applications lifespan. Users, however, can be surprisingly compassionate in the face of system outages, provided the user experience degrades gracefully.

Consider this scenario: you are using an application that allows you to browse a catalog of products and look for local stores that carry that product, along with important information such as its address, phone number, and store hours. Let's say the service that provides information about local stores becomes unavailable. This clearly impacts the user experience in a less-than-ideal way, but the application can handle the failure in more than one way. The worst way, which would probably result in the worst user experience, would be to allow the failure to cascade and take down the product catalog. A slightly better way would be to allow the user to continue searching for products, but when they go to find a local store that carries the product, they're informed via some kind of information box that the local store information is currently unavailable. This is frustrating, but at least they can still look at product information, such as price, models, and colors. It would be better still to recognize that the service was not operating and have some kind of informational banner informing the user that local store information is temporarily unavailable. With this information, we can inform the user of the situation, allowing them to decide whether they'd still like to go ahead and search for products. The experience is suboptimal, but we would avoid unnecessarily frustrating the user.

Verifying fault tolerance with Gameday exercises

This chapter contains recipes that should help you create more reliable, resilient microservice architectures. Each recipe documents a pattern or technique for anticipating and dealing with some kind of failure scenario. Our aim when building resilient systems is to tolerate failure with as little impact to our users as possible. Anticipating and designing for failure is essential when building distributed systems, but without verifying that our systems handle failure in the ways we expect, we aren't doing much more than hoping, and hope is definitely not a strategy!

When building systems, unit and functional tests are necessary parts of our confidence-building toolkit. However, these tools alone are not enough. Unit and functional tests work by isolating dependencies, good unit tests, for instance, don't rely on network conditions, and functional tests don't involve testing under production-level traffic conditions, instead focusing on various software components working together properly under ideal conditions. To gain more confidence in the fault tolerance of a system, it's necessary to observe it responding to failure in production.

Gameday exercises are another useful tool for building confidence in the resiliency of a system. These exercises involve forcing certain failure scenarios in production to verify that our assumptions about fault tolerance match reality. John Allspaw describes this practice in detail in his paper, *Fault Injection in Production*. If we accept that failure is impossible to avoid completely, it becomes sensible to force failure and observe how our system responds to it as a planned exercise. It's better to have a system fail for the first time while an entire team is watching and ready to take action, than at 3 a.m. when a system alert wakes up an on-call engineer.

Planning a Gameday exercise provides a large amount of value. Engineers should get together and brainstorm the various failure scenarios their service is likely to experience. Work should then be scheduled to try to reduce or eliminate the impact of those scenarios (that is, in the event of database failure, revert to a cache). Each Gameday exercise should have a planning document that describes the system being tested, the various failure scenarios, including steps that will be taken to simulate the failures, expectations surrounding how the system should respond to the failures, and the expected impact on users (if any). As the Gameday exercise proceeds, the team should work through each of the scenarios, documenting observations—it's important to ensure that metrics we expect to see emitted are being emitted, alerts that we expect to fire do indeed fire, and the failure is handled in the way we expect. As observations are made, document any differences between expectations and reality. These observations should become planned work to bridge the gap between our ideal world and the real world.

Instead of walking through code, this recipe will demonstrate a process and template that can be used to run Gameday exercises. The following is not the only way to conduct Gameday exercises, but one that should serve as a good starting point for your organization.

Prerequisites

As always, there are some prerequisites you should ensure you meet before attempting to run a Gameday exercise. Specifically, your teams should be used to instrumenting code with the necessary metrics and alerts to provide a good degree of observability into your production environment. Your teams should have experience working within a well-understood and practiced incident-response process that includes having regular retrospectives to continuously improve in light of production incidents.

Finally, your organization should be accustomed to talking openly about failure and unexpected production incidents, and be committed to processes that encourage continuous improvement. These prerequisites should suggest that your teams have the necessary organizational support and psychological safety to conduct these kinds of resiliency exercises.

How to do it...

1. The first step in a Gameday exercise is selecting a system that will be tested. When you're just getting started with Gamedays, it's wise to select a system that is well understood, has failed before, and has a limited blast radius in terms of the impact on users.

2. Once the service is selected, gather the team responsible for its development and operation, and start brainstorming different failure scenarios. If there is a data store, consider what could happen if it were suddenly unavailable due to a hardware failure. Perhaps the database could be shut down manually. What happens if the database is terminated in an unsafe way? The service runs in some kind of clustered configuration, so what happens if one node is removed from the load balancer? What happens when all nodes fail and are removed from the load-balancing pool? Another area to test is unexpected latency. In a distributed system, sufficiently high latency is impossible to distinguish from lack of service availability, so there are a number of interesting bugs that can lurk here. Getting the team together to discuss all of these scenarios (as well as others) can be a great way to learn more about a system. Document all of the scenarios that you plan to test.

3. Schedule a time and a room for the Gameday experiment (if you're a remote team, arrange for everyone to be on a video call together). Invite the team responsible for the service being tested, a representative from your customer support team, and any other stakeholders who are interested in seeing the experiment.

4. Using a template, such as the one included here, plan out in detail how the experiment is going to be conducted. On the day at the scheduled time, start with an overview of the system being tested. This is a good opportunity to ensure that everyone has a consistent view of how the system works. Then go through each scenario, assigning the actual action to someone on the team.

5. Document observations during the experiment, detailing how the system reacted to the failure injection.

6. In the event that observations made during the experiment are different than expectations, schedule follow-up tasks, in the form of tickets, for the team to correct the discrepancy.

A template for Gameday exercises

The following template can be used for planning and executing a Gameday exercise.

System: Message Service

System Overview:

A detailed description (possibly including diagrams) of the system under test. It's a good idea to document how requests are routed to the system, some of the major systems that interact with it, data stores it uses and their general configuration, and any downstream services it depends on.

Dashboards:

Links to important dashboards to watch while the Gameday exercise is underway.

Test Scenarios:

Scenario: Database becomes unavailable due to nodes being terminated.

Method:

Shut down database EC2 nodes manually using AWS CLI tools (include actual command).

Expectations:

List how you expect the service to react. Include details about expected changes in metrics, alerts that should be fired, system behavior, and user impact.

Observations:

Document observations during the actual test.

Follow-up Action Items:

Create tickets for any follow-up work that should be done as a result of the experiment.

Introducing automated chaos

Running manual Gameday exercises is a great way to introduce the practice of failure injection. Forcing failures in production helps build confidence in the resilience of systems and identifies opportunities for improvement. Gameday helps teams gain a better overall understanding of how their systems behave when confronted with a number of failure scenarios. As a team conducts more exercises, it will start to accumulate tools for performing common tasks, such as introducing latency in the network or spiking CPU usage. Tooling helps automate mundane tasks, improving the efficiency of Gameday exercises. There are a variety of open source and commercial tools designed to automate chaos engineering that teams can take advantage of right away.

Gameday exercises are planned and scheduled. Some organizations go one step further and introduce continuous failure injection as a way of ensuring that systems are handling common failure scenarios smoothly. In early 2011, Netflix announced the creation of the Simian Army—a suite of tools designed to inject common failures into a production environment. Arguably the most famous member of the Simian Army, Chaos Monkey, randomly shuts down nodes in a production environment. The Simian Army tools have been open sourced and are available to use in your own organization. They can be scheduled to run as part of a Gameday exercise, or set up to run on specific schedules (that is, Monday to Friday, 9 a.m. to 5 p.m., when on-call engineers are usually in the office).

Pioneers in this space, PagerDuty, have conducted "failure Fridays" since 2013. Every Friday, engineers get together to attack a specific service. Over time, engineers started building commands into their Chat Bot to perform common functions such as isolating a node from other network traffic, even adding a "roulette" command that would randomly select hosts for rebooting.

Hosted commercial services have been developed to help automate chaos engineering. Gremlin is a hosted product designed to help teams run Gameday exercises by providing access to a library of "attacks" executed through agents installed on nodes in your environment. Gremlin provides an API and a web interface that allows users to configure attacks designed to spike resource usage (CPU, memory, disk), simulate random failures by killing processes or rebooting hosts, and simulate common network conditions, such as latency and **Network Time Protocol (NTP)** drift. Having a product like Gremlin lowers the amount of upfront effort needed to start doing failure injection.

Another open source tool is the Chaos toolkit, a CLI tool designed to make it easier to design and run experiments. In this recipe, we'll install the Chaos toolkit and use it to execute a simple experiment against a hypothetical user service. The user service will be the same one we wrote in the *Improving performance with caching* recipe earlier in this chapter.

How to do it...

1. The Chaos toolkit is written in Python and can be installed using `pip`. We'll need a working Python3 environment. This recipe will assume you are installing it on macOS X using Homebrew. First, install pyen—a utility that supports managing multiple Python development environments, as shown here:

   ```
   $ brew install pyenv
   ```

2. Install Python3 by executing the following command line:

   ```
   $ pyenv install 3.4.2
   $ pyenv global 3.4.2
   ```

3. With a newly-installed Python3 environment, go ahead and install the Chaos toolkit by executing the following command line:

   ```
   $ pip install -U chaostoolkit
   ```

4. The Chaos toolkit uses the JSON files to describe experiments. Each experiment should have a title, description, and optionally some tags used to categorize experiments. The `steady-state-hypothesis` section describes how the service is expected to behave under normal conditions. In our situation, we assume that the service will return either `200` in the event that a user is found, or `404` in the event that a user has not been found:

   ```
   {
     "title": "Kill MySQL process",
     "description": "The user service uses a MySQL database to store
   user information. This experiment will test how the service behaves
   when the database is unavailable.",
     "tags": [
       "database", "mysql"
     ],
     "steady-state-hypothesis": {
       "title": "Service responds when MySQL is running",
       "probes": [
         {
           "type": "probe",
   ```

```
        "name": "service-is-running",
        "tolerance": [200, 404],
        "provider": {
          "type": "http",
          "url": "http://localhost:8080/users/12345"
        }
      }
    ]
  },
  "method": [
    {
      "name": "kill-mysql-process",
      "type": "action",
      "provider": {
        "type": "process",
        "path": "/usr/local/bin/mysql.server",
        "arguments": ["stop"],
        "timeout": 10
      }
    }
  ]
}
```

5. Run this experiment:

   ```
   $ chaos run
   ```

6. If successful, the output should indicate that the service responds well when MySQL is unavailable. However, in its current state, the experiment will leave MySQL stopped, which isn't ideal. Now you have something to fix, which is left as an exercise to the reader, and you can rerun your experiment. Congratulations! You just ran your first automated chaos experiment.

15
Security

In this chapter, we will cover the following recipes:

- Authenticating your microservices
- Securing containers
- Secure configuration
- Secure logging
- Infrastructure as Code

Introduction

As with many of the topics covered in this book, security in a microservice architecture is about trade-offs. In a microservice architecture, individual code bases have limited responsibilities. If an attacker is able to compromise a single running service, they will only be able to perform actions that are governed by that particular microservice. The distributed nature of a microservice architecture, however, means that there are more targets for an attacker to potentially exploit in services running in separate clusters. The network traffic between those clusters, including traffic between edge services and internal services, presents many opportunities for an attacker to discover vulnerabilities.

Because of the distributed nature of microservice architectures, network topology must be considered when configuring how services are able to communicate with one another. This concern exists in monolithic code bases as well, where a running instance of a single code base needs to communicate over the network with database servers, caches, load balancers, and so on. It could be argued that microservice architectures make these challenges more obvious and therefore force engineers to consider them earlier.

Security is a big topic. This chapter will discuss a number of good practices to consider when building, deploying, and operating microservices, but it's important to note that this is not an exhaustive list of considerations. Good API practices and defense in depth should be considered when developing any system and microservices are no exception. I heartily recommend **OWASP** (https://www.owasp.org/index.php/Main_Page) as a resource for learning more about web application security.

Authenticating your microservices

In `Chapter 2`, *Breaking the Monolith*, we introduced a Ruby on Rails code base that powers our fictional image-sharing application, `pichat`. The Rails code base authenticates each request by inspecting the Authorization header. If the header is present, the application attempts to decode it using a shared secret read from an environment variable (see the *Secure configuration* recipe). If the token provided in the Authorization header is valid, the decoded value contains contextual information about the user, including the user ID. That information is then used to retrieve the user from the database so that the application has context on the user making the request. If the Authorization header is missing or cannot be decoded successfully, the application raises an exception and returns an HTTP 401 to the caller, including an error message. In order to obtain a token to include in the Authorization header, a client application can send a `POST` request to the `/auth/login` endpoint with valid user credentials. The following CURL commands demonstrate this flow:

```
$ curl -D - -X POST http://localhost:9292/auth/login -
d'email=p@eval.ca&password=foobar123'

HTTP/1.1 200 OK
Content-Type: application/json; charset=utf-8
ETag: W/"3675d2006d59e01f8665f20ffef65fe7"
Cache-Control: max-age=0, private, must-revalidate
X-Request-Id: 6660a102-059f-4afe-b17c-99375db305dd
X-Runtime: 0.150903
Transfer-Encoding: chunked

{"auth_token":"eyJhbGciOiJIUzI1NiJ9.eyJ1c2VyX21kIjoxLCJleHAiOjE1MzE2ODUxNjR
9.vAToW_mWlOnr-GPzP79EvN62Q2MpsnLIYanz3MTbZ5Q"}
```

Now that we have a token, we can include it in the headers of subsequent requests:

```
$ curl -X POST -D - -H 'Authorization:
eyJhbGciOiJIUzI1NiJ9.eyJ1c2VyX21kIjoxLCJleHAiOjE1MzE2ODUxNjR9.vAToW_mWlOnr-
GPzP79EvN62Q2MpsnLIYanz3MTbZ5Q' http://localhost:9292/messages -
d'body=Hello&user_id=1'
```

```
HTTP/1.1 201 Created
Content-Type: application/json; charset=utf-8
ETag: W/"211cdab551e63ca48de48217357f1cf7"
Cache-Control: max-age=0, private, must-revalidate
X-Request-Id: 1525333c-dada-40ff-8c25-a0e7d151433c
X-Runtime: 0.019609
Transfer-Encoding: chunked
```

```
{"id":1,"body":"Hello","user_id":1,"created_at":"2018-07-14T20:08:19.369Z",
"updated_at":"2018-07-14T20:08:19.369Z","from_user_id":1}
```

Because `pichat-api` is a monolithic code base, it is playing many different roles to support this flow. It is acting as an Authorization service, an Authentication gateway, a user store, and an Authorization client. This kind of coupling of responsibilities is exactly what we want to avoid in a microservice architecture.

Luckily, it's easy to divide these responsibilities into separate code bases while keeping the flow the same. Encoding information in **JSON Web Tokens** (**JWT**) using a shared secret allows individual microservices to securely authenticate requests without having to make requests to a centralized authentication service for each request. Obtaining an authentication token can be the responsibility of a centralized service, but this fact can be made transparent to the client using an API Gateway or a backend for a frontend. The following diagram demonstrates how some of the responsibilities will be divided:

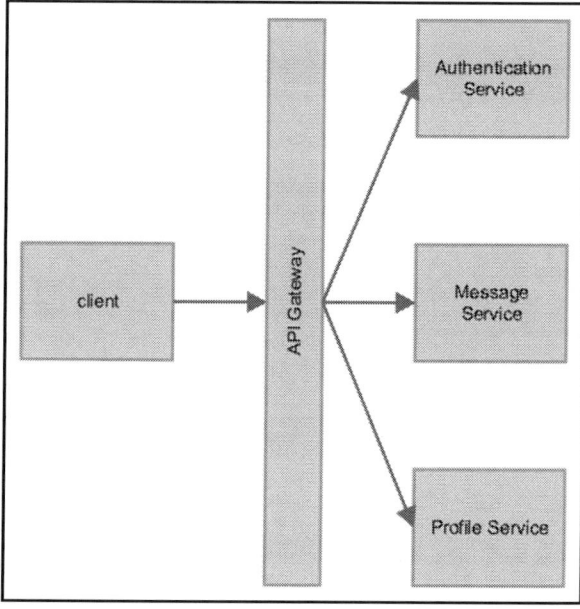

We will create an **Authentication Service** that handles user registration and exchanges credentials for a JWT. We will then create a simple **API Gateway** using the Zuul open source project that we covered in `Chapter 3`, *Edge Services*.

How to do it...

Let's have a look at the following steps:

1. Let's create the authentication service. Create a new Java project with the following `build.gradle` file:

```
group 'com.packtpub.microservices'
version '1.0-SNAPSHOT'

buildscript {
    repositories {
        mavenCentral()
    }
    dependencies {
        classpath group: 'org.springframework.boot', name: 'spring-boot-gradle-plugin', version: '1.5.9.RELEASE'
    }
}

apply plugin: 'java'
apply plugin: 'org.springframework.boot'
apply plugin: 'io.spring.dependency-management'

sourceCompatibility = 1.8

repositories {
    mavenCentral()
}

dependencies {
    compile group: 'org.springframework.boot', name: 'spring-boot-starter-web'
    compile group: 'org.springframework.security', name: 'spring-security-core'
    compile group: 'org.springframework.security', name: 'spring-security-config'
    compile group: 'org.springframework.boot', name: 'spring-boot-starter-data-jpa'
```

```
    compile group: 'io.jsonwebtoken', name: 'jjwt', version:
'0.9.1'
    compile group: 'mysql', name: 'mysql-connector-java'
    testCompile group: 'junit', name: 'junit', version: '4.12'
}
```

We'll be storing user credentials in a MySQL database, so we declare `mysql-connector-java` as a dependency. We'll also use an open source JWT library called `jjwt`.

> Storing user credentials is an important topic. User passwords should never be stored in plain text and many hashing algorithms, such as MD5 and SHA1, have been shown to be vulnerable to various brute force attacks. In this example, we'll be using `bcrypt`. In a real-world usage, we'd consider multiple hashing steps, such as hashing with SHA512 first and then running through `bcrypt`. We'd also consider adding a per-user salt. The **Open Web Application Security Project** has a lot of great recommendations for storing passwords: `https://www.owasp.org/index.php/Password_Storage_Cheat_Sheet`.

2. Create a new class called `Application`. It will contain our main method as well as `PasswordEncoder`:

```
package com.packtpub.microservices.ch06.auth;

import org.springframework.boot.SpringApplication;
import
org.springframework.boot.autoconfigure.SpringBootApplication;
import org.springframework.context.annotation.Bean;
import
org.springframework.security.crypto.bcrypt.BCryptPasswordEncoder;
import
org.springframework.security.crypto.password.PasswordEncoder;

@SpringBootApplication
public class Application {

    @Bean
    public PasswordEncoder passwordEncoder() {
        return new BCryptPasswordEncoder();
    }

    public static void main(String[] args) {
        SpringApplication.run(Application.class, args);
    }
}
```

3. We'll model the user credentials as a simple POJO with `email` and `password` fields. Create a new package called `com.packtpub.microservices.ch06.auth.models` and a new class called `UserCredential`:

```
package com.packtpub.microservices.ch06.auth.models;

import org.hibernate.annotations.GenericGenerator;

import javax.persistence.*;

@Entity
public class UserCredential {
    @Id
    @GeneratedValue(generator = "uuid")
    @GenericGenerator(name = "uuid", strategy = "uuid2")
    private String id;

    @Column(unique=true)
    private String email;

    private String password;

    public UserCredential(String email) {
        this.email = email;
    }

    public String getId() {
        return id;
    }

    public void setId(String id) {
        this.id = id;
    }

    public String getEmail() {
        return email;
    }

    public void setEmail(String email) {
        this.email = email;
    }

    public String getPassword() {
        return password;
    }
```

```
        public void setPassword(String password) {
            this.password = password;
        }
    }
```

4. Create a model to represent the response to successful login and registration requests. Successful responses will contain a JSON document containing a JWT. Create a new class called AuthenticationToken:

```
package com.packtpub.microservices.ch06.auth.models;

import com.fasterxml.jackson.annotation.JsonProperty;

public class AuthenticationToken {

    @JsonProperty("auth_token")
    private String authToken;

    public AuthenticationToken() {}

    public AuthenticationToken(String authToken) {
        this.authToken = authToken;
    }

    public String getAuthToken() {
        return this.authToken;
    }

    public void setAuthToken(String authToken) {
        this.authToken = authToken;
    }
}
```

5. The UserCredential class will be accessed using the Java Persistence API. To do this, we have to first create CrudRepository. Create a new package called com.packtpub.microservices.ch06.auth.data and a new class called UserCredentialRepository. In addition to inheriting from CrudRepository, we'll define a single method used to retrieve a UserCredential instance by email:

```
package com.packtpub.microservices.ch06.auth.data;

import com.packtpub.microservices.ch06.auth.models.UserCredential;
import org.springframework.data.repository.CrudRepository;

public interface UserCredentialRepository extends
CrudRepository<UserCredential, String> {
```

```
        UserCredential findByEmail(String email);
    }
```

6. When a user attempts to register or log in with invalid credentials, we want to return an HTTP 401 status code as well as a message indicating that they provided invalid credentials. In order to do this, we'll create a single exception that will be thrown in our controller methods:

```java
package com.packtpub.microservices.ch06.auth.exceptions;

import org.springframework.http.HttpStatus;
import org.springframework.web.bind.annotation.ResponseStatus;

@ResponseStatus(HttpStatus.UNAUTHORIZED)
public class InvalidCredentialsException extends Exception {
    public InvalidCredentialsException(String message) {
super(message);  }
    }
```

7. Create the controller. The login and registration endpoints will be served from a single controller. The registration method will simply validate input and create a new `UserCredential` instance, persisting it using the `CrudRepository` package we created earlier. It will then encode a JWT with the user ID of the newly registered user as the subject. The login method will verify the provided credentials and provide a JWT with the user ID as its subject. The controller will need access to `UserCredentialRepository` and `PasswordEncoder` defined in the main class. Create a new package called `com.packtpub.microservices.ch06.auth.controllers` and a new class called `UserCredentialController`:

```java
package com.packtpub.microservices.ch06.auth.controllers;

import
com.packtpub.microservices.ch06.auth.data.UserCredentialRepository;
import
com.packtpub.microservices.ch06.auth.exceptions.InvalidCredentialsE
xception;
import
com.packtpub.microservices.ch06.auth.models.AuthenticationToken;
import com.packtpub.microservices.ch06.auth.models.UserCredential;
import io.jsonwebtoken.JwtBuilder;
import io.jsonwebtoken.Jwts;
import io.jsonwebtoken.SignatureAlgorithm;
import org.springframework.beans.factory.annotation.Autowired;
import org.springframework.beans.factory.annotation.Value;
import
```

```
org.springframework.security.crypto.password.PasswordEncoder;
import org.springframework.web.bind.annotation.*;

import javax.crypto.spec.SecretKeySpec;
import javax.xml.bind.DatatypeConverter;
import java.security.Key;

@RestController
public class UserCredentialController {

    @Autowired
    private UserCredentialRepository userCredentialRepository;

    @Autowired
    private PasswordEncoder passwordEncoder;

    @Value("${secretKey}")
    private String keyString;

    private String encodeJwt(String userId) {
        System.out.println("SIGNING KEY: " + keyString);
        Key key = new SecretKeySpec(
                DatatypeConverter.parseBase64Binary(keyString),
                SignatureAlgorithm.HS256.getJcaName());

        JwtBuilder builder = Jwts.builder().setId(userId)
                .setSubject(userId)
                .setIssuer("authentication-service")
                .signWith(SignatureAlgorithm.HS256, key);

        return builder.compact();
    }


    @RequestMapping(path = "/register", method =
RequestMethod.POST, produces = "application/json")
    public AuthenticationToken register(@RequestParam String email,
@RequestParam String password, @RequestParam String
passwordConfirmation) throws InvalidCredentialsException {
        if (!password.equals(passwordConfirmation)) {
            throw new InvalidCredentialsException("Password and
confirmation do not match");
        }

        UserCredential cred = new UserCredential(email);
        cred.setPassword(passwordEncoder.encode(password));
        userCredentialRepository.save(cred);

        String jws = encodeJwt(cred.getId());
```

```
            return new AuthenticationToken(jws);
        }

        @RequestMapping(path = "/login", method = RequestMethod.POST,
    produces = "application/json")
        public AuthenticationToken login(@RequestParam String email,
    @RequestParam String password) throws InvalidCredentialsException {
            UserCredential user =
    userCredentialRepository.findByEmail(email);

            if (user == null || !passwordEncoder.matches(password,
    user.getPassword())) {
                throw new InvalidCredentialsException("Username or
    password invalid");
            }

            String jws = encodeJwt(user.getId());
            return new AuthenticationToken(jws);
        }
    }
```

8. Because we are connecting to a local database, and because we use a shared secret when signing JWTs, we need to create a small properties file. Create a file called `application.yml` in the `src/main/resources` directory:

```
server:
  port: 8081

spring:
  jpa.hibernate.ddl-auto: create
  datasource.url: jdbc:mysql://localhost:3306/user_credentials
  datasource.username: root
  datasource.password:

secretKey: supers3cr3t
```

Now that we have a functioning authentication service, the next step is to create a simple API Gateway using the open source gateway service, Zuul. In addition to routing requests to downstream services, the API Gateway will also use an authentication filter to verify that valid JWTs are passed in headers for requests that require authentication.

9. Create a new Java project with the following `build.gradle` file:

```
group 'com.packtpub.microservices'
version '1.0-SNAPSHOT'

buildscript {
    repositories {
        mavenCentral()
    }
    dependencies {
        classpath group: 'org.springframework.boot', name: 'spring-
boot-gradle-plugin', version: '1.5.9.RELEASE'
    }
}

apply plugin: 'java'
apply plugin: 'org.springframework.boot'
apply plugin: 'io.spring.dependency-management'

sourceCompatibility = 1.8
targetCompatibility = 1.8

repositories {
    mavenCentral()
}

dependencyManagement {
    imports {
        mavenBom 'org.springframework.cloud:spring-cloud-
netflix:1.4.4.RELEASE'
    }
}

dependencies {
    compile group: 'org.springframework.boot', name: 'spring-boot-
starter-web'
    compile group: 'org.springframework.cloud', name: 'spring-
cloud-starter-zuul'
    compile group: 'org.springframework.security', name: 'spring-
security-core'
    compile group: 'org.springframework.security', name: 'spring-
security-config'
    compile group: 'org.springframework.security', name: 'spring-
security-web'
    compile group: 'io.jsonwebtoken', name: 'jjwt', version:
'0.9.1'
    testCompile group: 'junit', name: 'junit', version: '4.12'
}
```

Note that we're using the same JWT library as the Authentication service.

10. Create a new package called `com.packtpub.microservices.ch06.gateway` and a new class called `Application`:

```
package com.packtpub.microservices.ch06.gateway;

import org.springframework.boot.SpringApplication;
import
org.springframework.boot.autoconfigure.SpringBootApplication;
import org.springframework.cloud.netflix.zuul.EnableZuulProxy;

@EnableZuulProxy
@SpringBootApplication
public class Application {
    public static void main(String[] args) {
        SpringApplication.run(Application.class, args);
    }
}
```

11. We'll create an authentication filter by creating a subclass of `OncePerRequestFilter`, which aims to provide a single execution per request dispatch. The filter will parse the JWT out of the Authorization header and try to decode it using a shared secret. If the JWT can be verified and decoded, we can be sure that it was encoded by an issuer that had access to the shared secret. We'll treat this as our trust boundary; anyone with access to the shared secret can be trusted, and therefore we can trust that the subject of the JWT is the ID of the authenticated user. Create a new class called `AuthenticationFilter`:

```
package com.packtpub.microservices.ch06.gateway;

import io.jsonwebtoken.Claims;
import io.jsonwebtoken.Jwts;
import
org.springframework.security.authentication.UsernamePasswordAuthent
icationToken;
import org.springframework.security.core.Authentication;
import
org.springframework.security.core.authority.SimpleGrantedAuthority;
import
org.springframework.security.core.context.SecurityContextHolder;
import org.springframework.web.filter.OncePerRequestFilter;
import javax.servlet.FilterChain;
import javax.servlet.ServletException;
import javax.servlet.http.HttpServletRequest;
import javax.servlet.http.HttpServletResponse;
import javax.xml.bind.DatatypeConverter;
```

```
import java.io.IOException;
import java.util.ArrayList;
import java.util.Optional;

public class AuthenticationFilter extends OncePerRequestFilter {

    private String signingSecret;

    AuthenticationFilter(String signingSecret) {
        this.signingSecret = signingSecret;
    }

    @Override
    protected void doFilterInternal(HttpServletRequest request,
HttpServletResponse response, FilterChain filterChain) throws
ServletException, IOException {
        Optional<String> token =
Optional.ofNullable(request.getHeader("Authorization"));
        Optional<Authentication> auth = token.filter(t ->
t.startsWith("Bearer")).flatMap(this::authentication);
        auth.ifPresent(a ->
SecurityContextHolder.getContext().setAuthentication(a));
        filterChain.doFilter(request, response);
    }

    private Optional<Authentication> authentication(String t) {
        System.out.println(signingSecret);
        String actualToken = t.substring("Bearer ".length());
        try {
            Claims claims = Jwts.parser()
.setSigningKey(DatatypeConverter.parseBase64Binary(signingSecret))
                    .parseClaimsJws(actualToken).getBody();
            Optional<String> userId =
Optional.ofNullable(claims.getSubject()).map(Object::toString);
            return userId.map(u -> new
UsernamePasswordAuthenticationToken(u, null, new
ArrayList<SimpleGrantedAuthority>()));
        } catch (Exception e) {
            return Optional.empty();
        }


    }
}
```

12. Wire this together with a security configuration for the API Gateway project. Create a new class called `SecurityConfig`:

```
package com.packtpub.microservices.ch06.gateway;

import org.springframework.beans.factory.annotation.Value;
import
org.springframework.security.config.annotation.web.builders.HttpSec
urity;
import
org.springframework.security.config.annotation.web.configuration.En
ableWebSecurity;
import
org.springframework.security.config.annotation.web.configuration.We
bSecurityConfigurerAdapter;
import
org.springframework.security.config.http.SessionCreationPolicy;
import
org.springframework.security.web.authentication.UsernamePasswordAut
henticationFilter;

import javax.servlet.http.HttpServletResponse;

@EnableWebSecurity
public class SecurityConfig extends WebSecurityConfigurerAdapter {

    @Value("${jwt.secret}")
    private String signingSecret;

    @Override
    protected void configure(HttpSecurity security) throws
Exception {
        security
            .csrf().disable()
            .logout().disable()
            .formLogin().disable()
.sessionManagement().sessionCreationPolicy(SessionCreationPolicy.ST
ATELESS)
            .and()
                .anonymous()
            .and()
                .exceptionHandling().authenticationEntryPoint(
                    (req, rsp, e) ->
rsp.sendError(HttpServletResponse.SC_UNAUTHORIZED))
            .and()
                .addFilterAfter(new
AuthenticationFilter(signingSecret),
                        UsernamePasswordAuthenticationFilter.class)
```

```
            .authorizeRequests()
            .antMatchers("/auth/**").permitAll()
            .antMatchers("/messages/**").authenticated()
            .antMatchers("/users/**").authenticated();
    }
}
```

As we can see, we're permitting any requests to the authentication service (requests prefixed with /auth/...). We require that requests to the users or messages service be authenticated.

13. We need a configuration file to store the shared secret as well as the routing information for the Zuul server. Create a file called application.yml in the src/main/resources directory:

```
server:
  port: 8080

jwt:
  secret: supers3cr3t

zuul:
  routes:
    authentication-service:
      path: /auth/**
      url: http://127.0.0.1:8081
    message-service:
      path: /messages/**
      url: http://127.0.0.1:8082
    user-service:
      path: /users/**
      url: http://127.0.0.1:8083
```

14. Now that we have a working authentication service and an API Gateway capable of verifying JWTs, we can test our authentication scheme by running the API Gateway, authentication service, and message service using the ports defined in the preceding configuration file. The following CURL requests now show that valid credentials can be exchanged for a JWT and the JWT can be used to access protected resources. We can also show that requests to protected resources are rejected without a valid JWT.

Note that in this example, the message service still doesn't do any authorization of requests. Anyone making an authenticated request could theoretically access anyone else's messages. The message service should be modified to check the user ID from the subject of the JWT and only allow access to messages belonging to that user.

15. We can use `curl` to test registering a new user account:

```
$ curl -X POST -D - http://localhost:8080/auth/register -
d'email=p@eval.ca&password=foobar123&passwordConfirmation=foobar123
'

HTTP/1.1 200
X-Content-Type-Options: nosniff
X-XSS-Protection: 1; mode=block
Cache-Control: no-cache, no-store, max-age=0, must-revalidate
Pragma: no-cache
Expires: 0
X-Frame-Options: DENY
X-Application-Context: application:8080
Date: Mon, 16 Jul 2018 03:27:17 GMT
Content-Type: application/json;charset=UTF-8
Transfer-Encoding: chunked
```

{"auth_token":"eyJhbGciOiJIUzI1NiJ9.eyJqdGkiOiJmYWQzMGZiMi03MzhmLTR
iM2QtYTIyZC0zZGNmN2NmNGQ1NGIiLCJzdWIiOiJmYWQzMGZiMi03MzhmLTRiM2QtYT
IyZC0zZGNmN2NmNGQ1NGIiLCJpc3MiOiJhdXRoZW50aWNhdGlvbi1zZXJ2aWNlIn0.T
zOKItjBU-AtRMqIB_D1n-qv6IO_zCBIK8ksGzsTC90"}

16. Now that we have a JWT, we can include it in the headers of requests to the message service to test that the API Gateway is able to verify and decode the token:

```
$ curl -D - - -H "Authorization: Bearer
eyJhbGciOiJIUzI1NiJ9.eyJqdGkiOiI3YmU4N2U3Mi03ZjhhLTQ3ZjktODk3NS1mYz
M5ZTE0NjNmODAiLCJzdWIiOiI3YmU4N2U3Mi03ZjhhLTQ3ZjktODk3NS1mYzM5ZTE0N
jNmODAiLCJpc3MiOiJhdXRoZW50aWNhdGlvbi1zZXJ2aWNlIn0.fpFbHhdSEVKk95m5
Q7iNjkKyM-eHkCGGKchTTKgbGWw" http://localhost:8080/messages/123

HTTP/1.1 404
X-Content-Type-Options: nosniff
X-XSS-Protection: 1; mode=block
Cache-Control: no-cache, no-store, max-age=0, must-revalidate
Pragma: no-cache
Expires: 0
X-Frame-Options: DENY
X-Application-Context: application:8080
```

```
Date: Mon, 16 Jul 2018 04:05:40 GMT
Content-Type: application/json;charset=UTF-8
Transfer-Encoding: chunked

{"timestamp":1532318740403,"status":404,"error":"Not
Found","exception":"com.packtpub.microservices.ch06.message.excepti
ons.MessageNotFoundException","message":"Message 123 could not be
found","path":"/123"}
```

The fact that we get a 404 from the message service shows that the request is getting to that service. If we modify the JWT in the request headers, we should get a 401:

```
$ curl -D - -H "Authorization: Bearer not-the-right-jwt"
http://localhost:8080/messages/123

HTTP/1.1 401
X-Content-Type-Options: nosniff
X-XSS-Protection: 1; mode=block
Cache-Control: no-cache, no-store, max-age=0, must-revalidate
Pragma: no-cache
Expires: 0
X-Frame-Options: DENY
Content-Type: application/json;charset=UTF-8
Transfer-Encoding: chunked
Date: Mon, 23 Jul 2018 04:06:47 GMT

{"timestamp":1532318807874,"status":401,"error":"Unauthorized","mes
sage":"No message available","path":"/messages/123"}
```

Securing containers

The advent of containers has solved many problems for organizations that are managing microservice architectures. Containers allow services to be bundled as a self-contained unit, and the software and its dependencies can be built as a single artifact and then shipped into any environment to be run or scheduled. Instead of relying on complicated configuration-management solutions to manage small changes to production systems, containers support the idea of immutable infrastructure; once the infrastructure is built, it does not have to be upgraded or maintained. Instead, you just build new infrastructure and throw away the old.

Containers also allow organizations to optimize their use of storage and compute resources. Because software can be built as containers, multiple applications can be running on a single virtual machine or piece of hardware, each unaware of the others' existence. While multi-tenancy has many advantages, having multiple services running on the same VM introduces new attack scenarios that a malicious user could exploit. If an attacker is able to exploit a vulnerability in one service, they may be able to use that exploit to attack services running on the same VM. In this kind of setup, by default, the cluster is treated as the security boundary; if you have access to the cluster, you must be trusted.

Depending on the needs of an organization, treating the cluster as the security boundary may not be sufficient and there may be a desire for more security and isolation between containers. The seccomp security facility was introduced into the Linux kernel in Version 2.6.12. It supports restricting the system calls that can be made from a process. Running containerized applications with a seccomp policy essentially sandboxes the service and any other process running in the container. In this recipe, we'll show you how to check that the seccomp is configured in your Linux kernel and demonstrate running a container with a custom seccomp policy.

How to do it...

1. In order to use a seccomp policy with a Docker container, you must be running the container on a host OS with a Linux kernel configured with seccomp support. To check this, you can search for CONFIG_SECCOMP in the kernel configuration file:

   ```
   $ grep CONFIG_SECCOMP= /boot/config-$(uname -r)
   CONFIG_SECCOMP=y
   ```

2. Now that we've verified that seccomp is enabled in the Linux kernel, we can take a look at the default profile that is packaged with Docker (https://github.com/ moby/moby/blob/master/profiles/seccomp/default.json). This default policy is sufficient for most needs and is fairly restrictive. If seccomp support is enabled, containers will be run with this policy.

3. To further verify that seccomp is configured and Docker is able to support it, we'll create a simple custom policy and then run a command in a container that demonstrates that the policy is being enforced. Create a file called policy.json:

   ```
   {
       "defaultAction": "SCMP_ACT_ALLOW",
       "syscalls": [
           {
               "name": "chown",
   ```

```
            "action": "SCMP_ACT_ERRNO"
        }
    ]
}
```

4. Now, run a container executing a shell and try to create a file, then change the ownership. The error message indicates that the container is being restricted by the seccomp policy:

```
$ docker run --rm -it --security-opt seccomp:policy.json busybox
/bin/sh
/ # touch foo
/ # chown root foo
chown: foo: Operation not permitted
```

Secure configuration

Services usually require some form of configuration. A service configuration stores all of the information that could potentially vary depending on the environment the service is deployed in. For example, when running a service locally on a developer's workstation, the service should probably connect to a database that is also running locally. In production, however, the service should connect to the production database. Common data stored in configuration includes the location of and credentials to data stores, access tokens, or other credentials for third-party services and operational information, such as where to send metrics or what values to use when initializing connection pools or configuring timeouts for network connections.

It's important to store configuration separately from code. When you make a configuration change, you should not have to commit a change to a source code repository, create a new build, and run a separate deploy. Ideally, there should be an easy way to change configuration without deploying a new version of a service. Storing configuration in code (for example, hard coding a password in a source code file) is also a bad practice from a security perspective. Anyone with access to the source code has access to the configuration, and in the case of secrets, this is rarely desired. It is a good practice to roll keys and credentials as often as possible, so that even if a secret is compromised or is vulnerable to being compromised, it will not be valid for very long. Hardcoding secrets makes this difficult, which in practice often means it won't happen.

A common best practice is to store configuration in environment variables. This is a good way to expose configuration values to a process in a way that can be changed easily depending on the environment a service is running in. Environment variables are good for non-secret configuration values, such as hostnames, timeouts, and log levels. Environment variables are not sufficient for storing secrets.

Storing secrets as environment variables makes the values accessible to any process running in the same container or process space as the service, which makes them susceptible to being intercepted. There are various solutions for storing secrets separately from the rest of an application's configuration. Applications deployed on a Kubernetes cluster can use a special object type called `secret`, which is intended for this purpose. Kubernetes secrets are encrypted using a private key residing on a master node while in transit between nodes, however, the secret is stored in plaintext at rest. Ideally, secrets should be stored as encrypted values and only decrypted by a process that is explicitly permitted to do so.

Vault is an open source project actively maintained by HashiCorp. Its purpose is to provide an easy-to-use system for storing and accessing secrets securely. In addition to secret-storage, Vault provides access-log auditing, fine-grained access-control, and easy rolling. In this recipe, we'll create a new service, called attachment-service, that is responsible for handling messages' image and video attachments. Attachment-service will use Vault to obtain valid AWS credentials used to access an S3 bucket when uploading photo and video files. The service will also use Vault to obtain database credentials to a MySQL database where attachment metadata will be stored. Non-sensitive configurations, such as the name of the database or the name of the S3 bucket to upload photos and videos to, will be made available to the service as environment variables.

How to do it...

In order to demonstrate using Vault to securely store sensitive configuration data, we'll first create an attachment service that stores sensitive information using environment variables. We'll then integrate Vault so that the same configuration is read from a secure store:

1. Create a new Java project called `attachment-service` with the following `build.gradle` file:

```
group 'com.packtpub.microservices'
version '1.0-SNAPSHOT'

buildscript {
    repositories {
        mavenCentral()
```

```
    }
    dependencies {
        classpath group: 'org.springframework.boot', name: 'spring-
boot-gradle-plugin', version: '1.5.9.RELEASE'
    }
}

apply plugin: 'java'
apply plugin: 'org.springframework.boot'
apply plugin: 'io.spring.dependency-management'

sourceCompatibility = 1.8

repositories {
    mavenCentral()
}

dependencies {
    compile group: 'org.springframework.boot', name: 'spring-boot-
starter-web'
    compile group: 'org.springframework.boot', name: 'spring-boot-
starter-data-jpa', version: '1.5.9.RELEASE'
    compile group: 'mysql', name: 'mysql-connector-java'
    compile group: 'com.amazonaws', name: 'aws-java-sdk-s3',
version: '1.11.375'
    testCompile group: 'junit', name: 'junit', version: '4.12'
}
```

2. Create a new package called
   com.packtpub.microservices.ch06.attachment and create a new class
   called Application, which will serve as our service's entry point. In addition to
   running our Spring Boot application, this class will expose one bean, which is the
   Amazon S3 client. Note that we're using the
   EnvironmentVariableCredentialsProvider class, which reads credentials
   from a set of environment variables for now, this is not what we want to do in
   production:

```
package com.packtpub.microservices.ch06.attachment;

import com.amazonaws.auth.EnvironmentVariableCredentialsProvider;
import com.amazonaws.regions.Regions;
import com.amazonaws.services.s3.AmazonS3;
import com.amazonaws.services.s3.AmazonS3ClientBuilder;

import org.springframework.boot.SpringApplication;
import
org.springframework.boot.autoconfigure.SpringBootApplication;
```

```
import org.springframework.context.annotation.Bean;

@SpringBootApplication
public class Application {

    @Bean
    public AmazonS3 getS3Client() {
        AmazonS3ClientBuilder client =
AmazonS3ClientBuilder.standard();
        return client.withCredentials(
            new
EnvironmentVariableCredentialsProvider()).withRegion(Regions.US_WES
T_2).build();
    }

    public static void main(String[] args) {
        SpringApplication.run(Application.class, args);
    }
}
```

3. Create a new package called
   com.packtpub.microservices.ch06.attachment.models and a new class
   called Attachment. This will be the representation of attachments that we store
   in a relational database:

```
package com.packtpub.microservices.ch06.attachment.models;

import org.hibernate.annotations.GenericGenerator;

import javax.persistence.Column;
import javax.persistence.Entity;
import javax.persistence.GeneratedValue;
import javax.persistence.Id;

@Entity
public class Attachment {

    @Id
    @GeneratedValue(generator = "uuid")
    @GenericGenerator(name = "uuid", strategy = "uuid2")
    private String id;

    @Column(unique = true)
    private String messageId;
    private String url;
    private String fileName;
    private Integer mediaType;
```

```java
    public Attachment(String messageId, String url, String
fileName, Integer mediaType) {
        this.messageId = messageId;
        this.url = url;
        this.fileName = fileName;
        this.mediaType = mediaType;
    }

    public String getId() {
        return id;
    }

    public void setId(String id) {
        this.id = id;
    }

    public String getMessageId() {
        return messageId;
    }

    public void setMessageId(String messageId) {
        this.messageId = messageId;
    }

    public String getUrl() {
        return url;
    }

    public void setUrl(String url) {
        this.url = url;
    }

    public String getFileName() {
        return fileName;
    }

    public void setFileName(String fileName) {
        this.fileName = fileName;
    }

    public Integer getMediaType() {
        return mediaType;
    }

    public void setMediaType(Integer mediaType) {
        this.mediaType = mediaType;
    }
}
```

4. In order to perform basic operations on the previously defined `Attachment`
   class, we'll create a new package called
   `com.packtpub.microservices.ch06.attachment.data` and an interface
   called `AttachmentRepository`, which extends `CrudRepository`. We'll also
   define one custom method signature that allows a caller to find all attachments
   related to a specific message:

```
package com.packtpub.microservices.ch06.attachment.data;

import
com.packtpub.microservices.ch06.attachment.models.Attachment;
import org.springframework.data.repository.CrudRepository;

import java.util.List;

public interface AttachmentRepository extends
CrudRepository<Attachment, String> {
    public List<Attachment> findByMessageId(String messageId);
}
```

5. We also need a way to model incoming requests. Our service will accept requests
   as JSON sent in the request body. The JSON object will have a file name and
   contain the file data as a Base64-encoded string. Create a new class called
   `AttachmentRequest` with the following definition:

```
package com.packtpub.microservices.ch06.attachment.models;

import com.fasterxml.jackson.annotation.JsonProperty;

import java.util.Map;

public class AttachmentRequest {
    private String fileName;

    private String data;

    public AttachmentRequest() {}

    public AttachmentRequest(String fileName, String data) {
        this.fileName = fileName;
        this.data = data;
    }

    public String getFileName() {
        return fileName;
    }
```

```
public void setFileName(String fileName) {
    this.fileName = fileName;
}

public String getData() {
    return data;
}

public void setData(String data) {
    this.data = data;
}

@JsonProperty("file")
private void unpackFileName(Map<String, String> file) {
    this.fileName = file.get("name");
    this.data = file.get("data");
}
}
```

6. In our controller, which we'll define next, we'll need to return an HTTP 404 response to callers if no attachments can be found for a particular message. In order to do this, create a new package called com.packtpub.microservices.ch06.attachment.exceptions and a new class called AttachmentNotFoundException:

```
package com.packtpub.microservices.ch06.attachment.exceptions;

import org.springframework.http.HttpStatus;
import org.springframework.web.bind.annotation.ResponseStatus;

@ResponseStatus(code = HttpStatus.NOT_FOUND, reason = "No
attachment(s) found")
public class AttachmentNotFoundException extends RuntimeException
{}
```

7. We'll put everything together in our controller. In this basic example, two methods are defined; one that lists attachments for a specific message and one that creates a new attachment. The attachment is uploaded to an Amazon S3 bucket, the name of which is specified in a configuration value. Create a new package called com.packtpub.microservices.ch06.attachment.controllers and a new class called AttachmentController:

```
package com.packtpub.microservices.ch06.attachment.controllers;

import com.amazonaws.services.s3.AmazonS3;
```

```
import com.amazonaws.services.s3.model.CannedAccessControlList;
import com.amazonaws.services.s3.model.ObjectMetadata;
import com.amazonaws.services.s3.model.PutObjectRequest;
import
com.packtpub.microservices.ch06.attachment.data.AttachmentRepositor
y;
import
com.packtpub.microservices.ch06.attachment.exceptions.AttachmentNot
FoundException;
import
com.packtpub.microservices.ch06.attachment.models.Attachment;
import
com.packtpub.microservices.ch06.attachment.models.AttachmentRequest
;
import org.apache.commons.codec.binary.Base64;
import org.springframework.beans.factory.annotation.Autowired;
import org.springframework.beans.factory.annotation.Value;
import org.springframework.web.bind.annotation.*;

import java.io.ByteArrayInputStream;
import java.io.InputStream;
import java.util.List;

@RestController
public class AttachmentController {

    @Autowired
    private AttachmentRepository attachmentRepository;

    @Autowired
    private AmazonS3 s3Client;

    @Value("${s3.bucket-name}")
    private String bucketName;

    @RequestMapping(path = "/message/{message_id}/attachments",
method = RequestMethod.GET, produces = "application/json")
    public List<Attachment>
getAttachments(@PathVariable("message_id") String messageId) {
        List<Attachment> attachments =
attachmentRepository.findByMessageId(messageId);
        if (attachments.isEmpty()) {
            throw new AttachmentNotFoundException();
        }
        return attachments;
    }

    @RequestMapping(path = "/message/{message_id}/attachments",
```

```
method = RequestMethod.POST, produces = "application/json")
    public Attachment create(@PathVariable("message_id") String
messageId, @RequestBody AttachmentRequest request) {

        byte[] byteArray = Base64.decodeBase64(request.getData());

        ObjectMetadata metadata = new ObjectMetadata();
        metadata.setContentLength(byteArray.length);
        metadata.setContentType("image/jpeg");
        metadata.setCacheControl("public, max-age=31536000");
        InputStream stream = new ByteArrayInputStream(byteArray);

        String fullyResolved = String.format("%s/%s", messageId,
request.getFileName());

        s3Client.putObject(
            new PutObjectRequest(bucketName, fullyResolved, stream,
metadata)
        .withCannedAcl(CannedAccessControlList.PublicRead));

        String url =
String.format("https://%s.s3.amazonaws.com/%s", bucketName,
fullyResolved);

        Attachment attachment = new Attachment(messageId, url,
request.getFileName(), 1);
        attachmentRepository.save(attachment);
        return attachment;
    }
}
```

8. In order for any of this to work, we have to create a properties file. Java properties files support a syntax for getting values from environment variables, which is shown in the following code. Create a new file in the src/main/resources directory called application.yml:

```
spring:
  jpa.hibernate.ddl-auto: create
  datasource.url: ${DATABASE_URL}
  datasource.username: ${DATABASE_USERNAME}
  datasource.password: ${DATABASE_PASSWORD}

s3:
  bucket-name: ${BUCKET_NAME}
```

This example works well enough. `EnvironmentVariableCredentialsProvider` in the AWS SDK expects `AWS_ACCESS_KEY_ID` and `AWS_SECRET_ACCESS_KEY` to be set, and we specify that a number of non-sensitive configuration values should be similarly read from environment variables. This is clearly better than hardcoding configuration values, but we're still exposing secrets to any process running in the same container or process space as our service. The environment variables also have to be set somewhere (by a configuration management system or specified in a Dockerfile), so we haven't solved the problem of storing sensitive secrets. Next, we'll modify our new service to read S3 credentials from Vault.

 In this recipe, we'll be running Vault in development mode. Installing Vault for production use is a big topic that cannot be properly covered in a single recipe. For the production use of Vault, please consult the excellent documentation available at `https://www.vaultproject.io/intro/index.html`.

9. Install `vault` on your local development machine. See `http://www.vaultproject.io` for instructions for any platform. If you are running macOS X and use **HomeBrew**, you can install Vault with a single command:

    ```
    $ brew install vault
    ```

10. Run the `vault server` in development mode, providing a simple-to-remember root token:

    ```
    $ vault server --dev --dev-root-token-
    id="00000000-0000-0000-0000-000000000000"
    ```

11. Enable a new instance of a `kv` secrets engine with a path specific to this service:

    ```
    $ vault secrets enable -path=secret/attachment-service
    ```

12. Write the AWS access key and secret pair to `vault` as secrets. Substitute the placeholders for your actual AWS access key ID and AWS secret access key:

    ```
    $ vault write secret/attachment-service
    attachment.awsAccessKeyId=<access-key>
    attachment.awsSecretAccessKey=<access-secret>
    ```

13. In order for our service to read these values from Vault, we'll use a library that simplifies Vault integration for Spring Boot applications. Modify our project's `build.gradle` file and add the following dependency:

```
group 'com.packtpub.microservices'
version '1.0-SNAPSHOT'

buildscript {
    repositories {
        mavenCentral()
    }
    dependencies {
        classpath group: 'org.springframework.boot', name: 'spring-
boot-gradle-plugin', version: '1.5.9.RELEASE'
    }
}

apply plugin: 'java'
apply plugin: 'org.springframework.boot'
apply plugin: 'io.spring.dependency-management'

sourceCompatibility = 1.8

repositories {
    mavenCentral()
}

dependencies {
    compile group: 'org.springframework.boot', name: 'spring-boot-
starter-web'
    compile group: 'org.springframework.boot', name: 'spring-boot-
starter-data-jpa', version: '1.5.9.RELEASE'
    compile group: 'org.springframework.cloud', name: 'spring-
cloud-starter-vault-config', version: '1.1.1.RELEASE'
    compile group: 'mysql', name: 'mysql-connector-java'
    compile group: 'com.amazonaws', name: 'aws-java-sdk-s3',
version: '1.11.375'
    testCompile group: 'junit', name: 'junit', version: '4.12'
}
```

14. Our application needs a configuration class to store values read from Vault. Create a new package called `com.packtpub.microservices.ch06.attachment.config` and a new class called `Configuration`:

```
package com.packtpub.microservices.ch06.attachment.config;

import
org.springframework.boot.context.properties.ConfigurationProperties
;

@ConfigurationProperties("attachment")
public class Configuration {

    private String awsAccessKeyId;

    private String awsSecretAccessKey;

    public String getAwsAccessKeyId() {
        return awsAccessKeyId;
    }

    public void setAwsAccessKeyId(String awsAccessKeyId) {
        this.awsAccessKeyId = awsAccessKeyId;
    }

    public String getAwsSecretAccessKey() {
        return awsSecretAccessKey;
    }

    public void setAwsSecretAccessKey(String awsSecretAccessKey) {
        this.awsSecretAccessKey = awsSecretAccessKey;
    }
}
```

15. Modify the `Application` class to create an instance of the class we just created. Then use the instance when creating the S3 client so that we can use credentials taken from Vault instead of environment variables:

```
package com.packtpub.microservices.ch06.attachment;

import com.amazonaws.auth.AWSCredentials;
import com.amazonaws.auth.AWSStaticCredentialsProvider;
import com.amazonaws.auth.BasicAWSCredentials;
import com.amazonaws.regions.Regions;
import com.amazonaws.services.s3.AmazonS3;
import com.amazonaws.services.s3.AmazonS3ClientBuilder;
```

```
import
com.packtpub.microservices.ch06.attachment.config.Configuration;
import org.springframework.boot.SpringApplication;
import
org.springframework.boot.autoconfigure.SpringBootApplication;
import
org.springframework.boot.context.properties.EnableConfigurationProp
erties;
import org.springframework.context.annotation.Bean;

@SpringBootApplication
@EnableConfigurationProperties(Configuration.class)
public class Application {

    private final Configuration config;

    public Application(Configuration config) {
        this.config = config;
    }

    @Bean
    public AmazonS3 getS3Client() {
        AmazonS3ClientBuilder client =
AmazonS3ClientBuilder.standard();
        AWSCredentials credentials = new
BasicAWSCredentials(config.getAwsAccessKeyId(),
config.getAwsSecretAccessKey());
        return client.withCredentials(
                new
AWSStaticCredentialsProvider(credentials)).withRegion(Regions.US_WE
ST_2).build();
    }

    public static void main(String[] args) {
        SpringApplication.run(Application.class, args);
    }
}
```

That's it! The attachment service is now configured to read AWS credentials from Vault.

Secure logging

Together with traces and metrics, logs are an essential component of an observable system (we'll discuss Observability more generally in `Chapter 16`, *Monitoring and Observability*). Logs are an ordered, timestamped sequence of events that originated in a particular system.

In a microservice architecture, the increased complexity of having multiple services makes having good logs essential. The exact criteria that makes logs good is subjective, but generally speaking, good logs should help an engineer piece together events that may have led to a specific error state or bug. Logs are usually organized by levels, a configurable toggle that allows a developer to instruct a service to be more or less verbose with the information sent to logs.

While essential for observing the behavior of systems in production, logs can also present privacy and security risks. Having too much information sent from systems to logs can give a would-be attacker information about users of your system, or sensitive information such as tokens or keys that can be used to attack other parts of your system. Having a microservice architecture spreads out this possible attack surface, making it even more important to have a carefully planned strategy for how your services should log information.

Infrastructure as Code

Microservices architectures typically require more frequent provisioning of compute resources. Having more nodes in a system increases the attack surface that an attacker could scan for possible vulnerabilities. One of the easiest ways to leave a system vulnerable is to lose track of the inventory and leave multiple, heterogeneous configurations active. Before configuration-management systems, such as, Puppet or Ansible were popular, it was common to have a set of custom shell scripts that would *bootstrap* new servers in a system. This worked well enough, but as the needs of the system grew, and the shell scripts were modified, it became unwieldy to bring older parts of the system up to date with the changing standards. This type of configuration drift would often leave legacy parts of a system vulnerable to attack. Configuration-management solved many of these problems by allowing teams to use code, usually with a declarative syntax, to describe how nodes in a system should be configured. Configuration-management systems typically did not deal with provisioning actual compute resources, such as compute nodes, data stores, or network storage.

Infrastructure as Code is the process of managing infrastructure-provisioning and maintenance through machine-readable code files rather than manually. Using code to describe the infrastructure allows for effective versioning, reviews, and rollbacks of changes to a system. Being able to automate the process of bringing up a database node or adding a compute node to a cluster frees developers up to worry about their applications, relatively assured that they are not leaving old configurations out in the wild. Together with immutable infrastructure, Infrastructure as Code provides an additional safety net against a system being compromised by vulnerable, forgotten components.

In this recipe, we'll demonstrate using *Terraform*, an open source tool created by HashiCorp, to provision a collection of AWS resources, including an EC2 instance and a Redis ElastiCache. We'll guarantee that resources provisioned with Terraform share configurations with regards to network access, backups, and other security considerations.

How to do it...

1. Before using terraform, you'll have to install it. Instructions are available on the project site, but if you are running macOS X and use HomeBrew (https://brew.sh/), you can issue the following command:

   $ brew install terraform

2. Create a new file called example.tf. This will contain configuration for our EC2 instance and ElastiCache instance. We'll use a default **Amazon Machine Image (AMI)** and enable daily snapshots that will be kept for five days:

```
provider "aws" {
    access_key = "ACCESS_KEY"
    secret_key = "SECRET_KEY"
    region = "us-east-1"
}

resource "aws_instance" "example" {
  ami             = "ami-b374d5a5"
  instance_type = "t2.micro"
}

resource "aws_elasticache_cluster" "example" {
  cluster_id            = "cluster-example"
  engine                = "redis"
  node_type             = "cache.m3.medium"
  num_cache_nodes       = 1
  parameter_group_name  = "default.redis3.2"
  port                  = 6379
  snapshot_window       = "05:00-09:00"
  snapshot_retention_limit = 5
}
```

Replace ACCESS_KEY and SECRET_KEY with a valid AWS access key pair.

3. Initialize terraform. This will install the AWS provider referenced in the preceding file:

```
$ terraform init
```

4. Terraform works by presenting an execution plan and then asking whether you'd like to proceed by applying the plan. Run the following command and type `yes` when prompted:

```
$ terraform apply

aws_instance.example: Refreshing state... (ID: i-09b5cf5ed923d60f4)
```

An execution plan has been generated and is shown in the following code. Resource actions are indicated with the following symbols: + `create`.

Terraform will perform the following actions:

```
+ aws_elasticache_cluster.example
      id: <computed>
      apply_immediately: <computed>
      availability_zone: <computed>
      az_mode: <computed>
      cache_nodes.#: <computed>
      cluster_address: <computed>
      cluster_id: "cluster-example"
      configuration_endpoint: <computed>
      engine: "redis"
      engine_version: <computed>
      maintenance_window: <computed>
      node_type: "cache.m3.medium"
      num_cache_nodes: "1"
      parameter_group_name: <computed>
      port: "6379"
      replication_group_id: <computed>
      security_group_ids.#: <computed>
      security_group_names.#: <computed>
      snapshot_retention_limit: "5"
      snapshot_window: "05:00-09:00"
      subnet_group_name: <computed>


Plan: 1 to add, 0 to change, 0 to destroy.
Do you want to perform these actions?
```

Terraform will perform the actions described earlier. Only `yes` will be accepted to approve:

```
Enter a value: yes
```

. . .

5. Log into your AWS management console and you'll see that a new Redis cluster and EC2 instance have been created. Terraform can also help you clean up. In order to destroy these two resources, run the destroy command and type in `yes` when prompted:

```
$ terraform destroy
```

Terraform is an incredibly powerful tool. In this recipe, we used it to create a single EC2 instance and an ElastiCache Cluster instance. You can do loads more with Terraform – the subject of Infrastructure as Code could fill a cookbook of its own. Thankfully, the docs provided by HashiCorp (`https://www.terraform.io/docs/index.html`) are excellent and I would recommend reading them.

Using an Infrastructure as Code solution will make provisioning and managing resources a much safer process, limiting the possibility of losing track of legacy infrastructure with out-of-date configurations.

Monitoring and Observability

16

In this chapter, we will cover the following recipes:

- Structured JSON logging
- Collecting metrics with StatsD and Graphite
- Collecting metrics with Prometheus
- Making debugging easier with tracing
- Alerting when something goes wrong

Introduction

Microservices add complexity to an architecture. With more moving parts in a system, monitoring and observing the behavior of the system becomes more important and more challenging. In a microservice architecture, failure conditions impacting one service can cascade in unexpected ways, impacting the system as a whole. A faulty switch somewhere in a datacenter may be causing unusually high latency for a service, perhaps resulting in intermittent timeouts in requests originating from the API Gateway, which may result in unexpected user impact, which results in an alert being fired. This kind of scenario is not uncommon in a microservice architecture and requires forethought so that engineers can easily determine the nature of customer-impacting incidents. Distributed systems are bound to experience certain failures and special consideration must be taken to build observability into systems.

Another shift that microservices have necessitated is the move to DevOps. Many traditional monitoring solutions were developed at a time when operations were the sole responsibility of a special and distinct group of system administrators or operations engineers. System administrators and operations engineers are often interested in system-level or host-level metrics, such as CPU, memory disk, and network usage. These metrics are important but only make up a small part of observability. **Observability** must also be considered by engineers writing microservices. It's equally important to use metrics to be able to observe events unique to a system, such as certain types of exceptions being thrown or the number of events emitted to a queue.

Planning for observability also gives us the information we need to effectively test systems in production. Ephemeral environments for staging and integration testing can be useful, but there are entire classes of failure states that they are unable to test for. As discussed in Chapter 14, *Reliability Patterns*, Gamedays and other forms of failure injection are critical for improving the resilience of systems. Observable systems lend themselves to this kind of testing, allowing engineers to gain confidence in our understanding of the system.

In this chapter, we'll introduce several tenants of monitoring and observability. We'll demonstrate how to modify our services to emit structured logs. We'll also take a look at metrics, using a number of different systems for collecting, aggregating, and visualizing metrics. Finally we'll look at tracing, a way to look at requests as they travel through various components of a system and alert us when user-impacting error conditions are detected.

Structured JSON logging

Outputting useful logs is a key part of building an observable service. What constitutes a useful log is subjective, but a good set of guidelines is that logs should contain timestamped information about key events in a system. A good logging system supports the notion of configurable log levels, so the amount of information sent to logs can be dialed up or down for a specific amount of time depending on the needs of engineers working with the system. For example, when testing a service against failure scenarios in production, it may be useful to turn up the log level and get more detail about events in the system.

The two most popular logging libraries for Java applications are **Log4j** (`https://logging.apache.org/log4j/2.x/`) and **Logback** (`https://logback.qos.ch/`). By default, both of these libraries will emit log entries in an unstructured format, usually space-separated fields including information such as a timestamp, log level, and message. This is useful, but especially so in a microservices architecture, where multiple services are emitting event logs possibly to a centralized log store; it's extremely useful to emit structured logs with some consistency.

JSON has become a common standard for passing messages between systems. Nearly every popular language has libraries for parsing and generating JSON. It's lightweight, yet structured, making it a good choice for data, such as event logs. Emitting event logs in JSON makes it easier to feed your service's logs into a centralized store and have log data analyzed and queried.

In this recipe, we'll modify our message-service to emit logs using the popular `logback` library for Java applications.

How to do it...

Let's have a look at the following steps:

1. Open the message-service project from `Chapter 15`, *Security*. The first change we'll make is to add the `logback` library to the `build.gradle` file:

```
group 'com.packtpub.microservices'
version '1.0-SNAPSHOT'

buildscript {
    repositories {
        mavenCentral()
    }
    dependencies {
        classpath group: 'org.springframework.boot', name: 'spring-
boot-gradle-plugin', version: '1.5.9.RELEASE'
    }
}

apply plugin: 'java'
apply plugin: 'org.springframework.boot'

sourceCompatibility = 1.8

repositories {
    mavenCentral()
```

```
    }

dependencies {
    compile group: 'org.springframework.boot', name: 'spring-boot-
    starter-web'
    compile group: 'io.github.resilience4j', name: 'resilience4j-
    circuitbreaker', version: '0.11.0'
    compile group: 'net.logstash.logback', name: 'logstash-logback-
    encoder', version: '4.7'
    testCompile group: 'junit', name: 'junit', version: '4.12'
}
```

2. Create a `logback.xml` configuration file. In the configuration file, we'll create a single logger, called `jsonLogger`, that references a single appender, called `consoleAppender`:

```
<?xml version="1.0" encoding="utf-8"?>
<configuration>
    <appender name="consoleAppender"
class="ch.qos.logback.core.ConsoleAppender">
        <encoder
class="net.logstash.logback.encoder.LogstashEncoder"/>
    </appender>
    <logger name="jsonLogger" additivity="false" level="DEBUG">
        <appender-ref ref="consoleAppender"/>
    </logger>
    <root level="INFO">
        <appender-ref ref="consoleAppender"/>
    </root>
</configuration>
```

3. Add a single sample log message to `Application.java` to test our new logging configuration:

```
package com.packtpub.microservices.ch07.message;

import
com.packtpub.microservices.ch07.message.clients.SocialGraphClient;
import org.apache.log4j.LogManager;
import org.apache.log4j.Logger;
import org.springframework.boot.SpringApplication;
import
org.springframework.boot.autoconfigure.SpringBootApplication;
import org.springframework.context.annotation.Bean;
import org.springframework.scheduling.annotation.EnableAsync;
import
org.springframework.scheduling.concurrent.ThreadPoolTaskExecutor;
```

```
import java.util.concurrent.Executor;

@SpringBootApplication
@EnableAsync
public class Application {

    private Logger logger =
LogManager.getLogger(Application.class);

    @Bean
    public MessageRepository messageRepository() {
        return new MessageRepository();
    }

    @Bean
    public SocialGraphClient socialGraphClient() {
        return new SocialGraphClient("http://localhost:4567");
    }

    public static void main(String[] args) {
        logger.info("Starting application");
        SpringApplication.run(Application.class, args);
    }

    @Bean
    public Executor asyncExecutor() {
        ThreadPoolTaskExecutor executor = new
ThreadPoolTaskExecutor();
        executor.setCorePoolSize(2);
        executor.setMaxPoolSize(2);
        executor.setQueueCapacity(500);
        executor.setThreadNamePrefix("SocialServiceCall-");
        executor.initialize();
        return executor;
    }
}
```

4. Run the application and see that log messages are now emitted in JSON:

```
$ ./gradlew bootRun

> Task :bootRun
{"@timestamp":"2018-08-09T22:08:22.959-05:00","@version":1,"message
":"Starting
application","logger_name":"com.packtpub.microservices.ch07.message
.Application","thread_name":"main","level":"INFO","level_value":200
00}
```

```
    .   ___                _          ___ _ _
   /\\ / ___'_ _ _ _ _(_)_ _  _ _ \ \ \ \
  ( ( )\___ | '_ | '_| | '_ \/ _` | \ \ \ \
   \\/  ___)| |_)| | | | | || (_| |  ) ) ) )
    '  |____| .__|_| |_|_| |_\__, | / / / /
   =========|_|==============|___/=/_/_/_/
   :: Spring Boot ::         (v1.5.9.RELEASE)
```

{"@timestamp":"2018-08-09T22:08:23.786-05:00","@version":1,"message":"Starting Application on fartlek.local with PID 82453 (/Users/posman/projects/microservices-cookbook/chapter16/message-service/build/classes/java/main started by posman in /Users/posman/projects/microservices-cookbook/chapter16/message-service)","logger_name":"com.packtpub.microservices.ch07.message.Application","thread_name":"main","level":"INFO","level_value":20000}

Collecting metrics with StatsD and Graphite

Metrics are numeric measurements over time. The most common types of metrics collected in our systems are counters, timers, and gauges. A counter is exactly what it sounds like, a value that is incremented a number of times over some time period. A timer can be used to measure recurring events in a system, such as the amount of time it takes to serve a request or perform a database query. Gauges are just arbitrary numeric values that can be recorded.

StatsD is an open source network daemon invented in 2011 at Etsy. Metrics data is pushed to a `statsd` server, often on the same server, which aggregates data before sending it on to a durable backend. One of the most common backends used with `statsd` is **Graphite**, an open source time-series storage engine and graphing tool. Together, Graphite and StatsD make up a very popular metrics stack. They're easy to get started with and enjoy large communities and a large selection of tools and libraries.

Spring Boot has a sub-project called **Actuator** that adds a number of production readiness features to a service. Actuator gives us our services certain metrics for free, together with a project called micrometer, Actuator enables a vendor-neutral API to various metric's backends. We'll use Actuator and micrometer in this recipe and the next one.

In this recipe, we'll add Actuator to the message-service we've worked with in previous recipes. We'll create a few custom metrics and demonstrate using `statsd` and `graphite` to graph metrics from our application. We'll run `statsd` and `graphite` locally in docker containers.

How to do it...

Let's look at the following steps:

1. Open the message-service project from previous recipes. We're going to upgrade the version of Spring Boot and add `actuator` and `micrometer` to our list of dependencies. Modify the `build.gradle` file to look like the following:

```
group 'com.packtpub.microservices'
version '1.0-SNAPSHOT'

buildscript {
    repositories {
        mavenCentral()
    }
    dependencies {
        classpath group: 'org.springframework.boot', name: 'spring-
boot-gradle-plugin', version: '2.0.4.RELEASE'
    }
}

apply plugin: 'java'
apply plugin: 'org.springframework.boot'

sourceCompatibility = 1.8

repositories {
    mavenCentral()
}

dependencies {
    compile group: 'org.springframework.boot', name: 'spring-boot-
starter-web', version: '2.0.4.RELEASE'
    compile group: 'org.springframework.boot', name: 'spring-boot-
starter-actuator', version: '2.0.4.RELEASE'
    compile group: 'io.micrometer', name: 'micrometer-core',
version: '1.0.6'
    compile group: 'io.micrometer', name: 'micrometer-registry-
statsd', version: '1.0.6'
    compile group: 'io.github.resilience4j', name: 'resilience4j-
circuitbreaker', version: '0.11.0'
    compile group: 'log4j', name: 'log4j', version: '1.2.17'
    compile group: 'net.logstash.logback', name: 'logstash-logback-
encoder', version: '5.2'
    testCompile group: 'junit', name: 'junit', version: '4.12'
}
```

2. Open `application.yml` in the `src/main/resources` directory and add the following:

```
server:
  port:
    8082

management:
  metrics:
    export:
      statsd:
        enabled: true
        flavor: "etsy"
        host:
          0.0.0.0
        port:
          8125
```

3. Our application now supports emitting metrics to a locally-running instance of `statsd`. Open `MessageController.java` and add the `Timed` annotation to the class as well as the `get` method:

```
package com.packtpub.microservices.ch07.message.controllers;

import com.packtpub.microservices.ch07.message.MessageRepository;
import
com.packtpub.microservices.ch07.message.clients.SocialGraphClient;
import
com.packtpub.microservices.ch07.message.exceptions.MessageNotFoundE
xception;
import
com.packtpub.microservices.ch07.message.exceptions.MessageSendForbi
ddenException;
import com.packtpub.microservices.ch07.message.models.Message;
import
com.packtpub.microservices.ch07.message.models.UserFriendships;
import io.micrometer.core.annotation.Timed;
import io.micrometer.statsd.StatsdMeterRegistry;
import org.springframework.beans.factory.annotation.Autowired;
import org.springframework.http.ResponseEntity;
import org.springframework.scheduling.annotation.Async;
import org.springframework.web.bind.annotation.*;
import org.springframework.web.client.RestTemplate;
import
org.springframework.web.servlet.support.ServletUriComponentsBuilder
;
```

```
import java.net.URI;
import java.util.List;
import java.util.concurrent.CompletableFuture;

@RestController
@Timed
public class MessageController {

    @Autowired
    private MessageRepository messagesStore;

    @Autowired
    private SocialGraphClient socialGraphClient;

    @Autowired
    private StatsdMeterRegistry registry;

    @Timed(value="get.messages")
    @RequestMapping(path = "/{id}", method = RequestMethod.GET,
produces = "application/json")
    public Message get(@PathVariable("id") String id) throws
MessageNotFoundException {
        registry.counter("get_messages").increment();
        return messagesStore.get(id);
    }

    @RequestMapping(path = "/", method = RequestMethod.POST,
produces = "application/json")
    public ResponseEntity<Message> send(@RequestBody Message
message) throws MessageSendForbiddenException {

        List<String> friendships =
socialGraphClient.getFriendships(message.getSender());
        if (!friendships.contains(message.getRecipient())) {
            throw new MessageSendForbiddenException("Must be
friends to send message");
        }

        Message saved = messagesStore.save(message);
        URI location = ServletUriComponentsBuilder
                .fromCurrentRequest().path("/{id}")
                .buildAndExpand(saved.getId()).toUri();
        return ResponseEntity.created(location).build();
    }

    @Async
    public CompletableFuture<Boolean> isFollowing(String fromUser,
String toUser) {
```

```
            String url = String.format(
    "http://localhost:4567/followings?user=%s&filter=%s",
                    fromUser, toUser);

            RestTemplate template = new RestTemplate();
            UserFriendships followings = template.getForObject(url,
    UserFriendships.class);

            return CompletableFuture.completedFuture(
                    followings.getFriendships().isEmpty()
            );
        }
    }
```

4. In order to demonstrate that metrics are actually being emitted, we'll run `statsd` and graphite locally in a docker container. Having installed `docker`, run the following command, which will pull down an image from `dockerhub` and run a container locally:

```
docker run -d --name graphite --restart=always \
   -p 80:80 -p 2003-2004:2003-2004 -p 2023-2024:2023-2024 \
   -p 8125:8125/udp -p 8126:8126 \
   hopsoft/graphite-statsd
```

5. Now, visit `http://localhost` to see your metrics!

Collecting metrics with Prometheus

Prometheus is an open source monitoring and alerting toolkit originally developed in 2012 at **SoundCloud**. It was inspired by Borgmon at Google. In contrast to the push model employed by systems such as `statsd`, Prometheus uses a pull model for collecting metrics. Instead of each service being responsible for pushing metrics to a `statsd` server, Prometheus is responsible for scraping an endpoint exposed by services that have metrics. This inversion of responsibilities provides some benefits when operating metrics at scale. Targets in Prometheus can be configured manually or via service discovery.

In contrast to the hierarchical format that systems such as Graphite use to store metrics data, Prometheus employs a multidimensional data model. Time-series data in Prometheus is identified by a metric name (such as `http_request_duration_seconds`) and one or more labels (such as `service=message-service` and `method=POST`). This format can make it easier to standardize metrics across a number of different applications, which is particularly valuable in a microservices architecture.

In this recipe, we'll continue to use message-service and the Actuator and micrometer libraries. We'll configure micrometer to use the Prometheus metrics registry and we'll expose an endpoint that Prometheus can scrape in order to collect metrics from our service. We'll then configure Prometheus to scrape the message-service (running locally) and run Prometheus locally to verify that we can query our metrics.

How to do it...

1. Open the message-service and edit `build.gradle` to include actuator and the micrometer-prometheus dependencies:

```
group 'com.packtpub.microservices'
version '1.0-SNAPSHOT'

buildscript {
    repositories {
        mavenCentral()
    }
    dependencies {
        classpath group: 'org.springframework.boot', name: 'spring-
boot-gradle-plugin', version: '2.0.4.RELEASE'
    }
}

apply plugin: 'java'
apply plugin: 'org.springframework.boot'

sourceCompatibility = 1.8

repositories {
    mavenCentral()
}

dependencies {
    compile group: 'org.springframework.boot', name: 'spring-boot-
starter-web', version: '2.0.4.RELEASE'
    compile group: 'org.springframework.boot', name: 'spring-boot-
starter-actuator', version: '2.0.4.RELEASE'
    compile group: 'io.micrometer', name: 'micrometer-core',
version: '1.0.6'
    compile group: 'io.micrometer', name: 'micrometer-registry-
prometheus', version: '1.0.6'
    compile group: 'io.github.resilience4j', name: 'resilience4j-
circuitbreaker', version: '0.11.0'
    compile group: 'log4j', name: 'log4j', version: '1.2.17'
```

```
        compile group: 'net.logstash.logback', name: 'logstash-logback-
    encoder', version: '5.2'
        testCompile group: 'junit', name: 'junit', version: '4.12'
    }
```

2. Add the following to `application.yml`. This will enable an endpoint that exposes metrics collected in the Prometheus metrics registry. Notice that we're opening another port for the management endpoints added by `actuator`:

```
server:
  port:
    8082

management:
  server:
    port:
      8081
  endpoint:
    metrics:
      enabled: true
    prometheus:
      enabled: true
  endpoints:
    web:
      base-path: "/manage"
      exposure:
        include: "*"
  metrics:
    export:
      prometheus:
        enabled: true
```

3. We can now test that our service is exposing metrics on the `/manage/prometheus` endpoint. Run the service and make the following `curl` request:

```
$ curl http://localhost:8081/manage/prometheus

# HELP tomcat_global_request_seconds
# TYPE tomcat_global_request_seconds summary
tomcat_global_request_seconds_count{name="http-nio-8082",} 0.0
tomcat_global_request_seconds_sum{name="http-nio-8082",} 0.0
# HELP tomcat_sessions_active_max
# TYPE tomcat_sessions_active_max gauge
tomcat_sessions_active_max 0.0
# HELP process_uptime_seconds The uptime of the Java virtual
machine
```

```
# TYPE process_uptime_seconds gauge
process_uptime_seconds 957.132
# HELP jvm_gc_live_data_size_bytes Size of old generation memory
pool after a full GC
# TYPE jvm_gc_live_data_size_bytes gauge
jvm_gc_live_data_size_bytes 1.9244032E7
```

4. Configure and run Prometheus in a docker container. Create a new file in the `/tmp` directory, called `prometheus.yml`, with information about our target:

```
# my global config
global:
  scrape_interval: 15s # Set the scrape interval to every 15
seconds. Default is every 1 minute.
  evaluation_interval: 15s # Evaluate rules every 15 seconds. The
default is every 1 minute.
  # scrape_timeout is set to the global default (10s).

# Alertmanager configuration
alerting:
  alertmanagers:
  - static_configs:
    - targets:
      # - alertmanager:9093

# Load rules once and periodically evaluate them according to the
global 'evaluation_interval'.
rule_files:
  # - "first_rules.yml"
  # - "second_rules.yml"

# A scrape configuration containing exactly one endpoint to scrape:
# Here it's Prometheus itself.
scrape_configs:
  # The job name is added as a label `job=<job_name>` to any
timeseries scraped from this config.
  - job_name: 'prometheus'

    # metrics_path defaults to '/metrics'
    # scheme defaults to 'http'.

    static_configs:
    - targets: ['localhost:9090']

  - job_name: 'message-service'
    metrics_path: '/manage/prometheus'
    static_configs:
    - targets: ['localhost:8081']
```

5. Download and extract the version of Prometheus for your platform. Instructions are on the Prometheus website (`https://prometheus.io/docs/introduction/first_steps/`). Run Prometheus with the configuration file we created in the previous step:

```
$ ./prometheus --config.file=/tmp/prometheus.yml
```

6. Open `http://localhost:9090` in your browser to issue Prometheus queries and see your metrics! Until you start making requests to your service, the only metrics you'll see will be the JVM and system metrics, but this should give you an idea of the kind of querying you can do with Prometheus and demonstrate how the scraper works.

Making debugging easier with tracing

In a microservices architecture, a single request can go through several different services and result in writes to several different data stores and event queues. When debugging a production incident, it isn't always clear whether a problem exists in one system or another. This lack of specificity means metrics and logs only form a small part of the picture. Sometimes we need to zoom out and look at the complete life cycle of a request from the user agent to a terminal service and back again.

In 2010, engineers at Google published a paper describing **Dapper** (`https://research.google.com/archive/papers/dapper-2010-1.pdf`), a large-scale distributed systems tracing infrastructure. The paper described how Google had been using an internally developed tracing system to aid in observing system behavior and debugging performance issues. This work inspired others, including engineers at Twitter who, in 2012, introduced an open source distributed tracing system called **Zipkin** (`https://blog.twitter.com/engineering/en_us/a/2012/distributed-systems-tracing-with-zipkin.html`). Zipkin started out as an implementation of the Dapper paper but evolved into a full set of tools for analyzing performance and inspecting requests to Twitter infrastructure.

All of the work going on in the tracing space made apparent a need for some kind of standardized API. The **OpenTracing** (`http://opentracing.io/`) framework is an attempt to do just that. OpenTracing defines a specification detailing a pan-language standard for traces. Many engineers from different companies have contributed to this effort, including the engineers at Uber who originally created Jaeger (`https://eng.uber.com/distributed-tracing/`), an open source, end-to-end distributed tracing system that conforms to the OpenTracing specification.

In this recipe, we'll modify our message-service to add support for tracing. We'll then run Jaeger in a docker container so that we can see a few traces in practice.

How to do it...

1. Open the message-service project and replace the contents of `build.gradle` with the following:

```
group 'com.packtpub.microservices'
version '1.0-SNAPSHOT'

buildscript {
    repositories {
        mavenCentral()
    }
    dependencies {
        classpath group: 'org.springframework.boot', name: 'spring-
boot-gradle-plugin', version: '2.0.4.RELEASE'
    }
}

apply plugin: 'java'
apply plugin: 'org.springframework.boot'

sourceCompatibility = 1.8

repositories {
    mavenCentral()
}

dependencies {
    compile group: 'org.springframework.boot', name: 'spring-boot-
starter-web', version: '2.0.4.RELEASE'
    compile group: 'org.springframework.boot', name: 'spring-boot-
starter-actuator', version: '2.0.4.RELEASE'
    compile group: 'io.micrometer', name: 'micrometer-core',
version: '1.0.6'
    compile group: 'io.micrometer', name: 'micrometer-registry-
statsd', version: '1.0.6'
    compile group: 'io.opentracing.contrib', name: 'opentracing-
spring-cloud-starter-jaeger', version: '0.1.13'
    compile group: 'io.github.resilience4j', name: 'resilience4j-
circuitbreaker', version: '0.11.0'
    compile group: 'log4j', name: 'log4j', version: '1.2.17'
    compile group: 'net.logstash.logback', name: 'logstash-logback-
```

```
encoder', version: '5.2'
    testCompile group: 'junit', name: 'junit', version: '4.12'
}
```

2. Open `application.yml` in the `src/main/resources` directory and add a section for `opentracing` configuration. Here we're configuring our `opentracing` implementation to connect to an instance of Jaeger running locally on port `6831`:

```
opentracing:
  jaeger:
    udp-sender:
      host: "localhost"
      port:
        6831

spring:
  application:
    name: "message-service"
```

3. In order to collect traces, we'll run an instance of Jaeger locally. Docker makes this easy with the following command:

```
docker run -d --name jaeger \
  -e COLLECTOR_ZIPKIN_HTTP_PORT=9411 \
  -p 5775:5775/udp \
  -p 6831:6831/udp \
  -p 6832:6832/udp \
  -p 5778:5778 \
  -p 16686:16686 \
  -p 14268:14268 \
  -p 9411:9411 \
  jaegertracing/all-in-one:latest
```

4. Run message-service and make a few example requests (even if they result in a 404). Open `http://localhost:16686` in your browser and you'll see Jaeger's web UI. Hit search and explore the trace data collected so far!

Alerting us when something goes wrong

If you're seriously looking at microservices, you're probably running a 24/7 service. Customers demand that your service is available to use at any time. Contrast this increase in the need for availability with the reality that distributed systems are constantly experiencing some kind of failure. No system is ever completely healthy.

Whether you have a monolith or microservices architecture, it is pointless to try to avoid production incidents altogether. Instead, you should try to optimize how you are able to respond to failures, limiting their impact on customers by reducing the time it takes to resolve them.

Reducing the time it takes to resolve incidents (often measured as mean time to resolve or MTTR) involves first reducing the **Mean Time To Detect (MTTD)**. Being able to accurately alert the right on-call engineer when a service is in a customer-impacting failure state is paramount to being able to maintain uptime. Good alerts should be actionable and urgent; if your system notifies on-call engineers when failures are either unactionable or non-urgent (not customer-impacting), you risk burning out on-call engineers and creating what is commonly referred to as alert fatigue. Alert fatigue is very real and can have a more catastrophic impact on uptime than any amount of software bugs or failing hardware. It is essential to continuously improve your system's alerting to get thresholds and other factors just right, to prevent false positives while maintaining alerting for truly customer-impacting incidents.

Alerting infrastructure is not something you want to build yourself. **PagerDuty** is an SaaS tool that allows you to create escalation policies and schedules for teams of engineers who are on-call for specific services. Using PagerDuty, you can set up a rotating schedule so that an engineer on a team of five, for example, can expect to be on-call one week in every five. Escalation policies allow you to configure a set of steps in case the on-call engineer is unavailable (perhaps they're driving their car on the freeway). Escalation policies are often configured to page a secondary on-call schedule, a manager, or even the entire team in the event that an incident goes unacknowledged for a certain amount of time. Using a system such as PagerDuty allows engineers on a team to enjoy much-needed off-call time while knowing that customer-impacting incidents will be responded to promptly.

Alerts can be configured manually using any number of supporting integrations, but this is time-consuming and error-prone. Instead, it's desirable to have a system that allows you to automate the creation and maintenance of alerts for your services. The Prometheus monitoring and alerting toolkit covered in this chapter includes a tool called Alertmanager which allows you to do just that. In this recipe, we'll modify our message-service to add alerts using Alertmanager. Specifically, we'll configure a single alert that fires when the average response time exceeds 500 ms for at least 5 minutes. We'll work from the version of message-service that already includes Prometheus metrics. We won't add any PagerDuty integration in this recipe, since that would require a PagerDuty account in order to follow along. PagerDuty has an excellent integration guide on its website. We'll configure `alertmanager` to send a simple WebHook-based alert.

How to do it...

Now, let's have a look at the following steps:

1. In a previous recipe, we configured Prometheus with a file called `prometheus.yml`. We'll need to add the `alertmanager` configuration to this file, so open it again and add the following:

```
# my global config
global:
  scrape_interval:     15s # Set the scrape interval to every 15
seconds. Default is every 1 minute.
  evaluation_interval: 15s # Evaluate rules every 15 seconds. The
default is every 1 minute.
  # scrape_timeout is set to the global default (10s).

# Alertmanager configuration
alerting:
  alertmanagers:
  - static_configs:
    - targets:
      - localhost:9093

# Load rules once and periodically evaluate them according to the
global 'evaluation_interval'.
rule_files:
    - "rules.yml"
  # - "first_rules.yml"
  # - "second_rules.yml"

# A scrape configuration containing exactly one endpoint to scrape:
# Here it's Prometheus itself.
scrape_configs:
  # The job name is added as a label `job=<job_name>` to any
timeseries scraped from this config.
  - job_name: 'prometheus'

    # metrics_path defaults to '/metrics'
    # scheme defaults to 'http'.

    static_configs:
    - targets: ['localhost:9090']

  - job_name: 'message-service'
    metrics_path: '/manage/prometheus'
    static_configs:
    - targets: ['localhost:8081']
```

2. Create a new file called /tmp/rules.yml. This file defines the rules we want Prometheus to be able to creates alerts for:

```
groups:
- name: message-service-latency
  rules:
  - alert: HighLatency
    expr: rate(http_server_requests_seconds_sum{job="message-
service", instance="localhost:8081"}[1m]) /
rate(http_server_requests_seconds_count{job="message-service",
instance="localhost:8081"}[1m]) > .5
    for: 1m
    labels:
      severity: 'critical'
    annotations:
      summary: High request latency
```

3. Create a new file called /tmp/alertmanager.yml. This is the file that will describe our alerting configuration. It is broken into a few different sections, global sets of certain configuration options that impact how alertmanager works. The section called receivers is where we configure our alert notification systems. In this case, it's a WebHook to a service running locally. This is just for demo purposes; we'll write a small ruby script that listens for HTTP requests and prints the payload to the standard output:

```
global:
  resolve_timeout: 5m

route:
  group_by: ['alertname']
  group_wait: 10s
  group_interval: 10s
  repeat_interval: 1h
  receiver: 'web.hook'

receivers:
- name: 'web.hook'
  webhook_configs:
  - url: 'http://127.0.0.1:4567/'
```

4. Here's the source code for the small ruby service that will print out our alerts:

```ruby
require 'sinatra'

post '/' do
    body = request.body.read()
    puts body
    return body
end
```

5. Run the ruby script, restart prometheus, and start alertmanager. With these three systems running, we'll be ready to test our alert:

```
$ ruby echo.rb
. . .

$ ./prometheus --config.file=/tmp/prometheus.yml

$ ./alertmanager --config.file=/tmp/alertmanager.yml
. . .
```

6. In order to get our alert to fire, open message-service and add the following line to MessageController.java. It's a single line that will force the controller to sleep for 600 milliseconds before returning a response. Note that this is above our threshold described in our rules configuration:

```java
@RequestMapping(path = "/{id}", method = RequestMethod.GET,
produces = "application/json")
public Message get(@PathVariable("id") String id) throws
MessageNotFoundException {
    try { Thread.sleep(600); } catch (InterruptedException e) }
e.printStackTrace(); }
    return messagesStore.get(id);
}
```

7. With that in place, run your updated message service and make a number of requests to it. After one minute, Prometheus should notify Alertmanager, which should then notify your local debug ruby service. Your alert is working!

17
Scaling

In this chapter, we will cover the following recipes:

- Load testing microservices with Vegeta
- Load testing microservices with Gatling
- Building auto-scaling clusters

Introduction

A significant advantage of using microservices over a monolith architecture is that microservices can be separately scaled to meet the unique traffic demands they serve. A service that must do work for every single request will have very different scaling needs than a service that only needs to perform work for specific kinds of request.

Because microservices encapsulate ownership over a single-domain entity, they can be load tested independently. They can also be configured to scale automatically based on demand. In this chapter, we'll discuss load testing using two different load testing tools and set up auto-scaling groups in AWS that can scale on demand. Finally, we'll discuss strategies for capacity-planning.

Load testing microservices with Vegeta

Load testing is an important part of predicting how your service is going to behave over time. When we are performing load testing, we shouldn't just ask simple questions, such as *"How many requests per second is our system capable of serving?"* Instead, we should try to understand how our whole system performs under various load conditions. In order to answer this question, we need to understand the infrastructure that makes up our system and the dependencies that a particular service has.

For example, is the service behind a load-balancer? How about a CDN? What other caching mechanisms are used? All of these questions and more can be answered by our systems having good observability.

Vegeta is an open source load testing utility designed to test HTTP services with a constant request rate. It's a versatile tool that can be used as a command-line utility or a library. In this recipe, we'll focus on using the command-line utility. Vegeta allows you to specify targets as URLs in a separate file—optionally with custom headers and request bodies—that can be used as an input to the command-line tool. The command-line tool can then attack the targets in the file, with various options to control the request rate and duration, as well as other variables.

In this recipe, we'll be using Vegeta to test the message-service we've been working with in previous chapters. We'll test a simple request path that includes creating a new message and retrieving a list of messages.

How to do it...

Let's have a look at the following steps:

1. We'll modify our message-service and add a new endpoint that allows us to query all messages for a particular user. This introduces the notion of an inbox, so we'll modify our `MessageRepository` class to add a new in-memory map of usernames to lists of messages, as shown in the following code. Note that in a production system, we'd choose a more durable and flexible store, but this will suffice for demonstration purposes:

```
package com.packtpub.microservices.ch08.message;

import
com.packtpub.microservices.ch08.message.exceptions.MessageNotFoundE
xception;
import com.packtpub.microservices.ch08.message.models.Message;

import java.util.*;
import java.util.concurrent.ConcurrentHashMap;

public class MessageRepository {

    private ConcurrentHashMap<String, Message> messages;
    private ConcurrentHashMap<String, List<Message>> inbox;

    public MessageRepository() {
        messages = new ConcurrentHashMap<>();
```

```
        inbox = new ConcurrentHashMap<>();
    }

    public Message save(Message message) {
        UUID uuid = UUID.randomUUID();
        Message saved = new Message(uuid.toString(),
message.getSender(), message.getRecipient(),
            message.getBody(), message.getAttachmentUri());
        messages.put(uuid.toString(), saved);
        List<Message> userInbox =
inbox.getOrDefault(message.getRecipient(), new ArrayList<>());
        userInbox.add(saved);
        inbox.put(message.getRecipient(), userInbox);
        return saved;
    }

    public Message get(String id) throws MessageNotFoundException {
        if (messages.containsKey(id)) {
            return messages.get(id);
        } else {
            throw new MessageNotFoundException("Message " + id + "
could not be found");
        }
    }

    public List<Message> getByUser(String userId) {
        return inbox.getOrDefault(userId, new ArrayList<>());
    }
}
```

2. Modify `MessageController` to add the endpoint itself:

```
package com.packtpub.microservices.ch08.message.controllers;

import com.packtpub.microservices.ch08.message.MessageRepository;
import
com.packtpub.microservices.ch08.message.clients.SocialGraphClient;
import
com.packtpub.microservices.ch08.message.exceptions.MessageNotFoundE
xception;
import
com.packtpub.microservices.ch08.message.exceptions.MessageSendForbi
ddenException;
import
com.packtpub.microservices.ch08.message.exceptions.MessagesNotFound
Exception;
import com.packtpub.microservices.ch08.message.models.Message;
import
```

```
com.packtpub.microservices.ch08.message.models.UserFriendships;
import org.springframework.beans.factory.annotation.Autowired;
import org.springframework.http.ResponseEntity;
import org.springframework.scheduling.annotation.Async;
import org.springframework.web.bind.annotation.*;
import org.springframework.web.client.RestTemplate;
import
org.springframework.web.servlet.support.ServletUriComponentsBuilder
;

import java.net.URI;
import java.util.List;
import java.util.concurrent.CompletableFuture;

@RestController
public class MessageController {

    @Autowired
    private MessageRepository messagesStore;

    @Autowired SocialGraphClient socialGraphClient;

    @RequestMapping(path = "/{id}", method = RequestMethod.GET,
produces = "application/json")
    public Message get(@PathVariable("id") String id) throws
MessageNotFoundException {
        return messagesStore.get(id);
    }

    @RequestMapping(path = "/", method = RequestMethod.POST,
produces = "application/json")
    public ResponseEntity<Message> send(@RequestBody Message
message) throws MessageSendForbiddenException {
        List<String> friendships =
socialGraphClient.getFriendships(message.getSender());

        if (!friendships.contains(message.getRecipient())) {
            throw new MessageSendForbiddenException("Must be
friends to send message");
        }

        Message saved = messagesStore.save(message);
        URI location = ServletUriComponentsBuilder
                .fromCurrentRequest().path("/{id}")
                .buildAndExpand(saved.getId()).toUri();
        return ResponseEntity.created(location).build();
    }
```

```
    @RequestMapping(path = "/user/{userId}", method =
RequestMethod.GET, produces = "application/json")
    public ResponseEntity<List<Message>>
getByUser(@PathVariable("userId") String userId) throws
MessageNotFoundException {
        List<Message> inbox = messagesStore.getByUser(userId);
        if (inbox.isEmpty()) {
            throw new MessageNotFoundException("No messages found
for user: " + userId);
        }
        return ResponseEntity.ok(inbox);
    }

    @Async
    public CompletableFuture<Boolean> isFollowing(String fromUser,
String toUser) {
        String url = String.format(
"http://localhost:4567/followings?user=%s&filter=%s",
                fromUser, toUser);

        RestTemplate template = new RestTemplate();
        UserFriendships followings = template.getForObject(url,
UserFriendships.class);

        return CompletableFuture.completedFuture(
                followings.getFriendships().isEmpty()
        );
    }
}
```

3. We'll need a mock socialgraph service, so create the following Ruby script in a file called `socialgraph.rb` and run it:

```
require 'sinatra'

get '/friendships/:user' do
    content_type :json
    {
        username: "user:32134",
        friendships: [
            "user:12345"
        ]
    }.to_json
end
```

4. Install `vegeta`. If you're on Mac OS X and have HomeBrew installed, you can just use the following:

```
$ brew update && brew install vegeta
```

5. Before we can launch an attach with `vegeta`, we'll need to create a `targets` file. The first request we'll make will create a message with the specified request body. The second request will get a list of messages by user ID. Create a file called `message-request-body.json`, as shown in the following code:

```
{
    "sender": "user:32134",
    "recipient": "user:12345",
    "body": "Hello there!",
    "attachment_uri": "http://foo.com/image.png"
}
```

6. Create another file called `targets.txt`, as shown in the following code:

```
POST http://localhost:8082/
Content-Type: application/json
@message-request-body.json

GET http://localhost:8082/user:12345
```

7. With both our message-service and our mock socialgraph service running, we're ready to load test these two services using the following code:

```
$ cat targets.txt| vegeta attack -duration=60s -rate=100 | vegeta
report -reporter=text

Requests        [total, rate]               6000, 100.01
Duration        [total, attack, wait]       1m0.004668981s,
59.99172349s,  12.945491ms
Latencies       [mean, 50, 95, 99, max]     10.683968ms, 5.598656ms,
35.108562ms,  98.290388ms,  425.186942ms
Bytes In        [total, mean]               667057195, 111176.20
Bytes Out       [total, mean]               420000, 70.00
Success         [ratio]                     99.80%
Status Codes    [code:count]                201:3000   500:12   200:2988
Error Set:
50
```

Experiment with different duration values and request rates to see how the behavior of the system changes. If you increase the rate to 1,000, what happens? Depending on hardware and other factors, it's possible that the single-threaded Ruby mock service will be overwhelmed and trip the circuit breaker we added to the message-service. This should change certain details, such as the success rate, so it's an important observation to make. What would happen if you load tested the mock Ruby service separately?

In this recipe, we load tested the message-service, which depends on the socialgraph service. Both services were running locally, which was necessary for demonstration purposes and gives us some insight into how the two systems behave. In a production system, it's vital to load test your services in production so that you include all of the infrastructure involved in serving requests (load balancers, caches, and so on). In a production system, you can also monitor dashboards and look for changes to how your system behaves under load conditions.

Load testing microservices with Gatling

Gatling is an open source load testing tool that allows users to script custom scenarios using a *Scala-based DSL*. Scenarios can go beyond simple straight path testing and involve multiple steps, even simulating user behavior, such as pauses and making decisions about how to proceed based on output in the test. Gatling can be used to automate the load testing of microservices or even browser-based web applications.

In the previous recipe, we used Vegeta to send a constant request rate to our message-service. Our request path created a new message and then retrieved all messages for a user. This method had the advantage of being able to test the response time of retrieving all messages for a user as the list of messages grew. Vegeta excels at this type of testing, but because it is fed attack targets from a static file, you cannot use Vegeta to build dynamic request paths based on the responses from previous requests.

Because Gatling uses a DSL to script load testing scenarios, it's possible to make a request, capture some element of the response, and use that output to make decisions about future requests. In this recipe, we'll use Gatling to script a load testing scenario that involves creating a message and then retrieving that specific message by its ID. This is a very different kind of test than what we did in the previous recipe, so it's a good opportunity to demonstrate the differences between Vegeta and Gatling.

How to do it...

Let's check the following steps:

1. Download `gatling` for your platform. Gatling is distributed as a ZIP bundle and is available for download at `https://gatling.io/download/`. Unzip the bundle into the directory of your choice:

   ```
   $ unzip gatling-charts-highcharts-bundle-2.3.1-bundle.zip
   ...
   $ cd gatling-charts-highcharts-bundle-2.3.1
   ```

2. Simulations for `gatling` are placed by default in the `user-files/simulations` directory. Create a new subdirectory called `messageservice` and a new file called `BasicSimulation.scala`. This is the file that contains the code that describes your scenario. In our scenario, we'll use the Gatling DSL to script a POST request to the create message endpoint followed by a GET request to the message endpoint, as shown in the following code:

   ```scala
   package messageservice

   import io.gatling.core.Predef._
   import io.gatling.http.Predef._
   import scala.concurrent.duration._

   class BasicSimulation extends Simulation {

     val httpConf = http
       .baseURL("http://localhost:8082")
       .acceptHeader("application/json")

     val scn = scenario("Create a message")
       .exec(
         http("createMessage")
           .post("/")
           .header("Content-Type", "application/json")
           .body(StringBody("""{"sender": "user:32134", "recipient":
   "user:12345", "body": "Hello there!", "attachment_uri":
   "http://foo.com/image.png"}"""))
               .check(header(HttpHeaderNames.Location).saveAs("location"))

       )
       .pause(1)
       .exec(
         http("getMessage")
   ```

```
                .get("${location}")
        )

    setUp(scn.inject(atOnceUsers(50)).protocols(httpConf))
}
```

3. Create the same mock Ruby service we used in the previous recipe and run it:

```
require 'sinatra'

get '/friendships/:user' do
    content_type :json
    {
        username: "user:32134",
        friendships: [
            "user:12345"
        ]
    }.to_json
end
```

4. Run the Ruby mock service as well as our message-service. From the Gatling directory, launch Gatling by running `bin/gatling.sh`. You'll be prompted to select a simulation to run. Choose `messageservice.BasicSimulation`:

```
$ bin/gatling.sh
GATLING_HOME is set to /Users/posman/projects/microservices-
cookbook/chapter17/gatling-charts-highcharts-bundle-2.3.1
Choose a simulation number:
    [0] computerdatabase.BasicSimulation
    [1] computerdatabase.advanced.AdvancedSimulationStep01
    [2] computerdatabase.advanced.AdvancedSimulationStep02
    [3] computerdatabase.advanced.AdvancedSimulationStep03
    [4] computerdatabase.advanced.AdvancedSimulationStep04
    [5] computerdatabase.advanced.AdvancedSimulationStep05
    [6] messageservice.BasicSimulation
6
Select simulation id (default is 'basicsimulation'). Accepted
characters are a-z, A-Z, 0-9, - and _

Select run description (optional)

Simulation messageservice.BasicSimulation started...
. .
```

5. The output will show some statistics about the results from the load test. Requests will be bucketed into under 800 ms, between 800 ms and 1,200 ms, and over 1,200 ms. A link to an HTML file will be displayed. Open it in a browser to see charts and other useful visualizations about your load test.

As we've seen in this recipe, Gatling offers a lot of flexibility in running load tests. With some clever scripting using the DSL, it's possible to more closely simulate production traffic by parsing log files and generating requests, making dynamic decisions based on latency, responses, or other elements of requests. Both Gatling and Vegeta are great load testing tools that you can use to explore how your systems operate under various load conditions.

Building auto-scaling clusters

With the advent of virtualization and the move to cloud-based infrastructure, applications can exist on elastic infrastructure designed to grow and shrink based on anticipated or measured traffic patterns. If your application experiences peak periods, you shouldn't have to provision full capacity during non-peak periods, wasting compute resources and money. From virtualization to containers and container schedulers, it's more and more common to have dynamic infrastructure that changes to accommodate the needs of your system.

Microservices are a natural fit for auto-scaling. Because we can scale separate parts of a system separately, it's easier to measure the scaling needs of a specific service and its dependencies.

There are many ways to create auto-scaling clusters. In the next chapter, we'll talk about container orchestration tools, but without skipping ahead, auto-scaling clusters can also be created in any cloud provider. In this recipe, we'll cover creating auto-scaling compute clusters using *Amazon Web Services*, particularly Amazon EC2 Auto Scaling. We'll create a cluster with multiple EC2 instances running our message-service behind an **Application Load Balancer (ALB)**. We'll configure out cluster to automatically add instances based on CPU utilization.

How to do it...

Let's check the following steps:

1. This recipe requires an AWS account. If you do not already have an AWS account, create one at `https://aws.amazon.com/premiumsupport/knowledge-center/create-and-activate-aws-account/` and create a set of access keys at `https://docs.aws.amazon.com/general/latest/gr/managing-aws-access-keys.html`. Install the `aws cli` utility. If you're on OS X and have HomeBrew installed, this can be done with the following:

   ```
   $ brew install aws
   ```

2. Configure the `aws` command-line utility, entering the access key you created:

   ```
   $ aws configure
   ```

3. Create a launch configuration. Launch configurations are templates used by auto-scaling groups when creating new instances. In this case, we've chosen an Amazon AMI and `t2.nano` as our EC2 instance type (see `https://aws.amazon.com/ec2/instance-types/` for more details), as shown in the following code:

   ```
   $ aws autoscaling create-launch-configuration --launch-
   configuration-name message-service-launch-configuration --image-id
   ari-f606f39f --instance-type t2.nano
   ```

4. Create the actual auto-scaling group. Auto-scaling groups have configurable maximum and minimum sizes that specify how much the auto-scaling group can shrink or grow based on demand. In this case, we'll create an auto-scaling group with a minimum of 1 instance and a maximum of 5 instances, as shown in the following code:

   ```
   $ aws autoscaling create-auto-scaling-group --auto-scaling-group-
   name message-service-asg --launch-configuration-name message-
   service-launch-configuration --max-size 5 --min-size 1 --
   availability-zones "us-east-1a"
   ```

5. We want the instances in our auto-scaling group to be accessible behind a load balancer, so we'll create that now:

```
$ aws elb create-load-balancer --load-balancer-name message-
service-lb --listeners
"Protocol=HTTP,LoadBalancerPort=80,InstanceProtocol=HTTP,InstancePo
rt=8082" --availability-zones us-east-1a

{
    "DNSName": "message-service-lb-1741394248.us-
east-1.elb.amazonaws.com"
}
```

6. In order to automatically scale our auto-scaling group, we need to define a metric. Clusters can be scaled based on memory, CPU utilization, or request rate. In this case, we're going to configure our scaling policy to use CPU utilization. If CPU utilization hits a 20% average, our auto-scaling group will create more instances. Create a file called `config.json`:

```
{
  "TargetValue": 20.0,
  "PredefinedMetricSpecification":
    {
      "PredefinedMetricType": "ASGAverageCPUUtilization"
    }
}
```

7. Attach the scaling policy to our auto-scaling group.

```
$ aws autoscaling put-scaling-policy --policy-name cpu20 --auto-
scaling-group-name message-service-asg --policy-type
TargetTrackingScaling --target-tracking-configuration
file://config.json
```

Our auto-scaling group is now configured to grow when CPU utilization exceeds a 20% average. Launch configurations can also include bootstrapping steps for installing and configuring your service—typically with some kind of configuration-management tool, such as **Chef** or **Puppet**—or it can be configured to pull a Docker image from a private Docker repository.

18
Deploying Microservices

In this chapter, we'll cover the following recipes:

- Configuring your service to run in a container
- Running multi-container applications with Docker Compose
- Deploying your service on Kubernetes
- Test releases with canary deployments

Introduction

The way we deliver software to users has changed dramatically over the years. In the not too distant past, it was common to deploy to production by running a shell script on a collection of servers that pulled an update from some kind of source control repository. The problems with this approach are clear—scaling this out was difficult, bootstrapping servers was error prone, and deployments could easily get stuck in an undesired state, resulting in unpredictable experiences for users.

The advent of configuration management systems, such as **Chef** or **Puppet**, improved this situation somewhat. Instead of having custom bash scripts or commands that ran on remote servers, remote servers could be tagged with a kind of role that instructed them on how to configure and install software. The declarative style of automating configuration was better suited for large-scale software deployments. Server automation tools such as **Fabric** or **Capistrano** were also adopted; they sought to automate the process of pushing code to production, and are still very popular today for applications that do not run in containers.

Containers have revolutionized the way we deliver software. Containers allow developers to package their code with all the dependencies, including libraries, the runtime, OS tools, and configurations. This allows code to be delivered without the need to configure the host server, which dramatically simplifies the process by removing the number of moving pieces.

The process of shipping services in containers has been referred to as **immutable infrastructure**, because once an image is built, it isn't typically changed; instead, new versions of a service result in a new image being built.

Another big change in how software is deployed is the popularization of the twelve-factor methodology (`https://12factor.net/`). **Twelve-factor** (or **12f**, as it is commonly written) is a set of guidelines originally written by engineers at Heroku. At their core, twelve-factor apps are designed to be loosely coupled with their environment, resulting in services that can be used along with various logging tools, configuration systems, package management systems, and source control systems. Arguably, the most universally adopted concepts employed by twelve-factor apps are that the configuration is accessed through environment variables and logs are output to standard out. As we saw in the previous chapters, this is how we've integrated with systems such as Vault. These chapters are worth a read, but we've already been following many concepts described in twelve-factor so far in this book.

In this chapter, we'll be discussing containers, orchestration, and scheduling, and various methods for safely shipping changes to users. This is a very active topic, and new techniques are being improvised and discussed, but the recipes in this chapter should serve as a good starting point, especially if you're accustomed to deploying monoliths on virtual machines or bare metal servers.

Configuring your service to run in a container

As we know, services are made up of source code and configurations. A service written in Java, for instance, can be packaged as a **Java Archive (JAR)** file containing compiled class files in Java bytecode, as well as resources such as configuration and properties files. Once packaged, the JAR file can then be executed on any machine running a **Java Virtual Machine (JVM)**.

In order for this to work, however, the machine that we want to run our service on must have a JVM installed. Oftentimes, it must be a specific version of the JVM. Additionally, the machine might need to have some other utilities installed, or it might need access to a shared filesystem. While these are not parts of the service themselves, they do make up what we refer to as the runtime environment of the service.

Linux containers are a technology that allow developers to package an application or service with its complete runtime environment. Containers separate out the runtime for a particular application from the runtime of the host machine that the container is running on.

This makes applications more portable, making it easier to move a service from one environment to another. An engineer can run a service on their laptop, then move it into a preproduction environment, and then into production, without changing the container itself. Containers also allow you to easily run multiple services on the same machine, therefore allowing much more flexibility in how application architectures are deployed and providing opportunities for operational cost optimization.

Docker is a container runtime and set of tools that allows you to create self-contained execution environments for your service. There are other popular container runtimes they are widely used today, but Docker is designed to make containers portable and flexible, making it an ideal choice for building containers for services.

In this recipe, we'll use Docker to create an image that packages our message-service. We'll do this by creating a `Dockerfile` file and using the Docker command-line utility to create an image and then run that image as a container.

How to do it...

The steps for this recipe are as follows:

1. First, open our message-service project from the previous chapters. Create a new file in the root of the project called `Dockerfile`:

   ```
   FROM openjdk:8-jdk-alpine
   VOLUME /tmp
   EXPOSE 8082
   ARG JAR_FILE=build/libs/message-service-1.0-SNAPSHOT.jar
   ADD ${JAR_FILE} app.jar
   ENTRYPOINT ["java","-Djava.security.egd=file:/dev/./urandom","-jar","/app.jar"]
   ```

2. The `Dockerfile` file defines the base image that we'll use to build our message-service image. In this case, we're basing our image off of an Alpine Linux image with OpenJDK 8. Next, we expose the port that our service binds to and define how to run our service after it's packaged as a JAR file. We're now ready to use the `Dockerfile` file to build an image. This is done with the following command:

   ```
   $ docker build . -t message-service:0.1.1
   ```

3. You can verify that the preceding command worked by running `docker images` and seeing ours listed. Now we're ready to run the message service by executing our service in a container. This is done with the `docker run` command. We'll also give it a port mapping and specify the image that we want to use to run our service:

```
$ docker run -p 0.0.0.0:8082:8082 message-service:0.1.1
```

Running multi-container applications with Docker Compose

Services rarely run in isolation. A microservice usually connects to a data store of some kind, and could have other runtime dependencies. In order to work on a microservice, it's necessary to run it locally on a developer's machine. Requiring engineers to manually install and manage all the runtime dependencies of a service in order to work on a microservice would be impractical and time consuming. Instead, we need a way to automatically manage runtime service dependencies.

Containers have made services more portable by packaging the runtime environment and configuration with the application code as a shippable artifact. In order to maximize the benefits of using containers for local development, it would be great to be able to declare all the dependencies and run them in separate containers. This is what Docker Compose is designed to do.

Docker Compose uses a declarative YAML configuration file to determine how an application should be executed in multiple containers. This makes it easy to quickly start up a service, a database, and any other runtime dependencies of the service in a way that makes local development especially easy.

In this recipe, we'll follow some of the steps from the previous recipe to create a `Dockerfile` file for the authentication-service project. We'll then create a Docker Compose file that specifies MySQL as a dependency of the authentication-service. We'll then look at how to configure our project and run it locally with one container running our application and another running a database server.

How to do it...

For this recipe, you need to perform the following steps:

1. Open the authentication-service project and create a new file called `Dockerfile`:

```
FROM openjdk:8-jdk-alpine
VOLUME /tmp
EXPOSE 8082
ARG JAR_FILE=build/libs/authentication-service-1.0-SNAPSHOT.jar
ADD ${JAR_FILE} app.jar
ENTRYPOINT ["java","-Djava.security.egd=file:/dev/./urandom","-jar","/app.jar"]
```

2. Docker Compose uses a file called `docker-compose.yml` to declare how containerized applications should be run:

```
version: '3'
services:
  authentication:
    build: .
    ports:
     - "8081:8081"
    links:
      - docker-mysql
    environment:
      DATABASE_HOST: 'docker-mysql'
      DATABASE_USER: 'root'
      DATABASE_PASSWORD: 'root'
      DATABASE_NAME: 'user_credentials'
      DATABASE_PORT: 3306
  docker-mysql:
    ports:
      - "3306:3306"
    image: mysql
    restart: always
    environment:
      MYSQL_ROOT_PASSWORD: 'root'
      MYSQL_DATABASE: 'user_credentials'
      MYSQL_ROOT_HOST: '%'
```

3. As we'll be connecting to the MySQL server running in the `docker-mysql` container, we'll need to modify our authentication-service configuration to use that host when connecting to MySQL:

```
server:
  port: 8081

spring:
  jpa.hibernate.ddl-auto: create
  datasource.url: jdbc:mysql://docker-mysql:3306/user_credentials
  datasource.username: root
  datasource.password: root

hibernate.dialect: org.hibernate.dialect.MySQLInnoDBDialect

secretKey: supers3cr3t
```

4. You can now run the authentication-service and MySQL with the following:

```
$ docker-compose up
Starting authentication-service_docker-mysql_1 ...
```

5. That's it! The authentication-service should now be running locally in a container.

Deploying your service on Kubernetes

Containers make services portable by allowing you to package code, dependencies, and the runtime environment together in one artifact. Deploying containers is generally easier than deploying applications that do not run in containers. The host does not need to have any special configuration or state; it just needs to be able to execute the container runtime. The ability to deploy one or more containers on a single host gave rise to another challenge when managing production environments—scheduling and orchestrating containers to run on specific hosts and manage scaling.

Kubernetes is an open source container orchestration tool. It is responsible for scheduling, managing, and scaling your containerized applications. With Kubernetes, you do not need to worry about deploying your container to one or more specific hosts. Instead, you declare what resources your container needs and let Kubernetes decide how to do the work (what host the container runs on, what services it runs alongside, and so on). Kubernetes grew out of the **Borg paper** (https://research.google.com/pubs/pub43438.html), published by engineers at Google, which described how they managed services in Google's data centers using the Borg cluster manager.

Kubernetes was started by Google as an open source project in 2014 and has enjoyed widespread adoption by organizations deploying code in containers.

Installing and managing a Kubernetes cluster is beyond the scope of this book. Luckily, a project called **Minikube** allows you to easily run a single-node Kubernetes cluster on your development machine. Even though the cluster only has one node, the way you interface with Kubernetes when deploying your service is generally the same, so the steps here can be followed for any Kubernetes cluster.

In this recipe, we'll install Minikube, start a single-node Kubernetes cluster, and deploy the `message-service` command we've worked with in previous chapters. We'll use the Kubernetes CLI tool (`kubectl`) to interface with Minikube.

How to do it...

For this recipe, you need to go through the following steps:

1. In order to demonstrate how to deploy our service to a `kubernetes` cluster, we'll be using a tool called `minikube`. The `minikube` tool makes it easy to run a single-node `kubernetes` cluster on a VM that can be run on a laptop or development machine. Install `minikube`. On macOS X, you can use HomeBrew to do this:

   ```
   $ brew install minikube
   ```

2. We'll also be using the `kubernetes` CLI tools in this recipe, so install those. On macOS X, using HomeBrew, you can type as follows:

   ```
   $ brew install kubernetes-cli
   ```

3. Now we're ready to start our single-node `kubernetes` cluster. You can do this by running `minikube start`:

   ```
   $ minikube start
   Starting local Kubernetes v1.10.0 cluster...
   Starting VM...
   Getting VM IP address...
   Moving files into cluster...
   Setting up certs...
   Connecting to cluster...
   Setting up kubeconfig...
   Starting cluster components...
   Kubectl is now configured to use the cluster.
   Loading cached images from config file
   ```

4. Next, set the `minikube` cluster up as the default configuration for the `kubectl` CLI tool:

```
$ kubectl config use-context minikube
Switched to context "minikube".
```

5. Verify that everything is configured properly by running the `cluster-info` command:

```
$ kubectl cluster-info
Kubernetes master is running at https://192.168.99.100:8443
KubeDNS is running at
https://192.168.99.100:8443/api/v1/namespaces/kube-system/services/
kube-dns:dns/proxy
```

To further debug and diagnose cluster problems, use `kubectl cluster-info dump`.

6. You should now be able to launch the `kubernetes` dashboard in a browser:

```
$ minikube dashboard
Waiting, endpoint for service is not ready yet...
Opening kubernetes dashboard in default browser...
```

7. The `minikube` tool uses a number of environment variables to configure the CLI client. Evaluate the environment variables with the following command:

```
$ eval $(minikube docker-env)
```

8. Next, we'll build the docker image for our service using the `Dockerfile` file created in the previous recipe:

```
$ docker build -t message-service:0.1.1
```

9. Finally, run the `message-service` command on the `kubernetes` cluster, telling `kubectl` the correct image to use and the port to expose:

```
$ kubectl run message-service --image=message-service:0.1.1 --
port=8082 --image-pull-policy=Never
```

10. We can verify that the `message-service` command is running in the `kubernetes` cluster by listing the pods on the cluster:

```
$ kubectl get pods
NAME READY STATUS RESTARTS AGE
message-service-87d85dd58-svzmj 1/1 Running 0 3s
```

11. In order to access the `message-service` command, we'll need to expose it as a new service:

```
$ kubectl expose deployment message-service --type=LoadBalancer
service/message-service exposed
```

12. We can verify the previous command by listing services on the `kubernetes` services:

```
$ kubectl get services

NAME TYPE CLUSTER-IP EXTERNAL-IP PORT(S) AGE
kubernetes ClusterIP 10.96.0.1 <none> 443/TCP 59d
message-service LoadBalancer 10.105.73.177 <pending> 8082:30382/TCP
4s
```

13. The `minikube` tool has a convenient command for accessing a service running on the `kubernetes` cluster. Running the following command will list the URL that the `message-service` command is running on:

```
$ minikube service list message-service
|-------------|----------------------|----------------------------
|
| NAMESPACE | NAME | URL |
|-------------|----------------------|----------------------------
|
| default | kubernetes | No node port |
| default | message-service | http://192.168.99.100:30382 |
| kube-system | kube-dns | No node port |
| kube-system | kubernetes-dashboard | http://192.168.99.100:30000
|
|-------------|----------------------|----------------------------
|
```

14. Use `curl` to try and make a request against the service to verify that it's working. Congratulations! You've deployed the `message-service` command on `kubernetes`.

Test releases with canary deployments

Improvements in best practices for deploying have greatly improved the stability of deploys over the years. Automating the repeatable steps, standardizing the way our application interacts with the runtime environment, and packaging our application code with the runtime environment have all made deployments safer and easier than they used to be.

Introducing new code to a production environment is not without risk, however. All the techniques discussed in this chapter help prevent predictable mistakes, but they do nothing to prevent actual software bugs from negatively impacting users of the software we write. Canary deployment is a technique for reducing this risk and increasing confidence in new code that is being deployed to production.

With a canary deployment, you begin by shipping your code to a small percentage of production traffic. You can then monitor metrics, logs, traces, or whatever other tools allow you to observe how your software is working. Once you are confident that things are going as they should, you can gradually increase the percentage of traffic that receives your updated version until all production traffic is being served by the newest release of your service.

The term **canary deployment** comes from a technique that coal miners used to use to protect themselves from carbon monoxide or methane poisoning. By having a canary in the mine, the toxic gases would kill the canary before the miners, giving the miners an early warning sign that they should get out. Similarly, canary deployments allow us to expose a subset of users to risk without impacting the rest of the production environment. Thankfully, no animals have to be harmed when deploying code to production environments.

Canary deployments used to be very difficult to get right. Teams shipping software in this way usually had to come up with some kind of feature-toggling solution that would gate requests to certain versions of the application being deployed. Thankfully, containers have made this much easier, and Kubernetes has made it even more so.

In this recipe, we'll deploy an update to our `message-service` application using a canary deployment. As Kubernetes is able to pull images from a Docker container registry, we'll run a registry locally. Normally, you'd use a self-hosted registry or a service such as *Docker Hub* or *Google Container Registry*. First, we'll ensure that we have a stable version of the `message-service` command running in `minikube`, then we'll introduce an update and gradually roll it out to 100% traffic.

How to do it...

Go through the following steps to set up a canary deployment:

1. Open the `message-service` project we've worked on in the previous recipes. Add the following `Dockerfile` file to the root directory of the project:

```
FROM openjdk:8-jdk-alpine
VOLUME /tmp
EXPOSE 8082
ARG JAR_FILE=build/libs/message-service-1.0-SNAPSHOT.jar
ADD ${JAR_FILE} app.jar
ENTRYPOINT ["java","-Djava.security.egd=file:/dev/./urandom","-
jar","/app.jar"]
```

2. In order for Kubernetes to know whether the service is running, we need to add a liveness probe endpoint. Open the `MessageController.java` file and add a method to respond to GET requests at the `/ping` path:

```
package com.packtpub.microservices.ch09.message.controllers;

import com.packtpub.microservices.ch09.message.MessageRepository;
import
com.packtpub.microservices.ch09.message.clients.SocialGraphClient;
import
com.packtpub.microservices.ch09.message.exceptions.MessageNotFoundE
xception;
import
com.packtpub.microservices.ch09.message.exceptions.MessageSendForbi
ddenException;
import com.packtpub.microservices.ch09.message.models.Message;
import
com.packtpub.microservices.ch09.message.models.UserFriendships;
import org.springframework.beans.factory.annotation.Autowired;
import org.springframework.http.ResponseEntity;
import org.springframework.scheduling.annotation.Async;
import org.springframework.web.bind.annotation.*;
import org.springframework.web.client.RestTemplate;
import
org.springframework.web.servlet.support.ServletUriComponentsBuilder
;

import java.net.URI;
import java.util.List;
import java.util.concurrent.CompletableFuture;

@RestController
```

```
public class MessageController {

    @Autowired
    private MessageRepository messagesStore;

    @Autowired
    private SocialGraphClient socialGraphClient;

    @RequestMapping(path = "/{id}", method = RequestMethod.GET,
produces = "application/json")
    public Message get(@PathVariable("id") String id) throws
MessageNotFoundException {
        return messagesStore.get(id);
    }

    @RequestMapping(path = "/ping", method = RequestMethod.GET)
    public String readinessProbe() {
        return "ok";
    }

    @RequestMapping(path = "/", method = RequestMethod.POST,
produces = "application/json")
    public ResponseEntity<Message> send(@RequestBody Message
message) throws MessageSendForbiddenException {
        List<String> friendships =
socialGraphClient.getFriendships(message.getSender());

        if (!friendships.contains(message.getRecipient())) {
            throw new MessageSendForbiddenException("Must be
friends to send message");
        }

        Message saved = messagesStore.save(message);
        URI location = ServletUriComponentsBuilder
                .fromCurrentRequest().path("/{id}")
                .buildAndExpand(saved.getId()).toUri();
        return ResponseEntity.created(location).build();
    }

    @RequestMapping(path = "/user/{userId}", method =
RequestMethod.GET, produces = "application/json")
    public ResponseEntity<List<Message>>
getByUser(@PathVariable("userId") String userId) throws
MessageNotFoundException  {
        List<Message> inbox = messagesStore.getByUser(userId);
        if (inbox.isEmpty()) {
            throw new MessageNotFoundException("No messages found
for user: " + userId);
```

```
        }
        return ResponseEntity.ok(inbox);
    }

    @Async
    public CompletableFuture<Boolean> isFollowing(String fromUser,
String toUser) {
        String url = String.format(
"http://localhost:4567/followings?user=%s&filter=%s",
                fromUser, toUser);

        RestTemplate template = new RestTemplate();
        UserFriendships followings = template.getForObject(url,
UserFriendships.class);

        return CompletableFuture.completedFuture(
                followings.getFriendships().isEmpty()
        );
    }
}
```

3. Let's start our container registry on port 5000:

```
$ docker run -d -p 5000:5000 --restart=always --name registry
registry:2
```

4. As we're using a local repository that is not configured with a valid SSL cert, start minikube with the ability to pull from insecure repositories:

```
$ minikube start --insecure-registry 127.0.0.1
```

5. Build the message-service docker image, and then push the image to the local container registry with the following commands:

```
$ docker build . -t message-service:0.1.1
...
$ docker tag message-service:0.1.1 localhost:5000/message-service
...
$ docker push localhost:5000/message-service
```

6. A **Kubernetes Deployment** object describes the desired state for a pod and ReplicaSet. In our deployment, we'll specify that we want three replicas of our message-service pod running at all times, and we'll specify the liveness probe that we created a few steps earlier. To create a deployment for our message-service, create a file called deployment.yaml with the following contents:

```
apiVersion: extensions/v1beta1
kind: Deployment
metadata:
  name: message-service
spec:
  replicas: 3
  template:
    metadata:
      labels:
        app: "message-service"
        track: "stable"
    spec:
      containers:
        - name: "message-service"
          image: "localhost:5000/message-service"
          imagePullPolicy: IfNotPresent
          ports:
            - containerPort: 8082
          livenessProbe:
            httpGet:
              path: /ping
              port: 8082
              scheme: HTTP
            initialDelaySeconds: 10
            periodSeconds: 30
            timeoutSeconds: 1
```

7. Next, using kubectl, we'll create our deployment object:

```
$ kubectl create -f deployment.yaml
```

8. You can now verify that our deployment is live and that Kubernetes is creating the pod replicas by running kubectl get pods:

```
$ kubectl get pods
```

9. Now that our application is running in Kubernetes, the next step is to create an update and roll it out to a subset of pods. First, we need to create a new docker image; in this case, we'll call it version 0.1.2 and push it to the local repository:

```
$ docker build . -t message-service:0.1.2
...
$ docker tag message-service:0.1.2 localhost:5000/message-service
$ docker push localhost:5000/message-service
```

10. We can now configure a deployment to run the newest version of our image before rolling it out to the rest of the pods.

Other Books You May Enjoy

If you enjoyed this book, you may be interested in these other books by Packt:

TypeScript Microservices
Parth Ghiya

ISBN: 978-1-78883-075-1

- Get acquainted with the fundamentals behind microservices.
- Explore the behavioral changes needed for moving from monolithic to microservices.
- Dive into reactive programming, TypeScript and Node.js to learn its fundamentals in microservices
- Understand and design a service gateway and service registry for your microservices.
- Maintain the state of microservice and handle dependencies.
- Perfect your microservice with unit testing and Integration testing
- Develop a microservice, secure it, deploy it, and then scale it

Microservice Patterns and Best Practices
Vinicius Feitosa Pacheco

ISBN: 978-1-78847-403-0

- How to break monolithic application into microservices
- Implement caching strategies, CQRS and event sourcing, and circuit breaker patterns
- Incorporate different microservice design patterns, such as shared data, aggregator, proxy, and chained
- Utilize consolidate testing patterns such as integration, signature, and monkey tests
- Secure microservices with JWT, API gateway, and single sign on
- Deploy microservices with continuous integration or delivery, Blue-Green deployment

Leave a review - let other readers know what you think

Please share your thoughts on this book with others by leaving a review on the site that you bought it from. If you purchased the book from Amazon, please leave us an honest review on this book's Amazon page. This is vital so that other potential readers can see and use your unbiased opinion to make purchasing decisions, we can understand what our customers think about our products, and our authors can see your feedback on the title that they have worked with Packt to create. It will only take a few minutes of your time, but is valuable to other potential customers, our authors, and Packt. Thank you!

Index

26605921R00323

Printed in Great Britain
by Amazon